Study Writing

A course in written English
for academic and professional purposes

Liz Hamp-Lyons
Ben Heasley

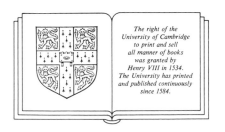

The right of the
University of Cambridge
to print and sell
all manner of books
was granted by
Henry VIII in 1534.
The University has printed
and published continuously
since 1584.

Cambridge University Press

Cambridge

London   New York   New Rochelle

Melbourne   Sydney

Published by the Press Syndicate of the University of Cambridge
The Pitt Building, Trumpington Street, Cambridge CB2 1RP
32 East 57th Street, New York, NY 10022, USA
10 Stamford Road, Oakleigh, Melbourne 3166, Australia

© Cambridge University Press 1987

First published 1987

Printed in Great Britain
by Scotprint Ltd, Musselburgh, Scotland

British Library cataloguing in publication data

Hamp-Lyons, Liz

Study writing: a course in written English
for academic and professional purposes.
1. English language – Text-books for
foreign speakers   2. English language –
Writing
I. Title   II. Heasley, Ben
808'.042   PE1128

ISBN 0 521 31558 1

SE

Contents

Part I

Part II

Teacher's guide

Thanks

Study Writing results from a long process of in-house materials development at the Institute for Applied Language Studies of the University of Edinburgh. An earlier writing course was developed by Gill Schärer and Ben Heasley as a pre-intermediate textbook presented in the form of a self-study programme. The evident need for material to help adult learners of English to write led Ben Heasley and Liz Hamp-Lyons to write a course commencing at post-intermediate level and intended for classroom use. The course was piloted at the IALS and revised as a result; it was piloted again at the IALS and elsewhere (a period during which Ben Heasley moved on to Ain Shams University, Egypt, and was able to bring a further dimension of experience to the book). This final version has, therefore, been extensively tried out.

We would like to record our debt of gratitude to Gill Schärer for her involvement in the early stages and for the use of several texts and tasks. Thanks are also due to:
- Clive Criper, Director of the Institute for Applied Language Studies, for his support of the project through all its stages;
- colleagues at the IALS, especially Tony Lynch, who oversaw the piloting with several generations of EAP students;
- colleagues at the Universities of Aston, Warwick and Essex who piloted later versions and provided feedback;
- Roger Bowers of the British Council for his detailed and constructive comments on two versions;
- Margaret Love, who has typed each version so patiently and excellently;
- Peter Donovan, Annemarie Young and Alison Baxter at CUP for their tremendous support and constructive advice throughout the project.

But thanks are due most of all to our families: Mike Lyons (and Christopher, who arrived on the scene between versions!); Hilda Heasley, Yana, Myles and Cian. Without their patience and the happiness they gave us we could never have persevered to this outcome.

An overview of unit contents

PART II

Unit			
10	Deciding how to organize the whole text	Text structure: Situation→ Problem→Solution→ Evaluation	Writer–reader relationship: the four co-operative principles
11	Developing text within an S→P→S→E framework	Text-based tasks focusing on:	situation problem solution evaluation
12	Text-based tasks without guidance		

To the teacher

Study Writing is designed for students of English as a foreign or second language at post-intermediate and advanced levels of proficiency in English. It is intended for anyone who wishes to learn English for academic or professional reasons. It has been trialled with students ranging in age from 17 to 50 from many different backgrounds.

Timing

The course provides about 40–60 hours of classwork. Not all students, however, will need to do every exercise of every unit. It is also assumed that some writing tasks will be assigned for homework. In general, we have erred on the side of providing too many rather than too few tasks, giving teachers considerable flexibility regarding the number of hours they will take to complete the course, depending on the exact needs of their own students. (See *Teacher's guide A (1)*.)

General principles

The course is based on an approach which emphasizes the discoursal and cognitive aspects of writing. Essentially we see writing as a form of problem-solving in which the writer faces two main tasks: (a) generating ideas in language, and (b) composing these ideas into a written structure adapted to the needs of the reader and the goals of the writer. This is why we ask students to think about different kinds of information and different ways of organizing writing. We believe that writing and reading are closely associated, and that a developing writer can learn a great deal from the study of sample texts from the writer's point of view. (See *Teacher's guide C*.)

Because we wish to emphasize the cognitive and discoursal aspects, we pay rather less attention to grammar, discussing only selected topics which experience suggests cause particular problems. This does *not* mean we think grammar is unimportant. On the contrary, without a solid basis of grammatical control, the student cannot hope to develop into an effective writer. But it is our view that error-free writing is less important than writing which addresses the topic clearly, develops it in a rational and relevant way, and takes account of the needs of the reader. Our experience agrees with the findings of many research studies: that once students are writing fluently and confidently, they will be more inclined and more able to write accurately.

Course organization

In Part I of the course, Units 1–9, a range of writing types are introduced and practised. In Part II we explore a framework for handling complete expository texts, both as reader and as writer. The final unit offers students the opportunity to think about writing in general as a creative process, and to explore some of the ways this process develops.

Units 1–9 have three main sections: *About writing* explores the principles of writing; *Using grammar in writing* focuses on aspects of grammar which are particularly critical for writing expository texts; and *Consolidation* gives students the opportunity to write long stretches of text under fewer constraints, applying what they have learned in the unit, and exercising their developing skill as a whole. The units in Part II, because they are dealing with the structure of whole texts, are not so readily divisible, and are structured differently from unit to unit.

General advice on teaching procedure

We do not believe that there is a 'right way' to teach writing, and we do believe that individual teachers should be allowed the freedom of making their own decisions. Nevertheless, the writers of a book always have certain ideas and assumptions which necessarily affect the book they write, so that it is easier to use the materials in some ways than others. We state our general views here in the hope that they will be helpful to the teacher seeking to understand why we have done this-or-that, and how *we* might teach it: this is not intended as a prescription of how any other teacher should do it.

Writing is clearly a complex process, and competent writing is frequently accepted as being the last language skill to be acquired (for native speakers of the language as well as for foreign/second language learners). Few people write spontaneously, and few feel comfortable with a formal writing task intended for the eyes of someone else. When the 'someone else' is a teacher, whose eye may be critical, and who indeed may assign a formal assessment to the written product, most people feel uncomfortable. It makes sense, then, that the atmosphere of the writing classroom should be warm and supportive, and non-threatening. It helps if teachers show willingness to write too, and to offer their attempts for class discussion along with those of the students; it helps if students can work together, assisting each other, pointing out strengths and weaknesses without taking or giving offence. Many of our tasks suggest working with a partner or in groups, and we see this work as very important: not only does it make the task livelier and more enjoyable, but it makes sure that students see that writing really is co-operative, a relationship between writer and reader. Usually the writer has to imagine a reader, but co-operative writing provides each writer with a reader and makes the writing task more realistic and more interactive.

Writing is commonly seen as a three-stage process: pre-writing, writing and rewriting. Although this is very much an oversimplification, it is a helpful one. In the past teachers concentrated on the end of the second stage, i.e. after the writing had been done. They did not see how they could intervene at the pre-writing and writing stages, and rewriting was seen only as 'correcting the mistakes'. We now understand the importance of all three stages as part of the writing process, and try to help students master the *process* by participating in it with them, rather than contenting ourselves with criticizing the *product*, i.e. the composition, without knowing much about how it was arrived at.

We have included a *Teacher's guide* at the back of the book, for those teachers who would like more detailed guidance on how to use the book, or/and about the teaching of writing in general. The topics covered in the guide are listed on the Contents page. There are also teaching notes on each unit (and on the *To the student* introduction) at the end of the guide.

To the student

About *Study Writing*

Before you begin to work with *Study Writing*, you probably have some questions you would like to ask about the course. Some of the questions students most often ask have been answered below. Of course, you will learn many more answers yourself as you study the course.

Q: Who is this course for?

A: It's for anyone who wants to study English seriously, who is adult (over about 17), and who is already able to write reasonably correct sentences in English but wants to be able to write longer pieces, paragraphs and complete texts, which are not only grammatically correct but also well-organized and informative. Most people who use this book will either be going to follow a course of study at a college or university which uses English, or planning to take an advanced examination in English.

Q: How will this course help me?

A: Firstly, it will give you practice in using many common ways of organizing texts as a whole (i.e. complete pieces of writing), and of organizing information within texts. Secondly, it will provide you with plenty of examples of different types of texts which other writers have produced and will help you to see the principles on which the organization of these texts is based. Thirdly, it will point out some of the most common grammatical difficulties which can prevent non-native writers of English from producing acceptable texts.

Q: Is learning to write English as difficult as it seems?

A: Well – it is very difficult to write like a Shakespeare or a D.H. Lawrence in a language which is not your own. But you are not aiming at great literature: you simply need to be able to write clear, accurate English which has a central idea and other related information and gets the meaning across to your readers. Because this type of English writing is highly structured and operates by rules or expectations which can be explained to you, and which you can see in example texts, it is much easier to learn than so-called 'creative writing' like novels, poetry and plays. Of course, information-based writing (usually called 'expository writing') is creative too: you take the ideas and information, apply the conventional patterns to them, but in your own way, so that you create a text which is unique to you.

Q: How is this course organized?

A: The course has two main Parts. In Part I, the main functional types of writing are introduced and practised. In Part II you will study the organization of texts in a different way, which will enable you to see each one more as a whole with parts than as a range of parts. Each Part is divided into several units, and there is a particular aspect of writing for you to concentrate on in each unit. You will also get opportunities to write whole texts throughout the course, so that you don't forget that the aspects you study are only parts of the whole skill of writing, and not the complete answer. The tasks you have to do become more difficult as the book progresses, until at the end you should be able to produce your own original text without any supports. The units in Part I have three main divisions: *About writing* tries to give you some insights into the process and structure of writing, and helps you to organize your own writing; *Using grammar in writing* focuses on one aspect of English grammar which is particularly helpful for writing expository texts; *Consolidation* provides the opportunity to put together everything you have learned in the unit, together with your other knowledge of writing in English, and allows you to show your skill in creating a short text of your own.

Q: Do I need to do anything else, apart from studying this course, in order to improve my writing ability?

A: While we sincerely believe that this course will help you become a competent writer, we are the first to acknowledge that there are limits to what any course can achieve. This limitation results from the fact that writing is such a complex activity that it cannot easily be broken down into a series of skills and subskills for teaching. While no course can ever teach you everything you need in order to become a competent writer, there is no reason why you cannot learn all there is to know about effective writing. To help you do just this, we include a *Study writing yourself* section in this introduction.

Study writing yourself

In this section we will concentrate on two ways in which you can help yourself learn to be a better writer.

1 One not so obvious approach to writing is through wide reading. Reading is essentially an attempt to find out why the writer bothered to write in the first place, i.e. to discover the writer's goal. To help readers achieve an understanding of her or his goal a writer must use some general framework to support whatever point she or he is trying to make. You will meet these frameworks in *Study Writing*. However, you can best appreciate how they can be varied to achieve different goals by studying other people's writings. In addition, you can best evaluate their relative effectiveness by examining how other writers use them. For example, if you want to compare two opposing viewpoints, do you present the one you favour first or last? The best way to answer this question is to examine what other competent writers do and then make up your own mind.

We could go on at great length about the advantages of wide reading and show how useful it is for learning grammar and vocabulary among other things. However, to do so would make this introduction unnecessarily long. We hope that what we have pointed out will convince you of the necessity of reading widely.

2 The most obvious way you can help yourself become a good writer is by writing. We strongly suggest that in addition to completing the tasks in *Study Writing* you also keep your own personal journal. Buy yourself an extra notebook, and try to write down some ideas every day, in English, about anything that interests you. Write down your opinions on life, love, the writing class, whatever interests you. As you write do not worry too much about putting your ideas in order, just let them flow; you will be surprised at what you will learn about your own thoughts, attitudes, feelings, etc. Neither should you worry about length; just keep going until the ideas stop. In some cases you may not produce more than a set of key-words, in others a set of notes, while, occasionally, you will surprise yourself by producing pages and pages of writing. The main purpose of this stage is to find out what you know/feel/etc. about the topic in hand.

The second stage is more difficult. Once a week, reread your journal, select one topic and rewrite it for a particular reader. This may be your teacher, a fellow student, or the whole class. You will need to think carefully about how to present your topic in such a way that your reader(s) can follow it. Instead of asking as you did in the first stage, 'What do I know about topic X?' you will have to ask yourself, 'What does my reader need to know about topic X?'

The transition from 'What do I know about X?' to 'What does my reader need to know?' is not an easy one to make, though it is a very necessary one. However, as with most things in life, once you begin to approach the problem, you will find a way through it.

Conclusion: How do you think you can become a 'good' writer of English?

So far, in this introduction, we have talked mainly about how *we* think you can become a 'good' writer of English. The time has now come for *you* to say how *you* think you can improve *your* writing.

Task

As your first attempt at keeping a journal we would like you to consider the following question:

What do I think will help me become a 'good' writer of English?
To start you off you might consider the following statements:

1 The most important thing for me is to study more grammar.
2 The most important thing for me is to have a good teacher.
3 The most important thing for me is to memorize useful expressions and sentences.
4 The most important thing for me is to read more.

5 The most important thing for me is to have a lot of practice in writing.
6 The most important thing for me is study more vocabulary.
7 The most important thing for me is to think about what makes writing effective.

When you have written up your journal, bring it to the next class and in groups of three or four discuss your beliefs. After the discussion, elect a spokesperson who will communicate your shared ideas to the class.

PART I

Unit 1 Spatial relationships

Introduction

Very often we have to describe in writing the location of a place, how a place is laid out or how a set of objects are connected (as in equipment for an experiment). In this unit we will look at some of the ways of describing spatial relationships. Spatial descriptions are often accompanied by a visual aid, such as a plan, map, or diagram.

Task 1

Read the following text by yourself and then look at the map which accompanies it. With a partner, discuss the text and the map and decide whether the map helps you to understand the text.

Acidic pollution

The discharge of waste from the production of titanium dioxide along the Humber estuary in Britain causes serious acidification of local waters, wipes out aquatic organisms and pollutes the beaches of Cleethorpes with acid and iron. The two main titanium dioxide plants in Britain are BTP Tioxide of Grimsby and LaPorte Industries of Stallingborough – both of them on the Humber estuary. Between them they discharge more than 60,000 m^3 of acidic waste daily. As a result, a long strip of land along the south bank of the estuary from Immingham to Cleethorpes has a brownish-red colour from the discharge.

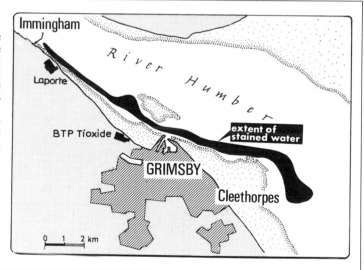

(*New Scientist*)

Not all texts describing spatial relations are accompanied by a map. For example, the writer of the following text, 'The Abraham Moss Centre', did not include a map. The text describes the location of a school and is part of the introduction to an educational research project.

Task 2

Read the passage and then:
a) make a note of the expressions which tell the reader where a place is;
b) using the information in the text, draw a simple map of the area;
c) say what you think the writer's aim was in producing this description;
d) say whether you can draw an accurate map on the basis of the information provided in the passage.

The Abraham Moss Centre

The Abraham Moss Centre is a low, white complex of buildings on the borders of Cheetham and Crumpsall, just to the north of the centre of Manchester. Although the site itself was industrial wasteland, it is in the heart of a residential district. Along one side of it runs a railway, but in every other direction it is surrounded by semi-detached and terraced housing of the inter-war years. Both Cheetham and Crumpsall were fairly prosperous Victorian developments, but Cheetham in particular has undergone extensive redevelopment.

(A.D. Edwards and V.J. Furlong *The Language of Teaching*)

Some of the expressions in the above text tell you *what* various places are, or were:
    'The Abraham Moss Centre is *a low, white complex of buildings*'.
Other expressions tell you *where* various places are, or were:
    'The Abraham Moss Centre . . . buildings *on the borders of Cheetham and Crumpsall*'.

Task 3

a) Add as many expressions of spatial relationships as you can to this illustration. Some you could use are:
opposite
between
beside
behind
(etc.)

b) Write four sentences to describe some spatial relationships between objects in the illustration, for example:
    The fountain is *in front of* the house.

About writing

There are basically two ways of organizing a description of a place. One way is to describe it as if it was being seen from the air (a bird's eye view). The other is to describe it from the point of view of a journey through it (a pedestrian's view). The description may need to be very detailed as, for example, when a novelist is describing a scene; or it can be rather general, as when a student is describing a geographical area as background to an agricultural experiment; or it can be very technical, as when an entomologist is describing the marking on a rare butterfly.

Task 4

Read this text, which describes a geographical area of East Africa, and then, working with another student:
a) decide whether it is written from a bird's eye view or from a pedestrian's view;
b) draw an outline map of the area to accompany the text;
c) decide what changes you would need to make in the text if you rewrote it from the other point of view.

As the Rift Valley sweeps northwards out of Kenya and into Ethiopia, it forms the spectacular Lake Turkana basin. The long, shallow waters of the lake, which stretches 155 miles north to south and up to 35 miles east to west, sparkle green in the tropical sun: someone called it the Jade Sea, a very apt name. At the south a barrier of small volcanic hills prevents the lake spreading further down into the arid lands of northern Kenya. From the west side rises the Rift Valley wall, a range of mountains with some peaks of more than 5000 feet. This is the land of the Turkana people, a tall, elegant pastoralist tribe. Beyond are the mountains and forests of Uganda. Pouring its silt-laden waters into the north end of the lake is the River Omo, a huge river that drains the Ethiopian Highlands to the north, and meanders tortuously as it nears its end at the border with Kenya where it reaches the Jade Sea. Where the river reaches the lake the sudden barrier to its progress forces it to dump its burden of silt, so creating an enormous delta.

(Adapted from R. Leakey and R. Lewin *People of the Lake*)

Task 5

The following text describes the same area as in Task 4, but in a different period of time and from a different point of view. Read the text and draw an outline map to accompany it. When you have completed your outline map, compare it with a map drawn by one other student.

Suppose now, we are back on the eastern shores of Lake Turkana $2\frac{1}{2}$ million years ago. Standing by the shores we would be aware of crocodiles basking in the tropical heat on sand-spits pointing finger-like into the shallow water. A little more than five miles away to the east savanna-covered hills rise up from the lake basin, sliced here and there by forest-filled valleys. At one point the hills are breached by what is obviously a large river that has snaked its way down from the Ethiopian mountains. Where the river reaches the flood-plain of the lake it shatters into a delta of countless streams, some small, some large, but each fringed by a line of trees and bushes.

As we walk up one of the stream beds – dry now because there has been no rain for months – we might hear the rustle of a pig in search of roots and vegetation in the undergrowth. As the tree-cover thickens we catch a glimpse of a colobus monkey retreating through the tree tops. Lower down, mangobeys feed on the ripening figs. In the seclusion of the surrounding bushes small groups of impala and water-buck move cautiously. From the top of a tree we could see out into the open, where herds of gazelle graze.

After going about a mile up the stream we come across a scene that is strangely familiar. Before us is a group of eight creatures – definitely human-like, but definitely not truly human – some on the stream bed and some on its sandy bank.

(Adapted from R. Leakey and R. Lewin *People of the Lake*)

In academic writing it is more usual to describe a place using the bird's eye technique (as was done in the text in Task 4). Such a description may or may not be accompanied by a visual (a map, photograph, etc.). In novels and other writing which emphasizes the human aspect of a description, the pedestrian's view technique is often used (as in the text in Task 5).

Task 6

This text is not a geographical description, but a set of instructions on how to set up the equipment needed in order to produce an unusual photograph. First read the text and then try to draw a diagram showing how the equipment should be set up. Then check your diagram with the one on page 19.

Making a physiograph using a camera

To make a physiograph, place the camera on the floor with its lens pointing directly upwards and lying immediately below the torch which has been suspended from a hook in the ceiling on a piece of string. Two other strings are hung from hooks several inches to either side of the main string to which they are connected at a point, say, three-quarters of the way down so that they form a V. The strings and the torch should be so arranged that when the torch is given its first swing to set it in motion the movement of the light comes within the area of the negative in the camera. Turn the torch on, turn the room light off, set the torch swinging and open the shutter. Using a fast film, the aperture may be set at about F/11 but the correct stop will have to be discovered experimentally by tests. After several minutes' exposure the track made by the swinging light will have produced a delightful linear pattern on the negative and this can be enlarged in the ordinary way to make a white linear design on a black background.

(E. de Marie *Photography*)

Visuals are used by writers to achieve different goals. Sometimes they are used only to break up pages of text. However, in academic writing they usually have a more informative purpose. Sometimes this purpose is to duplicate information given in a text in order to help the reader visualize the relations more clearly. This can be seen in the 'Making a physiograph' text and the diagram on page 19. The visual clarifies the rather complicated spatial relations set out in the text. It is a good example of the old saying that 'a picture (map/plan/diagram) is worth a thousand words'.

Visuals are also used to supplement texts, i.e. to add further information to the text or to emphasize a different aspect of the information given in the text.

Task 7

Read the text and decide whether the map which accompanies it contains supplementary or duplicate information, and whether it is essential to an understanding of the text.

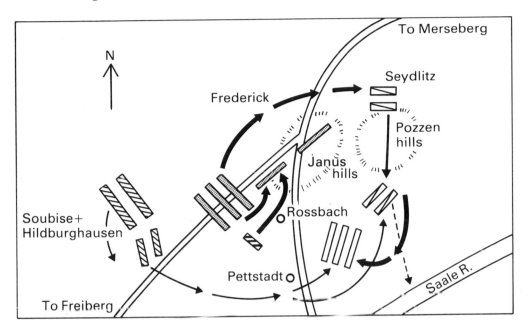

Rossbach *(The Seven Years War)*

Frederick II, the Great, faced his greatest peril in the summer of 1757. Prussia and its English ally had suffered successive defeats in the south (from Austria), west (from France), and east (from Russia). As the hostile ring tightened about him, the Prussian King rallied his forces and struck out to the west where the advance of 30,000 French and 11,000 Imperial troops of the Holy Roman Empire posed the greatest threat. In 12 days Frederick marched 170 miles to confront the invaders of Saxony at Rossbach, 26 miles southwest of Leipzig. The Prussians, reduced to 21,000 effective men by the forced march, camped northeast of the village.

On November 5 the allied commanders, the Prince de Soubise and the Prince of Saxe-Hildburghausen, resolved to crush Frederick with a large-scale turning movement against the Prussian left flank. Anticipating the manoeuver, Frederick deployed a small masking force to his front while his main body executed a leftward turning movement of its own behind a cover of hills. The ponderous allied columns, somewhat disorganised by a too-hasty march, suddenly received the full force of the Prussian blow on their right flank. Behind the fire of 18 heavy guns, Gen. Friedrich von Seydlitz' cavalry, followed by seven battalions of infantry, routed the enemy cavalry and then swooped down on the startled allied infantry. In 40 minutes the Prussian horsemen gunned and sabered the French and Imperials into wild flight. Most of the Prussian foot soldiers were still coming up when Soubise fled the field with 7,500 casualties, chiefly prisoners. The victors lost less than 600 men. Frederick's spectacular victory at Rossbach broke the advance from the west.

(D. Eggenberger *A Dictionary of Battles*)

Using grammar in writing

The most important information in a sentence very often appears at the beginning. This information may tell us what the sentence is about. For example, the sentence 'Zambia is a landlocked country' seems to be about Zambia. In this case 'Zambia' is also the subject of the sentence. However, in the sentence 'To the north lies Tanzania', 'To the north' is not the subject but is very important information as it locates the position of Tanzania in terms of some reference point which we already know.

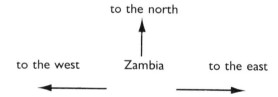

The organizing principle here is the points of the compass.

Task 8

Look at the following short texts and decide which is easier to understand.

i)   I live in Edinburgh. The capital of Scotland is Edinburgh. A part of the British Isles is Scotland.
ii) I live in Edinburgh. It is the capital of Scotland. Scotland is part of the British Isles.

Text (ii) is easier to understand because the writer uses the beginning of each sentence to lead into the next, guiding us through the text in a logical way.
    I→Edinburgh→It (Edinburgh)→Scotland→Scotland→British Isles
The organizing principle here is from part to whole.
   In spatial descriptions you will find that locational expressions often appear at the beginning of sentences in the text (e.g. *Beside the river, Further south*, etc.).

Task 9

Read the spatial description which follows and underline the locational
expressions that are used to guide the reader through the description.

Cairo: the modern city

The hub of the modern city of Cairo is the spacious
Midan el-Tahrir (Liberation Square). Here all the
city's main traffic arteries meet. – To the SW* of the
square are the Ministry of Foreign Affairs and the
Government Buildings, to the SE the American
University and the National Assembly. To the NW of
the square is the large range of buildings occupied
by the Egyptian Museum, which has the world's
largest and finest collection of Egyptian and Graeco-
Roman antiquities. Just beyond the Egyptian
Museum the Corniche el-Nil along the bank of the
Nile is lined by large modern hotels and prestige
buildings. In Shari Qasr el-Aini, which runs S from
Midan el-Tahrir, is the Ethnological Museum, and in
Shari el-Sheikh Rihan the Geological Museum. – To
the NE of the Midan el-Tahrir are the main commercial and shopping districts of the modern city, which
are entirely European in character. The goods sold in
the shops here are marked with fixed prices, which
cannot be reduced by bargaining like prices in the
bazaars.

* SW = south west; NE = north east etc.

(*Baedeker's AA Egypt*)

Descriptions of spatial locations are normally organized according to
conventional ways of looking at scenes. The most common conventions are:

general to particular
whole to part
large to small
outside to inside
top to bottom
left to right

The main point here is to be consistent. If you choose a particular convention,
use it throughout so as not to confuse the reader.

Task 10

a) Reread 'Cairo: the modern city' and state its organizing principle.
b) Draw a map of Cairo in as much detail as this text makes possible.

Task 11

a) Study the sketch map and then read the text which accompanies it. Notice how the writer has tried to organize both the whole text and each sentence, to guide your reading. Trace or copy out the map, then mark it with arrows (a red pen would be ideal) and number them to show the sequence in which the text describes it.

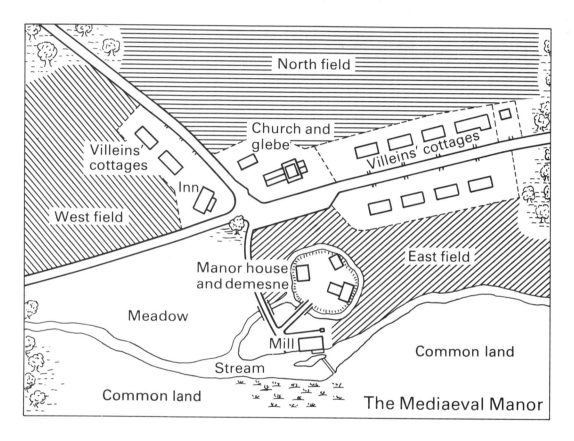

During the Middle Ages, the chief man of the village, or manor, was the lord of the manor. He owned his own piece of land on which he built his sturdy manor house. The lord's lands were known as the demesne and were usually walled, and separated from the rest of the village. The common lands of the manor were divided into three large fields: each field consisted of many long, narrow strips, and each villein (or villager) had a number of these strips, scattered about the field. Each year, wheat would be grown in one of the fields, barley or oats in another, and the third would be left uncultivated. A different field was left uncultivated each year to rest the soil.

The cottages of the villeins were built along the edges of

the fields beside the road, or track. These houses were simple buildings built of stone or wattle and daub (i.e. twigs and mud), and often had only one room. The church, with the priest's house and the glebe (the land belonging to the church) was in the middle of the village, frequently at a crossroads.

In addition to the fields of crops, the village had a hay meadow, usually near a stream. The hay was used for winter feed for the animals. The animals were kept on the common land on the outskirts of the village in good weather, and in bad weather they were brought into barns, or even into the villeins' houses.

(Adapted from J. Lockhart Whiteford *British History for the CSE Year*)

b) Reorganize the text, rewriting if necessary, so that it offers better guidance to the reader about the spatial relationships it describes.

Consolidation

A In some countries (the USA, for example) electric kettles are virtually unknown. Write a short text (imagine it is part of a letter to a penfriend in America) describing the main parts of an electric kettle and the way they fit together. The picture will help you.

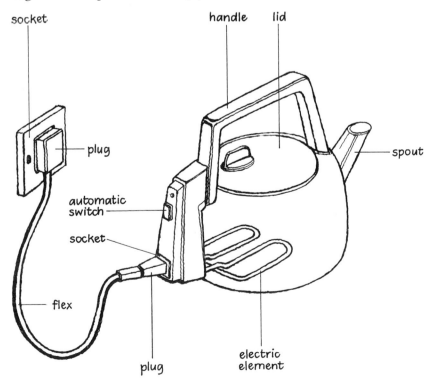

B   The outline map below shows the main car parks available to staff and
students of Edinburgh University. Write a text, intended to be part of a letter
to an overseas student planning to attend Edinburgh University, telling her
she will need to apply for a parking permit, and suggesting the best car parks.
Her classes will take place mainly in Adam Ferguson Building (marked AFB
and shaded black on the map, and located to the south-east of George
Square).

UNIVERSITY   OF   EDINBURGH

CAR PARKING AREAS

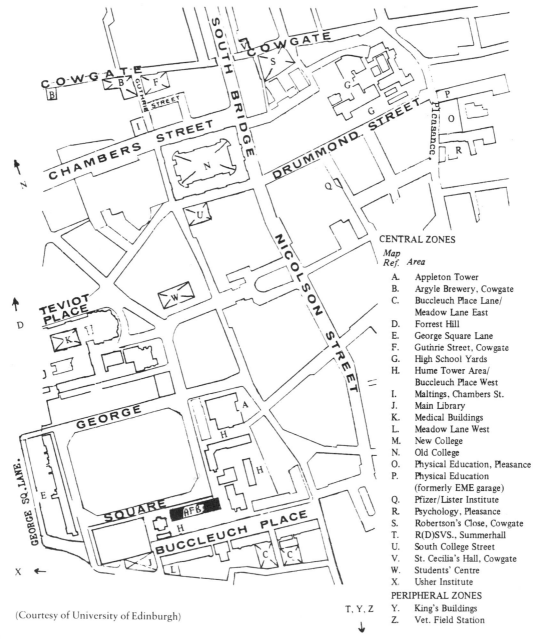

CENTRAL ZONES

Map Ref.	Area
A.	Appleton Tower
B.	Argyle Brewery, Cowgate
C.	Buccleuch Place Lane/ Meadow Lane East
D.	Forrest Hill
E.	George Square Lane
F.	Guthrie Street, Cowgate
G.	High School Yards
H.	Hume Tower Area/ Buccleuch Place West
I.	Maltings, Chambers St.
J.	Main Library
K.	Medical Buildings
L.	Meadow Lane West
M.	New College
N.	Old College
O.	Physical Education, Pleasance
P.	Physical Education (formerly EME garage)
Q.	Pfizer/Lister Institute
R.	Psychology, Pleasance
S.	Robertson's Close, Cowgate
T.	R(D)SVS., Summerhall
U.	South College Street
V.	St. Cecilia's Hall, Cowgate
W.	Students' Centre
X.	Usher Institute

PERIPHERAL ZONES

Y.	King's Buildings
Z.	Vet. Field Station

T, Y, Z

(Courtesy of University of Edinburgh)

C Imagine you are a dramatist. You have just written a drama, the major
portion of which is set in a living room just like the one pictured below.
Because dramatists never use pictures in their scripts, you have to write up
the stage scene. Organize the description from the audience's viewpoint (near
to far). Begin your description:

> We are looking at a living room . . .

Looking back

Now that you have completed this unit you should understand how texts are
organized according to a pedestrian's view and a bird's eye view. You should be
familiar with some expressions of location and understand how these are used
to guide a reader through a text; you should be able to use them in sentences and
text.

p. 12 Making a physiograph using a camera

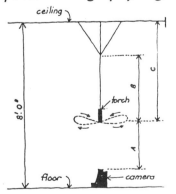

Making a physiograph: *A* is the distance between
camera lens and the light bulb of the swinging
torch; *B* is the distance between the light bulb
and the point in the string at which side strings
are fixed; *C* is the distance between light bulb
and ceiling. The relation between *B* and *C* sets
the pattern of the physiograph.

Unit 2   Class relationships (1) Classification

Introduction

People try to organize the world around them. One of the ways they do this is by looking for relationships among objects or ideas, and classifying them into groups according to their similarities and differences.

Task 1

The following is a set of English words given in no particular order (i.e. a list). Turn this list into a classification by ordering the words into groups. Be prepared to explain why you grouped them as you did:

lecturer	sleep	manager
son	intelligent	happy
enthuse	dream	scientist
old	sick	printer

You may have noticed that these data can be classified in several ways. The way you classify depends on what characteristics you think are important. In biology particular characteristics, such as the possession of bones, are used to define groups. Thus, for instance, animals with bones are generally classified as vertebrates. However, if we decided on some other characteristic (e.g. the possession of eyes) we should define a completely different group that included most (but not all) vertebrates, most insects, most crustaceans, some molluscs and some other invertebrates. A common way of classifying data is through a tree diagram, such as the one on page 21.

Task 2

The following sentences form a text which refers to the classification chart on page 21. However, except for the first sentence, they are not in the most logical order. Work with another student to try to agree on the best order for the numbered sentences, to form a complete text which fits the organization of the classification chart.

There are two classes of sugars, natural sugars and processed sugars.
i)   Fructose and glucose are difficult to buy on their own.
ii)   Raw cane sugar, white sugar and soft brown sugar are produced at different stages in the refining process.

iii)   The most widely consumed sugars are the end-product of the process, the white sugars.

iv)   Maple syrup, which is mostly sucrose and water, is very popular in North America. In Britain, you can buy it in health food shops.

v)   Soft brown sugar is made from either raw cane or white sugar, with molasses, treacle or syrup added.

vi)   Natural sugars are, however, of little significance to the consumer compared with the processed sugars.

vii) There are two types, Barbados and demerara.

viii) Honey is available in many forms, but they are all essentially the same, varying only in flavour and price.

ix)   Processed sugars can be classified according to the stage in the process at which they are produced.

x)   Raw cane sugar is an early stage in the process of making white sugar.

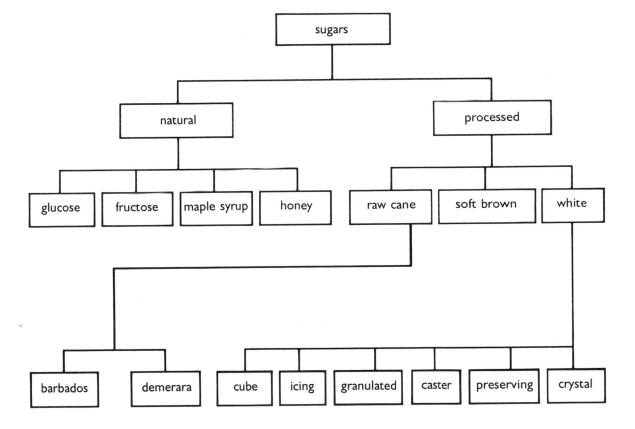

About writing

Decisions about what characteristics to use in forming a classification are usually partly based on convention (how others did it), and mainly based on your purpose in making the classification.

Task 3

When we think about education we usually think about formal schooling. But there are quite a variety of ways of becoming better educated.

a) Work with another student to add data of your own to the following list:

  Channels of Education
  i)   full-time schooling
  ii) correspondence courses
  iii) television broadcasts
  iv) ....
  v)   ....
  vi) ....
  (etc.)

b) Arrange the data logically into groups according to different criteria, e.g. cost, intensity, etc. Label each grouping clearly. Discuss your groupings with a partner.

In English, when we classify data and ideas, we divide all the information into categories. We do this in a logical way, but the logical ordering we choose depends on our purpose in making the classification. Some types of logical ordering are: time order (oldest to newest); general to particular hierarchy; and scale (examples of scales are importance (most important to least important), size (largest to smallest), familiarity (best-known to least-known)).

Task 4

What method of logical ordering (i.e. classification basis) was used in the diagram and text about sugars (Task 2)?

Task 5

What logical ordering is used here?

    Ms Alice Smith
    414 Oldfield Street
    Wilmington-on-Sea
    Blahshire
    England

Task 6

Choose a set of data about which you know quite a lot (e.g. difficulties of learning English; social, political or religious groups in your country) and classify these data according to a classification basis of your choice. Display the data in a logical diagram (like the 'sugars' diagram in Task 2). Show your diagram to a partner and ask her or him to identify the classification basis you used.

Using grammar in writing

You should have noticed in this unit so far that when we classify, we arrange members of a group, rather than parts relative to a whole as we did in Unit 1. The tables below show some of the most common language used in sentences which have classification as their purpose.

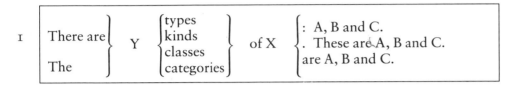

1
| There are ⎱ ⎰ The | Y | ⎧types⎫ ⎨kinds / classes⎬ ⎩categories⎭ | of X | ⎧ : A, B and C.⎫ ⎨ . These are A, B and C.⎬ ⎩ are A, B and C.⎭ |

2
| X ⎰consists of ⎱ ⎱can be divided into⎰ | Y | ⎧categories⎫ ⎨classes / kinds⎬ ⎩types⎭ | . These are A, B and C. : A, B and C. |

3
| A, B and C are | ⎧classes⎫ ⎨kinds / types⎬ ⎩categories⎭ | of X. |

Task 7

The table shows three major types of headaches and their symptoms. Write a text classifying the headaches, using the language of tables 1–3 above.

High Blood Pressure	Pain in forehead, sweating, anxiety, nausea, vomiting, confusion.
Allergy	Pressure on both sides of head, in forehead and behind eyes, sneezing, watery eyes.
Sinus	Frontal sinuses (forehead behind eyebrows): pain in forehead, temples, eyes; maxillary sinuses (cheekbones): pain in face, then forehead, upper jaw.

Task 8

Suppose that a developing country is considering ways of providing continuing education for its rural population. The group it is concerned with is small-scale farmers, who have had basic primary education and who are to be very important in a national drive to increase food production. You have been asked to be an Education Adviser to the Ministry of Education. Write a brief report to the Minister of Education, recommending which educational channel(s) should be used and why. Refer back to the work you did in Task 3 to help you.

Consolidation

A   Choose a classification basis for the people shown. Draw a simple tree diagram showing your classification, and then write a short text explaining the classification.

B   Use information from the two tables to write up a report intended for white-collar workers (e.g. bank staff, doctors) on the relationship between behaviour patterns and the risk of heart disease. Point out that they are likely to be classified as Type A and suggest how they might change their behaviour patterns to lower their risk of heart attack. (In describing the dangers of the types of heart disease you will probably choose to use a hierarchy based on a scale of frequency.)

BASIC PATTERNS OF BEHAVIOUR

Type	Characteristics
A	almost uncontrollable urge to compete chronic impatience and time-urgency staccato pattern of loud hurried speech strong tendency to interrupt almost unbearable discomfort at having to queue
B	relaxed, easy-going, free from competition, hostility and impatience

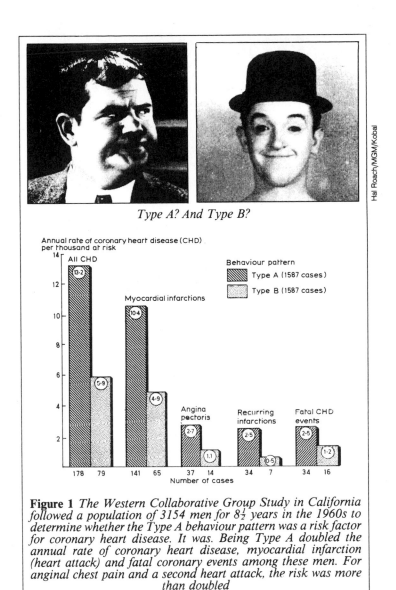

Type A? And Type B?

Figure 1 *The Western Collaborative Group Study in California followed a population of 3154 men for 8½ years in the 1960s to determine whether the Type A behaviour pattern was a risk factor for coronary heart disease. It was. Being Type A doubled the annual rate of coronary heart disease, myocardial infarction (heart attack) and fatal coronary events among these men. For anginal chest pain and a second heart attack, the risk was more than doubled*

(*New Scientist*)

C Think about your own special academic subject, or a special interest of yours. Try to draw a tree diagram classifying the various branches or sub-divisions that subject has (like the tree diagram on page 21). Then write a text to explain the basis or bases on which the subject is divided into these branches.

Looking back

Now that you have completed this unit you should understand what we mean in English by 'classification', and how data can be classified and arranged in diagrams and texts. You should be familiar with some expressions of classification and be able to use them in sentences and text.

Unit 3 Class relationships (2) Definition

Introduction

When we write we have to take into account the fact that our reader may not always understand the meaning of the more specialized words and expressions we wish to use. If we think this is the case, we will supply the reader with our definition of these terms. Here are some examples of writers defining terms for the reader:

1 In writing a paper on noise pollution, the writer needs to define the technical term 'perceived noise decibels' (PNdB):

> . . . aircraft noise is measured in PNdB (perceived noise decibels) – a unit which measures all the different sounds that make up a noise, and gives most importance to those that people actually find most annoying when they hear them.

2 Some words have different meanings in different special subjects, or have different meanings in different areas of one subject. These are often particularly difficult for the reader. In this example, the fairly common word 'interaction' is defined by the writer to make sure that both he and his readers are talking and thinking about the same thing:

> It will be convenient to end this introduction with some definitions that are implied in what has gone before and required for what is to follow. For the purpose of this report, interaction (that is, face-to-face interaction) may be roughly defined as the reciprocal influence of individuals upon one another's actions when in one another's immediate physical presence.

Task 1

Discuss the following sentences with a partner and decide which are acceptable definitions. Try to work out why the other definitions are not acceptable.

a) A capital city is like London.
b) A man is an animal with eight fingers and two thumbs.

c) Biochemistry is the study of biochemistry.
d) Socialism is what they have in the USSR.
e) Rust is a reddish brown coating formed on iron by the action of water and air.

Defining concrete terms is usually relatively easy. Such terms as 'copper', 'thermometer', etc. can usually be defined in the following way:

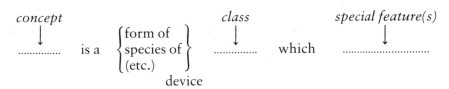

This definition structure is known as a *formal* definition.

Task 2

These formal definitions have their parts mixed up. See if you can rewrite them correctly. Check your rewritten sentences with one or two other students.

	concept	is	a/an/the	class	wh-word . . .
a)	a dentist	is	a	place	which is used in the manufacture of cloth
b)	copper	is	a	political system	which has four equal sides and four right angles
c)	an atom	is	a	plant	who takes care of people's teeth
d)	cotton	is	a	figure	which aims at public ownership of the means of production
e)	a restaurant	is	a	person	where food is bought and eaten
f)	a square	is	a	substance	that still has the same qualities, and can combine with other substances
g)	socialism	is	the	smallest piece of a simple substance	which is easily shaped, and allows heat and electricity to pass through it

Another definition structure, the *naming* definition, has the same parts but in a different order:

$$\underset{class}{\underbrace{\dots\dots\dots}} \begin{Bmatrix} who \\ which \end{Bmatrix} \underset{special\ feature(s)}{\underbrace{\dots\dots\dots\dots}}\ is\ \begin{Bmatrix} called \\ known\ as \\ (etc.) \end{Bmatrix} \underset{concept}{\underbrace{\dots\dots}}$$

> e.g. A person who studies living organisms is called a biologist.
>   A book which has soft covers and is relatively cheap is known as a paperback.

Many definitions can be written both ways.

Task 3

Not all the formal definitions in Task 2 can be rewritten as naming definitions. Rewrite those that can and suggest reasons why the remainder would make unsatisfactory naming definitions.

Task 4

Think of three ordinary subjects that you use or see every day. For each of them write both kinds of definition. Test them out on another student by blanking out the 'concept' word(s) and seeing whether she or he knows what you have defined.

> e.g. A writing instrument which contains a lead and can be erased by a rubber is called a . . .   (*pencil*)

In academic writing we tend to draw on other people's definitions of particular terms in order to help establish our own definition. When we follow this procedure we are obliged to make clear to the reader how we are using another writer's definition, i.e. do we accept it / accept part of it / reject it etc.?

Task 5

Read the following passage, which has been taken from an article called 'How animals learn: psychology vs ethology'. Then:
a) using information from the text, write a formal definition of a 'conditioned reflex';
b) using information from the text, write a definition of 'learning';
c) compare your definitions with those of another student.

> Until recently, learning was almost exclusively the prerogative of experimental psychologists, following the tradition established by I.P. Pavlov and his famous dogs. Pavlov found that dogs salivated when they heard a bell that signalled the arrival of food. Such a response was called a conditioned reflex and was supposed to demonstrate that the dog had in some way associated the bell with the food. Decades of subsequent research were based on the principle that all learning was a matter of forming associations between one stimulus and another, or between a stimulus and a response, under the influence of a "reinforcer" – reward or punishment. The animals that were studied were readily available and easy to handle in the lab – usually rats and pigeons.

(*New Scientist*)

Defining abstract concepts (words such as 'truth', 'beauty' and 'justice') is harder than defining concrete objects. Often such concepts cannot be adequately defined in a simple, one-sentence definition.

Task 6

What do you understand by the term 'social responsibility'? What does it involve? How do we recognize it? Who should be socially responsible?

Discuss these questions about social responsibility with some other students, then write your own definition of the term 'social responsibility' as you think it would be meant in a statement like:

Scientists, above all, should be socially responsible.

About writing

We have seen that to define something we need to name it, classify it, and state its most important (i.e. defining) characteristics. Because definitions are used to explain words we need, they are almost always only part of a text and not a whole text. We find definitions inside most serious writing, usually when something is being introduced for the first time.

Task 7

Read this text and find the definitions in it.

> The type of electricity that discharges from a solid material after it has been rubbed with another material is known as static electricity. One of the most common methods of demonstrating static electricity is by simply combing your hair. After it has passed through dry hair, a comb acquires the ability to attract small pieces of paper and similar objects to its surface. Two types of charge exist; no electrical phenomena are known that suggest the existence of more than these two types. Benjamin Franklin is responsible for the convention that an electrical charge is *negative* when it has been generated by rubber rubbed with fur, while the charge is *positive* when it has been generated from glass rubbed with silk. A charge generated in any other fashion can then be compared to these two results.
>
> The force of attraction, or the force of repulsion, of one type of charge for another one is called an electrostatic or coulombic force. Charles Coulomb first reported the results of such observations as a statement that has become known as *Coulomb's law*: Like charges repel: unlike charges attract.

Task 8

Rewrite Coulomb's law as a formal definition.

Task 9

Write formal definitions of:
a) static electricity;
b) positive charge;
c) electrostatic force.

Using grammar in writing

It is often necessary to expand the defining description of a concept by adding extra information to the definition. This can be done by using brackets or dashes. Study the examples.

1 A prehistoric animal is an animal which lived in a time before recorded history.
   A prehistoric animal (a brontosaurus, a pterodactyl, a mammoth, etc.) is an animal which lived in a time before recorded history.
2 Courtship is an innate pattern of behaviour which certain vertebrates carry out before mating.
   Courtship is an innate pattern of behaviour – such as dancing, preening, or bringing nesting materials – which certain vertebrates carry out before mating.

The additional information should be placed near the main information it clarifies.

Task 10

Use the information below these sentences to write expanded definitions of each underlined concept.

a) *Tungsten* is a metal which retains hardness at red heat.
    add: used in filaments in electric light bulbs
b) *A conversation* is a social event.
    add: two or more people speaking to each other

Task 11

Expand these definitions by adding your own examples; discuss the possibilities with another student.

a) Cereal is a plant which is grown to produce food.
b) A gas is a substance which is neither solid nor liquid.

A definition can also be expanded by giving an example of the use of the object or idea being defined, as in the example below:

> Aluminium is a metal which is light in weight. *Consequently, it is used in the manufacture of aircraft.*

When you expand a definition by giving an example of its use, you can use the following pattern:

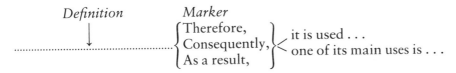

The decision whether to use a marker or not will depend on whether or not you think the reader needs to be *explicitly* told of the relationship between the definition and its use: in this case, that one is an effect of the other.

Task 12

Expand the following definitions by giving an example showing how the item being defined is used.

a) Glass is a substance which has the property of being transparent.
b) Stainless steel is an alloy which is resistant to corrosion.
c) A thermometer is a device for measuring temperature.

A definition can also be expanded by stating the main characteristics of the object or concept, as in the example below:

> Aluminium is a metal which is used in the manufacture of aircraft. *It is very light and resistant to corrosion.*

When you expand a definition by stating its characteristics, you may use explicit markers to show the relationship between the definition and its expansion:

> Aluminium is a metal which is used in the manufacture of aircraft *because* it is very light and resistant to corrosion.

In this case, one is a reason for the other.

Task 13

Expand the following definitions by stating the main characteristics of each item being defined.

a) Tobacco is a drug which is commonly used by human beings.
b) Cloth is a material made by weaving fibres such as wool, silk or cotton.
c) Binocular vision is that type of vision which allows distances to be judged and shapes to be perceived in depth.

In writing expanded definitions, *relative clauses* are very useful. Relative clauses allow a writer to avoid writing a series of very short sentences. They also allow the writer to show clearly which information she or he thinks is the most important and which is secondary. The information in the relative clause is always the secondary information. Look at these examples:

1 Aluminium, which is light and resistant to corrosion, is used in the manufacture of aircraft.
2 Aluminium, which is used in the manufacture of aircraft, is light and resistant to corrosion.

In the first example the *use* is the most important aspect for the writer, while in the second example the *characteristics* are most important.

Task 14

Use the notes, and other information if you wish, to write expanded definitions of each of the items in italics, using relative clause structures.

a) *caffeine* – substance – addictive – powerful effect on the heart – found in coffee

b) substance – not animal or plant – naturally occurring – includes ores, petroleum, natural gas and coal – often obtained by mining – *mineral*

c) *spacecraft* – vehicle – rocket engine – for travelling in space – capable of carrying astronauts – also known as spaceship – may carry missiles

Task 15

Complete the following short texts with the alternative that seems preferable to you.

a) Experimental psychology traditionally was interested in relationships between events. As a matter of fact . . .
    i)   the forming of associations between one stimulus and another was defined by such psychologists as learning.
    ii) learning was defined by such psychologists as a matter of forming associations between one stimulus and another.

b) People should use potassium bromide only under a doctor's direction because this form of bromide may cause skin rashes. It can also disturb the mind. . . .
    i)   Silver bromide is a form of bromide used in photography to make plates and film more sensitive to light.
    ii) In photography, a form of bromide called silver bromide is used to make plates and film more sensitive to light.

c) Brocade designs are woven by hand or machine into cloth to make fabrics for bedspreads, curtains, etc. . . .
    i)   Cloth that has designs woven into it with heavy yarns is called brocade.
    ii) Brocade is a cloth that has designs woven into it with heavy yarns.

d) Bubble gum (. . .) is a major cause of tooth decay among children.
    i)   bubble gum is a form of chewing gum
    ii) a form of chewing gum

Consolidation

A Study the expanded definition of 'civilization' below. Then write your own expanded definition of one of the following:

literacy   science
economics   medical ethics
agriculture   mechanics

> Civilization has received many definitions, but is often associated with cities. The words *civic, civil,* and *civilized* come from the Latin *civis* (citizen) and relate to obligations of people in a *civitas* (city-state). Civilization implies complex government. Usually a civilization also uses metals. Finally, a civilization develops arts of some maturity and creates some form of writing.

(Gerrit P. Judd *A History of Civilization*)

B Define, in at least three sentences, an abstract concept (e.g. 'beauty', 'honour', etc.) that has some influence on the way you live. Show your work to a partner and work together to judge how far your ideas have been communicated successfully. Make any changes necessary to enable your partner to fully understand your text.

C Quoted below you will find a passage from a well-known British novel, Lewis Carroll's *Through the Looking Glass*, in which Humpty Dumpty gives his opinions on defining words.

  1 Discuss Humpty Dumpty's ideas in groups of three or four. For example, can you use words in any way you want? Are there some words which can be used in different ways? Do some groups of people define particular words or groups of words in their own ways? If so, which words and in what ways?

". . . that shows that there are three hundred and sixty-four days when you might get un-birthday presents."

"Certainly," said Alice.

"And only one for birthday presents, you know. There's glory for you!"

"I don't know what you mean by 'glory'," Alice said.

Humpty Dumpty smiled contemptuously. "Of course you don't—till I tell you. I meant 'there's a nice knock-down argument for you!'"

"But 'glory' doesn't mean 'a nice knock-down argument'," Alice objected.

"When I use a word," Humpty Dumpty said, in rather a scornful tone, "it means just what I choose it to mean—neither more nor less."

"The question is," said Alice, "whether you *can* make words mean so many different things."

"The question is," said Humpty Dumpty, "which is to be master—that's all."

(Lewis Carroll *Through the Looking Glass*)

  2 Write a text giving your own views on how words and their meaning(s) might be defined and organized. What *is* meaning, anyway?

Looking back

Now that you have finished this unit you should understand how we use definitions in English, and should be able to recognize and produce them in sentences. You should also be familiar with ways of defining in texts.

Unit 4 Organizing texts (1) General–specific

Introduction

So far, we have concentrated on a number of purposes for which writing is used. We have examined some functions of informational writing, such as defining, and describing spatial relations, and have practised some organizational and grammatical areas which are particularly useful in expressing such ideas.

In this unit we are going to study an organizational principle of informational writing which can be used in organizing texts which have a wide variety of purposes. This is the *general–specific* pattern.

Generalizations are very important in writing. The sentence you have just read is a generalization and exemplifies one important function of generalizations: they are very useful in starting off a piece of writing / paragraph.

Task 1

With a partner, look at the following statements and identify:
a) the most general statement;
b) the most specific statement.

   i)   The results of an Edinburgh survey show that good language learners cope effectively with the emotional and motivational problems of language learning.
   ii) Most surveys show that many good language learners select goals and subgoals for themselves.
   iii) The majority of good language learners in the Edinburgh survey see language learning as a social process.
   iv) In a survey of good language learners taken in Edinburgh, 52% said they found talking to themselves to be a good way of learning how to talk in a foreign language.
   v)   One good learner, interviewed in the Edinburgh survey, claimed to have learned his English from watching television.

Generalizations allow a writer to introduce many points of detail in one statement (the generalization). Some or all of these can be developed later in the text, using information structures appropriate to the task, e.g. classifying, defining.

Task 2

Compose generalizations to cover the following sets of details.

a) Humans eat beef, pork, mutton, fish, fowl, etc.
b) Hinduism is a religion. Buddhism is a religion. Islam is a religion. Christianity is a religion.
c) Townsend's extensive study of poverty in the United Kingdom indicated that 57.2 per cent of those in households in poverty were women. In 1971 only 28 per cent of female employees, as against 62 per cent of male employees, were covered by an occupational pension scheme.
d) Computers are good at solving numerical problems. Computers are not good at tasks requiring common sense. Computers are good at selecting information. Computers are not good at tasks requiring imagination.

About writing

Generalizations are very powerful statements in that they can represent a large number of specific details. However, this necessarily means that they are rather vague. For example, if you read the generalization 'Reactions against technology are not new', you would expect the writer to support the generalization with some examples of 'old' reactions against technology. The text would have a *general–specific* pattern.

Task 3

Read this text and complete the diagram by filling in the numbers of appropriate sentences. You may need to use some numbers more than once.

Uses of Computers

(1) There are some tasks for which computers are eminently suited, and others at which they are no good at all.   (2) We know that they are very good at carrying out large computations – number crunching.   (3) They are very good at storing information (a passive task), and selecting parts of it (an active task).   (4) They are very good at trying an enormous number of possible combinations of conditions because they can sift through the possibilities at immense speed.

(5) Computers can run highly complex process plants in industry, for example, in chemical works.   (6) Raw materials are fed in at one end, and a product emerges at the other; in between there may be an infinity of combinations of temperatures, pressures and intermediate products, maintaining the balance of which is essential to getting what you want out of the plant.   (7) The whole process can be controlled by a computer, which monitors the variables, and makes adjustments accordingly.

(R. Dale and I. Williamson *The Myth of the Micro*)

generalization

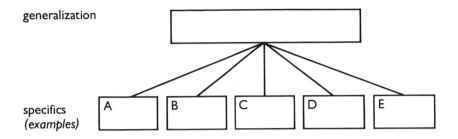

specifics
(examples)

Task 4

Rearrange the following sentences so that the resultant text follows a *general–specific* pattern.

i)   The defeat of France in the Napoleonic Wars is claimed to have been followed by a period of rampant mysticism including a wide resurgence of interest in astrology.

ii) George Orwell's *Nineteen Eighty-Four*, an equally damning indictment of the totalitarian possibilities contained in advanced technology, was written in the years immediately following the Second World War.

iii) Reactions against technology are not new.

iv) Throughout history man has been warned that he was creating forces he would be unable to control, that machines would eventually take over the planet and demand the total obedience of the human race (if, indeed, it was still allowed to exist), that to place one's faith in science and technology was to make a pact, like Faust, with the devil.

v)   Opposition to reason and to rationality, frequently embracing attacks on science and technology, has in particular been experienced by societies that have suffered a major upheaval or catastrophe.

vi) Oswald Spengler captured the imagination of a defeated Germany in 1920 with the publication of his *Decline of the West* and his prediction that 'Faustian man will be dragged to death by his own machine'.

(D. Dickson *Alternative Technology*)

Notice that, in this text (when the sentences have been rearranged), there is more than one sentence of generalization before the examples appear. The general sentences become more and more concrete until the specific examples are introduced by the phrase 'in particular'.

Task 5

Use information from the table below to write a text supporting the following generalization:

> 'Women constitute a disproportionately high percentage of low-paid workers in Britain today.'

You may also wish to put forward reasons as to why this is so. Discuss the generalization and the available information with another student before you begin to write.

	All women	**All men**	**Manual workers**		**Non-manual workers**	
			Women	**Men**	**Women**	**Men**
Table						
Earnings and hours worked by women and men in April 1979: adult employees in full-time employment whose pay was not affected by absence.						
Average gross weekly earnings (before tax or other deductions):	£63.00	£101.4	£55.2	£93.0	£66.0	£113.0
Proportion whose gross weekly earnings were:						
less than £50	29.9%	2.4%	41.1%	2.7%	25.7%	2.1%
less than £60	53.3%	8.1%	66.6%	9.6%	48.8%	6.1%
Average hours worked:	37.5	43.2	39.6	46.2	36.7	38.8
of which, overtime hours:	0.6	4.5	1.1	6.3	0.4	1.6
Average gross hourly earnings, excluding overtime pay and overtime hours:	£1.66	£2.32	£1.39	£1.98	£1.77	£2.90

Source: Summary Tables of *New Earnings Survey 1979*, in *Department of Employment Gazette*, October 1979, vol.87, no. 10, p.971.

Task 6

Use information from the table on page 39 to write a text supporting the following generalization:

> 'Inequality in wealth ownership continues to exist in contemporary Britain.'

Table

Estimated wealth of individuals in Great Britain, 1973.

Range of net capital value* (lower limit)	Number of cases (thousands)	Per cent	Amount (£ million)	Per cent
Nil	3,599	18.8	1,649	1.0
1,000	4,804	25.1	8,529	5.2
3,000	2,279	11.9	8,979	5.5
5,000	4,082	21.3	29,847	18.2
Under 10,000	14,764	77.1	49,006	29.9
10,000	2,229	11.6	27,738	16.9
15,000	782	4.1	13,854	8.5
20,000	1,044	5.5	30,723	18.8
50,000	211	1.1	13,109	8.0
100,000	79	0.4	10,025	6.1
200,000	31	0.2	19,414	11.8
Over 10,000	4,376	22.9	114,866	70.1
Total	19,140	100.0	163,872	100.0

* = 'net assets' or wealth.

Source: Inland Revenue, *Estimated Wealth of Individuals in Great Britain, 1973*, London, HMSO, 1975, table 1.

Examples are not the only kind of information which can follow a generalization. Sometimes a generalization provides a preview of the central points, which will be expanded in more detail in the rest of the text.

Task 7

Draw a diagram (like the one in Task 3) to show the general–specific structure of this extract.

> Stated simply, there are two habitats for plants and in each habitat raw materials are obtained differently. In land plants, oxygen and carbon dioxide enter through the pores in the leaves and stems. All the other raw materials are taken in from the soil through the roots. Plants that live in water are surrounded by dissolved raw materials which they take in all over their surfaces.

(British Museum *Nature at Work*)

Task 8

If you wanted to add the following detail to this text, *where* would you place it and why? Be prepared to justify your decision to a partner.

> *This wasteland comprises demolition sites and vacant plots usually owned by the local authority.*

The Wildlife of Britain's Wasteland

Many of Britain's industrial towns and cities are surrounded by wilderness, which sometimes has acquired the official designation of "urban common", but all of them have wasteland within their bounds which may be no less deserving of such recognition. Often they are left unused for years at a time, except, that is, for all those informal human activities, like adventure play, gypsy encampments, bonfires, dumping rubbish, and grazing goats, that are not allowed where the grass is mown and the trees are carefully planted. These impromptu "unofficial" urban commons often have a natural history that is both rich and unique to a particular area: a blend of wild animals and plants with "escapes" from gardens long gone. Citizens should see such areas as an asset, worthy of conservation.

(*New Scientist*)

Many types of detail may be introduced within the general–specific structure. In the text above we find details of definition ('This wasteland comprises . . .'); details of use ('Often they are left unused . . .'); and details of composition ('a blend of wild animals . . .').

Task 9

Discuss the information about Mauritius in the boxes with two or three other students. Decide how it can be organized in a general–specific pattern. Then use the information in the boxes to write a description of Mauritius, suitable for a secondary school textbook. Begin with a generalization.

Mauritius
At a glance

***** Excellent
**** Good
*** Fair
** Poor
* Appalling

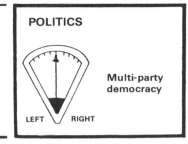

POLITICS

Multi-party democracy

LEFT RIGHT

SELF-RELIANCE
**

Food imports alone account for 25% of the total import bill

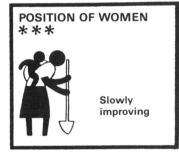

POSITION OF WOMEN
***

Slowly improving

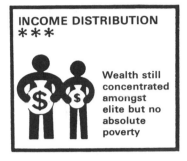

INCOME DISTRIBUTION
***

Wealth still concentrated amongst elite but no absolute poverty

LITERACY
****

72% for women and 86% for men

FREEDOM
****

No political prisoners. Absence of political and communal violence. Over 30 papers and magazines in publication

LIFE EXPECTANCY
****

66 years

(*New Internationalist*)

Using grammar in writing

In written English, the order in which groups of words appear makes a difference, sometimes a dramatic difference, to meaning. In speaking, we can make our meaning clear by repeating the same idea in different words, or by putting voice stress on certain words, but when we write, the words as they appear must be clear. Sometimes it is difficult to decide what word order to use, especially when referring to several things in the same sentence. Look at this example:

>   The morning when we were due to leave came at last.
>   The morning came at last when we were due to leave.

In speech, you could say either sentence and the hearer would probably know what you meant. In writing, however, you cannot take such a chance on being understood – only the first sentence is absolutely clear.

   A simple principle to help you decide on the order of word groups is:

>   What is most closely related in meaning should be closest within the sentence.

Task 10

Explain to a partner the differences in meaning between the two sentences in each of the following pairs.

a) Mary opened the door for the postman in a nightdress.
   Mary, in a nightdress, opened the door for the postman.
b) We rent rooms on the beach here.
   We rent rooms here on the beach.
c) By far the most widespread chemical elements are oxygen and silicon in the Earth's crust.
   By far the most widespread chemical elements in the Earth's crust are oxygen and silicon.

Sometimes more than one word-group order may be acceptable. In the sentence 'I watched him enter the bank through my binoculars', the correct order may be either:

1 Through my binoculars   I watched him   enter the bank.
   or
2 I watched him   through my binoculars   enter the bank.

Here 1 is better because 'I watched him' is closely related to *both* the other word groups. However, 1 gives emphasis to 'my binoculars' rather than 'I watched him', because the first part of an English sentence is considered emphatic: if you wanted to emphasize 'I watched him' you would choose 2.

Task 11

Underneath the following six sentences you will find six groups of words. Correctly add a different word group to each of the six sentences, making sure you follow the principle of word-group order given above.

a) He could not find a job.
b) In underdeveloped countries, the shortfall in food production in relation to population growth increases more and more.
c) The use of robots may change the workers' views.
d) People who tell you what you already know are bores.
e) The Trustees have decided to make available a sum of money for a travelling scholarship.
f) Coale and Hoover estimate that the proportion of children under fifteen in India in 1984 will be a third of the total population of the subcontinent.

in increasing numbers   *taking a low estimate only*
being over fifty   *such as those on the Indian subcontinent*
at great length   *each year*

When making decisions about the order of words in a sentence, it is also necessary to plan how the sentence will fit in with the preceding ones. Look at these two versions of the same text.

1 John was born in 1930. He lost his job this year. Being over 50, he cannot easily find another.
2 John was born in 1930. He lost his job this year. He cannot easily find another, being over 50.

Text 1 is preferable to text 2 for two reasons:
– 'Being over 50' is known information (born in 1930) and known information is usually placed at the beginning of a sentence.
– Text 2 has every sentence beginning with John; it lacks variety.

Task 12

Add the following expressions to the text below. The letter before each expression tells you to which sentence it belongs. Punctuate the completed text as necessary by adding capital letters, commas, etc.

a) as Egypt's population continues to expand
b) from 1960 to 1976
c) (both birth and death rates are lower than in rural areas)
d) in the areas
e) meanwhile
f) by the year 2000
g) by 2025
h) but

Cairo Population Outlook

(a) The urban centres suffer the additional burden of migration from the rural areas. (b) The percentage of Egypt's population living in Cairo rose from 14% to 22%, about half of the country's urban population. (c) The natural increase in Cairo is 2.5% annually, with migration adding another 0.6%. (d) The bulk of Cairo's growth has come around the city's boundaries. (e) Population growth in the city's centre dropped from 4.1% in the early 1960's to under 2% by the mid '70's as residential areas gave way to commercial and industrial development. (f) If present fertility and migration rates continue, the population of Cairo will almost double to 17.1 million. (g) Cairo would bulge with a staggering 39 million people – more than Egypt's entire population in 1975. (h) If an average of two children is achieved by 2000 the city's population would be 13.7, reaching 18.7 million by 2025.

(*Cairo Today*)

Consolidation

A Over half the world's rainforests have disappeared forever. The rest are in danger of disappearing in our lifetime. But rainforests have many advantages. Write a text on the topic 'How rainforests help man', using the outline information in the diagram tree (and remembering how information is classified). Define any terms you did not already know, the first time you use them.

B In groups of three, choose a generalization you feel you can support from the following list:

No man is an island.
If something can go wrong, it will.
The grass always looks greener on the other side of the hill.
All people are equal.

As a group write down as many ideas as you can that are relevant to the generalization. Try to group these ideas, defining them if necessary. Discuss how you might use them to write a text on your chosen topic. Finally write your own text individually.

C Using the information in this text, write a description of the findings of the study. Try to use a general–specific structure.

Cholesterol: the killer is convicted

A 10-year study of 3806 typical American men has shown that a cut in the cholesterol in their diet has saved lives.

Doctors have argued for years that America's predilection for food that is high in saturated fats is striking down men and women in their prime with heart disease, the country's biggest killer. High levels of cholesterol in the blood coat blood vessels with plaque, which causes angina and prompts surgery that costs billions of dollars each year.

But the hypothesis that low-fat diets and drugs could save lives had never been carefully tested – until the National Heart, Lung and Blood Institute began its study 10 years ago.

One group of subjects embarked on a low-fat diet supplemented by cholestyramine, a drug that attacks cholesterol, taken several times a day. The other group also dieted but, unknowingly, took a placebo instead of the drug. After one year, cholesterol levels dropped among both groups, but eventually the drug easily outperformed the diet, reducing the risk of heart disease by 19 per cent, and heart attacks by 24 per cent.

(*New Scientist*)

Looking back

Now that you have finished this unit you should be able to recognize generalizations and the details which support them. You should be able to write a simple text with a generalization supported by relevant specific details.

Unit 5 Class relationships (3) Comparison/contrast

Introduction

We have already seen that when we are writing informational (expository) texts we need to classify and define the concepts and objects we refer to. Classifications and definitions are both based on our recognition of the differences and similarities between objects and concepts. When we describe or discuss similarities, we are making *comparisons*. When we describe or discuss differences, we are making *contrasts*.

Task 1

For displaying similarities and differences, the matrix is very useful. Look at this example, then make the comparisons and contrasts requested below.

make	price	country of origin	engine size	m.p.g.*
Toyota	£5,200	Japan	999 cc	48
Volkswagen	£6,000	West Germany	1272 cc	40
Ford	£4,900	USA	1118 cc	48
Nissan	£5,200	Japan	988 cc	52

*m.p.g. = miles per gallon

a) Which two cars have the same petrol consumption?
b) Which two cars have the most characteristics in common?
c) Which two cars have the most differing characteristics?
d) Which Japanese car would be the better value?
e) Which car would be the best value?

Task 2

A report issued by the Royal College of Physicians in 1983, quoted in the *New Scientist*, stated that 'in Britain between 15 and 20 per cent of all deaths are caused by tobacco'. Look at the photographs on page 47. Write a short comparison/contrast of the image of cigarette smoking as presented through sporting events such as these with the image presented by the Royal College of Physicians' statement.

About writing

There are two main ways of logically developing a description based on comparison/contrast. The following text uses the first of these patterns, as you can see from the diagram on page 48.

Generalization {

All learning depends upon motivation, perception and exercise. The language learner's most important task is to internalise the basic patterns and to acquire a new system of language habits so that he/she can react automatically to the structural signals of the second language. This can be accomplished only by drill. Theoretical study of a language does not necessarily improve your ability to speak. *All this applies equally well to organic chemistry learning.* Structure recognition and structure drawing must be automatic and accurate. The eye must learn to assemble all cues, and size up just what has gone on in a given reaction – quickly, as a matter of habit. Obviously achieving this proficiency will also require drill.

Points relating to language learning {

Points relating to chemistry {

Pattern 1

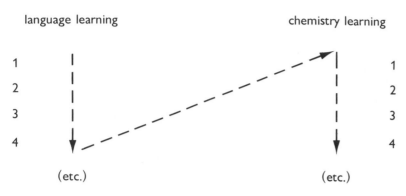

As can be seen from the diagram, the text first deals with language learning, giving all the available information, and then shows its similarity to the learning of organic chemistry, giving all the available information on that. The linking expression 'All this applies equally . . .' shows the comparison relationship between the two sets of details.

The next text, in contrast, is organized according to the second pattern, making its comparisons point by point, in pairs:

Generalization

management (1)

strikers (1)

management (2)

strikers (2)

> Television is generally biased against the workers. You can prove this any night by watching the news. When a strike is reported, a management representative will be interviewed in favourable surroundings (e.g. in his office). The strikers, however, will be interviewed all together out in the open. The manager will emerge as a polite, responsible, authoritative person, whereas the workers will emerge as people who shout and who all speak at the same time (as in polite and aggressive).

Pattern 2

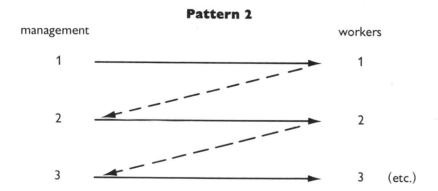

Whereas Pattern 1 moves vertically, Pattern 2 moves horizontally. Both patterns are equally acceptable, depending on the type and purpose of the text you are writing. Some people find Pattern 2 clearer because of the way it keeps reminding you of the comparison/contrast relationship. Sometimes, however, such continual reminders can become boring for the reader.

Task 3

Look at the text on tobacco you wrote (Task 2). Work with a partner to decide which pattern it follows.

Task 4

Look again at the matrix (Task 1) showing the price, engine size and m.p.g. of four cars.
a) Which organizational pattern would lead to the most easily understood text about the cars?
b) Write a text which makes clear the relative economy of the cars.
c) Compare your text with that of another student.

When you compare or contrast two or more items, you need to have a *measure* or *measures* on which to base each comparison/contrast. For example, in the 'cars' matrix the measures were price, country of origin, engine size and m.p.g.

Task 5

Study the following matrix, which shows the desirable and undesirable effects of some of the scientific developments of the last hundred years. Then write a text in which you discuss the desirability of innovation. Use examples from the table to support your arguments. Use either Pattern 1 or Pattern 2.

	Innovation	Long-term effects of innovation	
		desirable	*undesirable*
a)	antibiotics	diphtheria and other infections controlled	development of resistant strains of bacteria
b)	nuclear power	long-term energy supply assured	risk of radiation from system faults, leakage of stored wastes
c)	juggernaut lorries	reduced haulage costs	congestion on narrow roads and in towns, noise
d)	high-rise flats	higher densities of housing made possible	loneliness, communities broken up, vandalism

Using grammar in writing

There are many ways of expressing comparison and contrast; which way you use depends on your purpose. Let us compare the following sentences:

1 The Ford Sierra is cheaper than the Volkswagen Scirocco.
2 The Ford Sierra costs £6,600 whereas the Volkswagen Scirocco costs £7,100.

Both sentences say that the Ford Sierra is cheaper than the Volkswagen. However, they do this in different ways. Sentence 1 directly states that the Ford is cheaper than the Volkswagen but gives no evidence in the form of prices, whereas sentence 2 gives us the prices and indirectly states that the Ford is cheaper. Sentence 1 would be appropriate if the prices were already known to the reader (perhaps given in a table). Sentence 2 would be appropriate if the prices were not already known.

Task 6

Study the following sentences and:
a) circle the markers of comparison/contrast, as in the example below;
b) add at least two other sentences of your own, using different markers;
    (Markers are the words that tell you this is a comparison/contrast.)
c) read the sentences some other students have written.

Comparison
i)   (Both) tobacco (and) alcohol are injurious to health.
ii)   One language is as good as another.
iii) Cairo is no bigger than many European cities.
iv)   This book is the same price as many others.
v)   ....
vi)   ....

Contrast
i)   Arabic is read from right to left (whereas) English is read from left to right.
ii)   The Eiffel Tower is higher than the highest pyramid.
iii) While taxis are expensive, public transport is cheap.
iv)   Cairo differs from London in density of population.
v)   ....
vi)   ....

In the sentences above you have seen examples of comparison and of contrast within sentence structures. Table 1 on page 51 shows the common ways in which comparisons or contrasts can be expressed within sentences.

TABLE I

Comparison within sentences		Contrast within sentences	
A is like B A and B are similar A is similar to B A resembles B	with respect to cost.	A is unlike B A differs from B A and B differ A is different from B A contrasts with B	with respect to cost.
Both A and B cost £100. A is as costly as B. A is no more expensive than B. A costs the same as B.		A costs £100 whereas B costs £150. A costs £100, while B costs £150. A costs £100, but B costs £150. B is more expensive than A. A is not as expensive as B.	

As Table 2 shows, comparisons and contrasts can be made between sentences as well.

TABLE 2

Comparison between sentences	Contrast between sentences
A is expensive to buy. *Similarly*, it is expensive to operate. A is expensive to buy. *Likewise,* it is expensive to operate. A is expensive to buy. *Correspondingly*, it is expensive to operate.	A is expensive to buy. *On the other hand*, it is cheap to operate. A is expensive to buy. *In contrast*, it is cheap to operate. A is expensive to buy. *Conversely*, it is cheap to operate.

Task 7

Study the following sentences and:
a) circle the markers of comparison/contrast;
b) write at least two other pairs of sentences, using different markers;
c) read the sentences some other students have written.

Comparison
i)   Learning to drive a car requires a lot of patience. Similarly, learning a language requires a considerable amount of patience.
ii) Edinburgh as a major tourist centre invests large sums of money in preserving its ancient buildings. Cairo, likewise, has discovered that well-preserved ancient buildings are a considerable tourist attraction.
iii) ....

Contrast
i)   Japanese industry invests considerable sums of money in research and development. In contrast, British investment in this area is low.
ii) The majority of Egyptians practise Islam. On the other hand, there is also a large Christian minority.
iii) ....

Task 8

With a partner, look again at the text you wrote on the desirable and undesirable effects of scientific developments (Task 5). Discuss how your text can be improved by using suitable grammar techniques and logical connectors to make the information clearer. Then rewrite your text individually.

Task 9

You are going to read a text which contrasts the 'Western' idea of personal space with that of 'Easterners'. However, you only see one sentence at a time, and you must build up the text yourself by choosing the sentence which fits best with what comes before.

Read the beginning of the text and choose one sentence from the two which follow it. Keep choosing one sentence from each two, continuing the text as you think the writer might have written it.

Personal Space and Culture
Hall (1959) and others have commented on the different sense of space that Westerners and Easterners entertain.

(continue with one of the following)
a) When they speak with each other, Easterners tend to stand closer.
b) Easterners tend to stand closer when they speak to each other.

(continue with one of the following)
c) Westerners carry with them a spatial cocoon, on the other hand, that they do not like to see violated.
d) Westerners, on the other hand, carry with them a spatial cocoon that they do not like to see violated.

(continue with one of the following)
e) By a system of keeping reasonable distances between themselves and others, Westerners fill up beaches, buses – all public places in fact.
f) Westerners fill up beaches, buses – all public places in fact – by a system of keeping reasonable distances between themselves and others.

(continue with one of the following)
g) Deliberately choosing places near each other and even near crowded food stands or exits, an Egyptian beach fills up by "clumps".
h) An Egyptian beach fills up by "clumps", people deliberately choosing places near each other and even near crowded food stands or exits.

(continue with one of the following)
i) They enjoy the movement around them of other people and like to watch and interact with their neighbours.

j) Other people moving around them they enjoy and like to watch and interact with their neighbours.

(continue with one of the following)
k) By not speaking to those around them, Westerners forced to sit near each other effect privacy.
l) Westerners forced to sit near each other effect privacy by not speaking to those around them.

(continue with one of the following)
m) During illness the Westerner's desire for privacy becomes strongest.
n) The Westerner's desire for privacy becomes strongest during illness.

(continue with one of the following)
o) Then dominating the social context is his or her need to retreat and "sleep it off".
p) Then his or her need to retreat and "sleep it off" dominates the social context.

(continue with one of the following)
q) Egyptians, as might be expected, feel differently.
r) Egyptians feel differently, as might be expected.

(continue with one of the following)
s) They want the support of others, when they feel most vulnerable.
t) When they feel most vulnerable, they want the support of others.

(Adapted from A.B. Rugh *Family in Contemporary Egypt*)

Consolidation

A Using the information from the questionnaire shown below, compare and contrast Soviet and American children's responses to nuclear war. Be sure to include in your text possible reasons for the differing responses.

Do you think a nuclear war between the US and USSR will happen during your lifetime?

SOVIET		AMERICAN	
Yes	11.8%	Yes	38.5%
No	54.5%	No	16.0%
Uncertain	33.7%	Uncertain	44.5%

If there were a nuclear war, do you think that you and your family would survive?

SOVIET		AMERICAN	
Yes	2.9%	Yes	16.5%
No	80.7%	No	41.5%
Uncertain	16.4%	Uncertain	41.1%

If there were a nuclear war, do you think that the US and the USSR would survive it?

SOVIET		AMERICAN*	
Yes	6.1%	Yes	22.0%
No	78.9%	No	38.0%
Uncertain	15.0%	Uncertain	39.5%

Do you think nuclear war between the US and the USSR can be prevented?

SOVIET		AMERICAN	
Yes	93.3%	Yes	65.0%
No	2.8%	No	14.5%
Uncertain	3.9%	Uncertain	20.0%

American children were asked only about the survival of the US.

(*WorldPaper*)

B Write a text, based on the texts below, which answers the question:
   'Which is more effective in the Third World, radio or the press?'
Before you write you will need to make the following decisions:
  1 What measures will you use as your basis?
  2 Will you use Pattern 1 or Pattern 2 (or a mixed pattern, Pattern 3)?
  3 Who are you writing for, i.e. who is your reader?

THE RADIO

The world's entire population lives within transmitting distance of a radio signal. And the transistor revolution has greatly reduced the price of a set. No wonder the radio is becoming popular. In Africa the number of radio receivers has more than doubled in the 1970's to around 31 million. In Asia it shot up to 141 million and in Latin America to 87 million. In many regions community listenings are arranged with groups of villagers, students in schools or workers in factories, so they can discuss and act on the basis of broadcasts about farming, education or industrial safety.

But radio listening still lags far behind the industrial countries. There are nine sets for every 100 people of the Third World as against 70 per 100 in the developed world. The only area of the developing world where radios are reasonably plentiful is Latin America where there are 24 sets per 100 people.

Many developing countries also have insufficient transmission points. Compared to 13,400 broadcasting transmitters in the USA, Africa has only 790. As a result, an average African transmitter sends its signals over 100,000 square miles in comparison with 1,600 square miles for an average American transmitter. This means weak signals and lots of static for African listeners.

Number of radio receivers and their reach		
	Number of receivers (in millions)	Number of receivers per 1,000 people
World total	1,058	325
Africa	31	73
America	553	947
Asia	141	95
Europe	182	773
USSR	134	515
Developed countries	869	762
Developing countries	189	89
Africa (excluding Arab States)	20	62
Northern America	466	1,942
Latin America	87	252
Asia (excluding Arab States)	133	92
Arab States	19	130

Source: UNESCO Statistical Year Book, 1980

THE PRESS

Newspaper circulation in the Third World is minute. It averages about two copies per 100 people in Africa, and seven in both Asia and Latin America. In 34 of the smallest countries there are no daily newspapers.

Low circulation is due not only to poor literacy, but the high cost of production. Newsprint is manufactured in small quantities in the developing countries and the price of imported newsprint has escalated recently. The cost of distributing newspapers has also rocketed since the oil crisis of the early 1970's, because of their dependence on road transport.

So even the literate of the Third World find it difficult to regularly buy newspapers. The average Asian must work for three weeks to earn enough to buy a newspaper regularly for the year, while their counterparts in the West would earn enough in two and a half days.

Number and circulation of Daily papers		
	Number of Dailies	Number of copies per 1,000 people
World total	8,210	136
Africa	180	21
America	3,110	158
Asia	2,380	72
Europe	1,740	264
USSR	690	394
Developed countries	4,700	321
Developing countries	3,510	36
Africa (excluding Arab states)	150	15
Northern America	1,950	281
Latin America	1,160	72
Asia (excluding Arab States)	2,300	13
Arab States	110	30

Source: UNESCO Statistical Year Book, 1980

(New Internationalist)

C Discuss the following 'problems' with a partner or in a group.
   1 If you as a writer were presenting a comparison of two things, one of
      which is familiar to the reader, in which order would you present them:
      familiar followed by unfamiliar or unfamiliar followed by familiar? Why?
   2 If you were presenting a comparison of two proposals, solutions, etc., one
      of which you prefer, in which order would you present them: the preferred
      one followed by the other, or the other followed by the preferred one?
      Why?
   3 If, in a scientific report, you were presenting a set of advantages/
      disadvantages, in which order would you present them: advantage
      followed by disadvantage, or disadvantage followed by advantage? Why?

Work with a partner and choose a topic (for example, methods of heating a
house; sexual equality versus sex discrimination), then each write a text
following the principle you decided on in 1, 2 or 3 above. When you have
finished, discuss the texts written by yourself and your partner.

Looking back

Now that you have finished this unit you should recognize expressions of
comparison and contrast in sentences and text. You should recognize different
ways that texts structure comparison and contrast sequences, and you should be
able to produce simple texts of comparison and contrast containing suitable
expressions and having an appropriate structure.

Unit 6 Linear relationships (1) Time

Introduction

Every writer sometimes needs to write a time-based (chronological) sequence. Of course, historians do this often, but whether or not you are a historian you will occasionally want to describe a sequence of events in your writing. Chronological sequences can be written in different ways. In Western culture we normally think of time as moving forward in a straight line, and an expected chronological sequence follows this view of time and can be illustrated as follows:

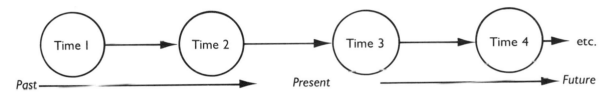

Time 1 is in the past, while Time 2 is also in the past but nearer the present than Time 1, and so on.

Task 1

Read the following text and use dates to complete the simple diagram which follows.

> ### By their garbage shall they be known
>
> As long ago as 1779 John Frere, High Sheriff of Suffolk, MP for Norwich, an English country gentleman, discovered at Hoxne, Suffolk, several bones from extinct animals associated with Stone Age flint implements. He published his findings in 1800. Frere's report was not really appreciated for another 60 years. But now Frere is known as the "founder of prehistoric archaeology".

(New Scientist)

⟫→

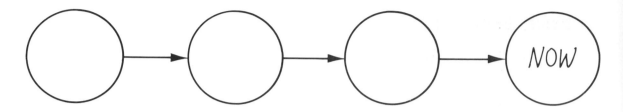

This simple time diagram shows time (in this case, historical dates) in natural order. Information and events are easiest to understand when they are presented in natural time order.

Task 2

In the text below, some of the information is not in an acceptable chronological order. Discuss with a partner what changes are necessary to put the information in an acceptable order.

> The production of silicon wafers containing integrated circuits is carried out mainly in the US. Cutting up these wafers into as many as 600 micro chips and maintaining and connecting them is labour intensive. In 1963, the major microelectronics companies set out in search of the cheapest labour power they could find to perform the labour intensive stages. They found the labour they were looking for in South East Asia, and the Fairchild company broke the ground by establishing an assembly factory in Hong Kong. By 1978, Malaysia, to take one example, had 69 microelectronic assembly plants, 20 of them owned by the biggest US companies.
>
> By the early 1970s Intel was building a thriving market in the US for its microprocessor, and other companies were beginning to build computer memories from microelectronic devices instead of the older hand-threaded core memories. This new level of integration led to a new wave of expansion between 1972 and 1974, this time into Malaysia, Thailand, the Philippines and Indonesia. The other major companies followed and, throughout the 1970s, Taiwan, South Korea and Singapore were favoured.

(Adapted from CSE Microelectronics Group *Microelectronics*)

About writing

As we live our daily lives, we see time as moving in one direction – past us into history, as we appear to move forward into the future. There is nothing we can do to change our relationship to time. However, when we write we can manipulate time if we wish, and move the writing backwards and forwards through time according to our purpose in writing.

Task 3

Read the following text and agree on answers to the questions below with one or two other students.

An Emigrant's Story

In 1847, Michael Moore, a poverty-stricken seventeen-year-old farm worker left Ireland for America. What the future held in store for him, he did not know. However, he did know that it could not be any worse than the past. He had grown up during the Great Famine in Ireland and had known what it was to be very hungry. He had watched his mother die of typhus a month before; his father had died a year after Michael was born. There was nothing now to keep him in Ireland and so, on a bright June morning, he stepped on board a ship bound for America. In years to come he would remember this moment.

---

a) Why do you think the writer starts with 1847 and then goes back into the past rather than starting in the past and ending up with 1847?
b) If the text were in the expected sequence, what verb tense would you expect to find used?
c) Which of the following tenses are used in the text? Present / present perfect / past / past perfect?

The writer of the above passage develops an unexpected sequence because he wants to highlight the fact that Michael Moore was forced to leave Ireland for America. The way Michael Moore's leaving is highlighted also captures our attention and makes us want to find out why he was leaving and why he was poverty-stricken. In general, writers use *unexpected* chronological sequences when they want to emphasize something *other than time*.

Task 4

Rewrite the 'Emigrant' text starting with Moore's early days in Ireland and ending with his departure from Ireland in 1847. Compare the two versions to decide which is the more interesting.

Task 5

+ *Write time phrase*

Complete this time diagram to show how the 'Land reform' text moves from one time period to another. Fill in the circles with paragraph numbers (two have been done for you). Where there is more than one time mentioned in a paragraph, the same paragraph may be entered in several columns. Check your answers with one or two other students.

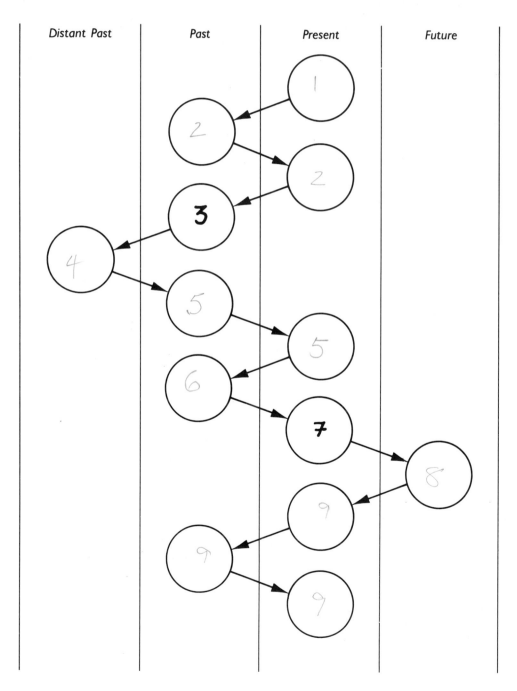

| Distant Past | Past | Present | Future |

LAND REFORM: Withering palms

1. Mauritania, on the west coast of Africa, has an interior with a large deposit of iron ore, nomads, oases, hundreds of thousands of date palms, and an awful lot of Sahara sand. Water, a scarce commodity, is the key to power.

2. The injection of a modern waterpump technology in the sixties into an already restive oasis society, according to a report in *Ceres* (No.76), has served to widen the gap between rich and poor date palm farmers.

3. At Atar oasis in 1965 there were about 10,000 date palm plantations. Most were in good shape with comparatively short trees set out in regular lines edged by simple irrigation ditches.

4. For centuries water had been raised from an underground table by the *chadouf*, which is a long pole on a central spindle with a heavy stone as a counterweight at one end and a water container at the other. The chadouf cannot draw water from a depth greater than the length of the pole and rope combined – about four metres.

5. A succession of drought years in the sixties saw the water table at Atar drop from four metres below the surface in 1960 to 20 metres. Only those plantations served by water pumps have survived.

6. The poorer farmers who could not afford to switch to motor pumps watched their plantations scorch and die. Then those with pumps faced another problem: maintenance.

7. The only pump maintenance shop is state-owned and employs only one man. There is no charge for repairs but the *Ceres* report describes the shop as 'depressing'. It says nothing is done to salvage parts from pumps beyond repair and that the place is 'inadequate for normal repairs'. This really means that when a pump breaks down the farmer has to buy another one or go out of business.

8. Possible solutions? Improve the repair shop, teach elementary pump maintenance to the planters, charge a fair price for repairs and ensure there is responsible supervision of the pump servicing facilities. But after that it's not so straightforward.

9. Atar is solidly controlled by the rich palm farmers who are not interested in water exploration or projects to improve irrigation to the drier and poorer plantations. Why should they be? In 1965 there were about 400,000 palms at Atar; today there are about half as many trees; and, not surprisingly, crop prices are higher.

(*New Internationalist*)

Using grammar in writing

You will have noticed that certain expressions like *in 1965*, *For centuries* and *in the sixties* help you recognize the natural time relationships between events. In general the verb form tells a reader that the writer is talking about the past, present or future, for example:

> *I walked to the University* = past

while a time expression indicates a more specific time in the past, present or future, for example:

> *I walked to the University yesterday* = past + particular time in past

⟫→

The more unusual the time sequence used in a text, the more you can expect to find specific time expressions to help you work out the time relationships. Here are some common time expressions which either mark a specific time (1) or show the relationship between times (2).

1 *Time Indicators*   then, just then, at that time, in those days, last Friday, next Easter, in 1983, at the beginning of June, at four o'clock, five years ago, (etc.)

2 *Time Relators*

Time before	until (then), by (then) before (then), up to that time, in the weeks/months/years leading up to, prior to, (etc.)
At the same time as	in the meantime, at that (very) moment, simultaneously, all the while, (etc.)
Time after	subsequently, afterwards, then, next, presently, after a while, later (on), in due course, eventually, finally, at last, in the long run, (etc.)

Task 6

Rewrite the text below so that instead of the time sequence 1948 → 1963 → 1969 it shows the sequence 1948 → 1969 → 1963.

In 1948, William Shocklay working in the laboratory of the Bell Telephone Company produced the first transistor. Years later, in 1963, Robert Noyce managed to put more than one transistor on the same small piece of silicon – integrating first two, then tens of transistors into complex current patterns and forming the basis of the integrated-circuit industry. Soon afterwards, in 1969, Ted Hoff, a research worker at Intel worked out a design which, for the first time, would put the complete workings of a basic computer processor on just one chip slightly less than a sixth of an inch long and an eighth of an inch wide.

(Adapted from CSE Microelectronics Group *Microelectronics*)

Task 7

Work with a partner to study this text and decide how the information can be reconstructed in natural time order. Check your results with another pair of students. When you are all agreed, you should each write up the text individually in natural time order, making any necessary changes.

Soon after the Cambrian explosion, 600 million years ago, the oceans teemed with different forms of life. By 500 million years ago there were vast herds of trilobites. But there are no trilobites alive today; there have been none for 200 million years. After the Cambrian explosion, species followed each other in rapid succession.

Before the Cambrian explosion species seem to have succeeded one another rather slowly. For most of the four billion years since the origin of life the dominant organisms were microscopic blue-green algae. By three billion years ago, a number of one-celled plants had joined together and the first multi-cellular organisms had evolved. By one billion years ago, plants, working cooperatively, had made a stunning change in the environment of the Earth. Green plants generate molecular oxygen, and a great many organisms, unable to cope with oxygen, perished. Less than ten million years ago, the first creatures who closely resembled human beings evolved. And then, only a few million years ago, the first true humans emerged.

(Adapted from Carl Sagan *Cosmos*)

Consolidation

A Read the text on pages 64–5, which appeared in the *Sunday Times* magazine and is about a paralysed woman's daily life. Then discuss the answers to these questions with a partner, or make notes.

1 The title of the text is 'A Life in the Day of . . .' A more normal title might be 'A Day in the Life of . . .': can you suggest why this rather strange title was chosen?

2 Because the text is about what Ann Armstrong does every day you probably expected to find a lot of verbs in the present tense (e.g. I wake up . . . I eat . . ., etc.). Does the writer use only verbs in the present tense? If not, what types of information do the sentences which use other tenses give us?

3 Why do you think the writer does not just present us with a list of sentences telling us what Ann Armstrong does every day?

4 When you have answered the other questions, write your own text about 'A Life in the Day of (yourself)'.

Ann Armstrong talks about life on a respirator.

A LIFE IN THE DAY OF
Ann Armstrong

" I love to wake up each morning to the sound of my husband's voice asking me, "Tea?" My reply is always an enthusiastic "Please". He supports my head in a comfortable position which enables me to drink from the cup that he holds to my lips. He is expert at this. We never spill a drop between us.

Thirty years ago, when I was a young and active mother of two small boys, Brian and Andrew, Ken had stood beside my bed with an early-morning cup of tea, wondering why I did not take it from him as usual. I wondered about that myself. Then I realised I could not move. I lay quietly waiting for my body to obey my brain. It seemed to be taking an interminable time. I was being distracted by the 'granddaddy' of all headaches. It felt as though someone was thumping the back of my head and neck with a sledgehammer and I could not put up my hand to defend myself.

Willingly, I allowed myself to be strapped on to a stretcher and rushed by ambulance along the jolting road from Newbury to Reading Isolation Hospital. The journey could have done me no good at all, but I needed to be slammed into an iron lung fast, so that my breathing could be done for me mechanically. My total repertoire of abilities had been locked in by catastrophic polio.

A respirator has 'breathed' me ever since. Down all those years the whooshing ship's engine kind of sound has gone on and on and on. At first it interfered with my thoughts and I kept remembering poems about the sea. Now I have learned to ignore it. Having dictated articles for national newspapers such as *The Times* and edited a magazine, *Responaut*, for disabled people, their families, engineers and medical staff for the 25 years since I founded it, I plan to spend the next 25 years tapping out books on my computer by sending it morse instructions with my toe.

The trick of surviving serenely the hateful reality of waking up each morning to the unbelievable fact that I still cannot move or breathe, is to take my cup for the day in small sips. I do not face in my mind the thought of another 30 years in one big, black immovable block – that way lies depression – but I can accept one more minute, one more hour or even one more day, especially if I can see a way through to being useful to the community to which I belong.

As I dare not catch cold, few visitors are allowed during the winter, so Ken has moved the bird-table close to my window. I can now share the antics of our mixed bag of wild birds – acrobatic blue tits, squabbling starlings and sparrows, bossy blackbirds and robins.

I have seen far too much of our excellent doctor these past few months. I am just recovering from a virus infection of my kidneys and throat. The medicine I drank so eagerly made my ears ring, so I stopped taking it. It was 50 per cent aspirin and known to cause tinnitus. I

Ann Armstrong, paralysed by polio, has spent the last 30 years on a respirator. She founded the magazine RESPONAUT in 1963 to enable disabled and non-disabled people to speak for themselves and bring about changes in the traditional image, language and lifestyles of the people concerned. She is married with two sons and lives in Newbury, Berkshire, with her husband Ken.

---

wonder how Jack Ashley puts up with this dreadful noise in his ears all the time? I found it hard to concentrate. I can only marvel at the superb introduction he has written for my new book, *Breath-of Life*.

The postman pushes through my letter-box packages and letters from distant friends in Canada, America, Australia, New Zealand, Hong Kong, Africa and both sides of the Iron Curtain. Ken opens the envelopes and hangs the letters up in front of me so that I can read them. I dictate a few words of reply and, before he leaves for work at the Council offices, Ken makes notes on the backs of the letters while waiting for Pam to arrive to take over the morning shift.

I delegate the domestic details to her and she fills the house with the smell of toast. This sharpens the appetite of my physiotherapist who arrives just as I am chewing my last crust. My physiotherapist keeps me stretched and supple. At this stage we do not look for any return of movement to my muscles. I am always hopeful, but I have had to accept that if my condition does not deteriorate, then that is progress.

The physiotherapist hands me back to Pam and we swallow a quick hot drink before the nurses come buzzing at the door. Two call every morning to 'breathe' me under the positive pressure mask, so that they can remove my cuirass [harness]. Then they treat the places where it bites me and I can do my daily breathing exercises to wash out excess carbon dioxide. I find all this activity very strenuous and am glad when it is over and I can settle down to computing a few ideas for my next book.

More cooking aromas drift in from the kitchen and Pam brings my lunch. I must not talk. My machine goes on breathing me relentlessly whether I need to swallow or not. I have swallowing difficulties and must make absolutely sure I despatch morsels of chewed food to my stomach only when my respiratory tract is closed. Carol takes over from

Pam. There will be even more aromatic smells from the kitchen as she cooks one of her famous curries. Meanwhile, Jean is desperately beavering away despatching the complimentary copies of our most recent issue of the *Responaut*.

In the evening Ken has to attend a council meeting. Rosemary arrives to type out the notes for my latest article and plans for the next *Responaut*. I switch on Radio 3 by pushing with my toe a button on the control panel at the foot of my bed. This gives me command over the television, radio, lamp, overhead light, computer, tape recorder, electric blanket and a series of battery-fed bells to various parts of the house. I can never be left alone and these bells are for summoning help when a second person is needed.

Ken arrives home about 9.30pm and takes over from Rosemary. We usually make or take phonecalls to or from our sons at this time. This brings them very close, now that they live away.

Ken will not eat his supper until he has completed my tucking-up routine. He rubs and exercises my limbs, settles me on a bedpan, then makes me straight in the bed, shakes up and rearranges my supporting cushions, washes where necessary, cleans my teeth, brushes and combs my hair, adjusts my cuirass, checks the air pressure and so on. The morning routine will be much the same.

It is bedtime. I have managed another productive day. I answered several letters, drafted a clutch of paragraphs for my next book, brought my diary up to date, made out a programme for this year's usual 10 meetings here of the Writers' Workshop, planned and listed jobs and meals, priced shopping lists for next week, arranged the helpers' rota and coped with all the demands on my day with much help from my friends.

I go to sleep. I am never disabled in my dreams . . .

(Sunday Times)

B Using the information from this diagram and text, write an account of the accident record of the Windscale nuclear processing plant. You can write your account from the point of view either of someone who is opposed to the use of nuclear processing plants, or of someone who is in favour of them. Discuss with your teacher / other students how best to achieve your goal of opposing or defending nuclear plants, given the information you have at your disposal.

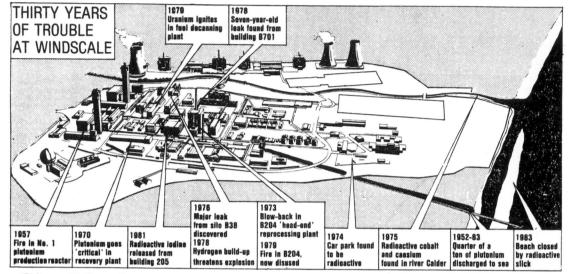

THIRTY YEARS OF TROUBLE AT WINDSCALE

1979 Uranium ignites in fuel decanning plant

1978 Seven-year-old leak found from building B701

1957 Fire in No. 1 plutonium production reactor

1970 Plutonium goes 'critical' in recovery plant

1981 Radioactive iodine released from building 205

1976 Major leak from silo B38 discovered
1978 Hydrogen build-up threatens explosion

1973 Blow-back in B204 'head-end' reprocessing plant
1979 Fire in B204, now disused

1974 Car park found to be radioactive

1975 Radioactive cobalt and caesium found in river Calder

1952-83 Quarter of a ton of plutonium discharged to sea

1983 Beach closed by radioactive slick

Call for atom plant probe

by GEOFFREY LEAN, Environment Correspondent

DR DAVID OWEN, the SDP leader, is pressing for an urgent investigation into Windscale, the controversial Cumbrian nuclear complex, where there have been more than 300 accidents since 1950.

He has written to Mrs Thatcher urging her to set up an 'independent committee of inquiry' into the plant, which last week was the centre of renewed public concern when the Government warned people to keep off beaches in the area. Dr Owen's initiative follows an exclusive report in *The Observer* that the Government is cracking down heavily on Windscale's discharges of radioactive waste to the sea, and attempts by Greenpeace, punished last week by a £50,000 fine, to plug the waste pipe.

But while he wants the discharges to be reduced to 'near zero,' Dr Owen is also taking the issue farther by pressing for a scrutiny of the accident-prone plant itself.

That is particularly significant, since in the past Dr Owen has been a robust defender of the nuclear industry. He is not in favour of closing Windscale, now renamed Sellafield, but believes that public confidence must be restored urgently if it is to remain open.

In his letter to the Prime Minister he says he is 'very concerned' that a series of incidents at the plant over the past few years 'has greatly weakened public confidence and se-

verely damaged the nuclear industry.'

An *Observer* investigation has established that there have been more than 300 accidents at Windscale since 1950. Since 1977 the plant has been responsible for nearly half the accidents in the whole of the British nuclear industry.

Disturbing

This disturbing record has attracted considerable pressure from the Nuclear Installations Inspectorate on British Nuclear Fuels Ltd, the nationalised firm that manages Windscale, to clean up the plant. About 400 buildings sprawl over the 485-acre site, which was once a munitions factory. Less than two years ago the inspectorate published a stinging report on the management of safety at Windscale.

Most of the recent incidents, it found, were caused by inadequate safety procedures, or by a failure to observe existing ones. Half the incidents resulted in the workers being exposed to, or contaminated by, radioactivity; a quarter by contamination above safety limits.

Several of them caused the inspectorate particular concern because they involved the failure or breach of a whole series of protective barriers and systems.

The report says: 'Our analysis revealed that such incidents might not have happened, or the consequences might have been mitigated, if in each case even one of the protective systems concerned had operated as intended.'

Thus silo 38 leaked radioactive caesium and strontium 90 (possibly for up to four years) before it was discovered in 1976; and two years later the same building was threatened by an explosion because of a build-up of hydrogen.

Both incidents were due to bad design, inadequate monitoring instruments, and inadequate arrangements for cooling and ventilation.

On Sunday, 4 February 1979 a fire started in a disused plant when oxy-acetylene equipment was being used to cut obsolete pipework. It was caused by failure to observe safety procedures.

When the fire started, the men found it hard to call the fire service because the fire alarm had been removed and the single telephone line to the fire station was engaged. And when the service finally arrived both their equipment and training were found to be defective.

The inspectorate's report showed that the maintenance of buildings at Windscale had been neglected and little money had been spent on repairs; that drawings were not kept up to date or were missing; that general housekeeping was poor; that the company had not kept up links with safety organisations; and that serious accidents were often partly caused by defective instruments, which had sometimes not been maintained or tested.

That was all at a time when the firm was improving safety standards, which had been allowed to deteriorate until the early 1970s.

Improvements continued throughout the decade, but by the end of it the inspectorate still found that industrial safety officers did not carry out systematic inspections, that workers did not understand the effects that radiation might have on them, and that managers were uncertain about who was responsible for inspecting some pipelines and drains carrying radioactive substances.

Under the inspectorate's pressure the management at Windscale has continued to make improvements, and most of the deficiencies identified in the report have now been put right.

But there is still concern about the state of much of the reprocessing and waste storage plant, which is old, initially designed at a time of laxer safety standards, and heavily labour intensive.

(*Observer*)

C Choose any time-based sequence with which you are familiar (e.g. making a cake; the life cycle of a butterfly; the life of a famous scientist, historian, politician; etc.). Try to describe this sequence to a partner very clearly so that she or he understands it properly. Answer all your partner's questions and make a note of any problems you had to solve. Then write a text about your sequence.

Looking back

Now that you have finished this unit you should be familiar with time expressions and time structure in texts. You should be able to write about events in their natural time order, and you should be able to write simple texts with an unusual time order.

Unit 7   Linear relationships (2) Process

Introduction

A process, like a chronological sequence, involves linear relationships. We think of processes as moving forward in a logical, step-by-step sequence. A process can usually be presented as a flow diagram. Look at this example:

Teacher Questioning

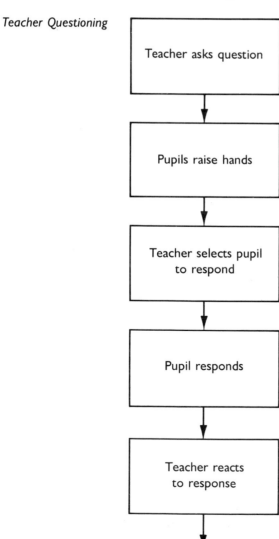

Task 1

Show the following partial process as a flow diagram by filling in the boxes.

> **Computing**
>
> To begin the process, information in a specially coded form is fed into the input unit. Next it is 'read' by a device which turns it into a series of electric impulses. The computer then 'writes' down this information, that is, transfers it to a storage unit. After this, depending on whether the information is data or instructions, further stages take place.

(R. Dale and I. Williamson *The Myth of the Micro*)

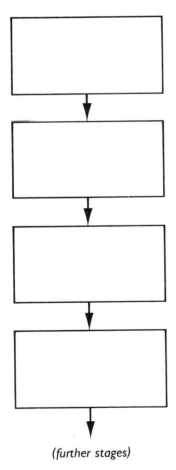

(further stages)

When you write up a process in a text, it will normally be in natural time order, i.e. starting at the beginning of the process and continuing step by step to the end, as in the example above.

Task 2

Use the flow diagram showing 'Teacher questioning' on page 68 as your basis for a text describing the process by which teachers ask and pupils answer questions. Then use the addition to the flow diagram, shown below, to add to your text a description of another possible part of the same process.

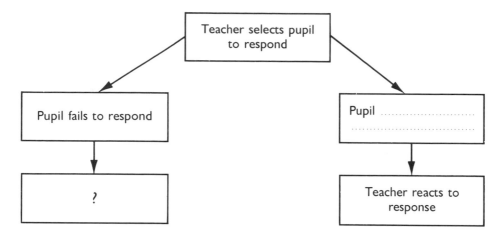

About writing

One obvious way of writing up a process would be to produce one sentence for each step in the process. This would give a text of five sentences for the text on computing, and seven sentences for Task 2. However, such a text would often seem very inexpert and boring; every sentence would state one step, and every sentence would have the same shape as the others. We often put several steps into one sentence, and we mark the steps to make them clear for the reader if we think it might be necessary.

When writing, as well as asking 'Have I got the information across?', you also have to ask 'Have I got the information across in a clear and interesting form?' To help yourself answer these questions, keep in mind the following principles of communication.

1   *The clarity principle*
    Make everything clear to your reader.
2   *The reality principle*
    Assume that your reader has a knowledge of the world and does not have to be told everything.

When judging whether you have been successful in conveying information about a process, the decisions you make about whether to use *sequencers*, and which ones to use, will be particularly important. Sequencers, such as *then*, *next*, *after this*, make clear the sequence in which events, or stages in a process, occur.

The table below gives some common sequencers used when describing a process:

Beginning	Middle steps	End
First Firstly To begin with Initially	Second(ly) Third(ly) (etc.) Next Then Subsequently After this Before this At the same time (etc.)	Lastly Finally

The sequencers are usually placed at, or near, the beginning of a sentence. This is quite logical when you consider that sequencers only work as signposts for the reader if they give *advance* warning of the need to recognize relationships.

Using the clarity principle, you might decide to use a sequencer to make each step of the process clear. On the other hand, using the reality principle, you might decide that sequencers are not needed because the process is described in natural time order and the reader's knowledge of the world will make the sequence clear to her or him.

Task 3

Look at the text below, and with a partner discuss which, if any, of the sequencers it contains are really necessary and if any are, why?

> One of the earliest attempts at solar heating was the Dover House, designed by Dr Maria Tilkes and Eleanor Raymond, and built in 1949. In this house, energy from the sun is absorbed by a large area of blackened metal sheets covered by double plates of glass. *Next*, the heat is carried away by air circulating behind the metal sheets. *After this*, it is stored chemically in large tanks containing Glauber's salt, a given volume of which can hold eight and a half times more heat than water. *Finally*, a fan blows the hot air from the storage to the various rooms in the house.

(Adapted from D. Dickson *Alternative Technology and the Politics of Technical Change*)

In general, readers expect that a process description will follow natural time order. When this happens, the reality principle suggests that there is little need for explicit sequencers. However, there are cases where the use of sequencers is absolutely necessary – when a writer leaves the real sequence in order to highlight an important point (i.e. when the process is not described in the order that it actually occurs in). In such cases, the clarity principle demands that sequencers make the correct order explicit.

Task 4

Read the following text and underline the sentence that contains an unexpected sequence.

One of the earliest attempts at solar heating was the Dover House, designed by Dr Maria Tilkes and Eleanor Raymond, and built in 1949. In this house, energy from the sun is absorbed by a large area of blackened metal sheets covered by double plates of glass. The heat is carried away by air circulating behind the metal sheets. Before the heat can be blown around the house it must first be stored in large tanks containing Glauber's salt, a given volume of which can hold eight and a half times more heat than water.

(D. Dickson *Alternative Technology and the Politics of Technical Change*)

This text departs from the sequence we found in the earlier version. It does this in order to highlight the storage stage. This unexpected sequence is clearly signposted by the explicit sequencers *Before* and *first*.

Task 5

Use the information in the following flow diagram to write a simple description of what happens before a motorist gets petrol. Try to highlight the fact that, in order to produce petrol, oil has to be refined. Think about whether/when you need to use sequencers. You do not have to use the same sequence in your text as in the flow diagram unless you want to. Compare your text with that of another student: they may be different but both may be satisfactory: can you see any reasons why?

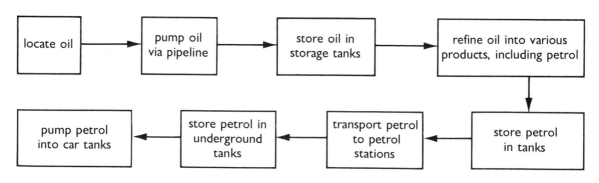

In addition to single word or short phrase sequencers, time clauses are also used as sequencers. Time clauses are most often marked by the use of *when, after, before*, and *while*.

Task 6

The following text describes the process of making new laws in the United Kingdom; it is a more detailed description than most of those you have met so far. Notice that the first paragraph is introductory, and the description of the process does not begin until the second paragraph. Read the text carefully and underline all the sequencers, of any type, that you find in it.

How Parliament Makes New Laws

1. New laws can originate in either the House of Lords or the House of Commons. A law which is being proposed is called a 'bill' until it is passed; then it becomes an 'act' of parliament.

2. To begin with the bill goes through the first reading. This just means that the title of the bill is announced and a time is set for it to be discussed. After this the second reading is really a debate. The bill may be rejected at this stage. If it is an important bill its rejection may cause the government to resign. On the other hand it may be passed, or there may be no vote. When this happens, it goes to the committee stage, where a small group of members (perhaps between 30 and 50), meet and discuss it in detail. When the committee has finished its work, it reports the bill with all the changes that have been made, to the House. This is called the report stage. The bill is discussed again, and more changes can be made. Then the bill is taken for its third reading, and a vote is taken. When it is passed, it goes to the other House, i.e. not the one it originated in. So if a bill started in the House of Commons it would at this point go to the House of Lords.

3. When the bill has been passed by both Houses, it goes to the Queen for the Royal Assent. A bill may not become law until the Royal Assent has been given, but this does not mean that the Queen decides on what will become law and what will not. It is understood that the Queen will always accept bills which have been passed by both Houses. When the Queen's consent has been given, the bill becomes an act, and everyone that it affects must obey the new law.

Task 7

Here is a flow diagram showing the stages in the process of turning a bill into an act. Note down the word or words used in the text 'How Parliament makes new laws' to link each stage to the one before it. Then discuss with another student the reason why each sequencer has been used.

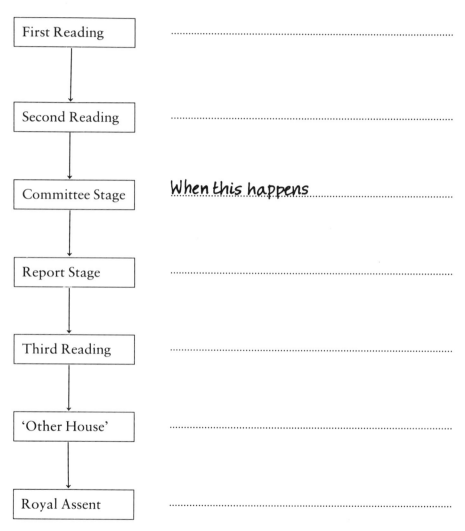

First Reading	....
Second Reading	....
Committee Stage	*When this happens* ....
Report Stage	....
Third Reading	....
'Other House'	....
Royal Assent	....

Using grammar in writing

The writing of a text about a process often involves the present simple tense of the passive voice. This is especially true in impersonal descriptions where the doers (agents) of the actions are not considered important enough to mention, or where there is no specific agent.

Task 8

Are we told who performs the action in these sentences? Underline any agents you find.

a) Sugar cane is harvested out in the fields.
b) Farm workers load it onto lorries.
c) The drivers bring the sugar cane to the factory.
d) The workers put the sugar cane into huge crushers which will crush it.
e) The sugar cane is crushed in the huge crushers.
f) These machines are regularly maintained.

When a description of a process is given, it is usually assumed that the process will be the same no matter who does it. The passive voice is frequently used, as this construction allows the choice of not mentioning the agent of the action. Sometimes, however, the clarity principle requires an agent to be stated, as in the following example:

> Once the diamonds are received by the diamond merchant, *highly skilled technicians* examine them for flaws and mark them preparatory to cutting.

In this case, the writer wants the reader to know that the agent is someone special, a highly skilled technician: the agent is important.

Task 9

This text describes a process for producing an alternative fuel for diesel engines.
a) With a partner, read the text and underline any agents you can find.
b) Also underline all uses of the passive voice.
c) Discuss the possible reasons for the writer's decisions about whether to use passive, or active + agent, in each case.

> In South Africa, researchers process sunflower oil to fuel diesel engines. An acid and a molecule are chemically combined to form an ester by removal of a water molecule. It is easy to do this: an acid is added to the oil, which is then heated to 30–40° for a few hours. The fuel mixture which is produced in this way possesses properties very similar to those of ordinary diesel fuel, but the mixture causes less exhaust smoke than diesel fuel, and can actually improve engine performance.
>
> In Brazil, researchers have carried out similar projects with processed vegetable oil.

(Adapted from *New Scientist*)

A description of a process is usually in the present simple of the passive voice, but if a time clause is used as a sequencer, the main verb of the time clause can be either in the *present simple* or *present perfect tense*. Whether the tense is active or passive voice depends on the writer's other decisions about the need for an agent, and what aspects of the process are being emphasized.

Task 10

The following time clauses are taken from the text on 'How Parliament makes new laws'. State why you think the writer chose the tense and voice that he did.

a) On the other hand it may be passed, or there may be no vote. *When this happens*, it goes to the committee stage . . .
b) When this happens it goes to the committee stage, where a small group of members (perhaps between 30 and 50), meet and discuss it in detail. *When the committee has finished its work*, it reports . . .
c) Then the bill is taken for its third reading, which is a debate, just like the second reading, and a vote is taken. *When it is passed*, it goes to the 'other House' . . .
d) It is understood that the Queen will always accept bills which have been passed by both Houses. *When the Queen's consent has been given*, the bill becomes an act . . .

In general descriptions of a process, the present simple tense of the passive voice is used (e.g. First, the material *is taken* . . .). When the present tense is used in this way, it is often called the *timeless present*, because its use does not mean that the process is happening at this moment, but that it happens in precisely this way, repeatedly, and on many occasions: in other words, no specific time reference is necessary. However, when the stages of a process are written up as a report, the report uses past tenses (e.g. First, the material *was taken* . . .). This is because one specific occurrence of the process, at a specific (past) time, is being reported.

Task 11

Use the information in the text 'How Parliament makes new laws' to write a *report* of the process which the 1981 Wildlife and Countryside Act went through before it was passed into law.

Consolidation

A Using the following flow diagram as your guide, write a description of the process of producing china cups. When you plan your text, consider:
1 making the text interesting with a variety of sentence types;
2 whether and when you need to use sequencers, and which ones to use;
3 choices of active or passive voice, and of tenses.

Write two paragraphs, and begin the second paragraph with 'After the rough edges are smoothed off, the cups . . .'.

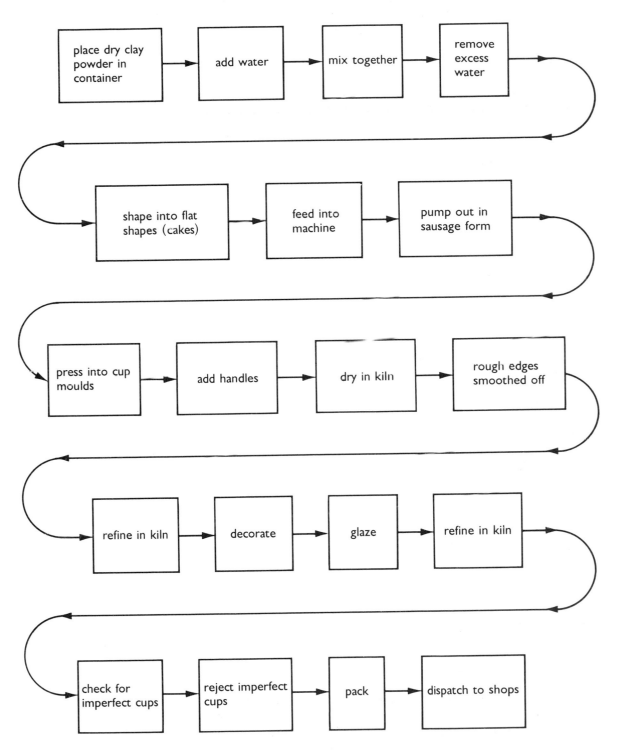

B The following diagram shows the braking system of a car. Use the information it contains (and get further information from textbooks or experts in mechanics if you wish) to write a short text explaining how a car braking system functions. Write a text suitable for schoolchildren in the first year of secondary/high school, taking an introductory science course.

Car braking system

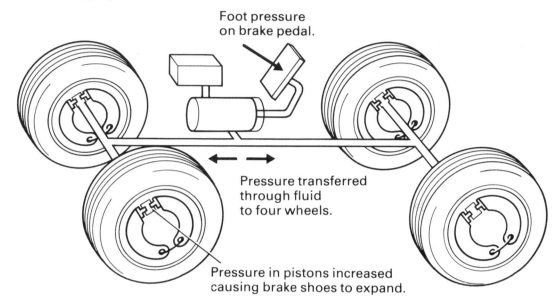

Foot pressure
on brake pedal.

Pressure transferred
through fluid
to four wheels.

Pressure in pistons increased
causing brake shoes to expand.

C Find out as much as you can about a process you are interested in, and write a text explaining it so that an intelligent adult could understand it. Illustrate with a diagram if you wish. When you plan your text, consider:
1   making the text interesting with a variety of sentence types;
2   the need to use sequencers, and which ones to use;
3   choices of active or passive voice, and of tenses.

Looking back

Now that you have finished this unit you should be able to write a text which sequences events in natural time order or unusual time order, using suitable time expressions, sequencers, and tenses. You should also be aware of when the passive voice might be needed.

Unit 8   Linear relationships (3) Cyclical process

Introduction

In the previous unit you learned how to write up a linear process, i.e. a process that consists of a series of stages and which has a beginning and an end. A natural process is more likely to be cyclical than linear. In a cyclical process there is no clear beginning or end, so that the cycle is continuously repeated. The diagram below should make the difference between the two types of process clear.

1   *A linear process*

2   *A cyclical process*

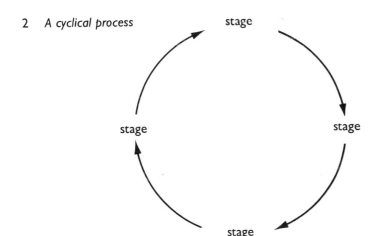

A cyclical process is described in much the same way as a linear process except that it is not always clear where the cycle begins.

Task 1

This flow diagram illustrates the nitrogen cycle. Nitrogen is essential for human, animal and plant life, and over 90% of the Earth's supply exists as a gas in the atmosphere. The diagram shows how nitrogen is provided to living organisms and then returned to the atmosphere. Below the flow diagram is a list of sentences describing the stages in the cycle. The sentences are not in an acceptable sequence. Using the flow diagram as a guide, match the sentences with the stages in the flow diagram to produce a text in acceptable sequence.

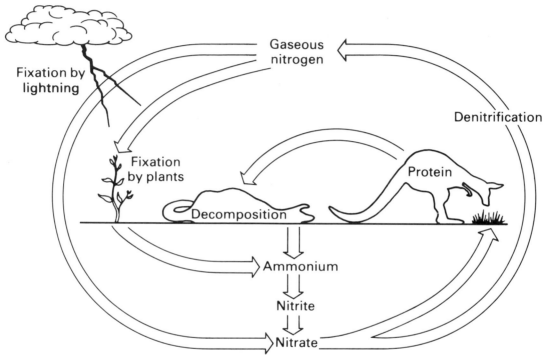

i)   Lightning contributes some nitrogen, in the form of nitrates, to the soil.
ii)   This gaseous nitrogen is returned to the atmosphere.
iii)   When animals eat the plants, the nitrogen they contain is synthesized into protein.
iv)   When plants or animals die, proteins are decomposed by bacteria into amino acids which are in turn broken down into ammonium.
v)   But at the source of most nitrogen is bacteria on plants, which 'fix' the nitrogen into ammonia.
vi)   The nitrates in the soil are absorbed by plant roots.
vii)   Some of the nitrates are degraded into nitrogen gas in the denitrification process.
viii) The ammonium is broken down into nitrites.
ix)   The ammonium resulting from decomposition returns to the nitrite – nitrate – protein cycle.
x)   The nitrites are converted into nitrates by soil bacteria.

About writing

When you write a text, it is usual to make the topic of the text very clear to your reader. This is done by stating the topic in a prominent position in the text, most frequently in the first sentence. A sentence which states the topic of a text, or of a paragraph or group of paragraphs, is called a *topic sentence*. (Sometimes this is known as the *thesis sentence*.)

Task 2

Study the following text and diagram, then:
a) underline the topic sentence of paragraph 1;
b) complete the topic sentence of paragraph 2;
c) write a third paragraph beginning with this topic sentence:
       'Bilharzia could be eradicated.'

1. Bilharzia is a disease found all over the world. It is spread by a small fluke, or flatworm (called schistosoma) which lives as a parasite in the water snail during one stage of its life-cycle, and in man during another stage. Three species cause human disease: one is found in parts of Africa, Spain and the Middle East, another in Africa and Central/South America and the last in the Far East. In these areas schistosoma eggs are present in slow-moving water.

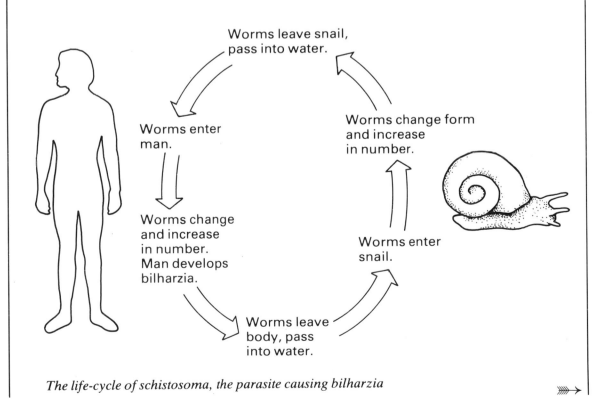

The life-cycle of schistosoma, the parasite causing bilharzia

81

2. The life cycle of schistosoma ....
The first stage takes place in the water. When the eggs hatch, the embryoes enter the bodies of water snails. They develop into worms inside the snails. Eventually the worms return to the water, and penetrate the skin of any person who happens to be standing in the water. Once inside the human body they move through the blood vessels to the liver. They remain in the liver until they are adult, and then move to the bladder, where they lay their eggs, causing severe inflammation. Finally the eggs are excreted into the water, and the cycle begins all over again.

Two common types of topic sentence are:
1 the generalization:
'Bilharzia is a disease found all over the world.'
2 the preview:
'The life cycle of schistosoma can be divided into two stages.'

Task 3

Study the following sentences and state which of them would make good topic sentences, i.e. which of them could easily be developed to form a paragraph.

a) The planet Venus is 26,000,000 miles away from Earth.
b) Generalizations are very useful in writing.
c) Motor cars are a form of transportation.
d) Recent changes in Egypt have affected women's roles in at least two potentially important ways.

Though it is not always necessary to begin each paragraph with a topic sentence, it is useful to do so when you are not completely certain of your ability as a writer. The advantage of beginning a paragraph with a topic sentence is that it provides both the writer and the reader with a clear aim, i.e. in the case of a generalization, examples will be required, and in the case of a preview, details will be forthcoming. For example, if the writer produces this as a topic sentence:

There are several parasites which are a danger to human beings.
then she or he is committed to producing further text about the topic of parasites of human beings. More than this, the reader will expect the writer to discuss specific parasites, and even more specifically, to discuss parasites which are a danger to human beings, including schistosoma. The specific information about what aspect(s) of the topic will be discussed in the text is known as the *main idea*. Often, the main idea is found in the topic sentence. In the sentence above, for example, 'parasites' is the topic and 'parasites *which are a danger to human beings*' is the main idea.

Task 4

Read the following texts; for each text, write down the topic sentence and put a box around the main idea.

a)

> We have only one clue as to how our Universe began. When starlight is passed through a spectroscope the bright spectral lines are displaced towards the red end of the spectrum. This red shift, due to the Doppler effect, tells us that the galaxies are rushing into space away from our galaxy. One explanation for this is that all matter in the universe started as a single, super-dense mass which exploded. This explanation is known as the 'big bang' theory.

b)

> There are two principal requirements for an explosive. First, it must remain stable unless it is struck or ignited, and then, once it is ignited, a chemical reaction must take place to cause heat and a large volume of gas to be produced in a very short time. In gunpowder, for example, the potassium nitrate, KNO_3, combines with the carbon in the charcoal to give carbon dioxide and some nitrogen gas.

c)

> All rocks were originally formed during the period when the Earth was molten and then cooled down. A great deal of this igneous (fire-made) rock still exists in its original stage. However, hard though it is, igneous rock breaks up into grains of sand in the course of millions of years of the action of wind and water, sun and ice. Some of this sand settled at the bottom of the sea and, over the ages, became pressed into hard rock forming strata of sedimentary rocks of varying thickness and composition, such as sandstone and limestone.

(*Penguin Book of the Physical World*)

In addition to providing the writer and the reader with a clear indication of what the text should be about, the topic sentence also indicates what the text will *not* be about: for example, if the topic sentence is:

There are several parasites which are a danger to human beings.

you will not expect to find a discussion of, for example, nuclear energy in the text! Using your topic sentence as guide to the rest of your writing helps you follow the third principle of communication.

3 *The relevance principle*
   Keep to your topic and your purpose for writing.

Task 5

Study the flow diagram and the text. Some of the sentences in the text should not be there: keep in mind the relevance principle, and discuss with a partner which sentences should be taken out.

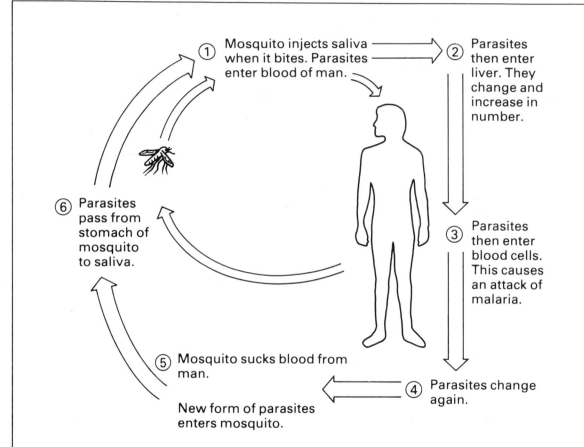

The life-cycle of the malaria parasite

Insects which transmit disease to man in their bites are called vectors, or carriers. Malaria is an example of a disease of this type. It is transmitted by a kind of mosquito called anopheles. Some diseases are transmitted by tiny water animals. The anopheles mosquito sucks blood from a person with malaria. Once in the stomach of the mosquito, the microbes multiply. House flies transmit microbes on their feet. The malaria microbes pass to the mosquito's mouth, and when the mosquito bites a person the malaria microbes pass into the person's blood. The parasites then enter the person's liver, in which they change and multiply. From there they pass into the blood cells, where they cause the malaria attack. The spread of insect-borne disease can be controlled.

Using grammar in writing

You have been studying various aspects of the grammar of writing, sometimes related to sentences and sometimes related to bigger elements of the text. Throughout this book you have seen examples of different sentence types: you have seen simple, compound and complex sentences. If you look back through some of the texts, you should be able to see that simple sentences (sentences with a single subject and a single verb) are used mainly to introduce a new idea, or to emphasize a point. They are less common in writing than in speech, and they often contain a long, complicated subject, for example:

> *The long-term goals of agricultural production, industrialization and population control in China* are commendable.

Compound sentences (sentences with two or more clauses joined by *and*, *but* or *or*) are also more common in speech than in writing. Compound sentences join together two closely related ideas in a way which indicates that both are equally important, for example:

> Western societies have always admired rainforests but have never understood them.

In writing, most sentences are complex sentences, especially in expository writing. This is because using complex sentences allows the writer to indicate a whole variety of relationships between ideas, and not simply list ideas as if they were unrelated (as would happen with a series of simple sentences) or link them together as if they were equally important (as with compound sentences). Here are just a few examples of complex sentences:

1 Switzerland, which is a small country with mountains, pine forests and lakes, is famous for winter sports, two of which are skiing and tobogganing.
2 Although Switzerland is famous for winter sports, visitors go to Switzerland in the summer too.
3 China has provided significant aid and technical assistance to other countries, both in quantity and quality, despite the fact that its annual income per head is less than £200.
4 It is surprising that the Arabian conquest of the Middle East took less than a century because the settled populations were large, well institutionalized and supported by the armies of Byzantium and Persia, while the Muslims were far fewer in number and had little in the way of weapons.

One type of complex sentence which is often found in texts designed to convey information is the sentence which contains a *relative clause*. A relative clause is a clause which contains additional information relating to the main clause of the sentence, for example:

RELATIVE CLAUSE

Endocrine glands, *which secrete into the blood*, are found in various parts of the body.

RELATIVE CLAUSE

A level *which has the fulcrum between load and effort* can be used to compare two masses.

Relative clauses which contain information *essential* to the meaning or purpose of the sentence are called *defining* relative clauses. Relative clauses containing information which, although useful, is *not essential* to the meaning or purpose of the sentence are called *non-defining* relative clauses. Non-defining relative clauses can be removed from the sentence without changing its meaning or making it ungrammatical, although of course the amount of information will be reduced. The first example on page 85 is a non-defining relative clause and the second example is a defining relative clause.

Task 6

The following sentences all contain a main clause and a defining relative clause:
a) find the main clause in each sentence and underline it;
b) explain to another student why the relative clause cannot be removed from the sentence.

i)   Barometers are meteorological instruments which measure atmospheric pressure.
ii) We shall here confine our description to specialized respiratory systems which involve only a part of the body.
iii) An aircraft flying at an altitude of 2,140 metres is subjected to pressures of 80 Kilonewtons per square metre.
iv) Just as remarkable as the evolutionary adaptation of the camel is the adaptation of the group of warm-blooded fish which includes shark, mackerel and tuna.
v)   Steels which have a carbon content of between 0.5 and 1.3% are known as high carbon steels.

The five sentences in Task 6 illustrate the fact that a defining relative clause limits the meaning of the sentence; without the limitation, the sentence becomes untrue, unclear or ungrammatical (or more than one of these).

In contrast, non-defining relative clauses provide *extra* information about the subject of the main clause. For example, in the sentence:

> Endocrine glands, which secrete into the blood, are found in various parts of the body.

the (non-defining) relative clause tells us what the endocrine glands *do*, i.e. their function.

Task 7

The following sentences all contain a main clause and a non-defining relative clause. For each sentence:
a) identify the main clause;
b) discuss with another student what function the non-defining relative clause has in each sentence.

i)   Valves, which are found in most veins, direct the blood flow.
ii) A common northern and eastern plant is the Indian-pipe, which is white while alive but black when dried.
iii) Some epiphytic orchids and other plants have aerial roots, which catch and absorb water from frequent tropical rains.

iv) The dominant aquatic vertebrates are the fishes, which are divided into two subclasses, the bony fishes and the cartilaginous fishes.

v) The kinetic energy of a fluid, due to its motion, is customarily measured with respect to the Earth's surface, which is assumed to have zero velocity.

Consolidation

A The following diagram shows a water treatment cycle. The basic idea behind this plan is to take used water, clean it and have it used again (and so on). Write a description of this cycle in order to persuade your town/city council to investigate the possibility of installing such a system. Consider the following factors when writing:
  1 the best point to enter the cycle, in order to explain it;
  2 the need to break down the cycle into stages, and the basis on which the stages might be defined;
  3 the need to use topic sentences for (a) the whole text and (b) each paragraph within the text;
  4 the need to vary sentence structure (i.e. simple/compound/complex).
Use the following as your title: 'Why waste used water?'

  When your text is finished show it to another student and ask her or him to comment on it, with the relevance, reality and clarity principles in mind.

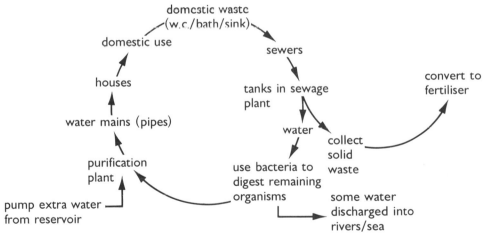

B It has often been claimed that a poverty cycle exists in society: that, in general, poor parents produce children who will be poor and who, in turn, will produce further children who will be poor, etc. In groups of five discuss this phenomenon. When you feel ready, write an individual text explaining the poverty cycle and stating your own opinions regarding its existence or not. Be sure to support any claims you make.

C In groups of three or four explore the notion of 'cycles', e.g. the seasons, day and night, life and death etc. What 'cycles' do you know? Can they be divided into classes? Can you define a cycle? When you have discussed all the ideas sufficiently, write an individual text on the theme of 'cycles'.

Looking back

Now that you have finished this unit you should be able to follow a text with a cyclical structure, and decide where to begin when writing a description of a cycle. You should be able to write clear and suitable topic sentences. You should recognize different sentence types: simple, compound and complex; and you should know how to use them appropriately. You should also be able to write complex sentences containing relative clauses of different kinds.

Unit 9   Linear relationships (4) Cause↔effect

Introduction

The attempt to analyse cause and effect is at the heart of all scientific disciplines. It is also a central concern of our daily lives. We see effects all the time: causes are harder to identify. Parents try to discover the cause of their children's behaviour (effects); political and economic experts speculate about the cause(s) of unemployment; the effects of drought in Africa are easy to see, but experts do not agree about the cause.

Cause and effect is a linear relationship; in real life causes always precede effects, as the following example shows.

Is cassava at the root of birth defects?

Cassava is the staple food of millions of people in Africa, Asia and South and Central America. Its swollen tuberous root can be boiled and mashed or grated to produce a meal, known as "farinha" in Brazil and "garri" in Nigeria, which can be cooked in small cakes. The root is also the source of the manufactured commodity, tapioca. A plot of cassava can be insurance against famine, because the crop can be left in the ground for two or three years without deterioration of the tubers and be almost immune to locust attack. But recent findings suggest that cassava may be responsible for birth defects.

It has other serious disadvantages. The tubers consist almost entirely of starch and are particularly low in protein, so enforced reliance on cassava leads to serious malnutrition. To make matters worse, some varieties, when grown under certain conditions of soil and climate, develop a high prussic acid content and become extremely poisonous to people and livestock if eaten raw. These tubers have to be laboriously prepared for consumption by prolonged and repeated boiling.

The new danger has emerged over the past few years in Nigeria. Doctors have begun to suspect that cassava, if eaten in large amounts during pregnancy, may cause deformities in the developing fetus; there appears to be a correlation between the cassava intake of pregnant women and the occurrence of various kinds of brain or other neuronal malformations in their babies.

(*New Scientist*)

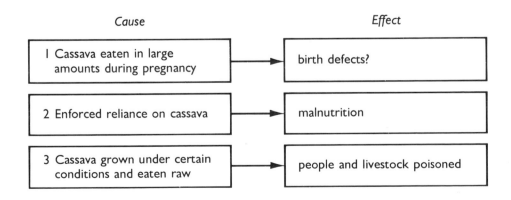

Cause		Effect
1 Cassava eaten in large amounts during pregnancy	→	birth defects?
2 Enforced reliance on cassava	→	malnutrition
3 Cassava grown under certain conditions and eaten raw	→	people and livestock poisoned

Task 1

Make a note of four expressions used by the writer in the 'Cassava' text to show a causal relationship.

About writing

Causes are very difficult to pin down with any degree of certainty. Firstly, the existence of a clear time relationship between two events (two events happening during the same period of time) does not necessarily mean that one is the cause of the other. Secondly, it is easy to confuse effect with cause. Even if the two events are so closely related in time that we can show that relationship statistically (i.e. we have a statistical correlation) it may be that both events are effects of the same cause: we must be careful not to make assumptions.

Task 2

Discuss the following in groups of three or four students.

a) There is a high positive statistical correlation between the asphalt on city streets being soft and people suffering from heatstroke. Does soft asphalt somehow cause heatstroke? If not, what *is* the relationship?
b) There is a high positive statistical correlation between the number of storks seen nesting in French villages and the number of births (human) recorded in the same communities. Do storks somehow cause babies to be born? Is there any cause↔effect relationship here?
c) Many pop stars suffer from partial deafness. Does poor hearing cause them to become pop stars? If not, what *is* the relationship?

This difficulty in assigning cause and effect is reflected in the fourth basic principle of communication:

4 *The honesty principle*
   Only say (or write) that for which you have evidence.

When you examine it, it is a very sensible principle, but one which is not always observed by many writers who prefer sweeping statements to carefully considered conclusions. An example of the honesty principle at work can be seen in the following conclusion from the text 'Is cassava at the root of birth defects?'

> 'But recent findings *suggest* that cassava *may be responsible* for birth defects.'

The use of the expressions *suggest* and *may be responsible* show that the writer's evidence is not 100% certain and, quite rightly, he does not attempt to draw conclusions which he cannot support: he is being honest with his readers. We have all observed someone, when speaking, 'bend' the truth to make their own position seem more favourable. They are much less likely to do this in writing, because the written word can more easily be held against them later.

Writers rarely actually lie, but the grammar of English makes it quite easy for them to vary their degree of commitment to the truth of a statement.

Task 3

a) Decide on an order for the sentences below, starting with the one which shows the most commitment to the statement and ending with the one which shows the least commitment.

   i)   The earth is probably round.
   ii)   The earth is possibly round.
   iii) The earth is round.
   iv)   Perhaps the earth is round.
   v)   The earth undoubtedly is round.
   vi)   It is said that the earth is round.

b) One of the sentences above uses a different method to reduce the degree of commitment to the truth of the statement. Which one? Explain how it is different.

The following table gives some guidelines on the language available for writers to state their *degree of certainty* or *degree of commitment*.

Degree of certainty/commitment	Verbs	Adverbs
complete	is (not) will (not) must (not)	certainly definitely clearly undoubtedly actually
partial ↗ strong ↘ less strong	can/cannot could (not) should (not) may (not) might (not)	probably (is) likely/unlikely presumably possibly perhaps
impersonal (i.e. no commitment of self)	It is said that. . . X reports that. . . There is evidence to suggest that. . . (etc.)	

Task 4

Each of the following sentences contains an inappropriate statement. Rewrite each sentence to conform with the honesty principle, i.e. so that its degree of personal or impersonal commitment agrees with reality. Check your rewritten sentences with those of another student.

i)   The earth is definitely flat.
ii) It will snow tomorrow.
iii) It is likely that inflation will fall to under 1% before the end of the year.
iv) Launching our nuclear waste into the atmosphere cannot cause any pollution for at least a million years.
v)   Eating apples makes you thin. I know that because my friend eats apples all the time and she is very thin.

Task 5

The confusion of cause and effect, and a lack of appreciation of the honesty principle, are both illustrated in the following extract from *The Twilight of the Idols, Or How to Philosophise with the Hammer* by the German philosopher Nietzsche, written in 1888.

a)   Read the text and then fill in the boxes in the sentences which follow.

> Everybody knows the book of the famous Cornoro, in which he recommends his slender diet as the recipe for a long, happy and also virtuous life. Few books have been so widely read, and to this day many thousand copies of it are still printed annually in England. I do not doubt that there is scarcely a single book [. . .] that has worked more mischief, shortened more lives, than this well-meant curiosity. The reason for this is the confusion of cause and effect. This worthy Italian saw the cause of his long life in his diet: whereas the prerequisites of long life, which are exceptional slowness of molecular change, and a low rate of expenditure of energy were the cause of his meagre diet. He was not at liberty to eat a small or a great amount. His frugality was not the result of his free choice, he would have been ill had he eaten more. [. . .] a scholar of the present day with his rapid consumption of nervous energy, would soon go to the dogs on Cornoro's diet.

(Nietzsche *The Twilight of the Idols, Or How to Philosophise with the Hammer*)

Cornoro believed that ⬚ resulted in ⬚ .

Nietzsche states that ⬚ and ⬚

are the causes of ⬚ and also of ⬚ .

b)   Rewrite the text stating the beliefs of both Cornoro and Nietzsche more honestly, i.e. as opinions rather than as facts.

Using grammar in writing

You will have seen several ways of expressing cause↔effect relationships already in this unit. In English, either the cause or the effect can be placed first in the sentence.

Task 6

Read the following text and note down three expressions used by the writer to show causality. Label cause (C) and effect (E) in each case to show which comes first in the sentence.

Pulmonary Tuberculosis

Pulmonary Tuberculosis is caused by infection of the lungs with the tubercle bacillus. Pulmonary lesions are due almost entirely to the human form of the tubercle bacillus, as distinct from the bovine type, which is mainly responsible for glandular and bovine tuberculosis. The bacilli lodge in the lungs and set up a chronic inflammation of a specific type. They produce areas of infiltration which have a characteristic tubercle formation; hence the name for the organism.

Task 7

In the text in Task 6 there are also some cause↔effect relationships which are not clearly marked by cause↔effect expressions. Find these relationships and rewrite the sentences which contain them so that the cause and effect are clearly marked.

Cause and effect are obviously closely related. The following sentences contain the same expression, yet one focuses on cause while the other focuses on effect.

1   Because of his depression,   he overate.
     (*cause of*)   (*effect*)

2   He overate because of his depression.
  (*effect of*)   (*cause*)

When you write about cause↔effect, you can decide for yourself whether the cause or the effect is most important to you, and that is what you will focus on.
   There are many ways of expressing causal relations in English. The simplest way of showing cause is:

because + clause (contains verb)
e.g. The war started *because the economic situation was desperate.*
because of / on account of + phrase (no verb)
e.g. The war started *because of / on account of the desperate economic situation.*

In speech *because* is the most common way of expressing causal relationships. However, writers use a wide variety of expressions for these relationships.

Task 8

Hospitals have to be particularly careful to avoid accidents of all kinds, and fire is a very serious danger in hospitals. The following text explains some ways in which fires in operating theatres can be avoided. Read the text, paying special attention to expressions showing cause↔effect relationships, then work with a partner to answer (a) and (b) below.

Industrial and Medical Hazards of Static Electricity

Although static electricity is of practical importance nowadays in only a few specialized applications, it can produce hazards in industry and in hospitals. If the charge built up to any great proportions, it would spark over to an uncharged conductor, and might set alight flammable materials in the process. A very dry atmosphere will help the build-up of charge and this is one of the reasons why a reasonably high relative humidity of around 65% should be maintained throughout any factory and hospital. In operating theatres the rubbing of overshoes on a composition floor or of gowns against a plastic table top can cause large charges to accumulate. Sparking here could cause the ignition of some of the volatile gases used in operational procedures, which would have serious results. The presence of an electric field may also cause the malfunction of delicate apparatus. The floors of an operating theatre should always be metallic, and there should be conducting paths from the top of the operating table to the floor. Casters on instrument tables must have conducting rubber tyres.

(Adapted from Morowitz *Life and the Physical Sciences*)

a) Underline the expressions which show cause↔effect relationships. Clearly label each cause (C) and effect (E).
b) Indicate the degree of certainty which the writer gives to these relationships, i.e. are the effects certain/probable/possible?

Task 9

Refer to the diagram to complete the following text about the erosion of the land caused by rivers and glaciers. You can make changes in the grammar of the text to express cause↔effect as you wish, but the facts must be correct.

When rain falls on mountains, it collects in depressions in the rock. The extreme cold .... the ice to freeze and glaciers to form. The ice melts and freezes again .... changes in temperature. Erosion of the rock of the mountain depression occurs .... the continual melting and refreezing, and is .... the action of wind moving the water. Eventually, the water wears away the rock enough .... a small stream which carries deposits of soil and rock which .... further erosion, gradually enlarging the stream bed. The weather, too, acts on rocks and soil, to split, break and wear away. The stream grows larger until eventually it reaches the old age stage. The silt from the river is deposited into the sea, ... sandbars, spits and promontories.

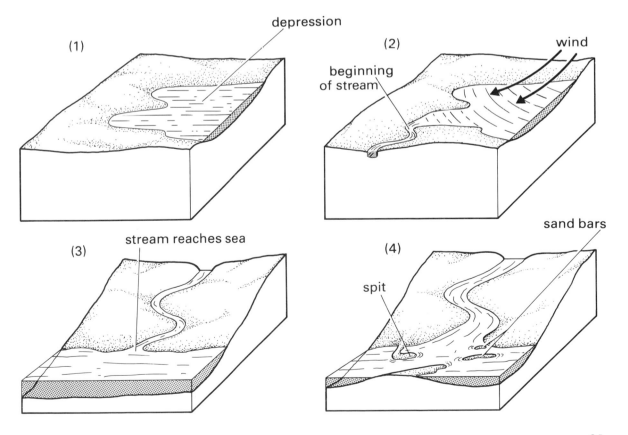

(1)   depression

(2)   wind
beginning of stream

(3)   stream reaches sea

(4)   sand bars
spit

Consolidation

A   Study the diagram and notes below, and discuss your interpretation with a partner or your teacher to make sure you have it correct. Do some other reading about the 'greenhouse effect' if you find it necessary. Then write a text with the title: 'The greenhouse effect: its causes and the dangers for the Earth's future'.

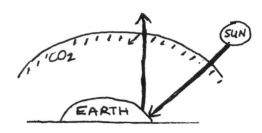

breathing → carbon dioxide (CO_2)
burning coal/oil, etc. → CO_2

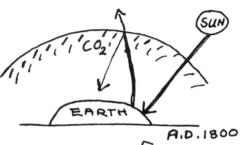

A.D.1800

plants 'breathing' → oxygen (O)
rainforests = huge resource to
              convert CO_2 → O
cutting rainforests → loss of O
burning trees produces CO_2

CO_2 gas traps heat in atmosphere
(glass traps heat in greenhouse
i.e. greenhouse effect)
more CO_2 ⟹ more heat in earth

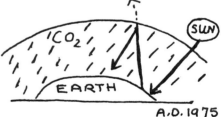

A.D.1975

B   Choose a scientific or sociological concept which involves at least one cause↔effect relationship, and investigate it to be sure you understand it clearly. Then write a text in which you describe this concept and make the causal relationship(s) clear. Write for an intelligent adult who is not familiar with this concept. Be sure to follow the honesty principle as well as the clarity, reality and relevance principles. Although your text is intended to be factual and informative, you should try to make it interesting too. Remember particularly to use a variety of sentence types; to provide clear topic sentences; and to support any generalizations you make.

C   Does viewing violence on television lead to a more violent society?
   1   Discuss this question with one or two other students, taking into account the views which follow.
   2   Use the discussion to help you plan and write an answer to the question, focusing in particular on possible causes and effects. Be careful to observe

the honesty principle, since you will have to take into account more than one point of view about this question.

> Watching violence on television is beneficial and helps decrease violent behaviour because viewers get rid of some of their own aggressive impulses through viewing and thereby reduce the likelihood that they will perform aggressive acts.

> Violence on television is different from real violence in that it is heavily ritualised. We know, as we approve of the death of the villain under a hail of police bullets, that we would not approve in the same way if a real-life villain were shot in front of us in real life.

> A number of cases have been reported of young children or teenagers duplicating a violent act previously seen on television. In fact, in one instance, the parents of a victim took legal action against a TV network, claiming that a programme shown during the hours when children were watching was responsible for a brutal attack on their 9 year old daughter. The three youngsters responsible admitted that they had copied the method of assault shown on the programme.

> I have read about studies which indicate that exposure to violence in the context of a TV drama decreases emotional responsiveness to real-life aggression in news films in both children and adults.

Looking back

Now that you have finished this unit you should be familiar with cause↔effect structures in text and with expressions which make different levels of claim about certainty. You should be able to produce texts which identify and express cause and effect accurately and clearly, using suitable expressions of certainty, and of cause↔effect.

PART II

Unit 10 Organizing texts (2) Structuring texts

Introduction

Various ways of organizing information into classifications, descriptions of processes, etc. were tried out in Part I. While all these information structures are important, they usually appear *within* larger texts rather than forming the basis for a complete text. Most texts have a complex structure that includes definitions, classifications, comparisons, etc., but as elements within the text, which has a larger overall purpose, usually to instruct or to inform. The way a complete text is organized will depend on the overall goal, the writer's prediction of the ability and knowledge of the reader, and the specific topic being written about.

Task 1

This text, which is about pulsars, is taken from the *Sunday Times* (London). As you can see from the heading, it is about a topic in astronomy, but because it is intended for a general audience of intelligent adults and not for astronomers you can expect it not to be very technical. The purpose of the article is to give information in an interesting way.

First, read the article. (Don't expect to have complete comprehension – a general understanding is sufficient.) Then complete the diagram using information from the text.

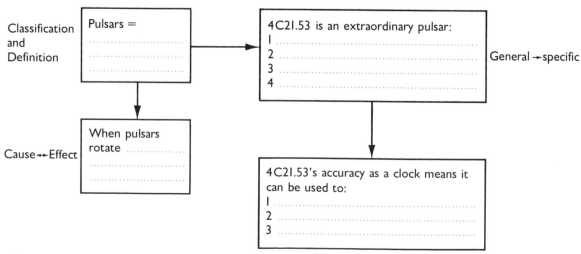

ASTRONOMY

The star that tells the time

A TINY STAR discovered three months ago looks like becoming the most accurate clock known to science, more precise than even the atomic clocks used as international time standards. Astronomers are looking into the possibilities of using it to fix the position of the earth with unprecedented accuracy, refine estimates of the masses of the outer planets, and detect so far hypothetical gravity waves.

The star was first recorded as 4C21.53 by radio astronomers at Cambridge some years ago, but it was not until last November that Donald Backer, of the University of California, discovered it was a pulsar, a type of star that sends out regular pulses of radio waves. Pulsars are the remains of supernovae (exploding stars) and matter in them is at an almost unimaginable state of compression in which a piece the size of a marble would weigh a thousand million tons. As the stars rotate, they send out beams of radio waves that sweep across the galaxy like the beam of a lighthouse.

However, 4C21.53 is an extraordinary object even by pulsar standards.

● It rotates 642 times a second, far faster than any other known pulsar.

● Although it is only about 10 kilometres across, its rotation is so rapid that its equator moves at a fifth of the speed of light.

● Its surface gravity is a million million million times that on earth, yet it is barely enough to hold the star together. If it turned only about three times faster it would break up.

● It has so far shown none of the small fluctuations in pulse rate characteristic of other pulsars. Hence its exceptional accuracy as a clock.

"The pulses are like a series of fence posts in space-time," says Professor Antony Hewish, the Cambridge radio astronomer who won the Nobel Prize in 1974 for the discovery of pulsars. "They might be used in a number of ways.

"For instance the earth's orbit is not a smooth ellipse. It is actually very complicated because of the effects of the other planets, and we cannot fix its position to better than a few kilometres. With the pulsar clock we could do better and then it would be possible to calculate the masses of the outer planets more accurately than at present. A quite different application would be the detection of gravity waves, which a lot of people have looked for, so far without success."

Bryan Silcock

(*Sunday Times*)

Task 2

Compare the way you filled in the boxes in Task 1 with another student's response, and try to reach an agreement about which is correct if you did not agree. Then write up what is in the boxes as a complete text. Try not to look at the original text while you are doing that.

Task 3

Oral rehydration therapy (ORT) is a very cheap way of helping some of the world's poorest people. This text about ORT has had its sentences typed in the wrong order. Work with a partner to decide on the correct order for the sentences. Make notes to remind yourselves what led you to choose the order you did.

i)   These deaths need not have occurred.

ii)   In 1984 alone, about half a million children were saved by this revolutionary technique.

iii) ORT, simply a drink of water, sugar and salt, costs practically nothing, and is simple enough for any parent to prepare.

iv)   Each year, more than four million young children die from diarrheal dehydration.

v)   Today, 38 nations have begun large-scale production of oral rehydration salts.

vi)   A revolutionary, low cost technique called oral rehydration therapy (ORT) could probably have saved their lives.

vii) Over the next five years, ORT could spread to half the world's families, saving the lives of some two million children each year.

Text structure

While informational texts in English use different combinations of the types of writing you have studied in Units 1–9, the structure of the text as a whole remains much the same. If this was not true it would be extremely difficult to read and write texts, since nothing would ever become predictable.

Task 4

The lines of this traditional nursery rhyme have been disorganized; try to rewrite it with the lines in their correct order. If there are generally recognizable structures for texts, it should be possible to agree on a sensible version of this text. Work with a partner, and check your recomposition with another pair of students afterwards.

> The Queen of Hearts
> And took them clean away
> He stole the tarts
>
> The Knave* of Hearts
> And beat the Knave full sore
> Called for the tarts
>
> The Knave of Hearts
> All on a summer's day
> She made some tarts
>
> The King of Hearts
> And vowed he'd steal no more
> Brought back the tarts.

*knave = a picture card in a deck of cards; (in old English) a dishonest man.

The reason it is possible to agree on a sensible version of the above rhyme is that it has a predictable text structure:

situation→problem→solution→evaluation

situation answers the question:
   'What are we talking about?'   In this text, the Queen's cakes.

problem answers the question:
   a) 'Why are we talking about this?'   Because there is a problem.
   b) 'What *is* the problem?'   In this text, the Knave stole the tarts.

solution answers the question:
   'What is to be / has been done?'   In this text the King calls for the tarts and beats the Knave.

evaluation answers the question:
   'How good is the solution?'   In this text apparently very good because the Knave promises never to steal again.

Task 5

This text has the *situation→problem→solution→evaluation* structure. First read the text quickly, then more carefully to identify the parts of its structure. Complete the flow diagram, working with a partner.

A green earth or a dry desert?
There may still be time to choose.

FOR MILLIONS OF YEARS, the tropical rain forests of South East Asia, South America, and Africa have been the earth's natural chemical laboratories, botanic gardens and zoos.

Today we are destroying them at such a rate that within 25 years only fragments will remain of the vast forests of Malaysia and Indonesia.

Because they grow mostly in poor tropical soil, relying upon a natural cycle between trees and animals for nourishment and replenishment, the forests cannot be replaced.

When the trees are felled, soil erosion begins and within a few years, the whole area that was once forest becomes wasteland.

We shall have lost for ever the earth's greatest treasure house of plants and animals; perhaps our most valuable resource for the future. And it is happening in areas where poverty already verges upon starvation. It is perhaps the world's most urgent conservation problem. The destruction is happening through ignorance, short-sightedness and ever increasing consumer demand. But it can be stopped if enough of us show enough concern.

How you can help.

In 1980 WWF and other international conservation bodies published the World Conservation Strategy. It is a programme for developing the world's natural resources without destroying them.

You can become part of a world movement which will see this plan become reality.

Join the World Wildlife Fund now. We need your voice and your financial support. Get in touch with your local WWF office for membership details or send your contribution direct to World Wildlife Fund at the address below. It may be the most important letter you'll ever write.

**WORLD WILDLIFE FUND – UK,
PANDA HOUSE,
11-13 OCKFORD ROAD,
GODALMING, SURREY GU7 1QU.**

 **WWF** © FOR WORLD CONSERVATION

Advertisement prepared as a public service by Ogilvy & Mather.

(New Scientist)

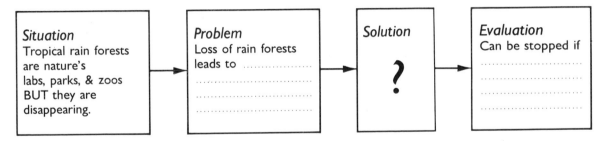

Situation	Problem	Solution	Evaluation
Tropical rain forests are nature's labs, parks, & zoos BUT they are disappearing.	Loss of rain forests leads to	?	Can be stopped if ....

Task 6

You have probably noticed that for many of the facsimile texts* in this book, there is a title or heading. Did you also notice that the heading has a general–specific relationship to the text? You can expect most complete informational texts to have a heading: why do you think this is? Discuss your ideas with a partner.

*facsimile texts = texts copied as they appeared in the original book or periodical

We have talked about *situation*, *problem*, *solution* and *evaluation* as if they are independent of people – individuals, groups, governments, etc. Clearly, however, a *problem* only exists in terms of how people see it; a *solution* is more or less acceptable to different people. Thus when there are several participants in the text, the structure becomes more complicated.

Read the following text to get a general idea of the complexity of S→P→S→E patterns which can be found in even quite a short text.

'Superbaby' turns superbust

JAKARTA—Mention the name of Lee Kuan Yew to female university graduates in Singapore, and many will angrily denounce the Singaporean Prime Minister's bold attempt at genetic engineering.

These women are the government's special targets in a campaign launched a year ago to encourage them to marry early and have children.

Despite mixed scientific evidence, Lee Kuan Yew is convinced that I.Q.'s and talent are genetically determined and can be inherited by children of intellectually superior parents. He sees it as the most promising way for Singapore to keep its edge, in the years to come, in the field of sophisticated new technology industries.

He underestimated, however, the free spirit of university-educated Singaporean women. Referring to the Prime Minister, one said, "He is living in the past. Women are not cattle to be manipulated for breeding."   —**Mochtar Lubis**

(*WorldPaper*)

In the text above, there are two main participants / groups of participants in the interaction: Lee Kuan Yew and female university graduates. Although the general situation is the same for both participants, their different places in society and different concerns lead to different specific situations.

Task 7

Complete the flow diagram to show what, according to the 'Superbaby' article, Lee Kuan Yew's situation is, how he sees the problem, what his solution is and how he evaluates his solution; use extracts from the text. Be careful: the S→P→S→E sequence does not always appear in chronological order in a text. Check your answer with at least one other student.

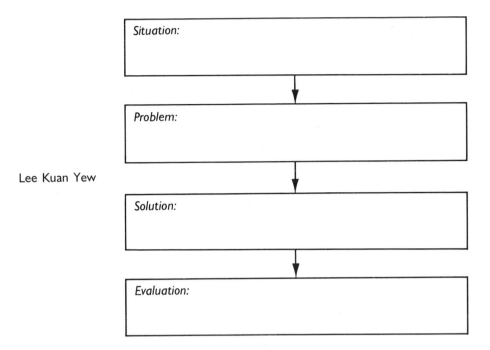

Lee Kuan Yew

Task 8

The other participants in the 'Superbaby' text, the female university graduates, do not see things in the same way as Lee Kuan Yew. Show the differences by completing the flow diagram, then check your answer with at least one other student.

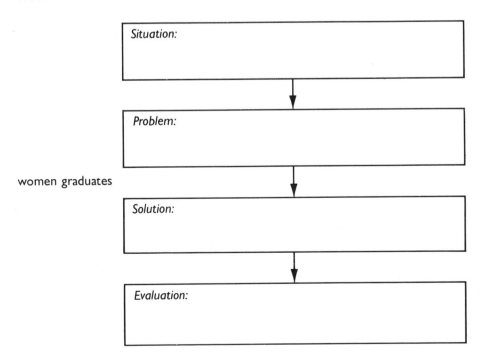

women graduates

Task 9

This text is more difficult than most of those you have seen, but the title gives you a clue to the problem to be presented and solved in the text. Extract the relevant information from the text in order to write your own short text, with an S→P→S→E structure, on the topic: 'What makes it possible for koalas to digest eucalyptus leaves?'

Why koalas like eucalyptus leaves

KOALAS are very particular about what they eat, devoting themselves entirely to a diet of the leaves of eucalyptus trees. But there are problems associated with an exclusive diet of leaves, especially if, like the koala, you happen to be a relatively small animal. One of these problems is that the leaves of trees are rich in fibre, and so resist digestion. Eucalyptus leaves are worse than most, for they contain large amounts of lignin—the indigestible, woody material found in the cell walls of many plants.

But there is another drawback for the fastidious koala. The ratio of an animal's gut volume to its energy requirements depends on body mass; the smaller it is, the lower the ratio. So diminutive leaf-eaters are likely to have difficulty processing sufficient quantities of their poor-quality food to meet their metabolic needs. On the whole, bigger animals make better browsers, which is not good news for a lightweight animal such as the koala.

S. J. Cork and T. J. Dawson of the University of New South Wales and I. D. Hume of the University of New England have made a study of the koala's digestion. They have identified three major factors that allow this marsupial to exploit its roughage-laden diet (*Journal of Comparative Physiology B*, vol 153, p 181).

In the first place, the koala has a discerning digestive system; like the rabbit, it can regulate the passage of food through its gut in a way that discriminates between particles of different sizes. The alimentary canal retains solutes and smaller, more digestible particles in the region of the caecum and colon, while expelling unwanted, coarser matter. This is probably a space-saving exercise; it has the effect of increasing the rate at which raw material can be fed into the system.

The second factor behind the koala's success is that it has a low overall requirement for metabolic energy, compared to other marsupials of similar size. So it saves

Fritz Prenzel/Bruce Coleman

Eucalyptus affects the parts other leaves cannot reach

on its fuel needs. In this respect, the koala is not dissimilar to another slow-moving, leaf eating mammal, the three-toed sloth.

Thirdly, eucalyptus leaves have hidden qualities. Despite the preponderance of lignin, such leaves are rich in digestible energy—especially in the form of lipids and phenols. Not all such resources are available to the koala's metabolic machinery; phenols and essential oils are excreted, for example. But some lipids are available, as are certain carbohydrates, such as sugar and starch. It is these compounds that satisfy the bulk of the koala's energy needs.

Surprisingly, constituents of the eucalyptus's cell walls, such as cellulose, are less important. Some cellulose is digested—with the help of microbes in the hind gut—but the koala's accomplishments in this field does not rival those of ruminants. □

(*New Scientist*)

Writer–reader relationship

In addition to following the conventions of text structure, writers also need to co-operate with their intended readers in various ways. These 'co-operative principles' are already known to you from earlier units:

1 Make everything clear to the reader but do not give more information than is necessary – clarity principle.
2 Assume that your readers know how the world works and do not need to be told everything *but* be sure to tell them anything you believe they will not know and need to know – reality principle.
3 Keep to your topic and your purpose for writing – relevance principle.
4 State only what you can provide evidence for – honesty principle.

While these co-operative principles are a matter of common sense, applying them in your own writing is not always easy. Apart from grammatical skill and good vocabulary, it requires control of the various information structures which you learned in Units 1–9 and an awareness of the possibilities for text structure which are available to a writer in English. The co-operative principles are not something which can be separated out: they are part of *everything* you write which is intended to be read and to convey information. They can be used with a series of *checks* which you can apply to what you have written to help you judge your own writing: is it clear? is it realistic? is it relevant? is it honest?

Task 10

In groups of three or four, discuss the text below, which deals with changes in levels of lead in petrol in Britain.

a) Apply the checks suggested above, of clarity, realism, relevance and honesty. Although the text was written for Scottish car drivers, you should be able to judge it fairly from your own point of view.
b) If this text was going to appear in a local newspaper in your country, in what ways (if any) would it be different (apart from being in a different language)? Rewrite as much of the text as necessary to make it suitable for publication in your country.

Taking the poison out of petrol
By J. C. BOWMAN, Our Motoring Correspondent

ALMOST without any impact or recognition, Britain has become a healthier, slightly less hazardous place in which to live and – particularly – breathe. From the beginning of this year, though many have had it a few weeks earlier, filling stations have been dispensing petrol with only 0.15 grammes of lead per litre instead of the previously permitted maximum of 0.40 grammes.

For the past 60 years or so, lead has been added to petrol because it improves its efficiency and makes it go further. It also helps to lubricate the engine valves. So why have you noticed no drop in performance or increase in fuel consumption since this major reduction in the amount of lead added?

The answer is in the blending at the refineries. By using

more high-grade spirit, octane ratings have been maintained at their previous levels. The saving in lead does not offset the extra cost of refining, so low-lead petrol is rather more expensive to produce: a consideration swallowed up by tumbling oil prices, with petrol reluctantly following suit.

The decision, on environmental and health grounds, to cut the lead content to its present level was taken in the late seventies. Getting rid of it altogether from petrol is a long-term goal so far as Britain is concerned, though it has already been achieved, almost in toto, in Japan while more than 60 per cent of petrol sold in the United States is lead-free.

It is more than a decade since the Americans decided to phase out leaded petrol but almost half the cars on their roads still use it. In the UK, there is a commitment to introduce unleaded petrol by October 1989 at latest. This coincides with an EEC deadline for the production of engines of more than two litres specially designed to run on unleaded petrol. For smaller engines, the proposed deadlines are 1991 or 1993, depending on the capacity.

In some European countries, particularly those like West Germany and Switzerland eager for tighter exhaust emission standards, unleaded petrol is already on sale to a limited extent. Apart from its general desirability, it is essential for cars with catalytic converters which are gradually being introduced in some larger cars to cut down the emission of noxious gases. Lead "poisons" the catalyst, making the converter useless.

Unleaded petrol, on the other hand, can harm some existing engines, damaging the valve seats. An increasing number of new cars, however, are suitable for a switch to lead-free petrol: many are German and Japanese models which run on two-star petrol and have hardened valve seats.

Ford's new range of lean-burn engines, including those for the latest Escort, Orion and 1.4 litre Fiesta models, are capable of running on unleaded fuel, with minor workshop adjustment. Later this year, 70 per cent of Fords produced in Britain and on the Continent will be able to run on unleaded petrol. By 1987, the Ford figure will rise to 100 per cent.

Refineries like BP's at Grangemouth are well prepared for a switch in production to unleaded petrol. It could be introduced long before 1989 if the will is there. Petrol companies believe there could be kudos in being the first to market unleaded petrol and are looking over each other's shoulders, not wishing to be caught napping.

Problems include cost and distribution. More crude oil is needed to produce the same amount of unleaded petrol, estimates of the additional cost ranging from 4p to 6p a gallon. The Government, it is now clear, is prepared to consider measures like differential rates of excise duty to wipe out the dis-incentive that higher-priced unleaded petrol would create.

For garage forecourts, the need to provide pumps for both leaded and unleaded petrol – as well as derv for the growing number of diesel cars – will probably mean that initially only the larger filling stations will provide it. For the unwary motorist there could be an increased risk of getting the wrong kind of fuel in the tank.

(*Scotsman*)

Unit 11   Organizing texts (3) Developing texts

Introduction

In Unit 10 you studied the useful *situation→problem→solution→evaluation*
(S→P→S→E) text structure by analysing and re-structuring some texts. While
you were working with those texts you probably learnt some general points:

1 The elements are not necessarily the same length as each other: it is possible
   to have a very short situation followed by a long discussion of the problem; or
   the reverse; etc.
2 Sometimes an element is omitted or only implied: the reality principle may
   tell the writer that an evaluation is not necessary; the writer may describe the
   situation and problem, then leave the reader to think about possible
   solutions; etc.
3 The elements may appear in a different order: this is most common when the
   problem is described before the situation which led to it, but other sequences
   may occur.

It is important to remember that texts are like people: each one is a little
different from every other one, but they all have certain characteristics in
common. Your job as a writer is to learn to control all the common
characteristics so that you can create texts which are individual and acceptable.

In this unit you will go another step towards this by working with incomplete
texts within the S→P→S→E framework, to complete them to your own
satisfaction and the satisfaction of readers.

Focus on situation

The part or parts of the text which focus on *situation* provide information about
the important question: what are we talking about? The amount of *situation*
information that needs to be presented to a reader depends on the writer's
judgement of the reader's background knowledge. We all have a strong
tendency to tell our readers only something they do not know. The danger is
that we assume readers have more background knowledge than they actually
have: the application of the *reality* principle needs to be carefully considered.
When in doubt, you are safer to include more information rather than leaving it
out.

Task 1

Read the two texts which follow: one is taken from the *Edinburgh Evening News*, a local newspaper, the other from a booklet produced by a British pressure group. The writers of the texts have made different assumptions about the readers' background knowledge, and therefore about the amount of *situation* information they needed to include. Read the texts and discuss with one or two other students whether these assumptions are justified or not.

Self-employed Carpenter.
Free estimates.   3368674

(*Edinburgh Evening News*)

RENEWABLE ENERGY

What is renewable energy?
We are already using up our fossil fuel reserves of coal, oil and natural gas. These fuels took millions of years to create. They are our precious *capital* and can never be replaced. They should be preserved for purposes for which it is difficult to find alternatives. In future we will need to start spending our energy *income*, and save our capital. By linking into the same energy network which powers the weather and climate, we might be able to use the sun, wind, waves and tides to help satisfy our energy needs. These are *renewable* sources. They serve as *income* and will never run out.

RENEWABLE ENERGY FOR BRITAIN:
The Outlook is Good

The British Isles are well placed to take advantage of the wind, waves and tides. There is potential for the use of green plants as biofuels, for geothermal and solar energy. Hydro-power at medium and small scales could also be developed.

(Lothian Energy Group *Living with Energy*)

Task 2

Use information from the diagram to write the *situation* part of the text, which has the title 'Are we wasting our energy resources?'.

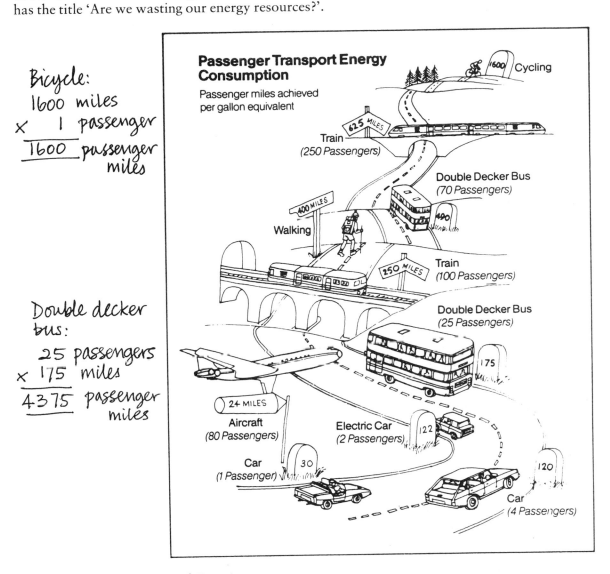

Bicycle:
1600 miles
× 1 passenger
1600 passenger
miles

Double decker
bus:
25 passengers
× 175 miles
4375 passenger
miles

(Lothian Energy Group *Living with Energy*)

In these days of rapid exhaustion of the world's non-renewable fossil fuel supplies, it is dangerously short-sighted to waste the precious energy resources we have. The energy at present consumed in moving people from one place to another varies enormously in .....

(*continue on a sheet of paper*)

Focus on problem

Einstein once said that the most important act of thinking a person can do is to define a problem, because anyone can work out a solution. The same can be said of the act of writing; until you can define for yourself the problem, you will find it very difficult to write.

The *problem* may be the first element of the text to be decided on, but as we have seen already, it is not usually the first part of the text to be presented to the reader. When it does appear first, it is usually for purposes of emphasis or special effect. In serious informational writing, the problem needs to be set within a context, a *situation*, for the reader.

Task 3

These two texts both give the greatest emphasis to the description of a problem, but one is light-hearted and the other is serious. Read the texts and discuss with one or two other students how clearly each problem has been described, what the purpose of each writer was in describing the problem, and whether you think the texts are successful in achieving those purposes.

DENTISTRY

No-drill thrill

THE DAY of the painless visit to the dentist – well, the 80% painless visit – is at hand. A chemical alternative to the dentist's drill has been developed in America, whereby decay is dissolved away rather than removed mechanically as at present (which, apart from hurting, carries the risk of damage to the healthy part of the tooth from heat and pressure). In 1,000-patient trials, drilling was reduced by 80% and pain-killing injections by 85%.

"We have been working on this for 15 years," says Professor Melvin Goldman, who with Dr Joseph Kronman developed the new method at Tufts University in Boston. "It took a lot of research to find a chemical that does the job, does not irritate soft tissues such as the inside of the lip, and is harmless if swallowed." The chemical they decided on, called N-chloro-alpha-aminobutyric acid, has been approved by the US Food and Drug Administration, the federal watchdog body.

The new procedure is to open up the cavity with a steel pick and then inject the chemical. Decayed tissue starts to dissolve after a few seconds, encouraged by gentle rubbing with the injector's tip. Some drilling may be required with awkward cavities, or when conventional filling materials – which do not adhere to the tooth and need an undercut hole – are used. But new filling materials, which adhere to teeth, make even this drilling unnecessary.

The new treatment is already available in America and Japan, and should be introduced in other countries soon.

Bryan Silcock

(*Sunday Times*)

DISCOVERY

Goodbye to sloppy gravy

SCIENCE has solved the perennial Teapot Problem, also known as the Gravy Boat Problem: what happens when you try to pour gravy gently so that your plate isn't swamped, but it runs back under the lip of the sauceboat and trickles onto the table. Ditto with pouring cream gently into coffee. The current issue of Scientific American reveals the authorised technique of dribble-free gravy-pouring.

Dr Joseph Keller, of New York University, measured the speeds of individual layers of liquid. He found that the lowest layer, nearest the spout, moved fastest; the uppermost layer moved slowest.

As speed increases in a fluid, pressure falls. Thus, the pressure is highest in the uppermost layer; it forces the liquid down and back against the spout.

Chemists have had the answer for years, dealing with dangerous liquids such as nitric acid. They simply hold a glass rod across the lip of the vessel as a guide for the liquid. To solve the gravy/cream/ tea problem, use a spoon in the same way.

Tony Osman

(*Sunday Times*)

Task 4

Read the *situation* paragraph which precedes the flow diagram. Then use the information in the diagram to help you write up the *problem* part of the text. In this case, the problem has a process organization.

Where Does It All Go?

The environmental face of salt applied to roads in winter is more complicated than was understood until recently. Environmentalists first noticed the death of plants beside the roads: this led them to investigate further and to discover just how widespread the problem arising from the widespread use of salt to prevent ice on roads really is.

⟫→

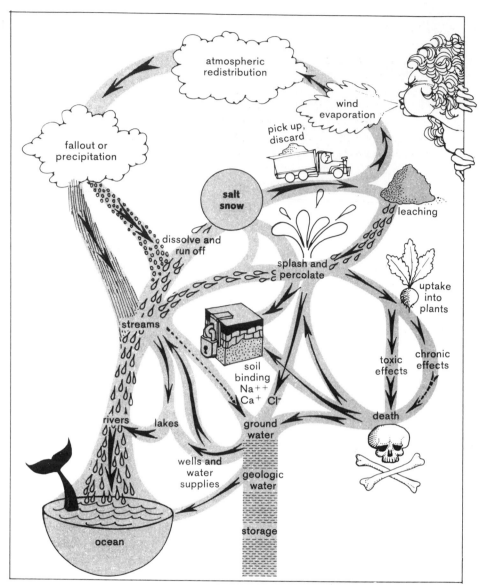

(R. Wagner *Environment and Man*)

Once a problem has been identified, it can either be evaluated (i.e. how serious a problem is it?), or a solution can be presented (i.e. how has it been / can it be solved?), and then the solution can be evaluated. This gives us two patterns, both of which are quite common:

We will look first at the simpler *problem→solution* structure.

Focus on solution

It is always possible to define a problem clearly, although sometimes the problem is so large and complex that it takes many people many years to learn all that is necessary to state the problem fully and accurately. Theoretical problems in the sciences (physics, chemistry, etc.) have exact solutions which can eventually be found. However, with real-life problems, an absolute solution is not always possible: a compromise solution often has to be found. For this reason some readers find the *solution* part of a text to be the least satisfactory. This may not be the fault of the writer, but a reflection of the facts of the subject written about.

Task 5

The following text describes a problem which is *not* a real-life problem – for us, anyway! Unlike a real-life problem it does have one solution (and only one). Discuss it with other students. Share your ideas to work out what the solution is.

TWO ODD COUPLES

In the early years of the 21st century the trend toward the unisex look and the blending of genders had reached so advanced a stage that it was almost impossible to tell males from females unless they were completely unclothed. Men and women looked alike, dressed alike, talked alike, thought alike, behaved alike.

Females regularly swallowed powerful male hormone pills that allowed them to grow beards and mustaches. Males just as regularly took female hormones to enlarge their breasts, slow the growth of facial hair, and raise the pitch of their voices. Both sexes usually wore tight-fitting pants to which were attached large, padded, ornamental codpieces. It was customary for men to have a small *M* embroidered on their codpiece, and for women to turn the *M* around to make a *W*.

During one of my infrequent out-of-body time travels, based on a secret meditation technique developed by Edgar Cayce Trance Laboratory, at Stanford Research International, I found myself strolling barefooted along the sunny oceanside of St. Augustine, Florida. The year was 2029. A pair of handsome youths walked toward me, one much taller than the other. Both had small blonde mustaches, and long yellow hair that bounced around their shoulders. They wore only bathing trunks so it was impossible to guess their sexes, although they held hands and acted very much like a couple in love.

We stopped to chat. Out-of-body journeys to the future

---

had become so commonplace by 2029 that the two youths seemed not at all surprised when I told them my real body was snoring on a bed in the mountains of western North Carolina, back in the year 1984.

"I assume one of you is male and the other female," I said, "but I don't know which is which."

"I'm the male," said the tall youth, smiling.

"And I'm the female," said the short one.

I should explain that when one's astral body is on a trip to another time or place, it acquires vigorous psychic powers. I could sense that at least one of the two was lying.

Impossible though it may seem, on the assumptions that one youth was male and the other female, and at least one lied, it is possible to deduce which sex belonged to which height. Solving the problem is such a delightful exercise in elementary logic that I urge you to work on it seriously before turning to the solution.*

*Solution on p. 118

(Martin Gardner in *Asimov's Science Fiction Magazine*)

Task 6

Read the (shortened) text below, then write a short paragraph of your own to suggest a solution to children's problems in understanding the special language of tests. Work alone.

When you have finished, compare your solution with that of one or two other students. Probably all your solutions are compromise solutions. Work together to write a paragraph which offers all of these solutions so that a reader would be able to choose among them.

There are clear indications from the National Child Development Study that poor physical home conditions are associated with declining levels of achievement. Poor housing, overcrowding and even lack of good bathroom facilities appear to be statistically related to behavioural differences such as a tendency to play truant frequently. These are, in turn, related to poor performance on tests of reading and arithmetic.

Language is another problem. Where English is not the mother tongue, children may have difficulties in trying to master a new language and the school curriculum at the same time. Where the first language is English, but a

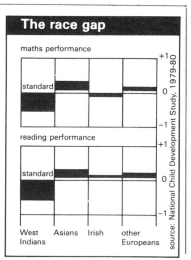

different dialect (for example, West Indian creole), teachers may underestimate a child's difficulty in speaking both their natural first dialect and the "standard" English of the classroom.

Selection procedures, including tests of "verbal reasoning", are almost certain to discriminate against minority groups with less competence in that kind of "test language". However able ethnic minority children might be, their talents are wasted if they cannot express themselves in terms understandable to examiners.

(*New Society*)

Focus on evaluation

It was pointed out earlier that *evaluation* can occur after either the *problem* or the *solution*. We will look now at evaluation of the problem.

Task 7

The following text begins with a generalization that suggests an evaluation of the problem of whether other people's tobacco smoke increases the risk of non-smokers getting cancer. The generalization is that it 'seems to'. Keeping in mind the honesty principle, read the text to find the specific evidence which will help you to evaluate the extent of the problem for yourself. Then use this evidence to write a one-paragraph summary (not more than 100 words) which honestly evaluates the problem.

Passive smoking may cause leukaemia

OTHER people's tobacco smoke seems to increase the chances of non-smokers getting a wide range of cancers. A new study in the US has found that leukaemia, for example, appears seven times more often among people who have spent their lives with smokers. Cancers of the cervix and breast were also strongly linked with "passive smoking".

The researchers, from the National Institute of Environmental Health Sciences, questioned more than 500 cancer patients about whether their parents and spouses smoked. They compared the results with those from a control group with similar jobs and smoking habits to the cancer patients.

The researchers reported in *The Lancet* last month that "overall cancer risk rose steadily and significantly with each additional household member who smoked over an individual's lifetime". They stress that the findings are preliminary, and require confirmation from other studies. But, "nonetheless, they suggest that effects of exposure to the cigarette smoking of others may be greater than has been previously suspected".   »»»→

Catherine Tate

People who had lived with one smoker (either parent or spouse) had 1·4 times the chances of contracting cancer as people with no such exposure. People who had lived with two smokers had 2·3 times the risk and those who had lived with three or more smokers had 2·6 times the risk. The trend applied to people who themselves smoked, as well as to those who did not smoke.

One surprising finding was that the risk of getting cancers not normally associated with smoking also rose among passive smokers. The risk of leukaemia rose 6·8 times among people who had lived with three smokers or more, the risk of breast cancer rose 3·3 times and the risk of cervical cancer increased 3·4 times.

Although passive smokers inhale less tobacco smoke, the researchers point out that the smoke they do breathe in is richer in many toxic chemicals. There is, for example, "three times as much benzo-a-pyrene, six times as much toluene and more than 50 times as much dimethylnitrosamine in a fixed volume of side-stream smoke in the gas phase as there is in cigarette smoke inhaled by the active smoker".

Past studies have found that byproducts of cigarette smoke, such as cotinine and thiocyanate, turn up in the blood, urine and saliva of non-smoking adults, children and fetuses that have been exposed to smokers. □

(*New Scientist*)

There are no real differences in the way the *evaluation* part of a text is organized and presented when it occurs after the *solution*.

Task 8

The advertisement below states a problem and offers a solution to it. Imagine that you are a journalist for a nurses' magazine: write a short report to appear in the magazine in which you evaluate Professor Potter's appliance and the solution it offers.

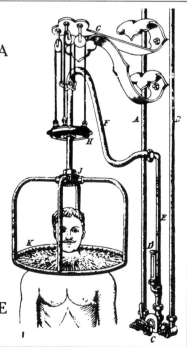

MEN. DO YOU SUFFER FROM A SHORT NECK?

Fear not,
RELIEF IS AT HAND.

PROFESSOR POTTER'S neck-lengthener is guaranteed to add INCHES to your height or YOUR MONEY BACK.

POTTER'S NECK-LENGTHENER: THE APPLIANCE OF SCIENCE

Task 9

Complete the following text by writing up the information in the table as the *evaluation* part of the text. Your evaluation will be personal, i.e. it will depend on the way you interpret the information available. It should not be longer than 100 words.

The Impact of Brezhnev

Leonid Brezhnev died in 1982. In looking back over his period as President of the Soviet Union — 1965 to 1982 — we ask ourselves what impact his years in office had on the ordinary citizens of the Soviet Union. The figures in the table, at the beginning of his Presidency and towards its end, permit a comparison of living standards.

Soviet Living Standards, 1965 and 1980		
Indicator	**1965**	**1980**
Monthly wage	96.5 roubles	168.5 roubles
Number of doctors	554,000	993,000
Families with TV sets	24 per cent	85 per cent
Families with refrigerators	11 per cent	84 per cent
Living space per person in towns	10 square metres	13.2 square metres
Consumption of meat per person	41 kilos	57 kilos
Consumption of vegetables per person	72 kilos	93 kilos
Consumption of potatoes per person	142 kilos	120 kilos
Consumption of bread per person	156 kilos	139 kilos

Source: Narodnoe Khoziaistvo SSSR v 1980. Statisticheskii ezhegodnik. Moscow. 1981

(*Guardian*)

It is not always possible to solve a problem fully or satisfactorily; probably the majority of solutions to real-life problems are only partial. Sometimes, evaluation of an apparent solution reveals another problem.

Task 10

We hear a great deal these days about the need to provide food for the world's starving millions. Read this text, then discuss the information it contains with a partner, and agree on an evaluation of the solution offered by the factory farming industry. Write up your evaluation individually.

Mark Gold on why developing countries don't need factory farming

Why do chickens cross the globe?

NOT content with its doubtful claim to produce cheap food for our own population, the factory farming industry also argues that "hungry nations are benefiting from advances made by the poultry industry". In fact, the proliferation of eggs in the Third World over the last decade represents an extremely disturbing development. Rather than helping the fight against malnutrition in "hungry nations", the spread of factory farming has, inevitably, added to the problem.

Large-scale intensive meat and poultry production is a waste of food resources. This is because more protein has to be fed to animals in the form of vegetable matter than can ever be recovered in the form of meat. Much of the food value is lost in the animal's process of digestion and cell replacement. Neither, in the case of broiler chicken, can one eat feathers, blood, feet, guts, or head. In all, about 44 per cent of the live animal is edible as meat.

This means one has to feed approximately 9–10 times as much food value to the animal than one can consume from the dead carcase. As a system for feeding the hungry, the effects can prove catastrophic. At times of crisis, as in Ethiopia this year, it is revealing that grain is the food of life.

Nevertheless, the huge increase in poultry production throughout Asia and Africa continues. Normally British or US firms are involved, either in selling stock, equipment, or expertise. For instance, an American based multinational has this year announced its involvement in projects in Zambia, Zimbabwe, Kenya, and Cameroon, as well as others in "early stages of development" in famine-stricken Sudan and Nigeria. Britain's largest suppliers of chicks, Ross Breeders, are also involved in projects all over the world.

Because such trade is good for exports, Western governments encourage it. Bangladesh, a country which could soon be suffering famine on the scale of Ethiopia, has joined the ranks of battery farmers. In 1979, a firm called Phoenix Poultry received a grant to set up a unit of 6,000 broiler birds and 18,000 laying hens. This almost doubled the number of poultry kept in the country in one swoop.

But Bangladesh lacks capital, energy, and food and has large numbers of unemployed. Such chicken-rearing demands an outlay of capital for building and machinery, extensive use of energy resources for automation, and involves feeding chicken with potential famine-relief protein food which is then inefficiently converted into meat or eggs.

The Food and Agriculture Organisation has found that the lunch bowl of a Bangladesh agricultural worker "contains a modest helping of plain boiled rice without meat, vegetables, or even sauce." Both the unemployed and women can hope for only half that quantity. Factory farming cannot alleviate such scarcity.

At present, one of Bangladesh's main imports is food grains, because the country is unable to grow enough food to feed its population. On what then can they possibly feed the chicken?

(*Guardian*)

Task 5 p.113, solution to Two Odd Couples
If the tall youth lied with the statement "I'm the male," then she is female, and the short male lied when he said "I'm the female." By similar reasoning, if the short youth lied, then the tall youth must also have lied. In brief, both lied. Therefore the tall one is the female and the short one is the male.

Unit 12 Organizing texts (4) Creating texts

In this last unit, you are provided with some written or visual material, and some tasks, but there is no guidance for completing the tasks. You are left to create your own texts.

You will probably want to discuss the material and/or tasks with one or more other students. Sharing ideas with others often helps you to clarify your own point of view. Discussing your first draft of a text with another student is also often helpful: it allows you to try out your text on a reader before your teacher sees it. Fellow students can point out weaknesses in the organization or argument; places where you need more or fewer ideas; language errors which interfere with your message; and so on. Exchanging drafts in this way can make your second draft, or editing of the first draft, easier and better.

If your teacher has not given you any more specific instructions, we suggest that you work through these tasks in the order in which they appear. If you want to be selective and not do all of them, we suggest you do not miss two in a row – they are designed to be more demanding as the unit progresses. Try to get feedback on one task before doing any major writing on the next one: you can use that feedback to create an even better text next time.

Task 1

Look at the photograph below. It shows passers-by who must have noticed the man lying on the pavement, but none of them have stopped to help him – to find out whether he is indeed ill, drunk or asleep.

Where is such a situation likely to occur? What could cause passers-by to ignore a man in such circumstances? What would be the best thing to do in these circumstances? Write a text, intended for your fellow students, in which you explain the picture and answer the questions above. Your text need not be longer than three (fairly short) paragraphs.

Task 2

This diagram shows how land rights were held in the feudal system. The feudal system in Britain existed hundreds of years ago, and in it land was given as a reward for service, and service had to be given in order to keep it. The system also involved the principle of 'serfdom', i.e. the workers, villeins or serfs who worked on a manor were regarded as the property of the manor. Write an explanatory text to accompany the diagram, intended for secondary school students. Keep your text fairly short and simple, but do not leave out any information.

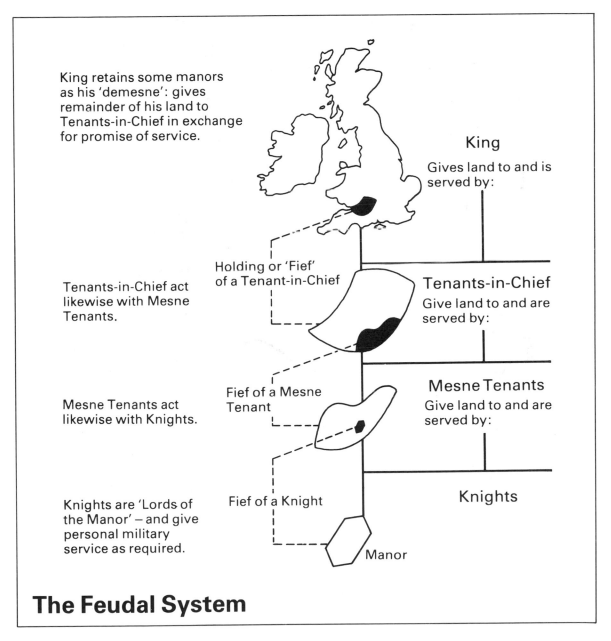

The Feudal System

Task 3

Culture shock happens when a person has to operate within a new set of cultural rules and values. Write a text, for American travellers to your country, alerting them to the existence of 'culture shock', and giving them some advice on how to cope with it.

Before you begin planning your essay, discuss the following texts with two or three other students. Consult also the text on pages 52–3.

a)

FAMILY AS SOCIAL GROUP

Egyptians tend to see themselves in relation to others, as members of groups, or in the context of their structural roles. They rarely think of themselves as individuals with unique potentials to develop or unique needs to satisfy.

A foreign television group was interviewing an employed middle-class woman for a documentary on Egyptian women. The foreigner phrased a question which was then translated into Arabic by a young blue-jeaned upper-class Egyptian. The subject of the interview had no trouble in answering questions about her work, her daily routines, her feelings about women working, and about the changes that had taken place in women's lives in Egypt. Then came the final question phrased by the foreigner as follows:

"Do you feel you have been able to realize your own identity within the modern context or if not how might you change your life to better realize that identity?" The translator, educated at the American University in Cairo, understood the question and put it to the woman in the best equivalent she was capable of. The subject answered:

"I am a mother, a wife, a grandmother, and a daughter to my mother who is still alive. I have no trouble being any of those things though there were times when my children were younger that it was hard for me to work and care for them properly." After several rephrasings of the question that emphasized her own needs as an individual, it became clear that she had difficulty in separating herself from her roles.

"But that is what I am," she insisted, "a mother, wife. . . ." She could express a momentary need for food, for drink, for a new dress but not for a long-term personal psychological or emotional need. The television people were disappointed by her answer. As they expressed it,

"Why isn't such a modern, articulate woman able to see beyond her position in the household?"

b)

The American, affected by a stomach disorder, had somehow stoically survived the morning inspecting a development project near a provincial town. Now he was feeling much worse and wanting only to return to his own bed and medicine. The head of the village council brought out a surprise picnic lunch for the twenty or so people congregated in the palm grove. The American sat dejectedly on the side unable to eat, becoming increasingly annoyed by the long dragged-out luncheon. There was a steady stream of jokes passing back and forth between Egyptians (all politely translated into English) and every few minutes the American was included in the joking – "Do you find our women beautiful? . . . Better than American women," they teased his wife. The banter was excruciating torture for the American.

"I feel sick," he finally said "and want to go home."

"Oh no, we will take you to our house, make some chicken broth for you and sit with you until you are better. We can't leave you alone." The American lost all patience and demanded to be taken back to the place in town where he was temporarily staying.

"Wait," his hosts said. "We are sending to the next town for some cola for you. It will make you feel better."

The American construed the encounter as a total lack of consideration for his need – to go home and sleep alone. The Egyptians felt they were doing everything they could to divert the American from his misery. They supported him with banter and good company giving up whatever else they might have had to do to stay with him.

c)

An American literature class in an Egyptian University had just finished Thoreau's *Walden*. The American professor had explained all the pertinent points of Thoreau's return to nature, his attempt at realizing self-sufficiency, his strong sense of individualism. The class was clearly uncomfortable with what they had been reading and were having difficulty in putting the book into some sort of familiar perspective.

"How do you feel about Thoreau, the man, and do you think that a life style like his would be appropriate in the Egyptian context?" the professor asked. Hands flew up and a number of answers came at once:

"He is a miser – he lacks generosity." The student based his comments on the lengthy accounting Thoreau made of all the materials he had bought to sustain himself in the woods. "What is the purpose of going off and living alone? What kind of life is that?" "Doesn't he have any family? He doesn't speak about them. How can he leave all his responsibilities behind like that?"

The consensus of the class was that Thoreau was not accomplishing anything useful by his anti-social behaviour; he had abrogated

> his role as a social being. He should in fact be considered "crazy" and would be so considered if he should try to live in this way in the Egyptian context. The concept of self-realization and self-reliance were totally lost on the students.

(A. B. Rugh *Family in Contemporary Egypt*)

Task 4

Refer to the (American) bar graphs below to write a report for publication in the magazine of the CCCC (Cigarettes Cause Cancer Campaign) on the data contained in the graphs.

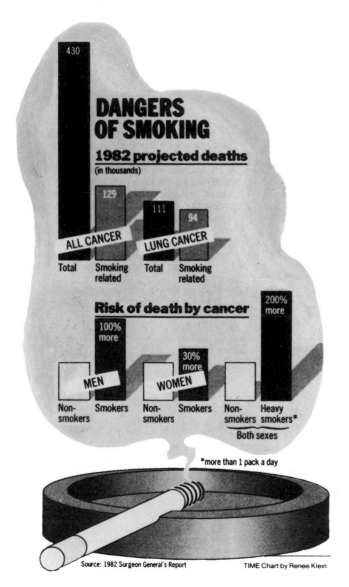

Task 5

Use the information in the map and accompanying text, and other information if you can find any, to help you write the text of a publicity leaflet for a group campaigning against nuclear plants in Britain (the woman in the picture below probably belongs to such a group).

A quarter of a ton of plutonium now lies at the bottom of the Irish Sea, discharged over the years from Windscale. It will remain intensely radioactive for almost a quarter of a million years. Animal experiments have shown that a fraction of a millionth of a gram, a bit of plutonium the size of a grain of pollen, can cause lung cancer. A lump of it the size of a grapefruit could, in theory, kill everyone on earth – though, in practice, it would be impossible to distribute it so finely that everyone received a fatal dose.

This map (right), based on official diagrams, shows where the plutonium has settled. The highest concentrations are near the end of the Windscale pipeline. It also demonstrates that it was a bad site to choose for such a highly polluting plant because it discharges into a relatively shallow sea, almost surrounded by land. This point has not been lost on the Irish Government, and this year the deputy Prime Minister asked Britain to close the pipeline.

Within the past year plutonium from Windscale has been identified as far away as the North Cape of Norway and even in the waters off Greenland.

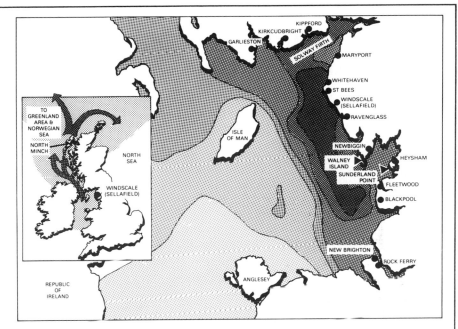

WARNING OBJECTS ON THIS BEACH MAY BE RADIOACTIVE

Windscale is the nucleus of atomic Britain; everything revolves around it. Built in the early 1950s on the site of an old munitions factory to provide plutonium for the young British nuclear weapons programme, it remains vital for the maintenance of an independent deterrent. And as the country's civilian nuclear network grew, it came to be seen as equally essential for reprocessing the waste of our nuclear power stations.

(Observer)

Task 6

Read the explanatory text and study the two diagrams, which show the diet of ordinary British people in 1939 and 1985. Consult an encyclopaedia or other reference book to find out what 'essential fats' are and what their function is. Then write a text intended for parents, to tell them what they should add to their children's meals to make sure they get a properly balanced diet.

HOW THE WHEEL OF HEALTH WORKS

THE 'WHEEL OF HEALTH' is a graphic representation of the amounts of nutrients we need, not just to survive, but to thrive. It is a map of nourishment, showing the quality of food eaten by a nation, a population group, or by an individual man, woman or child.

How does the wheel work? It is divided into 30 segments, representing essential nutrients and energy. We cannot do without essential nutrients, and they are not made within the body: we therefore have to eat them.

The simple key to the wheel is that the more its segments are filled in, the higher the quality of the food represented. Any segment incompletely filled shows food which is that extent short of the nutrient represented.

The large segment at the nine o'clock position shows energy, supplied by proteins, carbohydrates, fibres (only a small amount) and fats. Of these, proteins, starches (carbohydrate minus sugars), fibres and essential fats (basically the same as polyunsaturated fats) are represented on the wheel by the other four large segments. Sugars and saturated fats are harmful to health and are not represented. Amino acids are also not shown separately.

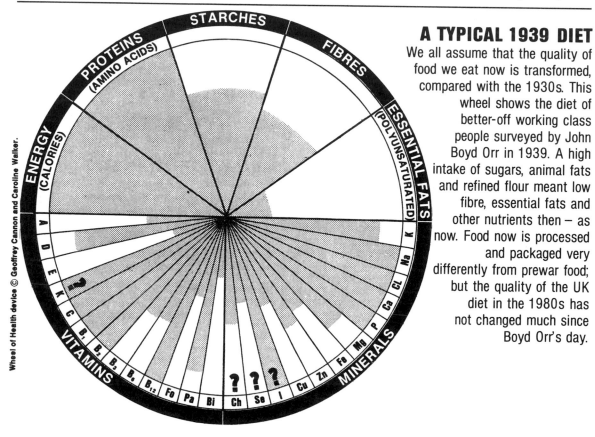

Wheel of Health device © Geoffrey Cannon and Caroline Walker.

A TYPICAL 1939 DIET

We all assume that the quality of food we eat now is transformed, compared with the 1930s. This wheel shows the diet of better-off working class people surveyed by John Boyd Orr in 1939. A high intake of sugars, animal fats and refined flour meant low fibre, essential fats and other nutrients then – as now. Food now is processed and packaged very differently from prewar food; but the quality of the UK diet in the 1980s has not changed much since Boyd Orr's day.

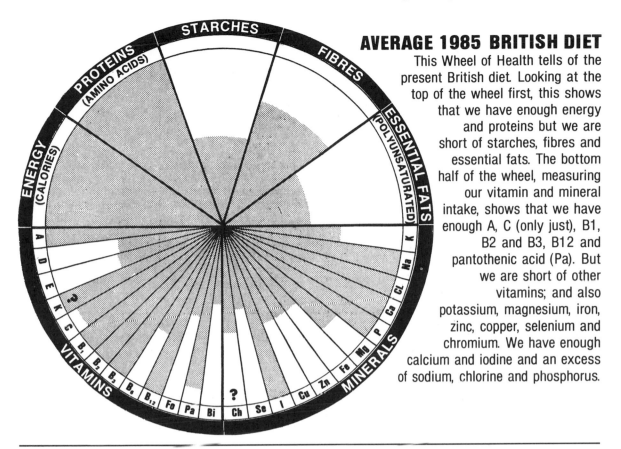

AVERAGE 1985 BRITISH DIET

This Wheel of Health tells of the present British diet. Looking at the top of the wheel first, this shows that we have enough energy and proteins but we are short of starches, fibres and essential fats. The bottom half of the wheel, measuring our vitamin and mineral intake, shows that we have enough A, C (only just), B1, B2 and B3, B12 and pantothenic acid (Pa). But we are short of other vitamins; and also potassium, magnesium, iron, zinc, copper, selenium and chromium. We have enough calcium and iodine and an excess of sodium, chlorine and phosphorus.

Vitamins (the 13 small segments making up the left-hand bottom quarter of the wheel) are essential nutrients needed in very small, varying amounts. As with all nutrients represented, the amounts of vitamins recommended as advisable for good health are all scaled so as to form the circumference of the wheel.

Minerals (the 12 small segments to the right of vitamins) may be inert or may be (like lead, for example) toxic in their effect. The 12 represented on the Wheel are all essential nutrients.

Scientists recommend the amounts of essential nutrients needed for good health by Recommended Daily Amounts (RDAs). In so far as any government has a national food and health policy, this is reflected in RDAs.

The RDAs used on the Wheel of Health are those published in 1980 by the National Academy of Sciences in the USA (energy, proteins, vitamins, minerals) together with other recommendations by the US Senate Committee on Nutrition and Human Needs (starches and essential fats) and the British NACNE committee (fibres).

(*Observer*)

127

Task 7

Use the diagram to write a report to the Nautical Institute on the safety risk involved in producing 'high-rise' car ferries. Begin your report as follows:

The development of bigger, more streamlined car ferries over the past two decades may have made it impossible to evacuate passengers safely in an emergency.

Here are some points to remember:

problems   *solutions?*
open-plan car decks   chutes
deck height→ladders   special helicopter deck
            ↘lifeboats
ferry may 'list'
winches too weak?

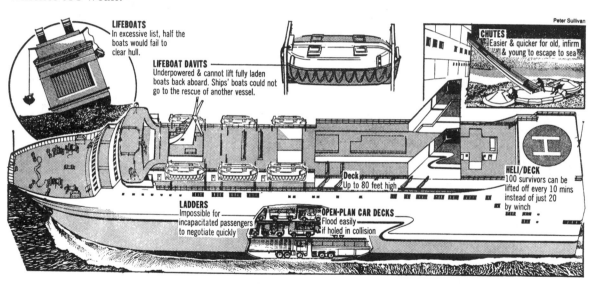

Task 8

In groups of three or four discuss the implications of 'electronic newspapers'. Refer to the newspaper material reproduced on pages 129–30. Some members of the group should concentrate on the problems associated with the older technology (*The Past*) – too many employees, complicated process, time-consuming process, expensive labour, etc. Others should concentrate on the problems of the new technology (*The Future*) – workers will lose jobs, trades will disappear, work will become less creative, machines will take over, etc.

   After you have finished your discussion write *one* of the following essays:

a) Why we need electronic newspapers.
b) Why we don't need electronic newspapers.

THE PAST

JOURNALISTS: Write articles illustrated by photographers and artists

LINOTYPE OPERATORS: Cast each separate letter from articles and advertisements

COMPOSITORS: take the metal type and the photographic blocks and fit them into a 'forme' the size of a newspaper page.

PROCESS make metal images, called blocks, of photographs and illustrations

READERS AND COPY READERS: copy readers read original copy, while readers make correction on page proofs.

STEREOTYPERS take impressions of forme called 'flong' from which a semi-cylindrical metal plate is cast with words, photos, and ads in mirror image.

ENGINEERS AND ELECTRICIANS: maintain and repair linotype machines presses and other machines.

DISTRIBUTION: oversee distribution to make sure right number of copies at right time and place.

MACHINE MINDERS AND ASSISTANTS: under surpervision of minders the machine assistants secure cast cylinder plates to presses, thread paper, start print run, repair breaks

PUBLISHERS: receive bundles of papers, supervise tying, load and drive vans.

THE SUNDAY TIMES

THE SUNDAY TIMES

THE FUTURE

JOURNALISTS: Write articles illustrated by photographers and artists. Typing story directly into the computer.

COMPUTER: sets type and designs page for printing plate.

PROCESS: make printing plates for presses.

PUBLISHERS: supervise tying, wrapping, loading and drive vans.

DISTRIBUTION: oversee distribution to make sure right number of copies at right time and place.

PRINTERS: secure plates to presses, thread paper, start print run repair breaks and maintain machines.

THE SUNDAY TIMES

America's papers show the way

● **More jobs, new papers, better papers: Frank Lipsius reports from New York**

THE new-technology revolution in American newspapers has brought increased circulations, a wider range of publications and an expansion of newspaper jobs – in spite of reduced manning in the composing rooms.

Payrolls in the publishing industry more than doubled in a decade from $3.1 billion in 1972 to $6.3 billion in 1981. Capital investment, largely as a result of re-equipment with new technology, doubled from $554m in 1972 to $1.02 billion in 1981.

Circulation of weekly newspapers has grown from 21m in 1960 to 49m in 1985. Big city dailies have remained relatively static, with total circulation going from 58m to 63m. Sunday papers, though, have grown more dramatically from 8.6m to 56m. This reflects the trend toward specialisation. Growth has been especially strong in the number and circulation of suburban and small-community newspapers. In 1965 there were only 357 semi-weekly papers; in 1982, 508.

There has also been a dramatic rise in newspapers circulating nationwide – something that hardly existed in the old days. The Wall Street Journal is producing regional editions that have catapulted it into becoming the nation's largest-circulation newspaper, a role formerly held by the New York Daily News. In addition, USA Today and the New York Times have used technological advances, particularly satellite-delivery of pages to regional production facilities, to achieve unprecedented growth.

A number of daily papers have added Sunday editions – made possible through the new technology – in response to demand from advertisers.

Total newspaper employment, according to government statistics, rose from 345,000 in 1965 to 443,000 in 1984 – and that figure does not fully cover the multitude of local papers. But the International Typographical Union, which formerly had a firm grip on nearly all printing jobs, has shrunk from over 100,000 in 1967 to 40,000 today, of whom about 4,000 are in fact retired members. The prospect is that the union may be reduced to 5,000 members in 1990.

According to Jim Cesnik of the 33,000-member journalists' union, the Newspaper Guild, employment of journalists has grown but not to the same extent as that of salespeople pushing advertising and circulation. The guild, however, has few members on the small local papers.

The New York Times spent $2m on radio advertising to boost home-delivery of the paper in the first nine months of 1985 – a campaign responding to a fall in the number of streetside news-stands. The general growth in circulations has helped increase advertising revenue among dailies from $15 billion in 1965 to $66 billion in 1982.

An interesting development noted by Charles Cole, a consultant to the 1,375-member American Newspaper Publishers Association, is that local newspapers have expanded their news-gathering teams, and some now send people abroad as well as having representatives in many American cities. Other departments in papers have also advanced, according to Cole. For example, mail rooms of many newspapers employ up to 25% more people handling the national advertising inserts that have become common. However, more automatic machinery may well reduce manning here.

(*Sunday Times*)

Task 9

Imagine you are Britain's Minister for Youth Employment. Use the information in the text and accompanying graphs to help you write a report to the Prime Minister explaining why you want to change the system of National Insurance contributions for the 16–19 age group. Find and include any other information you think you need.

Pay trap for job hunters

by David Lipsey

NEW evidence that the present structure of national insurance contributions hinders the creation of full-time jobs has been uncovered by the department of employment. It has persuaded employment ministers that lowering the contributions for low-paid 17–19-year-olds could provide a major boost to jobs for young people.

At present, employers pay no national insurance contribution (NIC) for an employee earning under £34 a week. At £34 a week, however, the employer has to contribute £3.55 and the employee £3.06.

The result, the government's family expenditure survey shows, is a great cluster of employees, mostly part-time women earning just under £34. By contrast, there are many fewer employees than expected earning £34–£40.

The department of employment concludes that the structure of the NIC is distorting the labour market, creating an artificial obstacle to full-time jobs. Young people, who would be the most likely takers of full-time jobs at these pay levels are the biggest sufferers, ministers believe.

Some 515,000 youngsters aged 16–19 are jobless, the latest official figures show. A further 688,300 aged between 20 and 24 are jobless (see graphic).

Better news for young people is that the youth opportunities scheme is creating at least 6,000 more new jobs than had previously been thought. The YOS gives a subsidy of £15 a week to employers who hire a youngster under 18 for a wage of less than £50 a week.

First indications were that 93% of these jobs would have been created anyway, without the subsidy.

>>>→

THE JOBLESS MILLIONS

UNEMPLOYED UNDER 25

figures in thousands

512,000
931,000
1,154,000
1,226,000
1,260,000

JAN 1980   JAN 1981   JAN 1982   JAN 1983   JAN 1984

Unemployment Benefit Attendance Card   UB40z

SURNAME   INITIALS

HOW OLD ARE THE JOBLESS?

Under 18	164·1
18-19	350·9
20-24	688·3
25-34	709·6
35-44	439·8
45-54	397·0
55-59	267·3
60+	33·5

figures in thousands

HOW LONG HAVE THEY BEEN OUT?

Up to 2	214·8
2-4	150·4
4-8	214·7
8-13	222·5
13-26	432·4
26-52	631·2
52+	1,234·4

WEEKS   figures in thousands

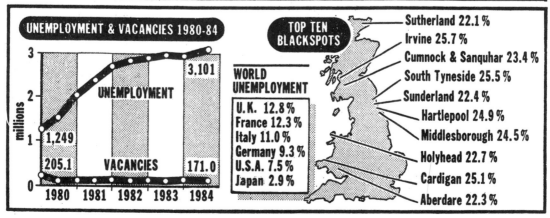

UNEMPLOYMENT & VACANCIES 1980-84

millions

UNEMPLOYMENT
1,249
3,101
VACANCIES
205.1
171.0

1980   1981   1982   1983   1984

TOP TEN BLACKSPOTS

WORLD UNEMPLOYMENT

U.K. 12.8%
France 12.3%
Italy 11.0%
Germany 9.3%
U.S.A. 7.5%
Japan 2.9%

Sutherland 22.1%
Irvine 25.7%
Cumnock & Sanquhar 23.4%
South Tyneside 25.5%
Sunderland 22.4%
Hartlepool 24.9%
Middlesborough 24.5%
Holyhead 22.7%
Cardigan 25.1%
Aberdare 22.3%

(*Sunday Times*)

Task 10

Choose your own material, visual or written or both, and write your own task instructions. Then do the task yourself. Use the experience you get from doing this to improve the task instructions, then give material and task to another student to do. When she or he has completed it, evaluate her or his text and discuss it.

A Structuring the writing sessions

1 The structure of the course

Fitting Study Writing *into your course*

It will take 40–60 class hours to cover the course, assuming a reasonable amount of homework and a selectivity in assigning tasks. However, should less time be available, you need to have a set of principles on which to base your decisions about how to work through the material. There are several possibilities.

a) As this is a writing course, and not a grammar course, the most obvious way to cut the time is to cut out the *Grammar in writing* sections. These sections are not intended to be the first introduction of a grammatical area, but a review of some particularly useful areas. Some classes will not need this review.

b) Some students may come to this course after one course focusing on writing; depending on the book they used, students may already be practised in functional writing (definitions, etc.). In this case it would make sense to concentrate on text structure (Part II) after a quick review of functions.

c) If it is felt that students would benefit from dealing with the relationship between grammar and writing, the *Grammar in writing* sections could provide the primary focus of a reduced course, with the *Consolidation* sections linking the grammar practice to writing development.

d) It may be felt that students primarily need to write *more*, in which case the *Consolidation* sections could provide the main route through the course with a quick review of the other sections in each unit as the need becomes evident.

Sequence or non-sequence?

By and large, though it is the easiest option, there is no particular merit in following the sequence of units in the course when there is no possibility of finishing it. It is of more benefit to the students to work through a complete body of material in a principled way, even though other whole areas are omitted. It is for this reason that we make the suggestions above. Obviously, the best way to use *Study Writing* is to use the whole book except when (as in the *Consolidations*) several options are provided to allow teacher and students room for choices based on personal taste.

Classwork vs homework

It will normally not be feasible to cover the course completely in class time. Consequently decisions need to be made regarding the amount and type of work assigned for homework. The amount will be determined by the time available and the appropriateness of the material for home study. Obvious candidates for homework are the longer tasks in each unit, particularly the *Consolidation* tasks. However, the other sections may also be given as home study since most of the answers to textual questions are given in the commentary.

It is difficult to generalize about homework as many factors are involved. For example, there may have been a prior decision to take a workshop approach to writing. In this case selections from the *Consolidation* sections may be written in class under supervision while the *Introduction* and *Grammar in writing* sections can be assigned as home study. If this approach is taken, sections assigned for out-of-class work should have been adequately prepared for in class.

Monolingual vs crosslingual treatments

The position taken in this coursebook is a monolingual one, i.e. we operate exclusively within one language – English in this case. However, it is also possible to adopt a crosslingual perspective, particularly if students have a language in common. Attention can then be drawn to the rhetorical conventions that operate in the first language in contrast to those that operate in academic writing in English. The value of such an analysis is that it draws attention to the known (the first language) and uses it as a bridge towards the unknown (writing in *English*).

2   The structure of the individual lesson

Pre-writing

This stage generally involves the writer in choosing a topic, or, if the topic has been assigned, in thinking about the topic and deciding on a way to respond to it, and selecting the appropriate ideas and information to use in a response. There are arguments in favour of a clearly laid-out topic being set, providing students with a strong structure to support the creative writing they will do, preventing them going astray because of irrelevance, poor organization of arguments, and so on. But there are also arguments in favour of leaving the task very vague, allowing students the space in which to think and create, to follow their own interests and ideas, to use their own knowledge and test out their developing skills without restrictions. We have tried, in our *Consolidation* tasks especially, to provide writing assignments of both kinds. Often the teacher will want to indicate to each student which task would be appropriate for her or him, but sometimes the students can be left to decide for themselves. There is no reason why every student should do the same task.

The pre-writing stage should be very active, with discussion of the topic area to make sure everyone has something to write about; students can be encouraged to bring additional reading material (not necessarily in English) to increase their familiarity with a topic area, and to work together exchanging factual information and opinions. Groups working on the same task can discuss the best way to approach the task, from the point of view of information structure, functional language needed, which arguments should come first, and so on.

Writing

There seems to be little point in using up classroom time with students working individually on a composition, and the teacher waiting passively for them to finish. If the teacher wants to set individual, unassisted writing tasks, these can be done as homework and then collected for marking. (A good deal of research has found that written work has to be handed back in the next lesson, with comments not just marks, for the marking to do any good.) Often, though, it is more effective for the students' learning, as well as easier on the teacher, to organize the writing stage as a *writing workshop*. In a writing workshop, the students work on their compositions in the classroom, but not silently and individually. They consult each other, or co-write (two or three students put together a single, co-operative, essay), while the teacher moves from student to student or group to group, reading over their shoulder what they are doing and providing feedback or answering questions. Questions might be about grammatical phrasing or lexical items, but they are just as likely to be about the strength or validity of a point, about the order in which to present information, or whether to begin a new paragraph. With more than 10–12 separate pieces of writing to keep track of, a writing workshop is difficult for the teacher to handle, so many teachers have part of the class doing this while the others work through controlled exercises, working ahead of the others or getting practice in a previous teaching point, or editing or proofreading a previous piece of writing. (Make sure it isn't always the quicker students who get the special attention of a workshop.)

Rewriting

Few of us, and few great writers, get it right first time. This does not only mean grammar, but all aspects of a piece of writing: the mood, the emphasis, the development, the choice of effective words and word combinations, etc. It is useful to distinguish two kinds of rewriting: editing and proofreading. The editing process is really an extension of the writing stage, involving the students in taking a critical look at their writing in order to be sure that the written product, the outcome of their writing process, is as they intended it to be. Often the students get so bound up in the creative process that they lose sight of their larger goal, the complete text. Editing permits them to make minor or major changes so that they have a text as close as they can make it to what they wanted to say. Proofreading simply means re-reading the text and correcting minor errors such as mis-spelling, verb tense consistency and stylistic features. Both editing and proofreading can be done co-operatively in the classroom, though proofreading requires little intervention from the teacher.

If you have access to word processors or micro-computers with word processing software, you will find that students are very motivated by creating their texts on a word processor. Word processors are very suitable for groups of not more than four students working on the co-operative creation of a text. Where the word processor really shows its advantages is in the ease with which errors can be corrected during proofreading; a little more skill with the programme will allow the students to reorganize the parts of the text, insert or delete sentences and paragraphs, and create headings, underline and highlight them as they polish their final products.

B   Making writing interactive

The interactive nature of writing is stressed in this book because writing for an audience causes problems for students on writing courses. In writing courses students often feel that they are somehow writing in a vacuum. This feeling is reinforced by the system of marking, which communicates to the student the sense that the marks are the only reason for writing. In this case a good piece of writing is one which attracts higher marks than previous ones, and not necessarily one which communicates with an audience. And yet, no-one really writes except *for* someone (even if that someone is only oneself, in the future, as with a diary).

By making writing conditions more interactive an awareness of audience is reinforced. In discussing a proposed piece of writing with another student, the student writer is forced to consider the audience and is more likely to adopt a reader-oriented approach to writing. It is important that the teacher should not be the only audience, because teachers are so often seen as critics and mark-givers. Writing for a variety of audiences develops flexibility and control in the writer. The following suggestions give only an indication of the variety of ways that interaction can be promoted in the writing class:

1   students in groups brainstorm a topic (i.e. collectively write down all the ideas that occur to them in connection with a given topic);

2   whole class discussion of how a given text might be adjusted for a different audience;

3   collaborative writing (i.e. two or more students work together to write a single, agreed, text);

4   whole class composition of short texts on the blackboard;

5   writing workshop (see *Teacher's guide A Structuring the writing sessions*, for a detailed description);

6   groups of students divide out the responsibility for different aspects of the research (information-finding for a text topic), then pool their results and work together to plan a text, which may be collaborative (3) or individual;

7   students exchange first drafts of a text and point out to each other changes which are needed to help the reader (e.g. better organization; paragraph divisions); they can also act as each other's editors (pointing out vocabulary repetitions, grammatical infelicities, spelling mistakes, etc.);

8   whole class examination of one or two texts (with names removed – photocopied, displayed on an overhead projector, or written onto the blackboard) from a specific point of view, e.g. ideas; text structure; grammar;

9   specification of an audience for a text, and making this as real as possible

(e.g. information about a topic another class is actually studying, which is then presented to them; class newspaper to be given to family and/or friends; explanation of a game which will then really be played);

10 specification of text type (e.g. report; newspaper article; set of instructions) which is appropriate to the purpose of the writing.

Making writing interactive requires imagination on the part of the teacher, but is rewarded by the imagination and enjoyment most students display in response.

C   Handling the reading texts

In *Study Writing* we provide texts for two main purposes: texts which are meant to be read primarily for the grammatical/rhetorical options they embody; and texts (mainly in the *Consolidation* sections) which should be read primarily for their content. Students must be made aware of this differential focus.

Texts which are presented for analyses of their grammatical/rhetorical options are often fragmentary, lacking in contexts and drawn from a wide range of specializations. For these reasons they are unsuitable as normal reading texts, i.e. texts to be read for content. When students are asked to read such texts they must be reminded of their purpose in reading. Otherwise they will get bogged down in the reading process and fail to perceive the teaching point, a particular information structure. Texts such as these are better skimmed rather than intensively read. Subsequent discussion should focus on the appropriateness, etc. of the information structure used rather than the content of the text.

Texts which are used as inputs for subsequent writings tasks need to be carefully prepared by the teacher to ensure that the content is understood by the students. This will usually involve informing students, where possible, of the context and likely readership of the article, some initial preparation of its content, glossing of key words coupled with recourse to the dictionary. The important point to remember is that reading in this case is an aid to writing and not meant to be an end in itself.

The view of reading which we put forward here is motivated by our perception of priorities: the more time spent reading in a writing class, the less time spent on writing. We acknowledge the beneficial effect of wide reading on the ability to write and feel that students should be encouraged in this, but not in the writing class.

To summarize, the following strategies are recommended:

Texts for analysis
1 Remind students of reading purpose.
2 Have students skim text for teaching point.
3 Focus discussion on teaching point.

Texts for ideas
1 Discuss context – type of publication, readership, background to content, etc.
2 Gloss difficult items / refer students to dictionary.
3 Discuss content, possible lines of development, etc.

D Analysing essay titles

Students often do less·well than they should on formal writing tasks, not because their writing skills are weak, but because they have not realized what it is they are asked to do. It is often helpful to teach them how to analyse essay titles. The analysis technique below has been tried out with a large and varied selection of essay titles.

1 **Topic** in an essay title is the same as 'topic' in a text, i.e. what, in the most general terms, the essay should be about. In the titles below the 'topic' appears in italics.
> *Happiness*
> *Pollution* is man's greatest enemy.
> Describe the life-cycle of *the moth*.
> Define a *fulcrum* and give at least two examples.
> Discuss the principal methods of controlling *noise at work*. Provide examples of each method.

2 **Focus** in an essay title is the detailed limitation of the topic: it tells the student more specifically, sometimes very specifically, what the essay should be about. In the titles below the 'focus', if there is one, appears in italics.
> Happiness (no focus)
> Pollution is *man's greatest enemy*.
> Describe *the life-cycle* of the moth.
> Define a fulcrum and give at least two examples. (no focus)
> Discuss *the principal methods of controlling* noise at work. Provide examples of each method.

3 **Comment** refers to the instruction word or phrase or (in some cases) more than one instruction: these instructions tell the student what text-type they should produce. Where applicable, the 'comment' is in italics in the examples:
> Happiness (no 'comment' – free response essay)
> Pollution is man's greatest enemy. (no 'comment' – but probably intended to be a discussion text)
> *Describe* the life-cycle of the moth.
> *Define* a fulcrum and *give* at least two *examples*. (two 'comment' requirements)
> *Discuss* the principal methods of controlling noise at work. *Provide examples* of each method. (two 'comment' requirements)

Here is a list of the most common *comment* key-words with an explanation for each:

Compare: requires an answer which sets items side by side and shows their similarities and differences. A balanced (fair, objective) answer is expected.

Contrast: requires an answer which points out only the differences between two items.

Criticize: requires an answer which points out mistakes or weaknesses, and which also indicates any favourable aspects of the subject of the question. It requires a balanced answer.

Define: requires an answer which explains the precise meaning of a concept: a definition answer will include definition structure, probably expanded.

Analyse: requires an answer which takes apart an idea, concept or statement in order to consider all the factors it consists of. Answers of this type should be very methodical and logically organized.

Discuss: requires an answer which explains an item or concept, and then gives details about it with supportive information, examples, points for and against, and explanations for the facts put forward. This is one of the most difficult types of essay question.

Evaluate: requires an answer which is similar to one with the key-word 'Discuss', but the conclusion in this type is expected to make a judgement, either 'pro' or 'contra' (for or against), the concept being discussed and evaluated.

Illustrate: requires an answer which consists mainly of examples to demonstrate or prove the subject of the question. It is often added to another instruction.

Justify: requires an answer which gives only the reasons *for* a position or argument. Note, however, that the proposition to be argued may be a *negative* one (e.g. Justify the abolition of the death penalty).

Prove/Disprove: both of these require answers which demonstrate the logical arguments and/or evidence connected with a proposition: *prove* requires the 'pro' points, and *disprove* requires the 'contra' points.

Summarize/Outline: require an answer which contains a summary of all the available information about a subject, i.e. only the main points and not the details should be included. Questions of this type often require short answers.

Trace: is found most frequently in historical questions (but not only in History courses); it requires the statement and brief description in logical or chronological order of the stages (steps) in the development of e.g. a theory, a person's life, a process, etc.

State: requires an answer which expresses the relevant points briefly and clearly without lengthy discussion or minor details.

Explain: requires an answer which offers a rather detailed and exact explanation of an idea or principle, or a set of reasons for a situation or attitude.

4   **Viewpoint** is an element of essay titles which often is not present. When it *is* present, it probably makes the whole task quite a lot more difficult. The term 'viewpoint' refers to the requirement, in the essay title, that the writer writes from a point of view dictated by the setter of the essay title. If the student does not really agree with that point of view it is difficult for her or him to write as if she or he does. All these titles contain a 'viewpoint' element:

Write a report arguing that smoking should be banned in all public places.
Show how over-population is a result of poverty rather than a cause.
'Violence on television and in films has encouraged violence among today's
    young people.' Give the reasons why the above statement is not true.
(Note that a title such as 'Pollution is man's greatest enemy' does not have a
'viewpoint' because the student can argue either for or against.)

To analyse the title, the students should follow these steps:
1 Identify the *Topic*.
2 Identify the *Focus* and be sure they are clear about how it relates to the *Topic*
   (is it an example of it? a stage in its sequence? the cause or an effect? one of
   the solutions to it as a problem? etc.).
3 Identify the *Comment* and be sure they know what this instruction requires
   them to do.
4 Check whether there is a *Viewpoint* and if so, if it is the same as their own. If
   it isn't, and there is a choice of tasks, they should avoid this one. If there isn't,
   they should plan very carefully *how* to answer the question with the required
   'viewpoint'.

In planning the essay, *Comment* decides the text-type (discussion, definition,
etc.); *Topic* determines the overall range of subject matter but *Focus* determines
the particular content; *Viewpoint* dictates which arguments, pro or con, to use;
the interaction between *Comment* and *Focus* will lead to decisions about the
organization of the essay.
Analysing the essay title only helps the student when:
a) the essay is a fairly formal one, with a clearly specified title (a lot of the
   Consolidation tasks in this book are *not* essay titles in the formal sense:
   because they were intended for discussion, group- or pair-work, several
   drafts before being assessed, etc., they often have rather long instructions
   and are left rather flexible in terms of what the student can do which will be
   considered acceptable);
b) the essay is expository, or information-based (stories, poems, etc. do not fit
   this analysis; completely open titles like the 'Happiness' one do not usefully
   fit either).
Obviously, an analysis of essay titles becomes most important when the student
is faced with test essays. It is only fair to give students enough practice *before*
they face real test essays; however, not all essay titles should be analysed in this
way or students might begin to think, wrongly, that there is never any room for
their own creativity in writing an essay. That would defeat what we hope is a
main purpose of this book.

E Providing feedback on written work

The feedback which the learner gets on her or his piece of writing plays a very important role, both in motivating further learning, and in ensuring that the learner's texts gradually come nearer and nearer to written fluency. It is important to divide this feedback into two types: formative and summative.

1   Formative feedback

The chief purpose of all types of formative feedback is to help learning proceed. Three 'stages' of formative feedback are suggested here, which differ in the amount of information they give the learner as opposed to the amount of self-correction they expect of the learner.

a) Correction

In this stage, the learner's errors are clearly identified on the paper, and they are corrected by the teacher, as in the following example:

> Britain can exchange their [*its*] ideas to [*with*] the [crossed out] different countrys [*tries*]. They also helps [*help*] the [crossed out] the underdeveloped countries. Day [crossed out] Britain is make [*making*] friendship [*friends*] with other countries through this programme. The [crossed out] Britain can able to [crossed out] distribute here [*her*] modern techniques to it [crossed out] of feeding and breeding of livestock to the different

Correction permits the learner to see exactly what was wrong and how it should be written, but it leaves no work for the learner to do.

b) Controlled correction

In this stage, the learner's errors are clearly indicated, but they are not corrected by the teacher. Instead, the teacher helps the learner to correct her or his own errors by stating in the margin what type of error she or he has made, as in the following example:

delete article
repeated
   subject ∧Britain ~~the~~ studying engineering in Britain
   is so ᵛadvantageous. / Because Britain
   is one of the industrial countries, and
s×2   labrotary equipiments are avaliable at s
   any institution in Britain.

Controlled correction gives learners plenty of support, and also leaves them with some work to do, in self-correction. The correction activity helps learners to remember the correct forms and avoid the same errors in future.

c) Guided correction

In this stage, there are two possibilities: either the locations of errors are pointed out but the learner is not told what types of errors they are; or the number and types of errors are indicated but the learner is not told exactly where they are. Both approaches guide the learner toward self-correction but require care and thought from the learner if the error is to be satisfactorily corrected.
   You can see both types of guided correction in the examples which follow:

v   we can easily get familiar with the real needs of practical
       industries.
           In addition to these advantages we can obtain the way
?m/v   how they find the due of new technologies and how they
P   think and how they solve ~~the way~~
                 the problem.

measure to be taken caused an excessive change
resulting in some serious problem.
Firstly, we lost ∧ senic beauty of mountains, rivers,
grassland etc, which are essential to our mental
health. We rush to the limited area and an
                             action
over crowd leads to further des~~troy~~ of nature.

Correction key: Most teachers want to develop their own system or code for
labelling learners' errors, depending on the specific recurrent problems which
they identify, but the following system is simple to use and simple for learners to
understand.

S   = spelling
C   = concord (agreement: subject and verb)
s/p = singular/plural
w/o = word order
T   = verb tense
V   = vocabulary, wrong word or usage
app = appropriacy (inappropriate style or register)
P   = punctuation (including capital letters)
Ir = irrelevant information
?M = meaning not clear
Λ   = word(s) missing

(J. Willis *Teaching English Through English*)

For teachers who are looking for a more detailed way of providing their learners
with formative feedback, the 'Formative Feedback Profile' on the next page will
be helpful. A profile like this allows the teacher to indicate for each individual
writer what her or his weaknesses are in specific areas. For example, a writer
may be 'Excellent' on *Ideas and Organization* but only 'Adequate' on *Surface
Features* due, perhaps, to problems with handwriting. There are so many
possible combinations using the Profile that every writer in a class could easily
get a different Profile: this makes the feedback to the learner really personal. By
keeping a copy of the Profile every time it is completed, as well as giving a copy
to the learner, the teacher is able to keep a record on each learner which will
make it possible to see how the learner develops and improves over time.

Teachers wishing to make multiple copies of *page 146 only* for the purpose of
providing feedback to their students need not obtain further permission from
the authors or publisher.

FORMATIVE FEEDBACK PROFILE

Communicative Quality	Excellent	★ a pleasure to read
	Very Good	★ causes the reader few difficulties
	Adequate	★ communicates although with some strain
	Fair	★ conveys its message with difficulty
	Weak	★ does not adequately convey its message
Ideas and Organization	Excellent	★ completely logical organizational structure; effective arguments and supporting material
	Very Good	★ good organizational structure; well-presented and relevant arguments and supporting material
	Adequate	★ clear but limited organizational structure; some arguments unsupported or material irrelevant
	Fair	★ logical breakdowns apparent; ideas inadequate and/or poorly organized
	Weak	★ logical organization absent; no suitable material
Grammar and Vocabulary	Excellent	★ wide range and fluent control of grammatical structures and vocabulary
	Very Good	★ effective use of an adequate range of grammatical structures and vocabulary
	Adequate	★ adequate range of grammatical structures and vocabulary, but could be used more effectively
	Fair	★ restricted range and uncertain control of grammatical structures and vocabulary
	Weak	★ grammatical structures not mastered and limited range of vocabulary
Surface Features	Excellent	★ handwriting, punctuation and spelling show no faults
	Very Good	★ occasional faults in handwriting and/or punctuation and/or spelling
	Adequate	★ handwriting and/or punctuation and/or spelling could be improved
	Fair	★ definite weaknesses in handwriting and/or punctuation and/or spelling
	Weak	★ little mastery of the conventions of handwriting or punctuation or spelling

2   Summative Feedback

This is more familiarly known to most of us as 'assessment', 'grading', 'marking' or even 'testing'. The chief purpose of summative feedback is to inform the teacher, the learner, and often others, as precisely as possible, how far the learner has progressed towards control over the written language. The judgements which are made are likely to appear in the learner's record where they may be referred to by headteachers, parents, higher education admissions personnel and other 'authorities'. Summative feedback does not have to be different from formative feedback, except that, once the judgement has been made and recorded there is nothing the learner can do to change it for the better, by rewriting or improving the text. The actual judgements which are made can be based on the same criteria as were used for formative feedback (and probably should be, to be fair to the learner). The judgements the teacher makes usually appear in the form of numbers such as 8/10, 12/20, 65/100, or grades such as A−; C+; F. This is in contrast to formative feedback which is usually in the form of descriptive comments. Many teachers develop their own summative feedback system, or are given one to use by their school: if you do not have a system already you can use the Formative Feedback Profile for summative purposes by assigning numerical or grade values to each level of each component. You will have to decide how much value to give to each component: we have found it works well to give twice as much weight to Communicative Quality, because it is the overall impression component and has most influence on readers.

   The problem with summative judgements is that they are not very reliable: they are influenced by factors such as handwriting, a knowledge of whether the learner works hard or is lazy, by the teacher's mood or tiredness, as well as by whether the learner was interested in the topic or was tired or worried that day, and so on. To be fair to everyone, these summative judgements should be based on a number of pieces of writing and not just one or two. These pieces should be on a range of topics, of different lengths, and under different conditions (for example, some might have been written for homework and some in class), and preferably over a period of time. Because everyone varies in how well they write depending on many factors, we can get the most accurate (which is the fairest) idea by judging as wide a variety as possible and averaging out the results. It is also fairest to get more than one teacher to do the judging whenever possible. Responding to a piece of writing is a personal thing as well as a professional one, and several personal responses give a better idea of how the writer's writing is seen by teacher-judges in general.

F   Teaching notes to individual units

To the student

It is essential that students are oriented to the writing course from the very beginning. It is also important to allow them the opportunity of exploring just what it is they want from a writing course. *To the student* provides for both of these possibilities.

Procedure

1 Students should be asked to read the *To the student* introduction and make their first journal entry before the writing class meets for its first session.
2 Begin the session with a discussion of their journal task: did they find it easy/useful/etc.? How much did they write? How long did it take?
3 Form students into groups of three or four and ask them to discuss what *they* can do to help themselves become 'good' writers. Tell them they will have to report their discussion to the class and consequently need to appoint a secretary/spokesperson.
4 Monitor the groupwork, show interest in the journals and generally help out where necessary.
5 Conduct a plenary session, making notes on the blackboard, where useful. Emphasize the link between the textbook and self-study / keeping a journal. Inform them of how you intend to structure the writing sessions – see *Teacher's guide A Structuring the writing sessions*.
6 Set out homework for the next session.

Notes

For further background on the value of journals in learning to write see:
Flower, Linda (1979) 'Writer-based prose: a cognitive basis for problems in writing', *College English* 41, 1:19–37. Reprinted in McKay, Sandra (ed.) (1984) *Composing in a Second Language*, Newbury House Publications Inc.
Spack, Ruth and Catherine Sadow (1983) 'Student-teacher working journals in ESL freshman composition', *TESOL Quarterly* 17, 4:575–594.

Unit 1   Spatial relationships

The aims of this unit are:
- to explore a number of conventions governing the description of spatial relationships;
- to examine the range of relationships that can hold between texts and visual materials;
- to study the role of sentence-initial position in the structuring of a written description;
- to provide practice in writing spatial descriptions.

Procedure

For this and *all* other units consult the *To the teacher* introduction and the *Teacher's guide A–E*.

Notes

Task 1:   Yes. The map helps a reader locate the area in question and gives the reader an indication of the extent of the pollution.

Task 2:   a) on the borders of Cheetham and Crumpsall; just to the north of the centre of Manchester; in the heart of a residential district; along one side of it; in every other direction it is surrounded by.

b) Example:

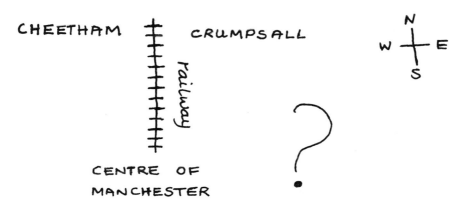

It is not clear if Cheetham is to the west or the east, or if the railway is to the west or to the east.

c) The writer's aim was to situate the school in its socio-economic context.

d) No.

Task 3:   a) Consult Leech, G. and J. Svartvik (1975) *A Communicative Grammar of English*: Part Three, Section A, *Place direction and distance*.

b) Answers should be grammatically and factually correct.

Task 4:   a) A bird's eye view.
        b) Example:

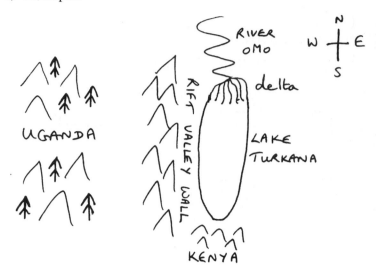

      c) The 'text' would circle the lake moving clockwise or anti-
          clockwise.

Task 5:   Example:

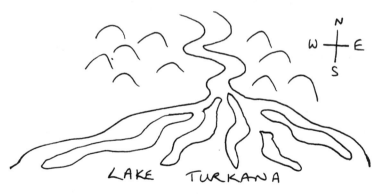

Task 6:   See text, p. 19.

Task 7:   The map contains supplementary information – the names of hills,
        towns, the river and details of troop movements.

Task 8:   See text (the answer is given in the following paragraph).

Task 9:   The hub; To the SW of the square; to the SE; To the NW of the square;
        Just beyond; along the bank of the Nile; In Shari Qasr el-Aini, which
        runs S from; in Shari el-Sheikh Rihan; To the NE.

Task 10: a) The organizing principle is from inside to outside; centre (hub) to
           periphery.

b) Example:

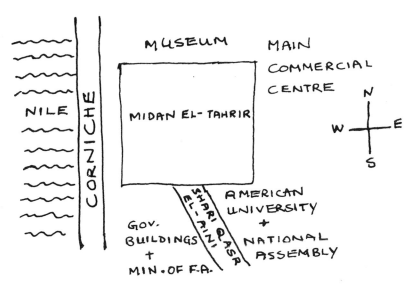

Task 11: a) Example:

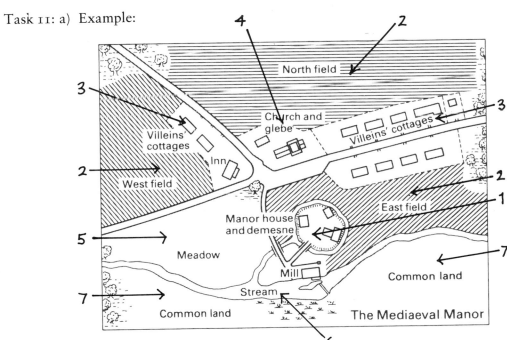

b) There are a number of possibilities. The best would probably be an
organization according to a centre-to-periphery plus clockwise or
anti-clockwise movement.

Consolidation: The Consolidation tasks in each unit are provided to offer a
choice of extended writing topics. Usually you will not want
every student to do every task.

Unit 2   Class relationships (1) Classification

The aims of this unit are:
– to introduce verbal and non-verbal means of classification;
– to relate classification to (a) convention (b) purpose;
– to explore grammatical exponents of classification;
– to practise writing texts based on classification.

Notes

Task 1: Accept any reasonable answer.

Task 2: Example:
(i), (iv), (viii), (vi), (ix), (ii), (x), (vii), (v), (iii).

Task 3: a) Some other possibilities are: evening classes – radio broadcasts – short intensive courses – self-study courses.
b) Accept any defensible grouping.

Task 4: General to particular.

Task 5: Smallest unit (house) to largest (country).

Task 6: Accept any well thought-out and reasonably complete answer.

Task 7: Example:
There are three major types of headaches. These are those caused by high blood pressure, allergy and sinus. Pain in the forehead, sweating, anxiety, nausea, vomiting and confusion are the major symptoms of the high blood pressure headache. Pressure on both sides of the head, in the forehead and behind the eyes, sneezing and watery eyes are the symptoms of an allergy headache. Sinus headache may be centred in the frontal sinuses, when pain is felt in the forehead, temples and eyes; or in the maxillary sinuses, when pain is located in the face, forehead and upper jaw.

Task 8: Many good answers are possible. These should be logically organized and contain reasonable data/reasons.

Unit 3   Class relationships (2) Definition

The aims of this unit are:
– to explore the relationship between the use of definitions and the writer's perception of the reader's needs;
– to introduce and practise the form of definitions;
– to introduce and practise the form of relative clauses;
– to demonstrate how sentences are linked to the preceding text via choices in information distribution;
– to practise writing texts involving definitions.

Notes

Task 1: Sentence (e) is an acceptable definition.

Task 2: a) A dentist is a person who takes care of people's teeth.
b) Copper is a substance which is easily shaped and allows heat and electricity to pass through it.
c) An atom is the smallest piece of a simple substance that still has the same qualities, and can combine with other substances.
d) Cotton is a plant which is used in the manufacture of cloth.
e) A restaurant is a place where food is bought and eaten.
f) A square is a figure which has four equal sides and four right angles.
g) Socialism is a political system which aims at public ownership of the means of production.

Task 3: a) A person who takes care of people's teeth is known as a dentist.
c) The smallest piece of a simple substance that still has the same qualities and can combine with other substances is called an atom.
f) A figure which has four equal sides and four right angles is called a square.
g) A political system which aims at public ownership of the means of production is known as socialism.

Task 4: Any definition which fits the required pattern and is not factually inaccurate will be acceptable.

Task 5: Examples:
a) A conditioned reflex is a response that always follows a particular stimulus.
b) Learning is a reinforced association between one stimulus and another, or between a stimulus and a response.

Task 6: Accept any reasonable content which fits the definition pattern.

Task 7: The type of electricity that discharges from a solid material after it has been rubbed with another material is known as static electricity.
(Benjamin Franklin is responsible for the convention that) an electrical charge is *negative* when it has been generated by rubber rubbed with fur, while the charge is *positive* when it has been generated from glass rubbed with silk.
The force of attraction, or the force of repulsion, of one type of charge for another one is called an electrostatic or coulombic force.

Task 8: Examples:
A charge's electrostatic force is its force of attraction or repulsion which either attracts like charges or repels unlike charges.
Like charges are electrostatic forces of the same type which repel each other; unlike charges are electrostatic forces of opposite type which attract each other.

Task 9:   Examples:
    a)   Static electricity is a form of electricity that discharges from a solid material after it has been rubbed with another material.
    b)   A positive charge is a type of charge generated from glass rubbed with silk.
    c)   Electrostatic force is the force of repulsion or attraction of one charge for another.

Task 10: Examples:
    a)   Tungsten is a metal – used for filaments in electric light bulbs – which retains hardness at red heat.
    b)   A conversation (two or more people speaking to each other) is a social event.

Task 11: Examples:
    a)   Cereal (wheat, oats, etc.) is a plant . . .
    b)   Gas (oxygen, helium, etc.) is a substance . . .

Task 12: Examples:
    a)   Glass is a substance which has the property of being transparent. Consequently it is used in the manufacture of windows and picture frames.
    b)   Stainless steel is an alloy which is resistant to corrosion and as a result is used in the manufacture of sinks.
    c)   A thermometer is a device for measuring temperature. As a result thermometers are widely used wherever there is a need to regulate temperatures.

Task 13: Examples:
    a)   Tobacco is a drug which is commonly used by human beings. Its main characteristic is that it induces a feeling of well-being. *or* Its main characteristic is the noxious vapour given off when it is burned.
    b)   Cloth, a material made by weaving fibres such as wool, silk or cotton, is light, strong and porous and hence is used in the manufacture of clothing.
    c)   Binocular vision is that type of vision which allows distances to be judged and shapes to be perceived in depth. It is a characteristic of all animate beings.

Task 14: Examples:
    a)   Caffeine is a type of addictive substance which exerts a powerful effect on the heart. It is found in coffee and tea.
    b)   Substances which are not animals or plants but which occur naturally (including ores, petroleum, natural gas, coal and other substances obtained by mining) are known as minerals.
    c)   A spacecraft is a rocket-propelled vehicle which is capable of carrying astronauts and/or missiles into space. It is also known as a spaceship.

Task 15: a) (ii) seems preferable in that learning is the topic of the sentence and topics have a tendency to take sentence-initial position.

      b) (ii) While silver bromide is the topic, the expression *In photography* serves to orient the reader to the topic (silver bromide from the point of view of photography) and hence takes initial position. As seen in Unit 1 locational expressions can work in the same way – 'To the SW lies . . .'

      c) (ii) Complex structures tend to be placed towards the end of sentences – the principle of end-weight.

      d) (ii)

For further reference see Leech G. and J. Svartvik (1975) *A Communicative Grammar of English*: Part Three, Section D, *Presenting and focusing information* and *Order and emphasis*.

Unit 4   Organizing texts (1) General–specific

The aims of this unit are:
– to introduce the general–specific pattern as a way of organizing part or whole texts;
– to provide practice in recognizing and using variations of this pattern;
– to explore the importance of word order within and between sentences;
– to provide practice in writing texts based on the general–specific pattern.

Notes

Task 1:   (a) (ii) and (b) (v)

Task 2:   Examples:
      a) Humans eat flesh. / Humans are carnivores.
      b) Hinduism, Buddhism, Islam and Christianity are the world's major religions.
      c) Women are more likely to suffer from poverty than men.
      d) Computers are good at some tasks but not at others.

Task 3:

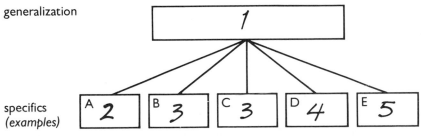

Task 4:   Original version (iii) (iv) (v) (i) (vi) (ii)

Tasks 5 and 6: Many acceptable texts are possible. Look for overall general–specific structure with factually accurate and sensible specific information.

Task 7:

Task 8:   After the first sentence.

Task 9:   A good answer will begin with a generalization about Mauritius (e.g. locating it; perhaps something with a definition structure). Then the general issues such as politics, freedom etc. will be introduced, and then particular issues (e.g. literacy, position of women).

Task 10: a) The postman was in a nightdress.
Mary was in a nightdress.
b) The rooms we rent are on the beach and we are here.
The rooms we rent are here and we are on the beach.
c) Oxygen and silicon are widespread everywhere.
Oxygen and silicon are widespread in the Earth's crust.

Task 11: Original versions:
a) *Being over fifty*, he could not find a job.
b) In underdeveloped countries, *such as those on the Indian sub-continent*, the shortfall . . .
c) The use of robots *in increasing numbers* may change . . .
d) People who tell you, *at great length*, what you . . .
e) The Trustees have decided to make available *each year* a sum . . .
f) *Taking a low estimate only*, Coale and Hoover estimate . . .

Task 12: Original version:
(a) *As Egypt's population continues to expand*, the urban centres . . . (b) *From 1960 to 1976* the percentage of Egypt's population . . . (c) The natural increase in Cairo is 2.5% annually, (*both birth and death rates are lower than in rural areas*), with migration . . . (d) The bulk of Cairo's growth has come *in the areas* around the city's boundaries. (e) *Meanwhile*, population growth in the city's centre . . . (f) If present fertility and migration rates continue, the population of Cairo will almost double to 17.1 million *by the year 2000*. (g) *By 2025* Cairo would . . . (h) *But* if an average . . .

Unit 5   Class relationships (3) Comparison/contrast

The aims of this unit are:
– to introduce the two main rhetorical patterns used in writing comparison/ contrast sequences;

– to explore grammatical exponents of comparison/contrast;
– to practise writing texts using comparison/contrast sequences.

Notes

Task 1: a) The Toyota and the Ford.
b) The Toyota and the Nissan.
c) The Volkswagen and the Ford.
d) The Nissan.
e) The Ford.

Task 2: Example:
Sporting events such as those shown in the photographs create an image of physical fitness, excitement and professionalism, whereas the statement by the Royal College of Physicians highlights the health risks of smoking. In addition, the link between smoking and sport is an indirect one, while the statement is very direct.

Task 3: Answer is dependent on student choice in Task 2.

Task 4: a) Probably Pattern 1 would be clearer in this case. It might be hard to write a good Pattern 2 text because of the very small bits of information to be fitted in – but students who do should have these texts accepted.
b) Relative economy would be highlighted and made clearest by making it the first point in each description, whether Pattern 1 or 2 is used.

Task 5: Many acceptable answers are possible. These should highlight the strongest desirable and undesirable effects by using the points in the best sequence, whichever pattern is chosen.

Task 6:
a) *Comparison*
  ii) (as) good (as)
  iii) (no) bigg (er) (than)
  iv) (same) price (as)

   Contrast
  ii) high (er) (than)
  iii) (while)
  iv) (differs from) London (in)

Task 7:
a) *Comparison*
  i) (similarly)
  ii) (likewise)

   Contrast
  i) (In contrast)
  ii) (On the other hand)

Task 8: You should use your discretion in looking at the two student texts. In general, any alterations that make the text better are acceptable.

Task 9: Original version:
(b) (d) (f) (h) (i) (l) (n) (p) (q) (t)
Throughout most of the passage the objects of contrast – Westerners and Easterners – are both grammatical subjects and themes. This ensures that they are seen as the central subjects/characters of the text, and also provides the reader with a consistent starting-off point for each stage of the contrast.

Unit 6   Linear relationships (1) Time

The aims of this unit are:
– to introduce expected and unexpected time ordering;
– to practise the use of time markers;
– to practise writing expected and unexpected sequences.

Notes

Task 1:

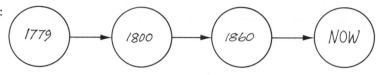

Task 2:   The last sentence of paragraph 1 should be the last sentence of
paragraph 2.

Task 3:   a)   The use of unexpected time sequence allows the writer to show the
relationships between events more strongly, making the text more
dramatic.
b)   Past simple.
c)   Past simple and past perfect.

Task 4:   One acceptable possibility is:
Michael Moore was a bright, poverty-stricken, seventeen-year-old farm
worker who grew up during the Great Famine in Ireland and knew what it
was to be very hungry. His father died in 1846; he watched his mother
die of typhus in May 1847. There was nothing to keep him in Ireland so,
on a bright June morning in 1847, he stepped on board a ship and left
Ireland for America. In years to come he would remember this moment.

Task 5:

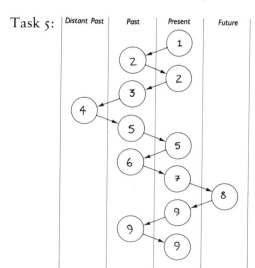

Task 6: Example:
 In 1948, William Shocklay . . . Long afterwards, in 1969, Ted Hoff . . . Hoff completed a process that had begun six years earlier, in 1963, when Robert Noyce managed . . .

Task 7: Natural time order is:
 Before the Cambrian explosion . . . For most of the four billion years . . . by three billion years ago . . . By one billion years ago . . . After the Cambrian explosion . . . and soon after (it), 600 million years ago . . . By 500 million years ago . . . But there are no trilobites . . . Green plants generate . . . Less than ten million years ago . . . And then, only a few million years ago . . .

 A few changes are necessary to get a good grammatical as well as correctly sequenced text, but not many. Students should be encouraged to make other changes if they think these would improve the resulting text.

Unit 7   Linear relationships (2) Process

The aims of this unit are:
– to introduce expected and unexpected process descriptions;
– to practise the use of sequencers;
– to practise writing process descriptions using active and passive voices;
– to practise writing expected and unexpected process descriptions.

Notes

Task 1: information coded→fed into input→read→written.

Task 2: All the information to do this adequately is provided in the two diagrams: look for a clear and accurate time sequence of information. Pupil response or failure to respond are concurrent; it makes best sense to write about 'pupil responds' first, as we think of this as the usual response, and to write about 'pupil fails to respond' second.

Task 3: They are not necessary for an understanding of the text as the text follows natural time order.

Task 4: Before the heat can be blown around . . .

Task 5: The need to refine oil is best highlighted by referring to petrol in the first sentence, then describing the oil refining process, then returning to petrol towards the end of the text. There are many possibilities with this structure.

Task 6: Then; To begin with; After this; When this happens; When the committee has finished its work; again; Then; When it is passed; at this point; When the bill has been passed; until; When the Queen's consent has been given.

Task 7: To begin with; After this; When this happens; When the committee has
finished its work; Then; When it is passed; When the bill has been
passed by both houses.

Task 8: a) no   d) workers
         b) farm workers   e) no
         c) drivers   f) no

Task 9: a) researchers; researchers; the mixture.
            N.B. 'by removal of a water molecule' refers to the method and not the
            agent.
         b) are chemically combined; is added; is heated; is produced.

Task 10: Accept any reasons the students can sensibly support.

Task 11: This is not nearly as difficult as the students might think, because they
can keep almost everything from the original text, replacing general
with specific terms, and omitting the general explanation, e.g. 'The
1981 Wildlife and Countryside Act originated in the House of
Commons, where it went through its first reading.' (etc.) The students
should be able to explain why they kept in or omitted any item of
information.

Unit 8   Linear relationships (3) Cyclical process

The aims of this unit are:
– to introduce cyclical process description;
– to practise using defining and non-defining relative clauses;
– to practise using coordination and subordination;
– to practise forming topic sentences;
– to practise writing cyclical process descriptions.

Notes

Task 1: Original version: (i) (x) (vi) (vii) (ii) (v) (ix) (iii) (viii) (iv)

Task 2: a) Bilharzia is a disease found all over the world.
         b) The life cycle of schistosoma can be divided into two main stages.
         c) Students need to use their own ideas about how bilharzia might be
            eradicated, as the solution is not provided. Some answers might be:
            humans should not stand in slow-moving water (this is not a very
            good answer because it would not *eradicate*); slow-moving water
            should be chemically treated to kill the water snails; scientists
            should find a chemical to kill the flatworms without killing the
            snails (etc.).

Task 3: (b) and (d) are good topic sentences.

Task 4: a) We have │only one clue │ as to how the Universe began.

   b) There are │ two principal requirements │ for an explosive.

   c) All rocks │ were originally formed │ during the period when the
      Earth was molten and then cooled down.

Task 5: Some diseases are transmitted by tiny water animals.
House flies transmit microbes on their feet.

Task 6: a) i) Barometers are meteorological instruments . . .
           ii) We shall here confine our description to specialized respiratory
               systems . . .
          iii) An aircraft [. . .] is subjected to pressures of 80 Kilonewtons per
               square metre.
           iv) Just as remarkable as the evolutionary adaptation of the camel
               is the adaptation of the group of warm-blooded fish . . .
            v) Steels [. . .] are known as high carbon steels.

Task 7: a) i) Valves [. . .] direct the blood flow.
           ii) A common northern and eastern plant is the Indian-pipe . . .
          iii) Some epiphytic orchids and other plants have aerial roots . . .
           iv) The dominant aquatic vertebrates are the fishes . . .
            v) The kinetic energy of a fluid, due to its motion, is customarily
               measured with respect to the Earth's surface . . .

Unit 9   Linear relationships (4) Cause↔effect

The aims of this unit are:
– to introduce the problematic nature of cause↔effect relationships;
– to explore rhetorical and grammatical ways of writing cause↔effect
  relationships;
– to practise writing cause↔effect sequences.

Notes

Task 1: because; may be responsible for; so; may cause.

Task 2: Examples:
   a) The heat of the sun causes both phenomena.
   b) Seems like a coincidence.
   c) Playing loud music may lead to partial deafness.

Task 3: a) (v) (iii) (i) (iv) (ii) (vi)
   b) (vi) The writer is merely reporting what has been said and does not
      necessarily support this view.

Task 4: Examples:
    i)   Some people think that the earth is definitely flat.
    ii) It might/could/may/etc. snow tomorrow.
    iii) My opinion is that inflation will fall to under 1% before the end of
        the year.
    iv) In the opinion of some experts, launching our nuclear waste into the
        atmosphere cannot cause any pollution for at least a million years.
    v)   My theory is that eating apples makes you thin.

Task 5: Example:
    a) Cornoro believed that *his slender diet* resulted in *long life*.
        Nietzsche states that *slowness of molecular change* and *a low rate of*
        expenditure of energy are the causes of the *slender diet* and also of *a*
        long life.
    b) Many different answers are possible. We expect them to be shorter
        and simpler, and without such exaggerated claims as 'everyone
        knows' and 'few books have . . .'. Students should include
        statements like, 'I believe that this book has caused a great deal of
        misunderstanding' and 'In my opinion, a scholar . . .'.

Task 6: Examples:
    – Pulmonary Tuberculosis (E) *is caused by* infection of the lungs (C) . . .
    – Pulmonary lesions (E) *are due almost entirely to* the human form of
      the tubercle bacillus (C) . . .
    – . . . the bovine type (C), which is *mainly responsible for* glandular
      and bovine tuberculosis (E) . . .
    – They produce . . . characteristic tubercle formation (C) *hence*
      the name for the organism (E).

Task 7: Examples:
The bacilli lodge in the lungs and cause a chronic inflammation of a specific type.
Another effect of the bacilli is that they produce areas of infiltration which
      have a characteristic tubercle formation.

Task 8: – static electricity (C) . . . can produce (*certain* E)
    N.B. This use of 'can' means 'is capable of . . .' and does not
    mean the same as 'may'.

    – If the charge built up to any great proportions (*conditional* C) it
      would spark (*certain* E) . . . and might set alight (*possible* E)

    – a very dry atmosphere (C) will help the build-up of charge (*certain* E)

    – the rubbing of (C) can cause large charges to accumulate (*certain* E –
      'can' = 'is capable of')

    – sparking here (C) could cause (*possible* E)

    – the ignition (C) would have serious results (*certain* E)

    – the presence of an electric field (C) may . . . cause the malfunction (*possible* E)

Task 9: N.B. The instructions tell students they can make grammatical changes; if they do so, they may end up with other correct answers, but here is the easiest:

When rain falls on mountains, it collects in depressions in the rock. The extreme cold *causes* the ice to freeze and glaciers to form. The ice melts and freezes again *with / due to* changes in temperature. Erosion of the rock of the mountain depression occurs *as a result of* the continual melting and refreezing, and is *worsened by / made worse by / increased by* the action of wind moving the water. Eventually, the water wears away the rock enough *to form* a small stream which carries deposits of soil and rock which *cause* further erosion, gradually enlarging the stream bed. The weather, too, acts on rocks and soil, to split, break and wear away. The stream grows larger until eventually it reaches the old age stage. The silt from the river is deposited into the sea, *resulting in* sandbars, spits and promontories.

Unit 10   Organizing texts (2) Structuring texts

The aims of this unit are:
- to add to the different ways of organizing and expressing different types of writing a basic pattern of overall text structure, in which all the writing types studied before can be used;
- to introduce a basic pattern of text structure;
- to indicate the variation that can be achieved with this structure.

Notes

Task 1: Example:

Pulsars =
1 A type of star that sends out regular pulses of radio waves.
2 The remains of supernovae.

When pulsars rotate they send out beams of radio waves that sweep across the galaxy.

4C21.53 is an extraordinary pulsar:
1 It rotates 642 times a second.
2 It rotates so rapidly that its equator moves at a fifth of the speed of light.
3 Its surface gravity is barely enough to hold the star together.
4 So far it has shown none of the small fluctuations characteristic of other pulsars.

4C21.53's accuracy as a clock means it can be used to:
1 fix the earth's position
2 calculate the masses of the outer planets
3 detect gravity waves

Task 2:   The texts will depend on filling in the boxes correctly, so this should be checked before the students are allowed to go very far with planning their actual text. Look for clear topic sentences to paragraphs and good general–specific structure within and between paragraphs.

Task 3:   Original version: (iv) (i) (vi) (iii) (ii) (v) (vii)

Task 4:   The Queen of Hearts
She made some tarts
All on a summer's day

The Knave of Hearts
He stole the tarts
And took them clean away

The King of Hearts
Called for the tarts
And beat the Knave full sore

The Knave of Hearts
Brought back the tarts
And vowed he'd steal no more

Task 5:   Example:

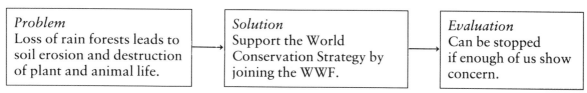

Task 6:   Students may make a number of suggestions, but the primary reason is that the headings help the reader know what to expect, help her or him to organize their mind about the subject of the text right from the beginning.

Task 7:   Example:

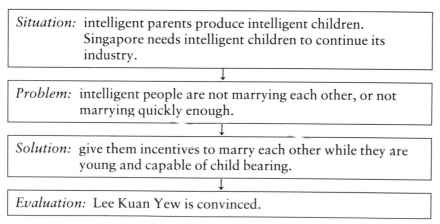

Task 8:   Example:

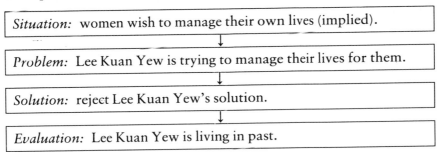

Situation: women wish to manage their own lives (implied).

Problem: Lee Kuan Yew is trying to manage their lives for them.

Solution: reject Lee Kuan Yew's solution.

Evaluation: Lee Kuan Yew is living in past.

Task 9:   Students can write any text which gets the right information in a well-organized way, but here is an example:
Koalas are able to digest eucalyptus leaves because of three major characteristics of their digestive systems. First, the koala's gut can discriminate between large and small food particles, keeping the small ones and eliminating the larger ones: this means it can eat very fast. Second, the koala has a low metabolic energy requirement, so it does not need as much food as some other animals. Third, eucalyptus leaves are rich in digestible energy, especially lipids and phenols. The lipids, and carbohydrates such as sugar and starch, satisfy the koala's energy needs.

Task 10: This discussion task should be quite straightforward; there are no right answers, only reasonable ones.

Unit 11   Organizing texts (3) Developing texts

The aims of this unit are:
– to provide more practice in writing the parts within the overall text structure introduced in Unit 10;
– to give more examples of how the parts of the text fit together, and of how writing types learned in Part I are used within the overall text;
– to allow students greater creativity in how they approach and fulfil written tasks.

Notes

Task 1:   The audience for the first would be only people actually looking for a carpenter, so all they really need is the phone number, and to know whether they can get estimates – so this is fine; the audience for the second one could be anyone vaguely interested in energy issues/problems, so much more information is needed.

Task 2:   This is very open-ended, but it is essential that the students get the facts right, i.e. that they do the maths for each form of transport and state the fuel consumption to miles travelled accurately for each, otherwise their description of the situation would be inaccurate. Note that they are not asked to suggest any solution or to make an evaluation.

Task 3:   Open-ended.

Task 4:   Example:
The problem with salting roads is that when it rains the salt dissolves and runs off into the soil. The salt which does not dissolve and run off is picked up on the wheels of vehicles and spread further. Salt also leaches out of salt piles stored near roads. Once the salt gets into the soil it travels into streams and rivers, and eventually evaporates into the atmosphere. This will result in salty rain. The salt is also evaporated from the roads and salt piles by wind straight into the atmosphere. Salt in soil is very harmful to plants.

Task 5:   Open-ended discussion. The answer is on p. 118.

Task 6:   The students will come up with their own suggestions for solutions. Some solutions might be to change the ways of testing so ethnic minority children are not discriminated against; to have special courses for ethnic minority children to teach them the skills that other children have; to improve home conditions; to spend more time on teaching them 'standard' English; etc. Note that students are not asked to evaluate, only to set out all the possible solutions so a reader could evaluate them.

Task 7:   Each student will create an individual text; the evidence they should be taking into account is:

leukemia 7 times more frequent among those close to smokers; cervical and breast cancer closely linked with passive smoking; 1.4 times higher chance of cancer if lived with one smoker; 2.3 times with two smokers; and 2.6 times with three or more smokers; worse for some cancers; studies found by-products of cigarette smoke in non-smoking adults, children and fetuses who had been exposed to smokers.

They should point out that the evidence is limited and preliminary, so they cannot be absolutely certain that the true facts are exactly these.

Task 8:   We would expect the students' open-ended writing to point out how silly this appliance is, and even that it is possibly dangerous.

Task 9:   Open-ended. Students should think about which of these indicators are more significant for living standards, and try to organize their text so that the most important aspects are treated first.

Task 10:   Open-ended. In making an evaluation of a topic like this, writers should make it clear why they feel as they do: often this is only partly because of what is written in the original text, and as much because of how they feel themselves, what their personal experience has been, how much they know about the topic, and so on.

Unit 12   Organizing texts (4) Creating texts

All the tasks in Unit 12 are open-ended. Encourage the students to think and talk about them fully before they begin to write. Sometimes the task needs, or would be improved by, information brought from elsewhere (the student's personal experience, or other reading material). Encourage them not to think of their first attempt as the last attempt, but to revise and then edit the text until it is really good. Try not to react to their first attempt as if it was a last attempt, either. In looking at the quality of what the students write, keep in mind this sequence of criteria:

– first, the content should be accurate (true);
– second, there should be enough content to fulfil the task properly (which means different numbers of points will be needed for different purposes);
– next, the information or opinions should be well-organized: the way it is organized will depend on the task and the type of writing being used in each part of the text (e.g. Pattern 1 or Pattern 2 of comparison/contrast);
– the parts of the text should be clearly related to each other, whether this is achieved by things like time sequencers or indicators of cause↔effect, or by a good grammatical control;
– the use of grammar need not be perfect, but should always be good enough for the reader to be able to read without being confused because grammar mistakes get in the way of the message: when deciding which mistakes are worth discussing and helping the student correct, think about their effect on communication of the message rather than thinking about grammar book accuracy;
– finally, look at punctuation (unless you found a punctuation error which got in the way of the message earlier), spelling and other 'mechanical' features – the student can usually clean these things up herself or himself once the message of the text is clear.

Acknowledgements

The authors and publishers are grateful to the following authors, publishers and others who have given permission for the use of copyright material identified in the text. It has not been possible to identify the sources of all the material used and in such cases the publishers would welcome information from copyright owners.

New Scientist pp. 8, 24–5, 29, 40, 45, 57, 75, 89, 104, 115–16 (These first appeared in *New Scientist*, London, the weekly review of science and technology.); A.D. Edwards and V.J. Furlong p. 9; Collins Publishers and Deborah Rogers Ltd pp. 10, 11; Penguin Books Ltd pp. 12, 19 from *Photography* by Eric de Mare (Penguin Handbooks, 1957, second edition 1958, third edition 1962, fourth edition 1968, fifth edition 1970, sixth edition 1975, seventh edition 1980, copyright © Eric de Mare, 1957, 1959, 1962, 1968, 1970, 1973, 1975, 1980), p. 26 from *The Presentation of Self in Everyday Life* by Erving Goffman (Allen Lane The Penguin Press, 1969, copyright © Erving Goffman, 1959), p. 83 from *Our Universe: How it Began* from *The Penguin Book of the Physical World*, editorial consultant Alan Isaacs (Penguin Books 1976, copyright © Penguin Books 1976), p. 92 from *The Twilight of the Idols/The Anti-Christ* by Friedrich Nietzsche, translated by R.J. Hollingdale (Penguin Classics, 1968, copyright © R.J. Hollingdale, 1968); Allen & Unwin and Dover Publications Inc. pp. 13–14; The Automobile Association and Jarrold printing p. 15; University of Edinburgh p. 18; The Kobal Collection (photograph) p. 25; Doubleday & Company Inc. p. 26; Macmillan Publishing Company p. 33 (Copyright © 1966 by Gerrit P. Judd. Reprinted by permission of the publisher.); W.H. Allen & Co. plc pp. 36, 69; David Dickson pp. 37, 71, 72; tables on pp. 38, 39 reproduced with the permission of the Controller of Her Majesty's Stationery Office; British Museum (Natural History) p. 39; the *New Internationalist* pp. 41, 54–5, 61; Earthlife p. 44; Sporting Pictures (UK) Ltd p. 47; Syracuse University Press pp. 52–3, 122–4; *WorldPaper* pp. 54, 102; CSE (The Conference of Socialist Economists, 25 Horsell Road, London N5 1XL) pp. 58, 62; Random House Inc. p. 63, reprinted by permission of the author and the author's agents, Scott Meredith Literary Agency Inc., 845 Third Avenue, New York, NY 10022; Times Newspapers Ltd pp. 64–5, 99, 110, 111, 128, 129–30, 131, 132; the *Observer* pp. 66–7, 125, 126–7; World Wildlife Fund p. 101; Bruce Coleman Ltd (photograph) p. 104; the *Scotsman* pp. 105–6; Lothian Energy Group pp. 108, 109; Martin Gardner pp. 113–14, 118; *New Society* pp. 114–15; Cath Tate (photograph) p. 115; the *Guardian* p. 117; Mark Gold p. 118; bar graphs on p. 124 copyright 1982 Time Inc. (All rights reserved. Reprinted by permission from *Time*.); Geoffrey Cannon pp. 126, 127; Longman p. 145.

Thanks to staff and students at the Cambridge Eurocentre for their cooperation in the photo session.

Drawings by Chris Evans pp. 9, 17, 19; David Mostyn p. 24.
Photograph on p. 120 by Jeremy Pembrey.
Artwork by Gecko Ltd and Wenham Arts
Book design by Peter Ducker MSTD

Pregnancy Loss and the Death of a Baby:

Guidelines for Professionals

Pregnancy loss is always something, it is never nothing and it could be everything.
The Reverend Peter Speck, Personal communication 1997

When your husband dies, you become a widow. When your wife dies, a widower. Children who lose their parents are called orphans. But we have no name for a parent who loses a child. (Miller and Ober 2002)

I never expected this to happen to me...I never dreamed that I would hear the two words "baby" and "died" in the same sentence. Mother

Pregnancy Loss and the Death of a Baby:

Guidelines for Professionals

3rd edition

Judith Schott, Alix Henley and Nancy Kohner

Published by Bosun Press
The Ferry Point
Ferry Lane
Shepperton on Thames
TW17 9LQ

First published in Great Britain in 2007
by Bosun Press on behalf of
Sands (the stillbirth and neonatal death charity)
28 Portland Place
London W1B 1LY

Tel: 020 7436 7940
Helpline: 020 7436 5881
Email: support@uk-sands.org
Website: www.uk-sands.org

ISBN-10: 0-9554243-2-1
ISBN-13: 978-0-9554243-2-8

Pregnancy Loss and the Death of a Baby: Guidelines for Professionals

Copyright © 2007 Sands

A CIP catalogue record for this book is available from the British Library.
Typeset in 11.5pt Minion
Printed in England by
The Cromwell Press Ltd

Book design and production by
FW Barter ARCA
Bosun Press
Email: info@bosunpress.com
www.bosunpress.com

The Sands Guidelines are a compilation of research findings and the guidance and feedback given to the Authors by health professionals, other relevant experts and bereaved parents. The Guidelines are not intended to be prescriptive directions defining a specific course of management or care, but are offered as an aid to good practice. They should not be relied on in isolation. Staff must make their own judgements and apply them where appropriate, taking into account professional guidance, Trust and other protocols and all the circumstances and facts of the particular case. Neither Sands nor the Authors shall be responsible or liable for any loss, damage, liability or claims (whether direct or indirect) that arise out of or in connection with the Guidelines.

CONTENTS

INTRODUCTION

As many readers will know, Nancy Kohner, who was closely involved with Sands for many years and who wrote the previous editions of the Sands Guidelines, died in March 2006 after a long illness. She was held in great respect and affection by health professionals across the UK, and is very much missed.

The Sands Guidelines were very close to Nancy's heart and we are privileged that she felt able to entrust them to us. We spent some time with Nancy discussing her plans for this edition, all of which we have incorporated. These were that: all childbearing losses, whenever and for whatever reason they occurred, should be included; it should be clear when the law applies and also when it does not; there should be more emphasis on ongoing care after a loss from primary care staff; the Guidelines should be fully referenced; and they should reflect the enormous changes that have taken place since the previous edition in 1995.

These changes have been considerable and complex and are reflected in the increased length of this edition. There are new laws, changes in professional guidance, regulations, and clinical care, and new ethical dilemmas. There have been many changes in the ways that health services are organised and structured. Public expectations and scrutiny of health care provision have also increased. In addition, there has been a great deal of research into, and increasing recognition of, the impact of a childbearing loss on parents and families, and the importance of the care that is offered.

Our research for this edition clearly shows that health care staff all over the UK are very aware of parents' needs and have adapted their procedures and care as a result. We have seen many examples of excellent practice and of pioneering ways of supporting parents who have had a childbearing loss. We have had contact with many health professionals who care passionately about providing sensitive care, and we are most grateful to those who shared with us their ideas, skills and ways of working, and their aspirations for further improvements.

However, these improvements are not universal. Even where standards are high, a change in staffing levels or the loss of experienced personnel can result in care that is less responsive to parents' needs. Pressure on the health care system and the increasing drive to cut costs mean that fewer members of staff are expected to deliver ever higher standards of care. Working with childbearing loss is stressful and time consuming, and demands great skill and sensitivity. Our one concern about these Guidelines is that, in defining good practice, we are placing an additional load on already overburdened staff.

On the positive side, a number of Trusts and Health Boards are already fulfilling many of the recommendations in this edition. Only some of these recommendations have direct cost implications. Others may require a review of the way that care is organised. Nearly all of them require staff to give time and thought to how they care for parents. We recognise that this is difficult in an increasingly hard-pressed service but we believe that, in the long run, time spent offering sensitive care at these critical times is an investment in the future health and wellbeing of parents. It can also reduce the incidence of complaints, litigation and adverse publicity.

The original Guidelines were based largely on the views and experiences of parents. This edition is based on research evidence and on discussions with health professionals of all the relevant disciplines, as well as on parents' views and experiences. To add immediacy to the text we have included quotes from parents who have had a childbearing loss. We are grateful to all the parents who have given us permission to use their words. Their names and, in some cases, the names of their babies are listed on pages 6, 7 and 8.

Each chapter has been read and commented on by at least five relevant experts whose names are listed on page 247 We owe them all a debt of gratitude for finding time in their busy schedules to give us their professional advice. We have done our best to balance the different views and feedback we have received. Each chapter has also been read and commented on by representatives of Sands. If there are errors or omissions, however, the responsibility is ours.

The speed of change means that these Guidelines will need to be updated more frequently than in the past. However, what will endure through all the changes that the future may bring, is the vital importance of parent-led care, choice, and the empathy, time and care that staff need to give to bereaved parents. These form the bedrock of the Sands Guidelines, originally researched and written by Nancy, to whom we all owe a debt of gratitude.

Judith Schott and Alix Henley

These Guidelines provide benchmarks for good practice but they are not set in stone. Although they are based on research and on what many parents have found helpful, some of the recommendations may be unacceptable to some women and their families. It is always important to find out from each parent what will be right for them. There may also be changes in professional standards and regulations and new legislation as well as new research and medical advances that may change practice. Staff should therefore use their professional judgement when deciding what to offer each woman and her family.

In order to ensure that staff are aware of any new issues and changes in regulations, professional guidance and practice relevant to the Sands Guidelines, essential updates will be posted on the Sands website. To access the webpage, go to www.uk-sands.org and click on **Improving Care** and then on **2007 Guidelines updates.**

TERMINOLOGY

We have used the phrase "childbearing loss" to cover all losses at any gestation and losses in the first few weeks after birth.

These Guidelines are intended for primary care staff as well as staff working in hospitals and clinics. They have been written both for trained and experienced professionals and for students and junior members of staff. For reasons of brevity and inclusion, we have used the word "staff" to denote all those professionals, including GPs, community midwives and health visitors, who organise and provide health care; receptionists and bereavement services officers; and everyone else who organises or provides care for parents who experience childbearing losses.

We have referred to midwives as "she", although we acknowledge that there are also male midwives. We have used "parents" to denote expectant and bereaved mothers and their partners. We recognise that some women will not have partners, and that others will have female partners who also need to be acknowledged and supported. We have included sections specifically on the needs of fathers as, until recently, men's needs when a pregnancy ends or a baby dies have received little recognition.

We have used the phrase "Trusts and Health Boards" because the rapid changes in the way that health services are structured and managed in England, Wales, Scotland and Northern Ireland make it impossible to use a phrase that covers all the bodies involved. However, the Guidelines are also applicable to Foundation Trusts, to independent health care establishments and to all other bodies that may be set up in the future to organise and provide care for women and families experiencing a childbearing loss.

ACKNOWLEDGEMENTS

We are extremely grateful to the many people who have helped us by sharing their expertise, and by reading and commenting on drafts of these Guidelines:

Lesley Allan, Clinical Nurse Specialist, Women's Health Unit, Wishaw General Hospital, Lanarkshire
Carolyn Basak, Midwifery and Women's Health Advisor, Royal College of Nursing
Ruth Bender Atik, National Director, The Miscarriage Association
Sue Benn, Patient Advice and Liaison Services, University College London Hospitals NHS Foundation Trust
Louise Boden, Chief Nurse, University College London Hospitals NHS Foundation Trust
Tony Brookes, Bereavement Services Manager, University Hospital of North Staffordshire
Sue Bush, King's College Hospital, London
Dr Alan Cameron, Consultant Obstetrician, Queen Mother's Hospital, Glasgow
Alistair Carmichael, Principal Procurator Fiscal, Deputy Policy Unit, Crown Office, Scotland
Carol Clay, Bereavement Co-ordinator, Twins and Multiple Births Association (TAMBA)
Dr Marta Cohen, Consultant Pathologist, Sheffield Children's Hospital NHS Trust
Ann Cowper, formerly Director of Midwifery Education, West Sussex College
Dianne Crowe, Specialist Nurse, Hexham General Hospital, Northumbria Healthcare Trust
Liz Davies, Director of UK Operations, Marie Stopes International
Jane Denton, Director, Multiple Births Foundation (MBF)
Joanie Dimavicius, Director, Concept Communications, founder and formerly director of ARC
Kathryn Druery, Clinical Specialist Midwife, Confidential Enquiry into Maternal and Child Health (CEMACH)
Sarah Falk, formerly hospital social worker, working with families
Dr Paula Fernandes, GP, The Hammersmith Surgery, Hammersmith, London
Jane Fisher, Director, Antenatal Results and Choices (ARC)
Joanne Fletcher, Consultant Nurse, Gynaecology, Royal Hallamshire Hospital, Sheffield
Sue Frame, Counsellor, Women and Children's Group, Queen Mary's Hospital, Sidcup
Ann Furedi, Chief Executive, British Pregnancy Advisory Service (bpas)
Alison Gibbs, Matron, Neonatal and Paediatric Services, Lincoln County Hospital
Annette Gilkeson, Assistant Deputy Registrar General, General Register Office, Northern Ireland
Penny Gillinson, founder of a neonatal parent support group
Janet Gladman, Midwife, Harrogate District General Hospital
Dr Kate Guthrie, Clinical Director, Sexual and Reproductive Health Partnership, Hull
Kathryn Gutteridge, Consultant Midwife, University Hospital of Leicester NHS Trust
Joe Harrison, Performance Manager, University College London Hospitals NHS Foundation Trust
Alex Horsfall, Bereavement Support Midwife, Bradford Teaching Hospitals
Annmarie Hughes, Miscarriage Nurse, Liverpool Women's Hospital
Rosemary Johnson, Antenatal Screening Co-ordinator, Wales
Dr J W Keeling, Consultant Paediatric Pathologist (retired), Edinburgh
Donna Kirwan, Antenatal Screening Co-ordinator, North West Region
Ruth Kirchmeier, Specialist Midwife, Fetal Medicine, Birmingham Women's Hospital
Dr Santina La Porta, GP, Tamworth House Medical Centre, Mitcham, Surrey
Rosemary Lee, formerly Chair, United Kingdom Association of Sonographers
Irene Lomas, Compton Health Centre, Ashbourne, Derbyshire
Dr Andrew Lyon, Consultant Neonatologist, Simpson Centre for Reproductive Health, Edinburgh
Dr Sheona Macleod, Compton Health Centre, Ashbourne, Derbyshire
Peter Mitchell, specialist in burial, excavation and exhumation
Samantha Murphy, PhD student, University of Surrey
Mandy Myers, Director of Nursing, British Pregnancy Advisory Service (bpas)
Professor Femi Oyebode, Head of Department of Psychiatry, University of Birmingham
Claire Painter, Lecturer in Women's Health, King's College, London

Lin Pavey, British Pregnancy Advisory Service (bpas)

Richard Pearse, Consultant Neonatal Paediatrician, The Jessop Hospital for Women, Sheffield

Nadia Permalloo, Antenatal Screening Co-ordinator, London Region

Justine Pepperell, Family Support Manager, BLISS the premature baby charity

Yvonne Ravizza, Casework Supervisor, General Register Office for Scotland

Anthony D G Roberts, Consultant Obstetrician and Gynaecologist, Queen's Hospital, Burton on Trent

Phyll Robson, Neonatal Bereavement Counsellor, North Cumbria Acute Hospitals Trust

The Reverend Peter Rowntree, Chaplain, University College London Hospitals NHS Foundation Trust

Dr Rosemary Scott, Consultant Histopathologist and Honorary Senior Lecturer, University College London

The Reverend Peter Speck

Dawn Squires, Manager, Eltham Crematorium, Eltham, Greenwich

Kate Stanton RGN, RSCN, NNEB, Derby Sands

Helen Statham, Senior Research Associate, Centre for Family Research, University of Cambridge

Dagmar Tapon, Genetic Counsellor, Queen Charlotte's and Chelsea Hospital, London

Elaine Thorp, Specialist Bereavement Midwife, Birmingham Women's Hospital and Vice Chair of Sands

Vivienne Traynor, General Register Office, Northern Ireland

David Trembath, Births, Deaths and Adoptions Branch, Office for National Statistics

Professor Cathy Warwick, Director of Midwifery, King's College Hospital, London

Dr Jane Weston-Baker, GP, North Road West Medical Centre, Plymouth

Angie Whitton, Clinical Nurse Specialist, Gynaecology, University Hospitals, Leicester

The Reverend Daphne Williams, Spiritual and Pastoral Care, The Whittington Hospital NHS Trust, London

Brenda Wilsher, Founder of Millie's Campaign

Dr Chris Wright, Consultant Paediatric Pathologist, The Royal Victoria Infirmary, Newcastle Upon Tyne

Our special thanks go to **Miss Gaye Henson,** Consultant Obstetrician, Whittington Hospital NHS Trust, who, in addition to her busy professional life, has supported us throughout, has alerted us to new issues, has read and commented on all the chapters, and has always been ready to answer our many questions.

The help and support we have received from the following people at Sands has been invaluable. In particular we thank: **Neal Long,** Director; **Elaine Thorp,** Vice Chair; **Erica Stewart**, Operations Manager; and **Kate Anker,** Trustee.

Sands also gratefully acknowledges the information and advice received from **Claire Stoneman** of Foot Anstey Solicitors who has edited the legal aspects of these Guidelines and who also obtained advice from O'Reilly Stewart Solicitors and Balfour Manson Solicitors in relation to legal issues affecting Northern Ireland and Scotland respectively.

Sands is very grateful to the organisations and Sands groups that have generously contributed to the costs of producing the Guidelines:

The Department of Health	**Farnborough Sands**
The Scottish Executive	**Glasgow Sands**
Ascot and Bracknell Sands	**Lewisham Sands**
Banff Sands	**North West Middlesex and South West Herts Sands**
Birmingham Sands	**Rochdale and Bury Sands**
Bromley Sands	**Tunbridge Wells Sands**
Bristol Sands	

We are most grateful to all the parents whose names are listed below, and to those who want to remain anonymous, for telling their stories and giving us permission to use their words in the text.

Dave Aylett, father of James who died on October 3rd 2003, and of Matthew and William.

Christine Bass, mother of Bobby Bass who died at 41 weeks of pregnancy.

Helen Batten, mother of Poppy who was born on April 19th 2000 and died on May 12th 2000, and of Amber, born on April 27th 2001, Scarlett, born on October 30th 2003, and Daisy, born on October 23rd 2006.

Lisa Beven, mother of Dominic, stillborn on June 5th 2003, and of Laurence.

Julia Bishop and Robin Wiltshire, parents of Louisa Hope, who died on October 18th 2003 aged 3 days, and of Natasha.

Nick and Ranj Brett, parents of 3 children, Saffia Brett 5 years old, Rishi Brett who was born January 31st 2003 and died after 2 days on February 2nd 2003, and Ranju Brett aged 15 months.

Claire Bruford, mother of twins who died at 9 weeks and 5 days gestation on June 20th 2006.

Vicky Burley Smith, mother of twins, Coran who died on June 19th 2005, and Ella who was born on September 4th 2005.

Patricia Calland, mother of Lily-anne who was born at 24 weeks on September 1st 2001 and died aged 5 days on September 6th 2001.

Jo Cameron, mother of Emmeline who was born at 24 weeks on August 31st 2006 and lived for a few hours.

Lee Cavalli, mother of Albie Nicholas who was stillborn on August 12th 2005, and of Stephen Henry and Matthew Lindsay.

Clare Chudley, mother of Kate Ella Chudley who had Edwards syndrome and who fell asleep on December 21st and was born on December 23rd 2003; of her twin, Thomas Morgan Chudley who was born December 23rd 2003; and of Adam Joshua Chudley who was born on June 3rd 2006.

Jennifer Cook, mother of David Paul who was born at 23 weeks on April 17th 2004 and lived for a few hours.

Sharon Darke, mother of twins, Charlie who was born on September 13th 1999 and died on September 19th 1999, and Joshua who was born on September 13th 1999 and died on September 25th 1999.

Mario Di Clemente, father of Leo who was born on January 27th 2003 and died on January 28th 2003, and of Luciano.

Sarah Cruikshank, mother of a baby who was miscarried at 8 weeks on November 17th 2004, and Jonathan who wanted to be a big brother.

Andrew Don, father of Lara Jean who died at 20 weeks some time between June 3rd and 4th 1997.

Julia Eilers, mother of Georgina who was stillborn at 34 weeks on September 30th 2001, and of Elizabeth.

Andrea English, mother of Matthew, born sleeping at 24 weeks of pregnancy on January 24th 2004.

Becci Eriksson, mother of Oskar who died during delivery on June 22nd 1999.

Shirley and Tim Gittoes, parents of Heulwen who was stillborn on January 14th 2001, and of Charlie and Joseph.

David Hansen, father of Calvin Baker Thayer-Hansen born still at 30 weeks on March 20th 2001, and of Calvin's younger siblings Zelda Dare and Orson Aurelius.

Louise Hogan, mother of Benjamin Hogan who was born sleeping on December 11th 2005, and of Eleanor Hogan.

Sarah Hughes, mother of Daniel Alexander who was stillborn on June 16th 2004, and of Samuel Elliott, born on May 11th 2005, and Holly Louise, born on September 20th 2006.

Karen and Angus Jones, parents of Rory Fabio who was stillborn on December 5th 1998, and of George and William.

Kerry Jones, mother of Bron Eiri who was born at full term on September 8th and died on 9th September 2002.

Dorothy and Arwel Jones-Williams, parents of Mariela who was stillborn at 41 weeks on May 18th 2004, and of twin boys, Leon and Ioan, born on May 24th 2005.

Donna Kiaie, mother of Max who was stillborn on 24th February 2005.

Joanne and Roberto Menichinelli, parents of Emma who was stillborn on December 3rd 2005 at 28 weeks of pregnancy.

Dawn and Darren Moore, parents of Frances Moore who was stillborn at 39 weeks on April 9th 2000.

Samantha Murphy, mother of Ann Rosemary who died at 27 weeks of pregnancy.

Gill Moore, mother of baby Georgina who was stillborn on March 24th 2002, and of Harriet born on November 30th 1995, and Fraser born on 16th February 1998.

Sandra Moseley, mother of Noah.

Marie Newton, mom of Rhiann and Iona born at 18 weeks August 26th 2001.

Jayne Owen, mother of Jack who was stillborn at nearly 21 weeks on April 8th 1999, of Grace Elizabeth Doreen who was stillborn at 35 weeks on September 19th 2004, and of Michael born on December 2nd 2000, and Joseph, born on October 10th 2006.

Colin and Cathy Pidgeon, parents of Daisy, stillborn at 30 weeks on Feb 10th 2006, and of Matthew and Rosie.

David and Linda Simmonds, parents of Hope and Faith, born and died on December 23rd 2003.

Kate Stanton, mother of Rose aged 4, and of Louis who was born full term on September 30th 2004, but was an undiagnosed breech, and due to a traumatic delivery died aged 20 hrs on October 1st 2004.

Kim and Matt Stephens, parents of Ned Stephens who was stillborn at 40 weeks on October 29th 2004, and of Charlie Stephens born on November 22nd 2005.

Suzie Tibbenham, mother of Kieran Tibbenham who was stillborn on September 8th 2001.

Amba Stephenson, mother of Abdullah Stephenson who was born on October 28th 2000 and died on October 31st 2000.

Deborah Styles, mother of Heather who was stillborn on October 14th 1998.

Alex and Sean Tuesley, parents of triplets born on June 21st 2002, Ben who was stillborn, and Eliot and Jake.

Sarah Turner, mother of Jennifer who was born asleep on July 7th 2004.

David Ward and Julia Gray, parents of Grace who was stillborn at 39 weeks on September 20th 1996.

Brenda Wilsher, grandmother of Millie Grace who was born on September 10th 2004 and died aged 9 hours and 32 minutes, and of Millie's brother James Isaac born safely on August 15th 2005.

Jackie Woodward, mother of Hannah Louise born on October 28th 2001 and died on November 28th 2001, and of Jessica born on August 27th 2003, and Matthew born on July 28th 2005.

PRINCIPLES OF GOOD PRACTICE

"Bereaved parents never forget the understanding, respect, and genuine warmth they received from caregivers, which can become as lasting and important as any other memories of their lost pregnancy or their baby's brief life." (Leon 1992)

1. Care should be parent-led. Identifying and meeting the needs of parents should be regarded as an investment in their future health and wellbeing.

2. Good care involves spending extra time with parents. This should be recognised by managers and staff.

3. Parents should always be treated with respect and dignity and should be supported with genuine sensitivity and empathy.

4. Each parent's personal preferences and cultural or religious needs should be taken into account.

5. Communication with parents should be clear, sensitive and honest, and should be tailored to meet individual needs. Trained interpreters and signers should be available for parents who need them.

6. It is not possible to predict the significance that a childbearing loss will have for individual parents. No assumptions should be made about the intensity and duration of grief that a parent will experience. It is important that staff accept, acknowledge and validate the feelings that individual parents are experiencing.

7. A father's grief may be as profound as that of the mother: his needs for support should be recognised and met. The needs of a partner in a same-sex couple should also be recognised and met.

8. Many childbearing losses involve periods of uncertainty. Staff should avoid giving reassurances that may turn out to be false. They should acknowledge the difficulty of living with uncertainty.

9. In any situation where there is a choice to be made, parents should be given the information they need, and should be supported and encouraged to make their own decisions about what happens to them and to their baby.

10. In addition to good emotional support, women should receive excellent physical care during and after a loss.

11. Women should be cared for in a place that is appropriate to their stage of pregnancy and the type of loss that they are experiencing.

12. Women and their partners should always be looked after by staff who are specifically trained to deal not only with their clinical care and physical, needs but also with their emotional needs.

13. Parents whose babies die in the second or third trimester should be offered opportunities to create memories. Their individual views and wishes should be respected.

14. The bodies of babies and fetal remains should be treated with respect at all times: arrangements for sensitive disposal and respectful funerals should be in place.

15. The hand-over of care from hospital to primary care staff should ensure that support and care for parents are seamless.

16. Ongoing support is an essential part of care and should be available to all those who want it, regardless of the timing or the type of loss that they have experienced. Support should continue to be available to all women and their partners during a subsequent pregnancy and after the birth of another baby.

17. All staff who care for parents during and after a loss should have opportunities to develop and update their knowledge and skills, and should have access to good support for themselves.

CHAPTER 1: PROVIDING INCLUSIVE CARE

> OTHER RELEVANT CHAPTERS:
> 2: HOLISTIC CARE
> 4: COMMUNICATION
> 5: COMMUNICATION ACROSS LANGUAGE AND OTHER BARRIERS

"Targeting care is about developing services that are effective for all women but particularly for those women who would not normally actively seek help and advice." Confidential Enquiry into Maternal and Child Health (CEMACH 2002)

Childbearing loss affects all social groups but is most likely to affect women who are socially disadvantaged, poor, excluded or vulnerable in other ways. For example, figures for England show that:

* Over one-third of all *stillbirths* and *neonatal deaths* are to mothers living in the most deprived geographical districts[1] (CEMACH 2006);

* Compared with "White" women, *stillbirth rates* for "Black" women are 2.8 times as high, for "Asian" women twice as high, and for "Chinese and other" women nearly twice as high[2] (CEMACH 2006);

* Compared with "White" women, *neonatal death rates* for "Black" women are 2.7 times as high, for "Asian" women 1.6 times as high, and for "Chinese and other" women nearly twice as high[2] (CEMACH 2006);

* *Stillbirth* rates for babies whose mothers are unmarried and who register the birth of their baby alone[3] are higher than stillbirth rates for babies whose parents are not married but who register the birth together. These, in turn, are higher than the rates for babies born to mothers who are married (ONS 2006);

* Levels of *perinatal mortality, stillbirth* and *infant mortality* are significantly higher among Gypsies and Irish Travellers (CRE 2006).

Women who are socially disadvantaged, poor, excluded or vulnerable in other ways are also more likely to die during pregnancy or childbirth, or following childbirth:

* Between 2000 and 2002, women living in the most deprived areas of England had a 45% higher death rate than women living in more affluent areas;

* Women living in families where both partners were unemployed, many of whom experienced features of social exclusion, were up to 20 times more likely to die than women from the more advantaged groups;

* Single mothers were three times more likely to die than those in stable relationships;

---

1   Compared with the expected one-fifth.
2   'Black' combines Black African, Black Caribbean and Black Other; 'Asian' combines Indian, Pakistani and Bangladeshi; 'Chinese and other' combines Chinese, 'Other' and mixed ethnic origin. These categories were selected from a list of possible options by women themselves.
3   These mothers are most likely to be living alone and to be unsupported.

- Women from ethnic groups other than "White" were, on average, three times more likely to die;
- Black African women, especially asylum seekers and newly arrived refugees, had a mortality rate seven times higher than "White" women and had major problems in accessing maternal health care (CEMACH 2004).

Women in the groups listed above are more likely, for various reasons, to find services unfamiliar, difficult or impossible to understand and use, frightening, insensitive or unhelpful. Special consideration and provision are therefore needed to ensure that, whether during an unproblematic pregnancy and birth, or at a time of pregnancy loss or the death of a baby, care reaches:

- Women who are homeless or living in poverty;
- Refugees and asylum seekers;
- Women who are using drugs;
- Women with a history of mental health problems;
- Women who have a physical or learning disability;
- Women who are experiencing domestic violence;
- Young teenage women;
- Women who speak and read little or no English;
- Black and minority ethnic women; and
- Women prisoners, who are more likely to come from disadvantaged backgrounds and to have multiple social problems which are compounded by the stigma of prison.

"Maternity services should be designed to be approachable and flexible enough to meet the needs of all women, including the vulnerable and hard to reach. Asylum seekers and refugees are a particularly vulnerable group and services need to respond to their needs."
(CEMACH 2004)

WORKING WITH DIFFERENCE
Discrimination
"All healthcare professionals should consider whether there are unrecognised but inherent racial prejudices within their own organisations, in terms of providing an equal service to all women." (CEMACH 2004)

Even in the caring professions there is evidence of prejudice, racism, stereotyping and hostility towards minority ethnic parents and parents of other marginalised groups (McLeish 2002: Davies and Bath 2001). Prejudice, stereotyping and discriminatory behaviour are always completely unprofessional. They prevent individual, parent-led care and increase the distress of bereaved families. Both direct and indirect racial discrimination are also illegal under the 1976 Race Relations Act (CRE 2002; CRE 1994).

Developing flexible and inclusive services

"Working with diversity is not about categorising people as "different" nor is it about treating them as special cases; it is about recognising and understanding each woman's individual needs, so as to be able to provide the same high standard of care for everyone."
Royal College of Midwives (RCM 2000)

Like other organisations, the health service has a culture which strongly affects the way that it organises and offers services. Trusts, Health Boards and managers should ensure that services are flexible and can be adapted to suit a range of different needs, and that systems and standard practices do not – either intentionally or unintentionally – discriminate against or exclude vulnerable women. Managers and staff need to look at the way they offer care, and to consider whether the services they offer are limited by assumptions about what women and families will or should want, or about how care should be provided.

Help for parents on low incomes

Trusts, Health Boards and managers should ensure that advice is offered to parents who have lost a baby, especially those on low incomes, about benefits and payments to which they may be entitled (see *Entitlement to time off work and benefits* in Chapter 13 and *Child benefit and other benefits* in Chapter 14).

Trusts, Health Boards and managers should also be aware of the costs that women – and couples – may incur if they have to travel a long way to access specialist care during pregnancy or to visit a baby in a specialist neonatal unit. Funding should be available to assist parents on low incomes.

Training and support for staff

Staff should be able to support each woman and family respectfully on their own terms, without stereotyping, labelling, or making judgments or assumptions. In order to do this, staff need training and other opportunities to:

- Identify their own culture-based values and assumptions and those of the organisation in which they work;

- Consider how these values and assumptions may affect their responses to parents who have different ways of life, values and wishes;

- Think about how they could find out about and respond to the needs and wishes of parents and families of different cultures.

Staff need to bear in mind that:

- The most reliable source of information about a woman's needs is the woman herself;

- It is never acceptable to assume what parents will want on the basis of their "background", circumstances, way of life, religion or "ethnic group", nor on the basis of the staff member's own culture or the culture of the workplace. It is always important to ask parents what they would find helpful and to check out any assumptions;

- People do not usually mind personal questions – provided that the reasons for asking them are explained, the questions are asked in a respectful and sensitive way, and staff then make a genuine attempt to use the answers to meet the parents' needs;

- Parents will not always know what is traditional or customary in their community when a woman experiences a childbearing loss. They may need time to think or to talk to family members and other people.

Trusts, Health Boards and managers should identify and train specialist midwives and nurses with skills in supporting vulnerable women with specific needs such as a sensory impairment, mental health problems, homelessness, domestic violence and substance misuse, as well as young teenage women, refugees and asylum seekers. In addition to offering support themselves, these midwives and nurses should be a resource for other members of staff.

Staff working with bereaved parents should receive robust support from their managers and colleagues, so that they feel able to adapt care and do things differently when this is what parents need.

CHAPTER 2: HOLISTIC CARE

OTHER RELEVANT CHAPTERS:
1: PROVIDING INCLUSIVE CARE
3: LOSS AND GRIEF
4: COMMUNICATION
5: COMMUNICATION ACROSS LANGUAGE AND OTHER BARRIERS
21: SUPPORT AND TRAINING FOR STAFF

Pregnancy loss or the death of a baby often shakes people's beliefs about the meaning and purpose of life and damages their self-esteem. In addition to physical and practical care, staff should aim to offer care that meets parents' personal, cultural, spiritual and religious needs.

CULTURAL NEEDS

Culture is a shared set of values, assumptions, perceptions and conventions that enable a group or community to function together. The simplest way to define culture is "how people do and view things". Everyone has a culture, and each person's culture is influenced by, for example, the group or community in which they grew up, their family heritage and social class, their religion, and the environment in which they live and work (Trompenaars 1993; Hofstede 1991).

Culture influences, at a very deep level, what each person feels is normal, acceptable, abnormal or unacceptable. It influences every aspect of daily life, including expectations of parenthood, reactions to pregnancy loss or the death of a baby, and how people understand and cope with these life-changing events (Cowles 1996; Murray Parkes 1985; Eisenbruch 1984).

However, it is important to stress that, although each person's behaviour is strongly influenced by culture, nobody is simply a package of culture. Culture is a framework, not a straitjacket. Everyone has their own unique personality and is affected by the myriad of different experiences and ideas that they encounter in their lives. Within any culture there is a very wide range of attitudes and opinions as well as differences based on, for example, social class, age, gender, religion and education.

All cultures are also constantly changing. In addition, individuals may, for various reasons, choose to do things that do not conform to the norms of their culture or religion. *It is impossible to guess, on the basis of the community or group in which they live or grew up, their way of life, their socio-economic status, religion or personal circumstances, what any parent will feel or want when their baby dies.*

The list overleaf includes some of the aspects of childbearing loss that may be affected by cultural and religious beliefs, attitudes and expectations. All parents – not only those in minority communities or those with a formal religion – are likely to have beliefs and expectations in relation to these areas. It is important to be alert to these and to try to find out what is important to each individual parent:

antenatal screening and diagnosis	expression of emotion
miscarriage	expectations of parenthood
termination	relationships between men and women
stillbirth	role of the father
labour and birth	families and decision making
support in labour	beliefs about the causes of childbearing losses
postnatal care	beliefs about death and life after death
neonatal death	post mortem examination
withholding and withdrawing life support	grief and mourning
disability and severe illness	funeral practices
infertility	

PERSONAL, SPIRITUAL AND RELIGIOUS NEEDS

The provision of spiritual and religious care has been accepted as an important part of health care since the inception of the NHS. Spirituality is not synonymous with religion, although some people express their spirituality through their religion. Spiritual care, which goes hand in hand with emotional support, should be available to everyone, whether or not they have a religious affiliation.

Spiritual and religious needs are highly individual. When faced with a crisis, people's beliefs, values and sense of self are often profoundly challenged and certainties may be swept away. Many parents who experience a pregnancy loss or the death of a baby feel isolated as they try to make sense of what may seem senseless. They ask questions such as "Why did this happen to me?", "What did I do wrong?", "Am I being punished in some way?", "How will other people see and react to me now?" and "How can I possibly cope with this?". Spiritual and religious beliefs and questions may become particularly important, even to people who do not normally consider themselves religious.

Offering care and support

Care can be offered by anyone – a member of the health care team, a counsellor or a chaplain. It is not usually necessary for the member of staff to share the religion or beliefs of the parent, though some parents may prefer to speak to someone who does share their beliefs.

The most important components of spiritual and personal care include the ability and willingness to stay with the person and, above all, *to listen with respect and with full attention.*

- Staff should avoid making any assumptions about a parent's beliefs or way of life;

- It is important that staff make no reference to their own beliefs or religious practices unless it is very clear that these are shared, or the parent asks;

- It is generally helpful to validate people's feelings. It is not helpful to make comparisons;

- Generalised reassurance – for example, that "everything will turn out all right", or that grief "will pass" – should be avoided;

- However, it may be helpful to acknowledge that the feelings a parent is experiencing are common to many grieving parents and are, in that sense, normal.

Offering this kind of care can be draining and may sometimes challenge the beliefs and assumptions of the caregiver. It takes generosity, insight and discipline to keep listening fully to people who are grieving, and to resist the temptation to reassure, find solutions, compare or talk about one's own experience and beliefs. It is important that staff are aware of and have an opportunity to meet their own personal and spiritual needs, that they know their own limits and receive good support.

Religious needs

Most people who have a strong religious faith have a set of beliefs and values that are woven into the fabric of their lives. These influence their views and reactions, and the meaning that they ascribe to what happens to them. People's religious beliefs may also determine their priorities and underlie many of their decisions.

A strong religious faith can be a great source of comfort and strength when life is difficult. It may give people purpose, courage and hope and can give meaning to hardship, suffering and tragedy. For many religious people, faith and acceptance of the power of God's will, sometimes called fatalism, helps them get on with their lives and cope with things as they happen. However, some people may doubt or lose their faith in the face of inexplicable tragedy. Some may be angry that such a thing could happen to them despite their faith.

It is important never to use generalisations about a particular religion or denomination as a basis for trying to anticipate the needs and wishes of individual parents. Within any religious group or denomination there are many different degrees of observance and practice and different points of view. Some traditions or practices may be important to individual parents and others may mean little. Sometimes parents themselves are surprised by what matters to them when faced with a childbearing loss.

People who make choices that are clearly against the precepts of their religion or of their community, may fear that their decision will cause conflict with more traditional family members. Strict confidentiality as well as respect for each individual's choices are essential.

Support Some parents may want the support of a religious leader from their own faith, and staff should offer to arrange this if necessary. The hospital chaplaincy (see below) can often provide contact details. This may be particularly important if there are religious ceremonies or rituals to be performed. However, in some communities, religious leaders are scholars who interpret religious teaching rather than offering pastoral care. Although many religious leaders have taken on a pastoral role, parents may not feel that their presence is required for prayers and ceremonies.

Religious rituals Rituals and ceremonies are important in most religions. For example: lighting candles, oil lamps or using incense; anointing with oil or holy water; praying; washing before prayer.

Religious rituals can have important spiritual, social and emotional significance and can be comforting even to people whose daily life takes little account of religion. Having a prescribed way of doing things may provide a framework for managing confusing and tragic situations.

Most religious rituals that parents might want to perform when a baby dies can be easily accommodated – and many may go unnoticed by staff. However, lamps, incense or candles often clash with institutional safety regulations. Some people may very much want to light a candle, for example, to symbolise the continuation of the spirit or to light the path for the soul. Their requests should be met with understanding and sympathy, and, wherever possible, accommodated safely.

Prayer Some people may want to pray alone or with family members, or with other members of their community. In addition to privacy and respect, people may want to:

- Wash before praying, usually under running water (for example most Muslims, some Jews, Hindus and Sikhs);
- Cover their heads or put on prayer shawls;
- Face in the direction of a holy place, for example Muslims and some Jews;
- Adopt certain positions while praying or meditating;
- Set up a small shrine.

A multi-faith room should be provided in the hospital for parents and families of all faiths and none.

Religious items – for example, holy books, pictures and statues; holy water that has been blessed or brought from a special place; prayer beads and religious medals; prayers or words from holy books or threads tied around a baby's wrist or fastened to clothes - should be treated with respect. They should be moved only if it is essential and then only with clean hands and placed somewhere safe and respectful. They should never be placed on the floor or near feet, shoes or soiled clothing. It is important to ask, if possible, before touching or moving a religious item. In some cases, religious items should only be touched by people of the same faith.

HOSPITAL CHAPLAINS

Chaplains who work in health care settings receive specialist training and gain experience of and insight into the very difficult personal, religious and ethical dilemmas that can arise in relation to childbearing loss. Parents, other family members and staff members sometimes find it particularly helpful to talk to a chaplain because he or she is not directly involved in clinical decisions and can bring a different perspective to the encounter. They may also feel that a chaplain has more time to sit with them and let them talk (McHaffie 2000).

Most parents have no experience of traditions and rituals associated with pregnancy loss or the death of a baby. Hospital chaplaincies in areas with a multi-faith population should include representatives of the main world faiths represented locally, so that they can provide support as well as help with religious questions and rituals to bereaved and anxious parents of different heritages (Sheikh et al 2004). They should also develop contacts with other local religious advisors and with non-religious advisors such as Humanists.

Much of this chapter is adapted from Schott and Henley (1996) and Henley and Schott (1999).

CHAPTER 3: LOSS AND GRIEF

A loss during pregnancy or around the time of birth is complex and unique (Hutti 2005). For the parents, it is the loss of a person who would have been, and may be the loss of hopes, dreams and expectations for the future. For many parents, losing a baby damages their self-esteem and self-confidence: they feel that they have failed. This may also be their first experience of loss and bereavement, and of the emotional chaos and devastation that can result.

CONCEPTS OF GRIEF

Grief is both universal and highly individual: people may have a wide range of feelings and physical reactions (Scrutton 1995: 13; Wortman and Silver 1989). Initially most people feel physically and emotionally shocked, even when the loss or death has been expected. They may feel numb and be unable to take in what has happened, or hear what is being said. They may experience physical reactions such as feeling shaky, cold, weak or breathless. These reactions may last for hours or days and may recur over the following weeks. Many people experience recurring waves of despair, sadness and crying spells. Some may find it hard to get organised or to see any purpose or meaning in life.

> *The pain of grief was so physical. My chest hurt, I could not move about and certainly could not think straight. Every now and then a wave of grief came crashing over me and all I could do was crouch down and scream until I was exhausted. Then there was calm until the next wave came.* Mother

> *I just feel so cheated, like part of me has died, and that my insides have been ripped out. I'm just so angry and all these feelings I have been told are natural.* Mother

People who are grieving commonly feel depressed and tearful. They may also feel guilty and resentful. They may be angry at the staff who were involved, relatives, friends, the person who has died or God (see also *Anger, blame and litigation* later). Sometimes the anger is turned inwards and the bereaved feel guilty and blame themselves, thinking, "If only I had...".

> *I blamed myself for the death of our baby, for drinking coffee, the occasional glass of wine, the prawn sandwich I had eaten.* Mother

> *Babies don't die for no reason. It was my responsibility, as Kieran's mother, to nurture my son through the first nine months of his life and to see him safely into this world. And even if you don't smoke, didn't drink, took all the multivitamins advised, avoided soft cheese and even hair dyes and nail varnish for fear of harmful chemicals - that guilt is still there. It was my responsibility and I failed.* Mother

The length and intensity of any individual's grief may be influenced by many factors, including their personality, circumstances, life experiences, attachment to this baby or this pregnancy, and the significance of the loss to them. Although many parents are devastated by their loss, some may see it as the end of a pregnancy rather than the loss of a life and may find it easier to move on (Leon 1992). In certain situations, for example, when there is a very poor prognosis antenatally or the baby is in neonatal intensive care, some parents may distance themselves and withdraw both physically and emotionally (Enkin et al 2000: 473).

Grief has been described as a series of "tasks", "stages" or "phases" through which people move, and these models can offer a useful foundation for thinking about grief. However, people do not necessarily experience the emotions that may be triggered by grief in a particular order; for each individual the experience is different and unpredictable. It is therefore unhelpful to impose a framework of "normal grieving" on bereaved parents, or to expect them to progress through a series of prescribed stages (Davies 2004; Wortman and Silver 1989; Murray Parkes 1985). Parents whose feelings and reactions do not fit into a formula may feel that there is something wrong with them; staff who expect a linear progression may consider parents' individual reactions abnormal, or discount them (Leon 1992). The most important thing is, as always, to listen to each person and to respond to their actual needs.

"Grief simply does not follow any kind of ordered, linear progression. If anything, the experiences of grief are better characterised in terms of wave after wave of violently contradictory emotional impulses." (Littlewood 1992)

The dual-process model of grief (Stroebe and Schut 1999) suggests that, rather than moving through stages or phases, bereaved people often move backwards and forwards, sometimes confronting their loss and emotions, and at other times putting grieving feelings aside and dealing with the demands of living.

> *My grief does not seem to leave me alone for very long and when it does leave me it only seems to do so because of the demands of my work ... It seems incredible that I should be able, or even willing, to carry on as normal. Sometimes I catch myself laughing and joking with work colleagues and feel as though I have let my little boy down.* Father

Although intense grief usually eases with time, many people find that it continues to return over months and years.

> *Now six months later, to most of the world I am just like any other mother of two healthy, lively young children. Inside I often fight to control my emotions and tears which seem triggered off by so many things.* Mother

Grief is like a wound that can be re-opened time and again (Cowles 1996). The date on which the dead baby was due, the anniversary of the death, other anniversaries, Mothers' and Fathers' days, festivals, celebrations and important life events, as well as certain sights, sounds and smells, may all trigger new waves of distress long after the actual loss. Memories of childbearing losses can also continue to surface many years later, especially during periods of stress or reflection (Dyson and While 1998).

I miss what might have been. I will never be able to pick them up and comfort them when they fall over. I will never get to see their paintings from the toddlers group or their first day at school and I will never get to see them playing with my daughter. Mother of twins

Resolution or continuing bonds?

Traditional models of grief generally assume that, after a period of time, the mourner should reach "resolution" and be able to "let go" of their emotional relationship with the person who has died. However, it is increasingly acknowledged that many bereaved people continue to feel a bond with the person who has died and he or she continues to be part of their lives. Studies confirm that many bereaved parents do not want to forget their dead babies: they may continue to feel a bond with them and find solace in doing so (Davies 2004; Wilson 2001; Walter 1999: xii; Klass 1996: 214–215).

Dear Charlie and Joshua, it is five years since you were born. You should both be starting school now. It seems longer ago now, but at other times not as long as five years. You have a younger sister Jessica, who is 4 and talks about you regularly, and a 2 year old brother Samuel, who doesn't really understand yet, but knows you are Mummy's babies. Mother of twins

At first we were terrified if at the end of the day we realised that we had not thought about her, in case that meant we were forgetting her; but as time went by we realised that not consciously thinking of her was fine, she would creep into our thoughts on her own. Mother

Culture and the *experience* of grief

Research indicates that grief is *experienced* in similar ways across all cultures, and that within each culture there is also a huge range of individual responses and many different ways of dealing with grief (Cowles 1996). However, although people's experience of grief is similar everywhere, the way that they explain the causes of their loss to themselves and how the loss fits into their system of values is influenced by culture and religion. Every culture and religion teaches different ways of understanding and dealing with the pain of loss.

Culture and the *expression* of grief

Although the *experience* of grief is similar across different cultures, the way that grief is *expressed* may not be. Unconscious cultural conditioning and social norms strongly determine the ways in which people express, or do not express, grief (Murray Parkes 1985). How bereaved people behave in public, the restrictions that they observe, the clothes they are expected to wear, how funerals are organised, and many other external expressions of grief are largely determined by culture and history. In some cultures and faiths there no formal grieving rituals following a childbearing loss.

Outward expressions of grief do not necessarily indicate what an individual is experiencing or what they need. Some cultures value stoicism in the face of adversity; some encourage private but not public expressions of grief; some value and encourage loud and open grieving; some consider wailing and crying in public distasteful and artificial; some consider that people should hide or suppress their grief because loss should be accepted without question as the will of God (Schott and Henley 1999: 217–220).

It is important to avoid assumptions about how a person feels based on the way they grieve, and to try to accept and adapt to their grieving style. A person who grieves silently and inwardly may appreciate the offer of an opportunity to talk about how they feel. People who express their feelings freely and openly should be offered time and privacy in which to do so.

GRIEF AND CHILDBEARING LOSSES

"Grief is what the person experiencing it says it is." (Mander 2005: 111)

It is impossible ever to predict the significance of a pregnancy loss or the death of a baby to any mother or father. The depth and length of parents' grief vary, and depend to some extent on their circumstances and experiences. A shorter gestation does not necessarily carry less emotional investment (Mander 2005: 41; Bagchi and Friedman 1999; Zeanah et al 1993). Peppers and Knapp (1980) found no significant differences in the grief responses of women who had had a miscarriage, a stillbirth or a neonatal death. Women who terminate a pregnancy for fetal abnormality, even when they feel that they have made the right decision, may experience grief that is as intense as the grief of women who have had a spontaneous perinatal loss (Zeanah et al 1993). Some women who have an early termination for reasons other than fetal abnormality may feel relief rather than grief. However, women who did not want a termination but felt that their personal circumstances left them no option may experience the termination as a bereavement.

Multiple pregnancies

Rates of pregnancy and childbearing loss are higher for parents expecting twins, and even higher for parents expecting three or more babies (ONS 2006). Parents with a multiple pregnancy who lose one or more of their babies at any stage in the pregnancy have to deal with the extreme complexity and difficulty of grieving for the child who has died while at the same time welcoming and caring for the surviving baby or babies, who may themselves be frail and vulnerable. This is an almost impossible task. Bryan (2002) states that for parents "the repercussions of the loss of one triplet may be as serious as the loss of a single-born child and often more complex".

Parents who are trying to care for a surviving baby while grieving for the baby or babies who have died (and perhaps organising a funeral and other practical tasks) may feel that they cannot enjoy or focus on the living baby as they should or would like to.

> *It was a difficult time, sharing the feelings of the joy of a new baby and mourning the loss of his beautiful twin sister. The first year was definitely the hardest, our friends and family could not possibly understand what we were going through.* Mother

Some parents may feel guilty about their grief and may worry about possible long-term effects on the relationship with the surviving baby. They may also be deeply anxious about his or her survival. In some cases, grieving is delayed or submerged while parents focus on the surviving baby or babies only to emerge or re-emerge later. Parents who were expecting twins or more babies also lose the excitement and special status generally given to parents expecting more than one baby. The birth of the surviving baby may be an anticlimax. If the pregnancy was the result of infertility treatment, some parents may also be angry at being prescribed a treatment that resulted in a higher order pregnancy and led to their babies' prematurity and death (MBF 1997a).

Although each baby is equally precious to the parents, those who have one or more surviving babies rarely receive the same degree of sympathy from other people for the baby or babies who have died. This is especially likely if the losses occurred before the birth (Pector and Levitin 2002). Well-meaning friends and relatives often focus on the surviving baby or babies and encourage and expect the parents to do the same. They may even try to comfort parents by pointing out that looking after several babies would have been difficult and stressful. They may discourage parents from grieving for or talking about the baby or babies who have died (MBF 2000). However, the presence of a living baby in no way lessens parents' grief for those who have died. It is very important that staff acknowledge all the babies – both those who have died and those who survive – and the difficulties that parents are likely to be experiencing, and that they allow parents to express their feelings of loss openly (MBF 1997a; Wilson et al 1982).

All staff who come into contact with the mother and the surviving baby or babies after the birth should be informed about the loss. If all the babies have been named, staff should refer to each baby – whether alive or dead – by his or her name (MBF 1997a) (see also Naming the baby in Chapter 12).

The conflicting emotions and mood swings that parents in this situation are likely to experience may persist for a very long time. Every event in the life of the surviving baby or babies – for example, birthdays, learning to walk and talk, festivals such as Christmas, milestones such as weaning, starting kindergarten, starting school – is also a reminder of the babies who have died and may trigger renewed grief. Because this is rarely understood, parents may mourn secretly and keep their memories and thoughts about their dead baby or babies to themselves.

Some time in the future, parents who lose one or more babies and also have one or more who survive, will have to decide whether, when, how and what to tell their surviving child or children about the circumstances of their birth.

> *Everyone was in so much shock as we had expected all three babies to be fine ... Feeling excited for two babies and sad for one baby was very hard and confusing. Our little man will always be loved and never be forgotten. Eliot and Jake are thriving now, and as they grow older we will ensure that they know they were triplets and that their brother Ben will always be with them.* Mother

There is some evidence that many multiples develop a relationship in the womb which would normally continue after birth, and that surviving children may have a sense of something missing (Bryan 2002; Leonard 2002). It is generally recommended that surviving children are told early about their dead siblings. It is easier for parents to discuss the dead baby or babies with the survivors if they have been named. It may also help, if the parents wish, to have copies of ultrasound scans, photographs or paintings of the dead baby or babies to discuss (MBF 2000) (see also *Creating memories* in Chapter 12).

For many parents it is important to know whether their same sex babies were identical (monozygotic). In some cases this may already be known. If not, a member of staff should discuss zygosity testing with the parents, as they may not think of it at the time. If the parents do not know whether or not the babies were identical, this may leave many unanswered questions and deep regret later. Knowing about the zygosity is an important part of creating memories of the dead twin and distinguishing between the two babies. As the surviving baby grows up, he or she may also want to know whether he or she had an identical twin. For most surviving twins this is very important to their sense of self and how they think of the brother or sister who died (Personal communication, MBF 2006). Knowing the zygosity is also essential for later genetic counselling if this is indicated. Mothers of dizygotic twins may want to know if they have an increased chance of having twins again in a future pregnancy.

Parents who lose all the babies in a multiple pregnancy may grieve more intensely and for longer than parents who lose a single baby. They grieve for each baby individually, not merely a "collective baby" and it is important that staff, too, distinguish and acknowledge each baby (Pector et al 2002). Swanson et al (2002) found that bereaved mothers of multiple babies scored higher on the Perinatal Grief Scale than bereaved mothers of single babies. They attribute this partly to the lack of acknowledgement of the grief that mothers of multiple babies experience. However, the grief of parents who have lost all their babies is likely to be better understood by other people than that of parents who have one or more surviving babies from a multiple pregnancy (MBF 1997a).

Fathers

My closest male friend John … gave me what I can only describe as the kind of hug only fathers can give their sons. I will be forever indebted to him. For that moment he could not change the pain but he carried some of it for just long enough when I could not. Father

The effects of childbearing losses on fathers have been largely ignored. It is often assumed that fathers do not bond with an unborn child and so are not as severely affected as mothers, especially in cases of early loss (Duncan 1995). However, recent research and much anecdotal evidence (for example, Don 2005; Di Clemente 2004 and Sands newsletters) show that many fathers respond to the loss of their baby with deep and intense grief. For example, Puddifoot and Johnson (1999) found that immediately following a miscarriage, fathers' "active grief" scores (that is, the distress due to the loss) were lower than those of their partners. However, they found unexpectedly high "delayed" effects and despair in some fathers several weeks later, especially in those who had seen the baby on ultrasound.

At the time of the loss many fathers feel helpless, frightened and angry at the pain and distress that the mother is experiencing (Bennett at al 2005). They may feel that they need to be strong and to focus on supporting her, because they recognise that for her the physical and emotional effects of the loss are almost always greater. They may also feel guilty and feel responsible for her unhappiness and physical distress.

I felt suffocated with grief. I could not bear my pain, but more, the pain my wife was suffering. I could not fix it. Father

In many cultures, gender conditioning affects men's ability to acknowledge their own needs and their willingness to seek support from other people. Consequently, men tend to be more isolated both socially and psychologically (Clare 2000: 85).

Grieving was hard because we did not seem to be able to communicate much and so did not really talk to each other about how we were feeling or how we were coping. I later discovered that my partner had started to drink and by the time I realised it, he had a serious drink problem. Mother

Many men rely on their partners for support and do not have a network of people to whom they can express their feelings. They may have nowhere to turn for help and support. When their partner is grieving, they also tend to feel the full force of her sorrow and anger. Family and friends often focus on the mother's needs and may not consider, or know how to deal with, the father's needs. All this may lead fathers to suppress or ignore their own feelings and needs, both at the time of the loss and later, and to feel excluded (Murphy 1998).

> *I was unable to give a name to my feelings let alone feel in a position to articulate them to anyone whatever their capacity. A supportive GP prescribed anti-depressants which I didn't think helped. I wasn't depressed. I was a bereaved Englishman.* Father

For most men, it is important that they are recognised and acknowledged – by their partners, by other family members and by staff – as parents who are grieving the loss of their baby and not simply as supporters and comforters (Samuelsson et al 2001). It is important to them to be able to protect their partner and also to be allowed to grieve in their own way and in their own time, without having to comply with other people's expectations of them. Conway and Russell (2000) found that many fathers received sub-optimal support from staff. When the father is present, he should be asked how he is and listened to in his own right (Wallerstedt and Higgins 1996). He should be actively included when information is given to the mother, and should be offered sensitive support and care as a bereaved parent as a matter of course.

Couples

> *The first few months were very hard. We seemed very separate and at times I wondered if we would ever get through this. But looking back on it now, I think it has made us stronger as a couple.* Mother

Grieving is very individual. Each parent is likely to have different perceptions of their loss and different ways of managing and expressing their feelings. A grieving mother and father often find that their needs and feelings do not coincide, and that it is hard to talk and to give each other support. Each may try to protect the other by keeping their more painful thoughts and feelings to themselves (Bennett et al 2005). As a result, each parent may feel increasingly lonely and isolated, and their relationship may become strained and difficult (Schaap et al 1997; Mander 2005: 118). In many cases the mother's grief persists for longer than the father's: he may feel ready – or be forced – to pick up the strings of his life before she does. This can lead to difficulties between them (Wallerstedt and Higgins 1996).

> *I think, if truth be told, we've probably moved a bit further apart. I don't think we communicated our experiences or how we were feeling particularly well. Maybe it's our inability to share how we feel, or maybe me just thinking I've shut that chapter door. I want to get on with life.* Father

Swanson (2003) found that, one year after their loss, some parents reported that their personal and sexual relationship with each other was more distant. These parents were also more depressed, anxious, confused and moody. However, those women who saw their partners as caring, and those couples who talked to each other about their feelings and experiences, perceived their relationship as closer. Statham et al (2001: 136) found that women who feel supported by their partners have higher emotional wellbeing.

It may help couples to know that:

- It can be very difficult for either parent to support the other when both are experiencing a crisis;

- It is common for people to react differently at different times, but that this does not mean that their partner does not care how they feel, nor does it mean that one of them cares more than the other about the loss;

- Although it can be difficult, taking time to listen to each other is helpful and important. Fathers who are anxious that talking may make things worse or make their partner cry more, may find it reassuring to know that talking does not cause the pain, rather it allows the pain to be expressed;

- Disparities in sexual desire may occur. Some women may see sex as a fearful reminder of their loss or think that their partner's desire for sex indicates a lack of feeling. On the other hand, some men see sex as a source of comfort and sharing (Hutti 2005; Wallerstedt and Higgins 1996).

Other children

Existing children are usually profoundly affected when their parents are grieving. Children born after a pregnancy loss may also be affected, because the experience of loss is likely to change the way that the parents view another pregnancy and the way they relate to future children.

Many people feel that children should be protected from the reality of death. There is some debate about whether young children grieve in the same way as older children or adults (Worden 1996: 9–17). Small children may also find it difficult to understand the meaning or permanence of death. However, there is no doubt that children of all ages are profoundly affected when the people on whom they most depend are grief stricken. Parents may become over-protective, or may be so devastated and preoccupied that their existing children feel excluded (Canadian Paediatric Society 2001). Children may respond to their own grief, or to the changes in the adults around them, by, for example, regressing to earlier behaviours, crying, clinging or becoming angry or difficult. All this increases the pressure on their parents and makes it even harder for them to cope. Children in this situation can be helped by long-term consistent support from another adult who is close to them and who is able to listen and respond to them. Parents should also be encouraged to inform the child's nursery or school, so that any changes in behaviour are seen in the context of the family's loss.

The decision to tell a child about a loss is very personal and will depend on several factors. Children who know that a new baby was expected should be told about the loss. Some parents may decide not to tell a child who does not yet know that their mother was pregnant. However, parents need to know that, whether children are told or not, they often sense when there is something wrong and their behaviour may change as a result.

When talking to a young child it is important to choose words that cannot be misinterpreted. For example, telling a young child that the dead baby is "sleeping" or has been "lost" could create great anxiety about going to sleep or getting lost. It is also important to recognise that most young children are ambivalent about the impending arrival of a sibling and, as a consequence, some may feel that the death is somehow their fault (Worden 1996: 120). They should be reassured that they are not to blame for the death of their baby brother or sister. Parents may need to explain to other family members and friends that children can be deeply affected by a loss and that this may affect their behaviour for some time.

Daisy had a massive impact on our family. Rosie, our one year old, was too young to understand what she'd lost. Matthew, her big brother, felt it very keenly and was very, very sad. Cathy and I were devastated – and could have been destroyed – by our grief. But with two tots depending on us, we couldn't let that happen. We sought out anything that could help us cope. Father

How and to what degree other children are involved after a childbearing loss depends to some extent on personal and cultural norms. Some parents actively include children, others try to shield children from death. Some parents encourage children to make their own choices about matters such as seeing the body, helping to plan the funeral and attending it, and visiting the grave. A small study (Wilson 2001) of the kinds of support that parents who belonged to a Sands group in Edinburgh gave their children identified three main categories:

- *Recognising and acknowledging the child's grief:* for example, telling children what is happening; understanding mood and behaviour changes as reactions to loss; listening and answering questions honestly, however difficult this might be, while trying not to burden children with their own grief;

- *Including the child in family rituals to do with the baby who has died:* for example, offering the child an opportunity to see and hold the baby; photographing them with the baby; including them in funeral or memorial services if they want to attend;

- *Keeping the baby's memory alive in the family:* for example, visiting the grave or crematorium garden; lighting candles in memory of the baby on anniversaries and at important festivals and celebrations.

Parents may find it useful to read leaflets produced by ARC, the Miscarriage Association, Sands and other voluntary organisations (see Appendix 2) on talking to children about a pregnancy loss. Some of these organisations publish books to help young children understand the concept of death and the feelings it can generate. If parents are still worried about how to support their other children, or are having difficulties, staff should offer to put them in touch with a counsellor or other professional who is experienced in the area of child bereavement.

Grandparents

Never underestimate what a grandparent goes through when a baby dies. For their suffering is doubled: they mourn for the child they will never get to see grow, and they watch their own child suffer the cruellest of agonies. They feel heartbroken, yet try to be strong. They see their own child's heartbreak and feel helpless. Father

As I was wheeled out of the delivery room, I saw my father pick up my baby boy, his grandson, and cradle him, sobbing quietly. Mother

Many grandparents are deeply affected and distressed by a childbearing loss. They may be shocked and frightened. If the baby had a genetic abnormality, some may also feel guilty. For some grandparents the loss also evokes painful memories of their own childbearing losses which were probably handled with far less sensitivity and awareness than is customary today. However, in most cases, grandparents and other family members are seen by staff merely as additional supporters for the parents and not as people who may be grieving and who may need help and support in their own right.

> *I have felt so helpless. I have been unable to "kiss it better" and make my daughter's pain go away, nothing can. I have simply held her hand and listened.* Grandmother

Provided the parents want them to be involved, grandparents may want to see and hold the baby and to participate in funerals and memorials. Involving the baby's grandparents and other family members at the time of the loss may also be a way of helping the parents in the future: other people who have seen the baby and were present at important events can share some of the parents' brief but crucial memories.

Other family members

Ideas about what constitutes a family vary from culture to culture. In the UK the family is most often taken to mean the parents (or parent) and their child or children. Other relatives may form the "extended family". In traditional Asian cultures, and many others, there is often no division between the immediate and extended family. Grandparents, aunts, uncles, siblings and cousins are all regarded as close family, and a new baby is usually considered an addition to the whole family. This means that a larger number of people may want to be directly involved and, provided the parents consent, their wishes should be accommodated as far as possible.

> *I can't believe how much the loss of my niece has affected me. Seeing my sister-in-law and my brother in such distress has been heartbreaking. I never realised how much you could miss someone that you have never known.* Aunt

In many cultures, pregnancy and childbirth and everything associated with them are traditionally women's responsibilities. Some women may not expect or want their husbands to be involved, and older female relatives may sometimes be more important in supporting a bereaved mother. Staff need to be sensitive to such differences and adapt their approach accordingly.

WITNESSING GRIEF AND OFFERING SUPPORT

Many factors make it hard for staff to witness the grief of others. Staff may:

- Feel helpless;
- Feel guilty for having let the parents down, even though they may have done their best;
- Be reminded of their own losses or losses that might happen to them (Worden 1991: 173–174);
- Have been conditioned by the culture of health care which demands detachment, and also focuses on doing things for people rather than just being with them;
- Feel that it is their duty to remove pain and distress, although this is impossible when people are grieving.

All this can make it tempting for staff to erect protective barriers and to keep an emotional distance.

Offering support

"The memories that parents take away from hospital are so important, as memories are all they have, and the professionals who were most involved are a major part of those memories."
(Personal communication, Joanie Dimavicius 2005)

Research consistently shows that, for most bereaved parents, one of the few positive memories they take away from their traumatic experience is the warmth and involvement of the staff who cared for them (Mander 2005: 73; Säflund et al 2004; McHaffie 2001: 216). Many parents are particularly grateful when staff take the initiative and offer them care and support without having to be asked (Statham et al 2001: 156).

A member of staff may be the only person who was with parents at very important moments; for example, during a scan, when the baby was born or when the baby died. Some parents may find it very helpful to talk through what happened with the member of staff who was there and to share their recollections of the experience.

Family members and friends are often anxious and shocked at the loss, or are themselves grieving, and may be unable to support the parents. Some family members and friends may not understand the significance of the loss to the parents, others may feel uncomfortable when it is discussed, may not know how to offer support, and may avoid them. Some people may blame the parents for their loss, or fear that their misfortune is catching. If the loss was due to termination, whatever the reason, some family members may strongly disapprove. In some communities, women who have lost a baby are traditionally excluded from family events and celebrations for some time. For all kinds of reasons, therefore, bereaved parents may receive little of the support they need from family and friends.

There are many ways in which staff members can offer support. The skill consists in being sensitive to what parents need at any particular time. Sometimes it is best just to listen, at other times it is appropriate to offer information or suggestions. Offering high-quality supportive care can be difficult, but this should not be a reason for staff to distance themselves or to be over-cautious about what they say and do (see *The importance of support* in Chapter 21).

It is always important to:

- Listen to parents – and be prepared to listen again and again;
- Treat parents as individuals and accept what they say without judgement;
- Acknowledge their feelings and respond with empathy;
- Remain calm when they express strong feelings;
- Express sympathy and sorrow when appropriate, but only if these are genuinely felt (Leon 1992);
- Avoid platitudes, comparisons and empty reassurances;
- Enable parents to have control over what happens and what they do whenever possible;
- Resist the temptation to give advice unless specifically asked;

- Arrange for ongoing support from community staff if the parents wish;
- Inform the parents, at an appropriate time, about sources of ongoing support such as counselling services and relevant voluntary organisations.

It can also help bereaved parents to know that it is normal to experience a whole range of physical as well as emotional reactions, that there is no "right" or "healthy" way to express or deal with profound grief, that grief can persist for much longer than most people expect, and that, although intense grief will normally subside over time, it can be triggered by, for example, anniversaries, festivals, and important family events (Mander 2005: 72; Dyson and While 1998; Leon 1992). At the same time, if the parents themselves are worried about how they are feeling, or feel that their grief is abnormal and debilitating, it is important to offer them help.

RECOGNISING COMPLICATED GRIEF

There is no universally accepted definition of normal grief, although it is widely agreed that the duration and intensity of grief following perinatal loss are often far longer than most people expect (Wallerstedt et al 2003). Such grief involves debilitating symptoms such as depression, anxiety, irritability, sleeping and eating disturbances, and preoccupation with the dead baby. In the early stages of a loss some women experience visual and auditory hallucinations, including hearing the baby cry or feeling the baby still kicking within them. Feelings such as failure, self-blame, helplessness and anger are also common and some parents may express anger towards staff and blame them for what has happened.

In most cases grief is "self-limiting" and decreases over time. However, although their feelings are no longer overwhelming, it is normal for many parents to continue to grieve for their baby for months or years and to experience resurgences of intense grief on anniversaries and other important occasions for up to ten years or more (Worden 1991: 89). Distress also often carries over into subsequent pregnancies (Hutti 2005) (see also *Care during another pregnancy* in Chapter 20).

In contrast to normal grief, complicated or "pathological" grief is generally characterised by prolonged, severe, debilitating and overwhelming symptoms, such as depression and an inability to cope with daily life. Condon (1987) suggests that after six months, although they are still grieving, parents should be more or less able to carry out normal family and work responsibilities. Parents who are unable to do this should be offered a referral for specialist help.

Predisposing factors for complicated grief include lack of social support, lack of perceived partner support, lower educational achievement, a high level of ambivalence about the pregnancy, and a history of mental health problems (Korenromp et al 2005; Hughes and Riches 2003; Condon 1987). People who have had other bereavements – for example, the loss of a parent or other family member, previous childbearing losses, other traumatic events – or who feel that their baby need not have died, may also be more severely affected (Worden 1991: 85). It has been suggested that the absence of a grief reaction may also indicate complicated or "pathological" grief, but systematic studies have not supported this theory (Hughes and Riches 2003; Wortman and Silver 1989). If there are no other symptoms, the absence of overt grief may simply be a preferred coping style.

Postnatal depression A childbearing loss does not exclude the possibility of the mother also suffering from postnatal depression. In a review of the literature on affective disorders following miscarriage, Klier et al (2002) state that it is both feasible and clinically useful to distinguish between grief and postnatal depression, even though depression is often a feature of grief.

Past history of mental illness Women who have a history of psychiatric illness, whether postpartum or not, are at greater risk of postpartum psychiatric illness including severe postnatal depression. Suicide is now recognised as a leading cause of maternal death (CEMACH 2004: Ch. 11A). It is important that women with a history of psychiatric illness are identified, and that those who become ill again after the birth are referred urgently for expert help.

Post traumatic stress disorder Grief following childbearing loss may also occasionally be accompanied by post traumatic stress disorder (PTSD). This is more likely to happen if the physical experience of the loss was traumatic or the mother's life was at risk (Hutti 2005; Korenromp et al 2005). Although the likelihood of PTSD appears to increase at later gestations, it can occur after loss at any stage in pregnancy (Engelhard et al 2001). Symptoms of PTSD may emerge at any time within six months and may include vivid flashbacks and nightmares accompanied by a replay of painful physical and emotional feelings, emotional numbness, intense aversion to and avoidance of babies or pregnant women, depression, irritability, edginess and/or exhaustion (RCP 2005; Condon 1987).

Domestic violence For some women, their grief is complicated by domestic violence. Violence may begin or escalate during pregnancy, and often becomes worse after the birth. In some cases the loss itself may have been caused by violence from a partner (DoH 2005a: 2.4; RCM 2006). In addition to physical injuries, women who experience domestic violence are likely to suffer from depression, anxiety, despair, post traumatic stress disorder and suicide attempts (DoH 2005a: 2.4).

Domestic violence is a difficult issue for many staff to raise with women (CEMACH 2004: Ch. 14). However, most women will not say that they are being abused unless they are specifically asked. Women are more likely to disclose abuse if they feel that the person asking is really interested and genuinely cares, and if they trust them (Mezey and Bewley 2000). It is important to ask questions about abuse only when the woman is not with her partner or another supporter, and when there is time to deal with whatever she says. Time should be made for this. If a woman speaks little or no English and her partner or a relative usually interprets for her, it is important that staff have at least one session alone with her, using a professional interpreter who understands the importance of confidentiality (RCM 2006).

All staff should have training to enable them to recognise and ask about the signs and symptoms of possible domestic violence, know what to say and do if a women says she is being abused, and respond in a way that is helpful to the woman. Whatever decision the woman makes about her future, staff should provide continuing support.

Good practice

It is important not to "pathologise" normal grief, nor to expect parents to fit into a prescribed pattern of grieving. However, staff, especially those working in primary care who have longer-term contact with parents, should ensure that parents who experience severe and debilitating symptoms over a prolonged period of time, those with symptoms of PTSD, and those who have been subjected to domestic violence are referred, with their consent, for specialist help.

ANGER, BLAME AND LITIGATION

Anger is a normal and common reaction to loss and may be directed towards the health professionals who were involved. Although it is difficult for staff to listen to parents who blame the hospital or a particular member of the health care team for what happened, it is important to do so. Some parents find it helpful to be able to express their anger and pain to someone who simply listens.

> *I was grief stricken, angry and desperate for someone to pay.* Father

It can be very hard to listen to anger without feeling threatened, becoming defensive or arguing. However, it is important that staff are able to remain calm. For parents, simply being able to express their anger to someone who listens can be a release, and this may be all that is needed.

Many parents remain angry simply because they were denied a compassionate response: no one said "I am so sorry your baby died" (Enkin et al 2000: 479). However, staff may be reluctant to use the phrase "I'm sorry" because they fear that this equates with an acknowledgement of guilt and may have legal implications. Ironically, bereaved parents may be so angered by this reluctance that they may in fact consider or even embark on litigation. It is important that staff understand that there is a difference between expressing sorrow and empathy for the distress that the parents have experienced, and apologising for negligence or poor care (Boyce et al 2002).

Complaints There may nevertheless be occasions when poor care has been a contributory factor or when staff have been negligent. It is essential not to assume that parents' complaints are always simply an expression of their grief. Parents who wish to make a complaint should be offered an opportunity to meet and talk to senior members of staff. When necessary, a formal complaints procedure should be instigated.

When investigating complaints from distressed parents and considering instituting changes in procedures, it is also important to bear in mind that what distresses one parent may be quite acceptable to others. Unless it is a matter of clinical safety or organisational failure, managers should think and consult carefully before imposing a wholesale change of practice on the basis of a single complaint, especially if there is good evidence that other parents are satisfied with current procedures and care.

SUPPORT AND TRAINING FOR STAFF

Trusts, Health Boards and managers should recognise that support following pregnancy and childbearing loss is an integral part of effective care for women and their families. Good support can improve long-term well being and prevent the need for costly intervention later (RCOG 2006; Swanson 1999; Moulder 1998: 222; Leoni 1997).

In order to offer appropriate care, staff need self-awareness and an understanding of the complex and varied experience of grief. They need to be able to set aside their personal feelings and beliefs and to focus on the needs of the parents. Staff in all disciplines should have access to flexible and responsive support systems – both informal and formal – and to training in caring for grieving parents (DoH 2005b: 8) (see also Chapter 21).

Trusts, Health Boards and managers should appoint and train specialist bereavement support staff (see *Bereavement nurses and midwives* in Chapter 4). These staff should be well supported by their managers and by colleagues.

CHAPTER 4: COMMUNICATION

> OTHER RELEVANT CHAPTERS:
> 1: PROVIDING INCLUSIVE CARE
> 3: LOSS AND GRIEF
> 5: COMMUNICATION ACROSS LANGUAGE AND OTHER BARRIERS

"In almost all the complaints we deal with we see an element of poor communication. Often communication is not what is complained about but the evidence emerges during the course of an investigation." (Personal communication, Office of the Parliamentary and Health Service Ombudsman 2005)

Communication is probably the single most important component of effective care. It underpins and colours everything that staff can offer. Excellent clinical care can be overshadowed by poor communication. Failures of communication are a significant cause of dissatisfaction and a common factor underlying many of the complaints about health care (Cockburn and Walters 1999) (see also *Anger, blame and litigation* in Chapter 3). Parents who are shocked, stressed and frightened are likely to be particularly sensitive to the way that staff communicate with them.

> *Everyone we came in contact with that night, the nurse, the registrar, the consultants, they were so fantastic. They took time to talk to me. And they really showed how upset they were as well.* Mother

The main aims of communication when dealing with childbearing losses are to:

- Discuss the current situation with the parents, so that they feel fully informed;
- Answer their questions and find out about their views and wishes;
- Explain available options and support them in making decisions; and
- Offer support.

Good communication builds trust, and parents need to feel able to trust the staff who are caring for them (Coulter et al 1999). Parents who have confidence in the staff and in their judgement and skills are also more likely to feel confident about their own ability to cope (McCourt and Pearce 2000).

Good communication includes:

- Choosing an appropriate place to talk;
- Allocating sufficient time;
- Introducing oneself, giving one's name and role;
- Including partners or others in the discussion if the woman wants them to be present;
- Giving clear, honest and succinct information;

- Using accessible and appropriate language and avoiding euphemisms;
- Listening attentively;
- Demonstrating sympathetic understanding of the impact of what is being said;
- Being aware of the messages that are conveyed by body language;
- Gauging how much information the parents can assimilate at any one time;
- Responding flexibly and sensitively to their specific needs;
- Remaining calm and supportive when they express strong emotions;
- Providing written information or information in other formats as a back-up to what has been discussed.

All staff who work with bereaved parents should receive training in the relevant communication skills (see *Staff training* in Chapter 21).

PLACE AND TIME

Discussions should, whenever possible, take place in a private place where they will not be overheard, overseen or interrupted. Women should not be expected to discuss their situation when they are partially clothed or when lying on an examination couch. Many units now have a quiet room for discussions, furnished like a sitting room and supplied with tissues and facilities for making tea and coffee.

It is essential that staff try to set aside uninterrupted time, away from phones, bleeps and the many distractions that occur in health care settings. Parents should be assured that the discussion can go on for as long as they need. However, it may be helpful to set a maximum time of an hour with the assurance that the parents can come back for further discussion if they want. After an hour, most people are exhausted, and discussion tends to become repetitive. If staff have only a short time to talk, they should tell parents at the beginning and arrange a specific time to talk further.

NON-VERBAL COMMUNICATION

Non-verbal cues such as posture, gestures, facial expression and tone of voice send powerful messages. People tend to discount a speaker's words if his or her body language "says" something different (Guirdham 1990: 117–22). Staff need to be aware of the non-verbal messages they may be sending, and also respond to parents' non-verbal cues.

Non-verbal signals differ in different cultures, and it can be difficult to interpret them correctly. Gestures and facial expressions can be misunderstood, especially when people are anxious and distressed. For example, in some cultures: smiling indicates shock, anger, embarrassment or grief; people use different non-verbal signals to show that they are listening and agreeing or disagreeing: shaking the head means yes and nodding means no.

When caring for parents of a culture different from their own, staff should be aware that their often unconscious assumptions, based on non-verbal cues, may be wrong. It may be helpful to ask other members of the same community or an interpreter how they would understand the person's behaviour (Henley and Schott 1999: 261–264).

Touch

The extent to which physical contact is permitted, between whom, and in what circumstances, varies between different cultures. In some cultures, touch is seen as friendly and positive, and it is appreciated if a familiar member of staff touches or hugs a distressed father or mother. In other cultures, touching or hugging is seen as intrusive and impolite. In some cultures, it is acceptable for members of the same sex to touch each other in public; in others it is acceptable for members of the opposite sex. In some cultures, any physical contact between men and women who are not married to each other is forbidden.

Within cultures, individual preferences about touch also vary a great deal. Some people are comfortable with physical contact, others find it unpleasant. It is important for staff to be aware of their own preferences and assumptions in relation to touch, and to try to assess whether touch is acceptable and appropriate with individual parents.

Eye contact

In some cultures, looking people in the eye is believed to indicate honesty and straightforwardness; in others it is challenging and disrespectful. Most people in Arab cultures share a great deal of eye contact and may regard lack of eye contact as rude (Argyle 1975). In British-English culture[1], a certain amount of eye contact is required, but too much makes many people uncomfortable. Most British-English people make eye contact at the beginning and then let their gaze drift to the side periodically to avoid "staring the other person out". In many other cultures, including that of the Indian subcontinent, direct eye contact is generally regarded as aggressive and offensive. Some African Caribbean men may also avoid direct eye contact, and this may be misinterpreted as rudeness or arrogance. In some cultures eye contact between men and women is seen as flirtatious or threatening. Men of these communities who do not make eye contact with women are not usually being rude or evasive, but respectful. Some very orthodox Jewish men will not look directly at women outside their immediate family.

CHOOSING WORDS

Language should be tailored to the parents' existing level of knowledge. Staff should also try not to add inadvertently to parents' distress by using words that, although clinically correct, can be misconstrued by parents. For example, under British law, a baby born dead before 24 weeks gestation has no legal status: staff have traditionally used the term "miscarriage" or "abortion" for all losses up to this date. However, to most parents a miscarriage implies a much earlier loss and does not acknowledge the magnitude and sadness of losing a baby in the second trimester. Using "miscarriage" for these losses hurts. Medical jargon should be avoided unless both parents are familiar with it.

- The RCOG (2006) suggests that, when talking to parents, staff should use "miscarriage" for the medical term "spontaneous abortion"; "incomplete miscarriage" for "incomplete abortion"; and "delayed miscarriage", "silent miscarriage" or early fetal demise instead of "missed abortion", "missed miscarriage" and "anembryonic pregnancy". Terms such as "pregnancy failure", "abnormal pregnancy", "blighted ovum" and "incompetent cervix" should normally be avoided, and "miscarriage with infection" should be used instead of "septic abortion";

---

1   The term British-English is used here to describe the predominant communication style in the UK. Although there are differences between communication styles in the different countries and regions of the UK, the differences between British-English and the traditional communications styles of minority groups in the UK are more significant.

- Most parents after 14 to 16 weeks prefer staff to use the word "stillbirth", because it indicates that they understand the meaning of the loss (Hutchon 1998);

- When caring for parents experiencing a spontaneous miscarriage at any gestation, staff should listen carefully to the words that the woman and her partner use and use these words in discussions and explanations. For example, although it may be clinically correct to talk about the products of conception, the embryo or the fetus, most women talk about their baby from the beginning of the pregnancy and can be upset and hurt by clinical terms;

- The choice of words to use with women who are having a termination is more problematic. As always, it is important to listen to and use the words that the woman uses herself. In general, parents who are terminating a pregnancy for fetal abnormality are likely to welcome the acknowledgement that they are losing a baby and would probably prefer staff to refer to their baby. In contrast, many women who are having a termination for reasons other than fetal abnormality may prefer to distance themselves from what is happening. They may want the event to remain unacknowledged and undefined (Moulder 1998: 84). With them it may be more appropriate to use words such as "the pregnancy" and "the contents of the womb".

Staff also need to think about the possible impact on parents of the words and phrases they use when talking to each other. A sentence that seems inoffensive and practical when said to a colleague may be devastating to grieving parents.

Our baby was born at 24 weeks and died a few hours later. We each spent some time with her and eventually, exhausted, drifted into sleep in the early hours. At 3am we were woken by a midwife who said, "Have you finished with your baby? If so I'll put her back in the fridge." I was shocked at what had been said so I quickly had to put it to the back of my mind as I did not want to contemplate our baby "in a fridge", it was too heartbreaking to dwell on. I did wonder if it would have been better to just take care of her and tell me when I woke that I could ask to see her again at any time. Mother

GIVING INFORMATION
At every stage, parents should be given as much information as they want about:

- What has happened, is happening and is likely to happen;

- Practical matters, procedures and arrangements; and

- The choices that are open to them.

Diagnoses, decisions, and procedures should all be explained and discussed, and uncertainties acknowledged. Parents' questions should be welcomed, and answered directly and honestly. Staff should also try to be sensitive to questions that parents may want to ask but find difficult to express, and should encourage them to say what is on their minds.

They never did anything without telling us what they were doing. Mother

People have different approaches to making decisions. For example, some like to have a great deal of detail, some are satisfied with a summary, and a few may want very little (Marteau et al 2001; Niven 1992: 62). Everybody should be given the basic facts, but the depth and detail should be tailored to individual wishes. It is also important to bear in mind that parents whose first language is not English may be reluctant to ask for information in case they are seen as difficult or as questioning the authority of staff (Ahmed at al 2005). This does not mean that they do not want the same information as other parents.

If possible, parents should receive information from a relatively small number of staff who are familiar with their situation and who know what they have already been told. It is extremely distressing for anxious parents to receive inconsistent or contradictory information. If parents have to see many different staff, perhaps in different locations, it is particularly important to ensure excellent communication between staff.

Parents may need to be warned of the pitfalls of searching the internet for information and of believing all that is written there. It can be helpful to guide them to reliable sites such as those provided by some teaching hospitals, professional medical bodies and the relevant voluntary support charities.

LISTENING

"The patient teaches, the care-giver learns." (Source unknown)

Communication should be a two-way process: *listening* with sensitivity and with complete respect is as important as *saying* things well.

Many parents who have lost a baby at any gestation want and need to talk about what has happened, often several times. Simply listening, however difficult, can be extremely helpful (see also *Support and listening* in Chapter 13).

Listening well involves:

- Looking attentive, keeping one's eyes on the speaker;
- Not interrupting or moving on to a new issue until the speaker has said all that they want to;
- Taking the speaker's concerns seriously;
- Asking clarifying questions if necessary, being careful not to sound challenging;
- If appropriate, reflecting back to the speaker a summary of what has been said, so that the speaker can either confirm or clarify it.

You need somebody to just sit with you and talk you through all these different feelings that you've got. One midwife was very good: she'd come in and sit with us and talk for a little while and then she'd go off again. Mother

Practical concerns In addition to their physical and emotional needs, parents may have urgent practical concerns which should also be taken seriously. These could include, for example, the care of other children; taking time off work for a large number of different appointments, with consequent loss of income; and paying for the travel involved in frequent visits to hospital. It is important to ask about these and, where possible, to try to arrange appointments at times that minimise inconvenience and travel and other costs (Statham et al 2001: 182). Parents, especially those who are living in poverty, may need information about the benefits they are entitled to (see *Entitlement to time off work and benefits* in Chapter 13 and *Child benefit and other benefits* in Chapter 14). Information about benefits is also available on the Sands website (see Appendix 2).

BREAKING BAD NEWS

Breaking bad news is extremely difficult and stressful. Although breaking bad news well cannot reduce the pain that parents feel, doing it badly is likely to increase both their immediate and their long-term distress. Statham et al (2001: 54 and 263) found that, even when parents had been devastated by receiving bad news during pregnancy, if they felt that it had been given with warmth and affection and that they had been treated with respect and sensitivity, most had positive memories and were grateful to the staff responsible. In contrast, parents had only bad memories if the information was given badly, or if the person giving it seemed not to understand the significance of what he or she was saying, was excessively blunt, or was not supportive. In one study, women who were very dissatisfied with the way they were told that their unborn baby had an abnormality had lower emotional wellbeing than other women a year after the event (Statham et al 2001: 144).

Parents should be told as soon as something worrying is suspected, even if it is not yet confirmed or certain. They often sense from the reactions of staff that something might be wrong, and they have a right to be told about any concerns when they arise, even if these later turn out to be groundless. If parents feel that staff are not being open and honest with them, their trust is reduced and their anxiety increased.

In general, parents appreciate an indication that the member of staff understands the impact of what they are saying. Phrases such as "I am afraid it is bad news..."; "I am sorry to say that the results are not what we expected..."; or "I am afraid this is not the news you wanted…" may be helpful. Staff should:

- Ensure that parents have sufficient time to take in what they have been told, to formulate their questions, and to express their concerns;

- Balance honesty and realism with sensitivity and support;

- Say when things are not certain and acknowledge the difficulty for parents of tolerating this;

- Express sympathy and sadness.

If the member of staff who is with the parents at the time cannot give them accurate or sufficient information, he or she should say so and should arrange for them to see someone else as soon as possible. Parents should not be given information that they may later discover is incorrect (Statham et al 2001: 266).

Except in an emergency, a woman who is alone should be asked if she would like to call her partner or a relative or friend to support her, and whether she would like to wait until they arrive before the problem is explained in detail. See also *Giving results over the phone* in Chapter 7.

People who are shocked and upset often find it hard to take in and remember what they are being told. They may only hear the first one or two things that are said and then think about the impact of these, ignoring anything else that is said. Repeated discussions may be necessary, particularly if there is a lot of information to convey. One way of ensuring that parents can recall everything that was said is to tape the discussion and give them the cassette to play later.

If there is a lot to discuss, staff should begin by dealing with the immediate issues and be prepared to leave less pressing ones until later, depending on how the parents react and how much they want to know immediately. It is important to watch for signs of distress and exhaustion and to suggest that the parents might like to take a break and continue the discussion later or on another day. It may sometimes be helpful to repeat information or phrase it in different ways to help the parents absorb it. Most parents also appreciate a written note of the key points to take away with them. They should also be given contact details for sources of support both during and out of office hours.

Parents need to know what will happen next and when it will happen (Buckman 1992: 79). Appointments for further information, investigations or procedures should be made with the minimum delay, and staff should acknowledge the difficulty and stress of even a short wait. The staff to whom the parents are referred should be informed, so that they know why the parents have come and can greet them accordingly (Statham et al 2001: 178).

If a woman is going home alone after receiving worrying or bad news, staff should suggest that she might like to call somebody to accompany her. This is especially important if she came by car, as driving when shocked and upset can be dangerous.

Dealing with parents' reactions

For staff, one of the hardest aspects of breaking bad news to parents is not knowing how they will react and having to deal with their responses. These may include, for example, stunned silence, disbelief, distress, anger, blame, guilt or tears. Distress and grief are very hard to witness, especially for people who have been trained to solve problems, find solutions and ease pain.

There is a tendency to react to tears as one does to a haemorrhage. However, crying is a release, and parents value the support of staff who can cope with their tears without embarrassment (Fallowfield 1993). Many people react to bad news and shock with anger, and look for someone to blame: this should not be taken personally (Buckman 1996:174–175). Remaining calm and supportive and allowing parents simply to express their pain and to cry can be very helpful (see also *Anger, blame and litigation* in Chapter 3).

FACILITATING INFORMED CHOICE

"*...an informed choice or decision has two core characteristics; first, it is based on relevant, good quality information, and second, the resulting choice reflects the decision-maker's values.*" (Marteau et al 2001)

Parents experiencing or facing perinatal loss may have to make a number of difficult decisions, none of which they will have expected or wanted to make. For example, depending on the situation, they may need to decide:

- who should be present during a scan for an abnormality or problem
- whether to have further tests
- whether to terminate the pregnancy
- how to dispose of the products of conception
- whether to consent to feticide
- whether to see and hold the baby

- whether to have time alone with the baby
- whether to take handprints and footprints
- whether to photograph the baby
- whether to involve other family members, and what to tell them
- whether to involve a religious leader
- whether to cut a lock of the baby's hair
- whether to withdraw life support from the baby
- when to leave the hospital
- whether to name the baby
- whether to take the baby home
- whether to have a post mortem examination
- whether to have a funeral or other ceremony

When people have to make decisions in unfamiliar and stressful situations, it is helpful to:

- Provide information that is accurate and objective, including the potential advantages, disadvantages and side effects;

- Be sensitive and gentle;

- Whenever possible, offer choices well in advance of the event. Except in emergencies, women should not be expected to make decisions in a hurry nor, for example, when they are still drowsy from the effects of drugs or a general anaesthetic;

- Deal with one decision at a time. If parents have to take several decisions, it may be helpful to break down each one into steps – whom to involve, what happens first, how much time there will be (Fonda Allen 1995);

- Use clear, unambiguous language. Chitty et al (1996) cite the case of a couple whose unborn baby had a lethal abnormality and who came to the labour ward not realising that the "induction" they had agreed to was in reality a termination;

- Sympathetically acknowledge the difficulties and pressures of the parents' situation;

- Wait quietly while they formulate their ideas, then listen with complete respect to what they have to say and, wherever possible, arrange for what they want, unless there are safety or legal considerations.

Parents need impartial and objective information in order to make informed choices that are consistent with their own values, their views of their obligations as parents, and their knowledge of their own situation and capabilities (Rempel et al 2004). Staff need to be aware of their own values and beliefs, and what they would decide, so that they can be sure that these are not influencing the information they give.

The degree to which parents want decision-making to be shared or guided will vary. Some parents prefer to make decisions completely independently once they have the necessary information. Others prefer to work out what they want to do with input and help from staff; some may want staff whom they trust to suggest what they should do, or expect a paternal doctor–patient relationship (Williams et al 2002; McHaffie 2001: 141–146). Some parents may want to ask advice from, or turn decision-making over to, older family members, the men in the family or religious advisers. In this case it is important that staff clarify with the parents as soon as possible what the roles of any additional participants should be (Nuffield 2006: 2.48).

If parents turn to staff for advice and guidance, it can be tempting to "help" them by steering them towards the option that the member of staff favours, or that is usual practice in the unit. However, this may not be the right decision for the parents in the long term and may cause lasting regret and guilt. It reduces their autonomy and may damage their confidence and feelings of self-worth (Edwards NP 2004: 8 and 20). At such a traumatic time it can also be particularly difficult for parents to refuse what they may perceive as instructions or recommendations from staff (Lundqvist et al 2002).

Parents need to feel guided, assisted and listened to, but not directed or controlled, and certainly not abandoned. One way to help is tentatively to offer examples of things that other parents have done. For example, "There are several options, some parents choose … Others decide …". Such examples may help parents to clarify what they do not want as well as what they do want. Unless a decision is needed urgently, parents should be given time to take in the information and to think through what they want to do without feeling any pressure (Statham et al 2001: 51). Some parents may want to be left alone for a while to talk privately. Some may want to go home to think and to come back for another appointment within the next few days. Some may change their minds several times before they finally decide what to do.

Information and consent

Whenever there is a decision to be made, the mother (before the birth) and parents (after the birth) should be supported and encouraged to think about what would be the best thing to do. They are the only people who can say what they want and they will have to live with the consequences.

Consent to interventions during pregnancy and labour must be given by the mother. Unless her mental capacity is impaired, her decisions override those of the staff and the baby's father (Nuffield 2006: 9.7). Once a baby is born, regardless of the gestation, parents and staff owe a duty of care to the baby. The mother no longer has exclusive responsibility for decision making, though the parents' views should be taken into account (Nuffield 2006 9:12, 9.18 and 9.28).

Before seeking a woman's formal consent for a test, treatment, intervention or operation, it is important to ensure that she fully understands the purpose of the intervention, what it will involve, the risks and benefits, possible consequences, and options and possible consequences if consent is withheld. If she is not offered as much information as she reasonably needs to make her decision, and in a form that she can understand, her consent may not be valid (DoH 2001a).

Consent forms should be available in all the main languages spoken in the area, and staff should check whether or not the woman can read and understand the form (DoH 2003b: 10). If necessary, an interpreter should be provided and/or information should be made available by other means such as video or audiotape (see *Written information and information in other formats* later).

Some women who normally make decisions jointly, or whose husbands or older male or female relatives normally make such decisions, may want their approval and support before deciding whether to have a test, treatment, intervention or operation. In this case, with the woman's consent, information about the purpose of what is proposed, what it will involve, risks and benefits, possible consequences and any alternatives should be made available to the other people involved. However, it is important always to ensure that the woman gives or refuses consent in her own right. It is also important not to assume on the basis of a woman's ethnicity that she does not want to make an independent decision (Schott and Henley 1996: 157).

Teamwork and keeping records

Implementing informed choice requires all the staff involved to work in a co-ordinated way and to communicate well. It is essential that parents do not receive conflicting information, and that once a decision is made it is recorded and is normally not raised again unless the parents themselves wish to raise it (see also *Checklists* in Chapter 12). If parents are repeatedly asked about a decision they have already made, they may feel that staff are questioning their decision and may lose confidence. Careful written records should be kept of all decisions and discussions, and all staff should check the notes regularly to ensure that they know what decisions the parents have made.

SUPPORT

Many bereaved parents simply want to talk with someone supportive. They may find it helpful to talk with someone they already know; for example, a nurse or midwife, their GP or a hospital doctor, a health visitor, chaplain or social worker. These may all be able to listen and help, and should have training to enable them to do so, though they are unlikely to be trained professional counsellors. Some parents also get valuable support and information from national charities with local groups, such as Sands, the Miscarriage Association and ARC (Antenatal Results and Choices).

Counselling

A smaller number of women, their partners and possibly other family members may want, at some stage, to see a professional counsellor. Parents themselves may be aware that they are experiencing difficulties and may ask for this kind of help. Alternatively, staff who are caring for parents may think that counselling could be helpful and may suggest it to them.

A counsellor has a relationship with parents that is different and preferably separate from parents' relationships with other members of staff. He or she can help parents to express, and gain some understanding of how they feel and, perhaps, find their own ways to manage their situation. Parents may see a counsellor for one session or for a number of sessions over a period of time. Sometimes it is helpful for a woman to see a counsellor alone; sometimes it is helpful for a couple to see a counsellor together.

Some hospitals have a counsellor who specialises in perinatal or childbearing losses. However, some parents find it too painful to return to the hospital where they lost their baby and they should be able to access professional counselling services in a more neutral environment. Some general practices employ a counsellor who will take referrals from the primary health care team. Counselling may also be available through a local bereavement service. All counsellors who support parents after a childbearing loss need to be knowledgeable about the specific issues that such losses involve.

After a termination for fetal abnormality and, when appropriate, after other losses, parents should also be offered a referral for genetic counselling.

BEREAVEMENT NURSES AND MIDWIVES

In some Trusts and Health Boards, one or more nurses and/or midwives are specially designated and trained to care for and support bereaved parents. They are responsible for offering emotional support and practical guidance, for co-ordinating care and communication, and for ensuring that complex procedures and paperwork are meticulously completed.

For parents, a specialist bereavement nurse or midwife is someone consistent and experienced to whom they can relate, who understands what needs to be done, and who can explain the options to them. They have a known person to contact whenever they have questions or requests, or simply want to talk.

A bereavement nurse or midwife should also be responsible for training, updating and supporting other members of staff who care for bereaved parents. This avoids the potential disadvantage of other people in the team or unit feeling inexperienced or de-skilled. In addition, the bereavement nurse or midwife should be involved in helping to ensure high standards of bereavement care and in establishing policies that ensure excellent co-ordination and communication between departments and with primary care staff.

It is generally best to have more than one specialist bereavement nurse or midwife:

- No single member of staff can suit all parents, and it is important that parents are cared for by someone with whom they feel comfortable;

- A single member of staff who cares for all bereaved parents is likely sometimes to feel overloaded, overwhelmed and isolated;

- Parents are still provided for if one member of the specialist bereavement team is sick or away.

- Two or more specialist bereavement nurses or midwives can offer each other support and time for reflection.

GOOD COMMUNICATION BETWEEN STAFF

Parents who experience a childbearing loss are uniquely sensitive to gaps in care and to thoughtless treatment that adds to their distress.

> *The anaesthetist who came to put in my epidural knew my baby had died. But he didn't say anything about it at all. Just joked and chatted as though nothing bad had happened.* Mother

If staff do not know about the parents' situation they cannot respond appropriately. It is therefore essential that all the staff whom parents encounter are well informed about their situation.

Because most events in maternity care are problem-free and have a happy outcome, staff generally approach expectant and new parents assuming that all is well. Parents who are experiencing a childbearing loss find it difficult and painful to have to explain their situation to a series of members of staff, or at a reception desk in front of a queue of expectant parents. If anxious or distressed parents are referred to another department, the staff there should normally be warned, so that they can intercept and greet them when they arrive. Receptionists and ward clerks should also be informed: they are often the first people whom parents meet. There should be a system for informing antenatal education staff, so that they do not send the parents an invitation to classes.

Communication and the duty of confidentiality

Although most people accept that information about them will be shared between different members of the health care team, and will be passed on to other health professionals who are, or will be, involved in their care, they nevertheless have a right to object and therefore should always be informed (GMC 2004; NMC 2004:8; DoH 2003a: 12). Even if information does not appear to staff to be sensitive, it may be very sensitive to an individual parent in their particular circumstances (DoH 2003a: 25). Staff have a duty of confidentiality to all women, including young women under the age of 16 (DoH 2004a).

A formal discussion or written consent to pass on information is not usually necessary. For example, it is enough for a member of staff to tell women that they will phone ahead to the relevant department or ward so that they are expected, or that it is customary to inform the GP, the community midwives and the health visitors so that they can offer appropriate care and support. This gives each woman an opportunity to say if she does not want this to happen.

In some situations, however, it may be especially important to check before passing on information to primary care staff. For example:

- Although most women expect their GP to be kept informed, they may not expect community midwives or health visitors to be informed, especially if they have not yet met them;

- Women who choose to terminate a pregnancy for reasons other than fetal abnormality may not want their GP to be informed at all. Some units inform the GP only if he or she referred the woman to them;

- Women who live in a conservative religious community and whose GP shares their faith may not want their decision to terminate a pregnancy, for any reason, to be passed on.

If women do not want information about them to be passed on to their GP or to other staff, this must be respected. This is no different from a woman exercising her right to refuse treatment (DoH 2003a: 32). If the refusal will negatively affect her care or reduce the options open to her, this must be clearly explained. It may be possible to find out why she does not want the information passed on and to allay her concerns or work out a compromise. It is important to explain that she can change her mind if she wants, and to record the discussion and final decision in the notes (DoH 2003a: 23–24).

Communication between hospitals

When a woman or a sick baby is transferred from one unit to another, medical records, requests for care and details of investigations, test results and treatment should be passed on straight away. All units should have procedures in place to ensure that the transfer of information is prompt and efficient, and a designated member of staff should be responsible for ensuring that this happens in each case.

All medical records should accompany a baby who is being transferred. As a minimum standard, a woman who is being referred should be given a written summary to hand to the staff, who should be expecting her. Parents should also be told which unit to contact if problems arise, and should be given written information about how to get in touch with the relevant department.

Communication between hospital and community staff

Community staff who do not know about a problem in pregnancy or the loss of a baby cannot offer the help and support that most parents want. Statham et al (2003), in a study of communication of prenatal diagnosis results to primary care staff, found that communication was patchy and unsystematic. Many of those community staff who did receive information did not know what action they should then take. In the case of rare abnormalities, some community staff knew too little about the abnormality to be able to offer informed support. Women were also visited by or encountered community staff who had not been informed about their loss, and who inadvertently said things that were inappropriate or deeply painful.

Provided the woman has been asked and does not object (see above), relevant community professionals should be promptly informed of the loss of a pregnancy (including early loss) or the death of a baby. A designated member of the hospital staff should be responsible for this. A checklist of people to inform, attached to the mother's notes, is a good way to ensure that community professionals have the information they need. The list should include the mother's GP and possibly her community midwife and health visitor. They should be informed:

- By telephone, before discharge;
- As soon as possible afterwards by letter, giving a full history. Post mortem investigation results (if applicable) should be sent later.

Information should not be faxed or emailed unless confidentiality can be guaranteed.

Community staff should know whom they can contact at the hospital in order to obtain information. Women should know if this contact is being made.

Hospital Trusts, Health Boards and managers should agree policies with Primary Care Trusts to ensure that, unless a woman objects, her GP and other relevant community staff are informed promptly about a loss during pregnancy, birth or afterwards, or about a diagnosis of fetal abnormality, and about the treatment and care she has received.

For most parents it is important that they are *offered* care and emotional support by community staff, rather than having to ask for it (Statham et al 2001: 156). The appropriate primary care staff should therefore take the initiative to make contact. They should have training on offering support to bereaved parents (see also *Staff training* in Chapter 21).

WRITTEN INFORMATION AND INFORMATION IN OTHER FORMATS

Verbal explanations and information are essential for effective care. However, people's ability to listen and remember what they are told is limited, especially when they are frightened, in pain, or grieving. Written information should not be used instead of face-to-face discussion, but it can be an extremely useful resource which staff can go through with parents, if this is helpful, and which parents can look at in their own time and refer to when they need it.

If people have difficulty reading or understanding written material, it may be helpful to offer to go through it with them. Information should also be available in other formats, such as large print, Braille, DVDs, cassettes, CDs, pictures etc. (For material in different languages, see overleaf).

Many Primary Care Trusts, Hospital Trusts and Health Boards produce their own leaflets and other material giving both general information and also specific information about different conditions, local services and arrangements. Some use material produced by voluntary support groups. All material should be checked on a regular basis to ensure that the information is consistent, up to date, relevant and easy to read. Material should also be available in the main languages spoken locally and in formats suitable for parents with a sensory impairment (see *Parents with a sensory impairment* in Chapter 5).

Producing written information and information in other formats

Successful leaflets and other materials require considerable thought and planning. Materials should be developed in consultation with the relevant experts, and with a range of people who have used the services and with parent representatives from different communities. People should be asked what they would want to know before a draft is produced, rather than simply presented with a draft to review. In one study of patients' views of written materials dealing with particular health problems, patients appreciated materials that gave them a sense of empowerment, reassured them that they were not alone in experiencing symptoms, gave them ideas for self-help, and suggested questions that they could ask (Coulter et al 1999).

The content should be objective, factual and evidence based. Common concerns and misconceptions should be addressed. Where relevant, risks and benefits should be described honestly, and uncertainties should be acknowledged frankly. If research evidence is used as the basis of recommendations, the sources should be given. This is especially important if the material is being used to enable people to make choices or to give informed consent. Sources of further information should also be given for parents who want to know more (Coulter et al 1999).

The language should be in plain English, using everyday language and short sentences. They should also be produced in the main languages spoken locally. When producing translated leaflets and other materials, the content should be developed with members of the relevant communities: simple translation from an English version is unlikely to be successful, especially in the difficult area of childbearing loss. Additional information may be necessary, and changes may be needed to accommodate cultural differences.

The tone should convey respect for readers and also encourage autonomy and participation in decision making. It is important not to sound patronising or bossy. For example, to avoid telling parents how they will feel, it may be helpful to use a format such as "Some parents feel X and others feel Y". Question and answer formats are also effective, using questions that parents themselves might ask.

The layout should be clear and uncluttered. The title should reflect the contents. Each topic should begin with a clear heading. Important information should be highlighted or boxed.

Illustrations can be used if they will increase understanding, but it is important to check with parent representatives that these are acceptable and helpful. Pink and blue should be avoided, and careful thought given to any design features and logos, other than the standard logo of the Trust, Health Board or hospital. People's tastes vary enormously, and what might seem comforting and appealing to some, might be off-putting for others. In order to be inclusive, religious symbols should be avoided.

All materials should be piloted with, and evaluated by, parents and/or their representatives, to ensure that the content is adequate and the language is clear before the materials become a standard part of care.

All leaflets and other materials should be dated (if possible with the date on which they will be reviewed and updated), and should include the name and contact details of the Trust, clinic or department that issued them. They should be reproduced in such a way that every copy looks clean and fresh. Poor quality photocopies are unacceptable.

CHAPTER 5: COMMUNICATION ACROSS LANGUAGE AND OTHER BARRIERS

OTHER RELEVANT CHAPTERS:
1: PROVIDING INCLUSIVE CARE
3: LOSS AND GRIEF
4: COMMUNICATION

Most of this chapter deals with caring for people whose first language is not English. The final section covers caring for parents with a sensory impairment. Although the approaches that help parents whose first language is not English and those parents who have a sensory impairment may be different, the problems that they experience in accessing and benefiting from care can be very similar.

PARENTS WHO SPEAK LITTLE OR NO ENGLISH

Studies confirm that people who speak little or no English are generally given less information, offered fewer choices, and feel powerless and extremely vulnerable. They are often unable to understand what is done to them and why. They cannot ask questions, voice worries or concerns, discuss important issues, make decisions or give properly informed or valid consent. Language barriers are usually far more significant obstacles to good-quality care than possible cultural differences (Roberts et al 2005; Sheldon 2005; Davies and Bath 2001).

Staff, too, are likely to become frustrated, stressed and exasperated if they cannot understand what a person is trying to tell them and are not sure that their message has got through. They often feel that they cannot give the care they want to give or use their skills properly. They are forced to compromise and lower their standards. If they know that they cannot communicate properly they may give up trying, and focus instead on carrying out essential practical tasks as fast as possible, often without explanation or discussion (Bulman and McCourt 2002). Trying to communicate across a language barrier takes a good deal more time and effort. Hard-pressed staff can find it difficult to conceal irritation and resentment. Language difficulties can also lead to negative judgements and stereotyping (Roberts et al 2005).

Even if people usually speak English well, distress and anxiety can drastically affect their ability to understand and express themselves. Staff caring for parents who do not speak fluent English should have easy access to trained and experienced interpreters. An interpreter can translate what is said and can also help explain to both staff and parents any cultural and other differences that may be hindering understanding.

THE PROVISION OF INTERPRETERS

Under Section 20 of the Race Relations Act 1976, it is illegal knowingly to provide an inferior quality of care to a particular racial minority group. The failure to provide interpreters for a minority group many of whose members speak little English could be construed as illegal. This is reinforced by Articles 10 and 14 of the Human Rights Act 1998 (Hewson 2004: 54).

Government codes of practice (for example, DoH 2003b: 10) and other official documents often stress the importance of having trained professional interpreters to interpret between parents and staff whenever important or difficult issues are discussed, or valid consent is required. However, provision is still inadequate, especially in areas with smaller minority communities and for languages that are less common. Staff often have to work through interpreters who are not properly trained or supported, or through family members or friends whose own English may be poor.

Providing interpreters for parents who speak little or no English is an essential part of safe and effective care. Although it may not always be possible always to have interpreters for all the languages spoken, Trusts, Health Boards and managers should provide the best and most comprehensive service possible:

- All Trusts and Health Boards should employ trained, professional interpreters to translate for the main groups in their area whose mother tongue is not English. For other minority language speakers, they should organise access to interpreters through outside agencies, or use telephone interpreting services if the discussion is fairly straightforward (see later). In some areas, bilingual linkworkers who can support, guide and act as advocates for women and their partners, as well as interpreting, are employed as part of the maternity care team;

- Interpreters should be available for the use of all staff, including primary care staff who work in clinics and who visit families at home;

- All staff should be trained in working with interpreters (see *Working with an interpreter* later);

- All staff should know how to contact interpreters for the different languages spoken locally. They should know how to book an interpreter in advance for a planned appointment, and how to contact one in an emergency. They should be encouraged to use interpreters whenever necessary, and especially for any discussion that is likely to be complicated, difficult or distressing. When an interpreter has been booked, clinic staff and receptionists should try to ensure that the woman is seen as soon as both she and the interpreter arrive, so that the interpreter's scarce time is not wasted;

- Wherever possible, leaflets and materials in other formats should be available in the parents' first language as a back-up (see *Written information and information in other formats* in Chapter 4.)

COMMUNICATING IF THERE IS NO INTERPRETER

Grief, anxiety, illness, exhaustion and shock all affect people's ability to communicate in their own language; the effects are even worse when trying to communicate in another language. Even parents whose English is normally good may be unable to understand what is said or to express themselves. All staff should have training in how to communicate across a language barrier when there is no interpreter.

Reducing stress

Reducing unnecessary stress is both important in itself and can help improve two-way communication. It can help if staff:

- Greet the person and introduce themselves;

- Ensure that they have parents' names right and are using and pronouncing them correctly;

- Allow more time and try to avoid showing that time is short. Signs of pressure or impatience increase anxiety and further impede communication;

- Use a reassuring tone of voice and sympathetic manner, so that parents know that the member of staff is trying to help even if they cannot understand what he or she says;

- Use non-verbal signals such as smiling, eye contact and touching, while bearing in mind cultural conventions (see also Non-verbal communication in Chapter 4);

- Convey support and respect by carrying out all interventions as gently and respect fully as possible;

- Encourage parents to ask when they have not understood, and be willing to explain things more than once if necessary;

- Watch for signs of weariness. All sides have to concentrate more when communicating across a language barrier and everyone gets tired more quickly. It is usually best to wind up the interview and fix another time to talk, or to take a break and continue the discussion later;

- Try to ensure continuity of carers. Familiarity with one or two members of health staff helps reduce parents' anxiety and reduces the number of times that they have to repeat the same information. Over time, parents and the staff caring for them can often work out ways of understanding each other better. Continuity of carers also helps all women, but perhaps particularly those who speak little or no English, to feel that they are the focus of care, have choices and control, and are better supported (McCourt and Pearce 2000);

- Keep accurate written records of what has been discussed and decisions that have been taken, so that different members of staff do not have to keep asking the same questions.

Modifying language to be more easily understood

In order to increase the amount that the parents understand, it is generally helpful to:

- Avoid speaking louder than usual. It is helpful, however, to speak clearly and perhaps more slowly, depending on the language ability of the parent;

- Be succinct and clear but try not to condense what has to be said. Denser language is more difficult to understand. It is helpful to break up what needs to be said into simple small components and use a short sentence for each one;

- Avoid using "pidgin" or broken English: it is not easier for people to understand and may give offence. Instead, make sure that the most important words in each sentence are clear;

- Listen for the words the parents use and understand, and try to use the same words. People who are learning a new language often understand everyday words and topics, but are unlikely to understand the words used to discuss subjects such as pregnancy, labour, birth and illness. It is particularly important to avoid hospital and clinical jargon and confusing euphemisms;

- Draw diagrams or point things out on a picture, where possible, rather than simply relying on spoken words. However, drawing an image of the human body might be unacceptable to some conservative Muslims. Staff should check first;

- When explaining something complicated, stop and plan what to say and in what order, dealing with one subject at a time, choosing words carefully, and pausing to check that the parents have understood, before moving on to a new subject. When giving instructions, it is helpful to give them in the order in which things need to be done.

Checking genuine understanding

Many people who have picked up English are good at social conversation and everyday topics and sound quite fluent. However, they may get completely lost when discussing unfamiliar topics, especially if they are anxious and upset. It is very important to take time to check understanding at each stage.

"A single mother with fairly good English was told that her baby girl was being transferred from the regional neonatal intensive care unit back to the special care unit at her local hospital. The staff thought the mother understood that the baby was being transferred because she was dying. But the mother thought it meant she was getting better. When the baby's condition deteriorated the mother was devastated and wanted her to go back to intensive care. The staff realised she had no idea that her baby was going to die."
(Personal communication, BLISS 2006)

Yes and No When checking understanding, it is helpful to try to avoid asking questions that can be answered with "Yes". "Yes", or its equivalent, is usually the first word that anyone learns in a new language, but it does not necessarily indicate understanding or agreement. There is always a strong temptation for people whose English is not very good to say "Yes", especially when talking to busy staff, to avoid causing exasperation and bad feeling. But it is dangerous to assume that "Yes" in these circumstances means yes.

Instead, "Yes" often means something like:

"Yes, I'm listening and I'm trying to understand."

"Yes, I want to be helpful even though I don't understand."

"Yes, I am listening; I don't understand but I know you mean well."

"Yes, I'm listening; I don't understand but I don't think I ever will and if I say yes we might be able to end this conversation."

If possible, questions should be worded so that they really check understanding. For example, instead of, "Do you understand?" it may be better to ask parents to say what they have understood.

Many people feel that saying "No" directly, particularly to a person in authority, is rude. They may use other indirect but polite ways of refusing a request or answering a question negatively. These may include not responding to the request, changing the subject, asking for time to think, making a non-committal reply, or using a polite phrase that insiders understand as meaning "No" but is less offensive. Parents should be gently encouraged to ask whenever they do not fully understand something, but staff should recognise that this can be difficult.

Helping parents remember what has been discussed

If a person does not understand what is said to them, or is straining to understand it, they cannot remember it. It is almost always helpful to write down the key points clearly and in plain English. Even if the parents cannot read it themselves they can usually find someone who can. If communication is clearly not working it is essential to arrange for a further discussion using a trained interpreter.

INTERPRETERS

"No agency can provide a fair or effective service to people with whom it cannot communicate." (Shackman 1984: 4)

What an interpreter does

Interpreting is extremely complex and demanding. Although many people believe that an interpreter can, or should, simply relay words accurately backwards and forwards between two people, the reality of even simple "word-for-word" interpreting is very different. Few words mean exactly the same thing in both languages, especially if the languages belong to different "language families". Important words and ideas, colloquial expressions, and technical and medical terms often have no straightforward equivalent in the other language and may need a long explanation. Word order and the order in which ideas are sequenced in different languages differ.

In addition to translating words, an interpreter often needs to explain unfamiliar cultural concepts and assumptions, and local practices, in both directions, and to translate the implications behind what people say, as well as the literal meaning. In addition, she[1] must be aware of and, when necessary, try to redress the imbalance of power between parents and staff, deciding when it is necessary to act as an advocate for the parents or to request more information on their behalf, and when to play a neutral role. In some cases, she may have to challenge racism, stereotyping and discrimination by staff, although her own status within the health care system is often very low.

As well as being responsible for accurately translating complex information and choices in both directions, an interpreter working with parents who are going through childbearing loss usually bears the full brunt of their emotions. Distressed and confused parents often see an interpreter as a key source of comfort, information and advice, expecting her to act as a friend and as an advocate for them with health care staff, and to provide ongoing emotional support (Sheldon 2005). The interpreter is therefore the fulcrum in a complex and difficult triangular relationship (see Figure 1 overleaf).

---

1   The interpreter is referred to in these Guidelines as 'she'. Women should always have access to a female interpreter. In some cases it may be necessary to provide a male interpreter to interpret for a bereaved father.

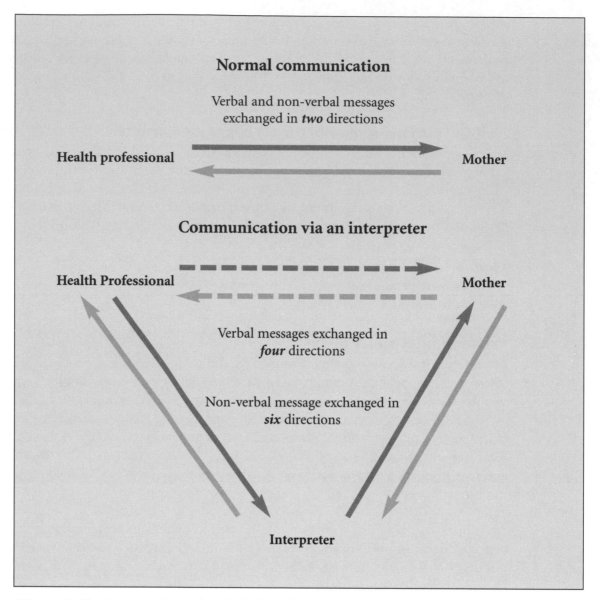

Normal communication

Verbal and non-verbal messages
exchanged in *two* directions

Health professional　　　　　　　　　　　　　　**Mother**

Communication via an interpreter

Health Professional　　　　　　　　　　　　　　**Mother**

Verbal messages exchanged in
four directions

Non-verbal message exchanged in
six directions

Interpreter

Figure 1: The interpreting triangle (adapted from Henley and Schott 1999)

Every member of staff looking after parents who do not speak fluent English should have access to a professional interpreter who:

- Is trained and experienced in health care interpreting and in interpreting for people who are bereaved;

- Is perfectly fluent in both English and the parents' mother tongue and can interpret professionally and accurately, without evident embarrassment or distress, while also supporting and listening to the parents;

- Understands clinical terminology and health care systems, and can explain these as necessary;

- Understands grief and grieving, the principles of giving support, how to break bad news, how to deal with strong emotions, and can translate these between cultures;

- Can work with other staff as part of a team to give the best possible care to parents;

- Can encourage parents to ask for the care, information and support they want and need;

- Is acceptable to the parents and can be trusted to maintain total confidentiality about the interview and everything that was said or happened during it (see *Confidentiality* below);

- Has access to good support for herself, because the emotional and practical demands of interpreting in these situations are extreme *(Support for interpreters below).*

Confidentiality

Confidentiality is essential in all health interpreting. If parents do not trust the person who is interpreting for them, they are unlikely to answer important questions fully or truthfully, or ask for what they really want. They must be certain that absolutely everything they say will be kept totally confidential. This is particularly important if they live in a small community where gossip travels fast. If there is a social stigma attached to a failed pregnancy, fetal abnormality or termination, or if parents choose to do something that goes against their family's or community's cultural or religious norms, total confidentiality is even more important.

Staff must therefore be able to assure parents with complete confidence that the interpreter will not mention the interview to anyone, will not reveal what was said during the interview to anyone else, and will not discuss the interview with the parents at a later date unless they themselves wish to discuss it.

Support for interpreters

"During the delivery you see dead babies delivered and then ten minutes later you are bleeped and you have to go to another call. There is no support at all and you have to keep your emotions inside of you until the end of the day." Interpreter (Sheldon 2005)

Interpreters need the same support and supervision as other staff who work closely with parents who experience a childbearing loss (see Chapter 21). However, many interpreters work in isolation, often on a sessional basis, and are completely unsupported. Some are untrained and very few receive continuing professional development. Because there is usually a shortage of interpreters, many work under extreme pressure with little or no time between consultations, and without breaks. They are rarely recognised or valued as part of a team, or included in support meetings for other staff (Sheldon 2005).

Like all staff caring for parents experiencing childbearing loss, interpreters should receive basic practical and emotional support from their managers and colleagues, regular opportunities to debrief and to discuss particularly difficult or complicated situations, and easy access to individual counselling if it is needed (Sheldon 2005).

WORKING WELL WITH AN INTERPRETER

For staff, working well with an interpreter involves a difficult balance between:

- Retaining overall responsibility for the discussion;

- Ensuring that the parents get the care they need and want, and can make fully informed choices; and

- Helping the interpreter to work effectively and to use her skills and knowledge to the full.

All this requires careful management. The good practice outlined below can help to make working with an interpreter go well. In addition, it is important that staff continue to follow the basic principles of good communication set out in Chapter 4.

Wherever possible, the family should have the same interpreter in all their contacts with hospital and community staff, at least at the time of the loss, during the period immediately afterwards, and during discussions about post mortem results, and genetic counselling.

Beforehand

Before working with an interpreter, especially for the first time, the doctor, nurse or midwife should discuss and agree with her how to manage the session. This includes:

- Explaining the purpose of the session;

- Making it clear that the interpreter is valued as a colleague and as a key contributor to the successful outcome of the discussion. She should be encouraged to explain cultural or other issues that arise on either side, and to intervene if people talk too fast or don't pause often enough. If she needs to have a longer conversation with one side, she should summarise what she is saying to the other;

- Checking whether she has constraints on her time, for example an appointment with another family elsewhere in the hospital;

- Checking with her how to pronounce and use the parents' names correctly;

- Discussing how the interpreter and the other staff present should respond if the parents become obviously upset. It is very difficult and even counter-productive for an interpreter to ignore parents' distress and continue translating mechanically.

At the beginning of the interview

It may be necessary, especially if this is the first session, to:

- Check that the interpreter really understands and speaks the parents' language and (if appropriate) dialect. For example, not all the languages of the Indian subcontinent that are spoken in Britain are mutually comprehensible. People who speak one Chinese dialect do not necessarily speak another;

- Explain to the parents the roles of the member of staff and the interpreter: make it clear that the interpreter will translate everything that is said in both directions and that she will not give advice other than that given by the member of staff (Permalloo 2006);

- Check whether the parents trust and feel able to talk openly to the interpreter. Ask her to explain the code of confidentiality to the parents, and assure them she will not repeat to anyone else anything that is discussed, or raise the subject with them again unless they wish her to;

- Allow time for the parents and the interpreter to get to know each other, possibly on their own. Many people find it discourteous and uncomfortable to go straight into the content of a discussion with a stranger, especially at a time of anxiety and distress. The parents may need to talk to the interpreter and feel comfortable with her before they can reveal personal information to her. When working with a larger family group, the interpreter may need to take time to establish credibility with each generation (Ahmed et al 1982).

During the conversation

- The member of the health care staff is still responsible for the care and wellbeing of the parents and should try to behave as normally as possible – for example, greeting the parents, facing them during the discussion, and speaking directly to them rather than to the interpreter. It is important to try not to become physically or emotionally distanced from the parents because the discussion is through an interpreter;

- The member of staff should try to use all their normal communication skills, listening, observing, responding, explaining and checking, speaking simple jargon-free English that is easier for the interpreter to translate, and breaking up what is said into translatable chunks;

- Everyone always understands more of a foreign language than they can speak. The simpler and clearer the English, the more likely the parents are to understand some of what is said. If the parents' English is fairly good, it may be possible to agree to converse in English, asking the interpreter just to listen for and help with any misunderstandings;

- It is necessary to allow at least twice as long for the discussion. Every word has to go via the interpreter in both directions (see Figure 1 earlier). Discussions with parents in this situation are bound to include unfamiliar words, procedures or ideas, and the interpreter may have to do a lot of explaining;

- Sometimes the interpreter may need to have a conversation with the parents alone, or with the member of staff, to make sure that they have completely understood each other or to clarify a point of translation. Provided the interpreter explains what is going on to each side, it is important to let this happen;

- At the end of the interview, it is a good idea to encourage the interpreter to talk generally to the parents to find out if they have any other worries or problems, and to translate these for the member of staff.

Afterwards

It can be very useful to talk to the interpreter about how the discussion went, and to ask for any insights or information she was unable to mention at the time. Because the interpreter bears the direct impact of the parents' emotions, and may herself be upset by the discussion, it may also be important to spend some time with her and to offer her support.

HOSPITAL LISTS OF BILINGUAL STAFF

Many hospitals have a list of bilingual staff members who can be called upon to translate in those languages where there is no interpreter. It is important that everyone on the list is both a trained health professional *and* genuinely bilingual. It is not acceptable to use non-professional staff to interpret.

Interpreting is a skill in its own right. Even though they are bilingual and trained in their profession, staff may need additional training in interpreting skills, including opportunities to discuss the demands of interpreting. It is also important to check that bilingual staff are genuinely willing to act as interpreters and that their career development and prospects will not be adversely affected if they are frequently asked to take time out to interpret.

SESSIONAL INTERPRETERS

Trusts and clinics that do not have their own trained full- or part-time interpreter in a particular language should contact their local council or other local provider for interpreters. Sessional interpreters who are interpreting for parents who are experiencing a childbearing loss must be very well briefed. It is important to check that they are acceptable to the parents and that total confidentiality can be ensured. They may need a good deal of professional support over the days and weeks in which they are involved with the parents (see also *Support for interpreters* earlier).

TELEPHONE INTERPRETING SERVICES

Telephone interpreting services can be useful for emergency and out-of-hours interpreting, consultations in languages for which there is no professional interpreter available locally, and consultations for which it has not been possible to book a professional interpreter in advance (Pointon 1996). However, telephone interpreting services are expensive, and are also unlikely to be suitable for the complex and sensitive discussions and exchanges of information that are necessary with parents who are likely to be shocked and distressed. In these situations a face-to-face interpreter is essential.

To help ensure successful telephone interpreting, staff should:

- Introduce themselves and the mother – or parents – to the interpreter;
- Explain the situation, their role and the purpose of the call to the interpreter;
- Allow the interpreter time to say who they are and explain their role;
- Avoid or explain technical terms and abbreviations unless the interpreter is familiar with this area of health care;
- Speak clearly and break up questions or information into short points;
- Check or rephrase if there might have been a misunderstanding;
- Pause frequently and long enough for the interpreter to translate.

WORKING WITH INFORMAL INTERPRETERS

Because of the shortage of professional interpreters in the health service, it is sometimes necessary to use an untrained or informal interpreter. For example, when a father speaks better English than his partner, staff often use him to interpret. However, even if his English is fluent enough to deal with the specialist language required, he is likely to find it almost impossible to interpret properly while at the same time coping with the distress and shock of his own loss. As a result, the baby's mother may receive only a partial explanation or may be unable to participate fully in any discussion. Couples should always be offered the help of a trained interpreter, even if one parent speaks English.

Informal interpreters have been found to be significantly more likely to make general mistakes in translating, and, in particular, to make mistakes that have potential or actual negative consequences (Flores et al 2003). If an informal interpreter has been used as an emergency measure, or there are any doubts about the accuracy of the translation, how the interview went, or whether fully informed consent has been given for any procedures, it is important to get a professional interpreter as soon as possible to review what has been said. However, a few parents may prefer to have a family member to translate for them, rather than expose themselves to a professional but unknown interpreter, especially if they have worries about confidentiality.

Except in extreme emergencies, it is *never* acceptable to use a child or a teenager to interpret for parents who are experiencing a perinatal loss. The long-term consequences of doing so, for both the young person and the family, can be extremely damaging. "It is not appropriate for a child to translate intimate details about his or her mother, and is unfair on both the woman and the child" (CEMACH 2004: Chap. 1).

When managing communication through an informal interpreter, staff should:

- *Listen carefully to the person's command of English* and decide how much it is reasonable to expect him or her to translate. Many people with patchy English end up interpreting for relatives and friends simply because there is no one else to do it. Because most people understand more of a language than they can speak, some people can translate from English into their first language but not from their first language into English;

- *Try to simplify the language they use* to make it easier to translate (see above), and watch carefully to see how much information is getting across. It may be necessary to cover only essential details and to leave important issues until a trained interpreter is available;

- *Find out what the interpreter's relationship is to the parents.* The person who has come to interpret for them may be a close relative, a distant relative, a friend, an acquaintance, a neighbour, a community worker, or someone who charges a fee for interpreting. The interpreter's relationship with the parents will affect what he or she can be asked to translate and what the parents are willing to say. In most cases, a man who is not the woman's partner will not feel able to translate intimate subjects or to be present during examinations or labour;

- *Be aware that the parents may not want the interpreter to know everything about them.* If the parents do not like or feel comfortable with the person acting as interpreter, need to discuss personal matters, or do not trust the interpreter to keep the discussion confidential or to translate their wishes accurately, they may not feel able to discuss things fully or truthfully. For example, they might fear that the interpreter will disapprove or will tell other people;

- *Find out whether there are things that the interpreter feels unable to interpret.* An untrained interpreter may be too embarrassed to discuss some things with the parents, may disagree strongly with some of what is to be translated, or may find the information so distressing that they cannot bear to translate it. They may deliberately select what they translate so as to avoid alarming the parents. If the interpreter is part of the family and will themselves be closely affected by what they translate, they may need care and support in their own right. Their ability to interpret will be affected if they become distressed;

- *Encourage the interpreter to relay the questions and information to and fro rather than answer for the parents.* Most informal interpreters find it very hard to stick to the discipline of interpreting and to relay questions and information without joining in the discussion. They may start answering for the other person if they think they know the answer;

- *Help the interpreter to do as good a job as possible* and to find out if he or she is worried about translating in this situation. It may help to spend time explaining the content and purpose of the discussion beforehand, and to find out if the interpreter feels able to manage the situation. If there are things the interpreter does not understand or is not sure how to translate, he or she should be encouraged to say so;

- *Thank the interpreter.* It is very important that the staff make it clear that they realise that the situation is not ideal and are grateful for the interpreter's help, rather than blaming the interpreter for having come along to translate, or resenting the fact that he or she cannot do it better.

Mis-translations can have serious clinical consequences, and can cause great distress to parents and families. It is necessary to get a professional interpreter as soon as possible if there seem to have been misunderstandings or inadequate translations.
(This section is adapted from Schott and Henley 1996, and Henley and Schott 1999.)

PARENTS WITH A SENSORY IMPAIRMENT

This section covers some of the things that staff should be aware of when caring for people who are deaf or hard of hearing, or for people who are blind or partially sighted. Because there are many different degrees of sight and hearing impairment, and because each person has their own preferred ways of managing their disability, staff should never assume that they can anticipate what any individual needs. The person with the disability is the expert, so it is important to ask them about their preferences and needs, and *to record these in a prominent place in the notes*. This should reduce the frequency with which parents have to explain their needs to different members of staff.

The legal framework

The Disability Discrimination Act (1995 amended 2005) gives people with disabilities the right to equal access to all areas of life. The Act also applies to Scotland and, subject to modifications contained in Section 8, to Northern Ireland.

Organisations and companies that provide goods, facilities and services to the public, such as health care providers, have "a duty to make reasonable adjustments" to ensure that people with disabilities can benefit from services in the same way as those who are able-bodied. The Act does not define "reasonable adjustments", but a new Code of Conduct – *Rights of Access: Services to the Public, Public Authority Functions, Private Clubs and Premises* – that came into force in December 2006 gives examples of adjustments. These include:

- Improving access routes and ensuring that they are free from clutter;
- Redecorating parts of the premises to give better contrast to someone with a visual impairment;
- Modifying equipment, for example providing telephones with text displays;
- Making written material available in forms such as Braille.

CARING FOR PARENTS WHO ARE DEAF OR HARD OF HEARING

There are about 9 million deaf and hard of hearing people in the UK and the number is rising (RNID undated). People who are deaf or hard of hearing may use a hearing aid, lip reading, sign language, an induction loop, or a combination of these.

Although it is not possible to ensure that signers for the deaf are always available, Trusts, Health Boards and managers should provide the best and most comprehensive service possible. Many of the issues discussed above in relation to interpreters also apply if a signer is used; for example, the importance of confidentiality, the need for additional time, and for staff to be trained in working well with a signer.

In addition it is helpful to:

- Find out how the person would like to be alerted when they are called in for a consultation;
- Allow more time;
- Choose a quiet, well-lit place to talk, and avoid sitting or standing in front of a window or strong light;
- Face the person and maintain eye contact when speaking to them;
- Avoid wearing a mask when speaking to a person with a hearing impairment;
- Avoid shouting, speaking slowly or exaggerating speech or facial expressions;
- Use clear, simple, everyday language;
- Check that the person has understood (see *Checking genuine understanding* earlier) and, if they have not, phrase the information in a different way;
- If necessary, write things down using everyday language and clear handwriting;
- Remember that they may not hear fire alarms or public address announcements.

There should be at least one member of staff who has had basic deaf awareness training and can advise and help other members of staff.

In some cases a woman may bring someone to sign for her. If necessary, staff should be able to book trained signers. Different countries have different sign languages, so, before booking a trained signer, it is important to check that she uses British sign language. If her first language is not English, she may use the sign language used in her country of origin.

If the woman is accompanied by a hearing person or someone who is signing for her, it is important to focus on the woman and not only on the hearing person or the signer. Signing does not "translate" word for word, and communication takes longer because each message that passes between the speaker and the recipient first has to be "interpreted" (see *Working well with an interpreter* earlier).

Staff should also have access to induction loops and RNID Typetalk, which allows communication between textphones and telephones. Staff need to allow time for the message to be converted from speech into Typetalk and then back again. For more information, contact the Royal National Institute for Deaf People (RNID) (see Appendix 2).

CARING FOR PARENTS WHO ARE BLIND OR PARTIALLY SIGHTED

People who are blind or partially sighted have the same need for information as everyone else. They also need to be able to move around and orientate themselves in an unfamiliar environment such as a hospital.

Written information should be available in different formats. No single method suits everyone, and people may use different methods at different times, depending on the circumstances.

- Many partially sighted people can read print but can find it difficult and tiring, especially if the document is long. A larger font (from a minimum of 14 point up to 22 point) makes written information more accessible to some partially sighted people;

- Braille (a system of raised dots that is "read" with the fingers, used by around 20,000 people in the UK) can be produced in-house or by a transcription agency;

- Information can also be provided on audiotapes.

For more information on how to create large-print formats and audiotapes, and on other methods of providing information to people who are blind or partially sighted, see the *See it right guidelines*, available from the Royal National Institute for the Blind (RNIB) (see Appendix 2).

Getting around There are many simple things that staff can do to help blind and partially sighted people get around a new environment and to feel included and accepted. For example:

- Making sure that there are no obstacles near entrances, reception desks, in corridors, departments or on wards;

- Ensuring that signs are in large print, with good colour contrast between the print and the background, and are positioned at eye level. It may be helpful to have some signs in Braille.

A blank wall in an open area may not be visible to some people and there is a risk that they may accidentally walk into it. Pictures or posters on blank walls, and markings at eye level on glass walls and doors can prevent accidents.

When offering assistance or caring for a blind or partially sighted person, staff should:

- Greet the person and introduce themselves;

- Offer assistance and wait for a response. If help is accepted, the member of staff should walk slightly in front, offering their arm. It is important to remember that not everyone with a sight problem wants to be guided;

- Always look ahead and describe any obstacles;

- Tell the person when approaching steps, stairs or slopes and say whether the stairs go up or down. The person with impaired sight should be on the side with a handrail;

- Place the person's hand on the back of the chair when offering a seat.

Orientating and including People who are blind or partially sighted need to know about their surroundings and to feel included in what is going on around them. It is important to start by asking each person how they like to familiarise themselves with their surroundings and then to use their preferred approach. For example, staff should:

- Make sure they know where things such as call bells, light switches, bedside locker, water jug and radio are;

- If necessary, help the person to arrange their belongings;

- Always put things back in the same place;

- Show the person how to get to the bathroom, toilet and day room;

- Ensure that no obstacles are left in the way;

- Introduce the person to those around them, giving names and their position, for example, "Sarah Smith is in the bed on your left and Mina Patel is in the bed opposite yours";

- Say who they are each time they are nearby;

- Say when they are leaving, so that the person does not find themselves talking to thin air;

- Make sure the person knows where drinks or food have been put;

- Ensure that the porter knows that the person has a sight problem if they have to go to another department;

- Avoid making assumptions; for example, a mother who is blind or who has impaired sight may still want photographs of her baby, so that she can show them to other people (see also *Creating memories* in Chapter 12).

The above section is adapted with permission from "Access to Services" produced by Altnagelvin Hospitals, Londonderry, Northern Ireland.

CHAPTER 6: TERMINATION OF PREGNANCY FOR REASONS OTHER THAN ABNORMALITY

OTHER RELEVANT CHAPTERS:
1: PROVIDING INCLUSIVE CARE
3: LOSS AND GRIEF
4: COMMUNICATION
5: COMMUNICATION ACROSS LANGUAGE AND OTHER BARRIERS

This chapter is included because termination for reasons other than abnormality is one of the most commonly performed procedures in Great Britain (RCOG 2004a), and at least one-third of British women will have had an abortion by the time they are 45 (Birth Control Trust 1997, cited in RCOG 2004a). It is important to ensure that women who make what is often a very hard decision are treated with respect and care.

However, termination on these grounds is covered separately in these Guidelines from other childbearing losses because some of the issues involved are different from other losses.

Termination and the law

Termination has been legal in certain circumstances in England, Scotland and Wales since 1967 (see Chapter 23). The circumstances in which termination is permitted in England, Scotland and Wales are similar to those in most other European countries (BMA 2005: 28–33).

The 1967 Abortion Act does not extend to Northern Ireland where termination is permitted only if the woman's life is at risk and in some cases of fetal abnormality. However, women from Northern Ireland may travel to the mainland to have a termination.

Why women choose to have a termination

There are many reasons why women may terminate a healthy pregnancy. These include:

- Unprotected sexual intercourse resulting in an unwanted pregnancy;
- Contraceptive failure;
- Relationship difficulties or breakdown;
- Inability to cope with a baby at this point;
- Financial constraints that would affect the woman's existing children.

For many women the decision to have a termination is the result of a combination of factors.

Young women and termination

Women under 16 are deemed to be able to give consent to treatment if they are found to be competent. It is considered good practice for staff to use the criteria of competence ("Gillick competence") outlined by Lord Fraser in 1985 in the House of Lords ruling on Gillick v. West Norfolk and Wisbech Area Health Authority and the Department of Health and Social Security 1986 Appeal Cases 112 (RCN 2003).

Younger women are entitled to the same confidentiality as older women. However, "the vast majority of young women tell an adult and are supported in the abortion process" (MSI 2005). In 2005 the termination rate for young women aged under 16 was 3.7 for every 1,000 young women in this age group (DoH 2006b).

The timing of termination

The earlier in pregnancy a termination is performed, the lower the risk of complications (RCOG 2004b). The trend is towards early termination: in 2005, 89 per cent of terminations were carried out at under 13 weeks' gestation; 67 per cent of these early terminations were carried out at under 10 weeks' gestation (DoH 2006b). The few women who request terminations later on in pregnancy do so because "they have specific circumstances that drive them to conclude that it is better if their pregnancy does not result in a child" (Furedi 2001).

A study of women undergoing late terminations (between 19 and 24 weeks' gestation), carried out by Marie Stopes International (MSI 2005), found that women do not take the decision to have a late termination lightly and that there are various reasons why women may present late. These include:

- Women not recognising the symptoms of pregnancy or attributing them to physiological factors such as irregular periods or the menopause, the consequence of their contraceptive method, or a recent pregnancy;

- Women experiencing significant difficulties in obtain a referral and getting appointments;

- In a small number of cases, women being in denial or facing a significant change in circumstances which forces them to re-think their situation – for example, domestic violence (MSI 2005);

- A few women not realising that there is a time limit and that they need to seek a termination early on in their pregnancy (BMA 2005).

These findings indicate that there will always be some women who request a late termination, though better and swifter access to services has the potential to reduce their number.

ACCESS TO SERVICES

"Where women meet the legal criteria for abortion, and have decided to terminate their pregnancy, delays should be kept to a minimum. Removing obstacles that cause delay and ensuring adequate service provision for earlier abortions could reduce the number of second trimester abortions." British Medical Association (BMA 2005)

To minimise delays in referral for termination, Primary Care Trusts should consider setting up contracts with service providers that enable women to access termination services directly without having to be referred. Whatever the access route, it should be widely publicised. Where direct access is not possible, referrals should be made without delay. Health service staff should not delay referral either by omission or commission (see *Conscientious objection* in Chapter 23).

The RCOG (2004a) recommends that:

- Women who request a termination should, whenever possible, be offered an assessment appointment within 5 days of referral;

- The maximum delay in offering an appointment should be less than 14 days;

- The termination should be carried out within 7 days of the consultation at which the decision to carry it out was made;

- The maximum delay in carrying out the termination should be 21 days from the date of consultation.

All hospital and clinics that carry out terminations should have clear policies on which methods they offer and the gestation limit for each method. Any unit that does not carry out terminations up to the legal limit of 24 weeks' gestation must refer women immediately. Units offering late termination should make sure that all health service staff who may refer women for late termination know about their services.

Trusts and Health Boards should ensure that there is provision within the NHS for women with pre-existing health problems who want or need a termination. These women cannot usually be cared for by independent service providers, because they require specialist medical care as well as a termination. Adequate NHS provision would cut the delay between referral and termination that these women often experience, reducing the number of terminations late in the second trimester.

Because not all independent service providers carry out terminations up to the 24 week-limit, and those that do have limited capacity, it is often difficult to arrange an appointment within the time limit. If a woman cannot access local services, she may have to travel considerable distances and incur the costs of travel, overnight stays and, in some instances, childcare while she is away from home. This may make late termination unaffordable for some women.

Trusts, Health Boards and managers should consider commissioning a centralised booking system to cover all local service providers that carry out terminations after 20 weeks' gestation. This would speed up referrals for women who are nearing the end of the second trimester. Trusts and Health Boards should also be aware of the costs that women may incur if they have to travel a long way to access late terminations. Funding should be available to assist women who are on low incomes.

If a pregnant woman presents at or beyond the legal limit for termination, staff should explain to her that she should get antenatal care as soon as possible, because this is important both for her own wellbeing and for that of her unborn baby. She should be told how she can access antenatal care and, with her consent, the clinic staff should arrange for her to be referred.

Standards of care

Wherever women are seen and cared for, staff should be appropriately trained and qualified, be sympathetic towards them, and have no objection to termination. Ideally, women having a termination should not be cared for at any stage in the same place as women who are continuing their pregnancies. Their privacy and dignity should be protected and, whenever possible, female staff should be available to care for women who, for religious or cultural reasons, prefer this. Trained interpreters who have no objection to termination for reasons other than abnormality, and whose confidentiality can be absolutely assured, should be available for women who speak little or no English (RCOG 2004a).

Conscientious objection

Doctors and other health service staff who have a conscientious objection to termination should arrange for women who are seeking a termination to be referred immediately to a colleague who is known to be willing to provide this service (BMA 2005: 3; GMC 2001; RCOG 1996).

Women who undergo termination of pregnancy for any reason should not be cared for by staff who might disapprove of the choices they have made and might be ambivalent about providing care (Marshall and Raynor 2002; Statham 2002). Managers should allocate staff who are sympathetic to the choices women have made. This both protects the interests of the woman and respects the right of members of staff to follow their conscience. The Nursing and Midwifery Council (NMC 2006) states that "Registrants who raise a conscientious objection to being involved in certain aspects of care or treatment must do so at the earliest possible time, in order for managers to arrange alternative arrangements" (see also Conscientious objection in Chapter 23).

Before a termination

In addition to a medical assessment of the grounds for a termination, each woman should have an opportunity to reflect on her situation and her decision with a member of staff who has counselling skills. She should also have access to written material and/or material in other formats about alternatives to a termination, such as having the baby adopted. Women who remain ambivalent about their decision can be given an appointment for admission but must be told that they can postpone or cancel their admission at any time (DoH 2001a: 10–11).

In addition, each woman should receive detailed verbal and written information or material in other formats about:

- The tests and examinations that will precede the termination, what these involve and why they are done. Women who will be scanned should be told that they need not see the picture on the screen unless they want to;

- The methods of termination that are appropriate for her stage of pregnancy. If a choice of method or of anaesthetic is available, the benefits, potential side effects, risks – including possible effects on future fertility – and possible failure rates should be explained and choices offered;

- How long she will stay in the unit if she is admitted for surgery or for an early or late medical termination, and what arrangements she should make for returning home afterwards;

- What to expect physically and emotionally after the termination;

- The arrangements for follow-up.

Care at home

Women who have had a surgical termination, and women who go home during a medical termination, should be given written and verbal information about how to take care of themselves at home, symptoms that may require medical attention, and whom they should call if problems arise. They should also be given the number of a 24-hour telephone helpline. Urgent clinical assessment and emergency gynaecological admission must be available.

In addition, every woman should be given a letter summarising the procedure she is undergoing or has undergone, so that any practitioner she consults about complications knows what has been done (RCOG 2002: 16). Some women do not want any information passed on to their GP: it is always important to check before doing so (see *Communication and the duty of confidentiality* in Chapter 4).

Aftercare

All women should be offered advice about resuming sexual intercourse and about contraceptive methods. Some women will welcome advice and discussion. They may want to discuss alternative methods if the pregnancy was due to contraceptive failure. Others may feel that raising the subject at this time is insensitive, or that they simply do not want to know about contraception at that point. However, it is important not to miss an opportunity to offer information. Women who do not want to discuss contraception should be given written information and/or material in other formats about the choice of methods and, when they are ready, where they can access contraceptive services.

All staff working in termination services, especially those who are responsible for counselling women before and after the procedure, should be able to give women accurate and up-to-date information about the different methods of contraception. The contracts of some Primary Care Trusts limit the types of contraception that independent sector providers can offer. Wherever possible, contracts should enable these providers to offer women their contraceptive method of choice as part of their care, without their having to go elsewhere.

Each woman should also be given written information or material in other formats about sources of support and counselling and how to access these services. Many women feel relief after a termination and may not need to talk about their feelings; others may feel sad and tearful. It has been suggested that the rates of psychological disturbance and self-harm are higher among women who have had a termination when compared both with women who give birth and with non-pregnant women of a similar age. However, the RCOG notes that this does not imply a causal association and may reflect a continuation of pre-existing psychological difficulties (RCOG 2004a: 16.9).

Zolese and Blacker (1992) point out that the termination of an "unwanted" pregnancy is in itself therapeutic, and conclude that marked psychological disturbance following a termination occurs in only a minority of women. They found that certain groups are at risk. These include women with a previous psychiatric history, younger women with poor social support, multiparous women, and women in communities where termination is strongly disapproved of. It is important to identify women in these situations, so that they can be offered appropriate support and treatment.

SENSITIVE DISPOSAL

Sensitive disposal of fetal remains and fetuses delivered before 24 weeks' gestation is now accepted good practice (see *Policies and practice* in Chapter 17). However, there is anecdotal evidence from health care staff that the vast majority of women who terminate their pregnancy in these circumstances do not want to discuss what happens to the products of the pregnancy.

To date, there has been no research to determine whether women would want to know about the method of disposal, or what their reactions would be if the subject were raised. Because there is no evidence to suggest that discussion would be beneficial, many staff are understandably reluctant or unwilling to confront women with questions or information about disposal. Trusts that already have contracts with local funeral directors and crematoria can easily ensure that the products of pregnancy are disposed of respectfully. At present this is neither practical nor affordable for independent service providers.

One way of ensuring that information about disposal is available to those women who want it is to include it in the written information or material in other formats that all women receive about their care. Individual women can then choose whether to raise the issue with staff. It is important that staff know about the method of disposal used by their unit, so that they can give accurate information if asked. Staff should also know how to advise women who express specific wishes in regard to the disposal of the fetal remains and who want to make arrangements themselves.

CHAPTER 7: ANTENATAL SCREENING, DIAGNOSTIC TESTS AND PROCEDURES

> OTHER RELEVANT CHAPTERS:
> 1: PROVIDING INCLUSIVE CARE
> 2: HOLISTIC CARE
> 3: LOSS AND GRIEF
> 4: COMMUNICATION
> 5: COMMUNICATION ACROSS LANGUAGE AND OTHER BARRIERS

This chapter deals with good practice in relation to antenatal screening and diagnosis, including the information and support that women and couples need when deciding whether to accept testing, and if and when the results present them with difficult and painful choices.

"Screening is more than applying a screening test. It is a programme which needs clear management, monitoring and quality assurance. Those offered screening must be able to make informed choices and have their decisions respected."
Department of Health (DoH 1998: 3.7.1)

Screening and diagnostic testing are a widely accepted and increasing part of care during pregnancy, yet few women or their families are prepared for the dilemmas and choices that can result. When a test or other procedure appears to be a standard part of care and receives institutional support, women generally accept it without question and assume that it is beneficial (Press and Browner 1997). However, a procedure that most parents assume will be straightforward may precipitate a cascade of agonising decisions about further diagnostic testing, and sometimes a decision about continuing with the pregnancy. The ever-widening scope of antenatal screening and testing also creates increasing ethical dilemmas and pressures for staff.

Trusts and Health Boards should have a protocol covering antenatal screening and testing that stresses the importance of informed choice. The protocol should also ensure that staff provide information that is consistent, reliable, up-to-date and clear. Parents should be given information verbally and in written or other formats, and they should be informed of results as soon as possible.

Trusts and Health Boards should have a policy that ensures prompt and accurate communication between the different specialties involved in screening and diagnostic testing; for example, midwifery, obstetrics, haematology, gynaecology nursing and genetic counselling. Good co-ordination and regular communication between specialties are essential to make sure that policies and procedures are coherent and offer the best possible service to parents, and that the information given to parents by staff in different specialities is consistent.

CONSENT

"If we value women's ability to make informed choices about prenatal tests as highly as we value reliable laboratory tests, evidence-based quality standards need to be developed for the information and support women are given at all stages of the process of prenatal testing." (Marteau and Dormandy 2001)

Consent must always be sought and documented before any screening or diagnostic test is performed. Staff must make it clear that all antenatal screening is optional.

Most women who have a partner will want their partner to understand what the tests involve and what the consequences might be, and many couples will make joint decisions. However, it is the woman who has the legal right to decide which screening and diagnostic tests she will (or will not) have during pregnancy, and her decision must be accepted. For this reason, this chapter refers mainly to women rather than to couples or partners. Nevertheless, the partner should always be included if the woman wants this.

> *For many men pregnancy is not just something that happens to their wife or partner. It happens to the two of them.* Father

Before being asked if she wants to consent, each woman must be given objective, factual information about:

- What the test is for, how it is done, what it might detect and any risks;
- Whether it is a screening or a diagnostic test and the relevant implications;
- What the test may find (for example, risk levels or definite diagnosis), and the accuracy and reliability of what may be found;
- The possible implications if an abnormality is suspected or detected;
- Any further tests that might be needed to confirm or clarify the results;
- Any other information that the test may provide;
- How long she will have to wait for a result, and when and how it will be given to her (UKNSC undated; Marteau and Dormandy 2001).

Staff should give each woman written information to supplement the discussion. Information should be available in the languages commonly spoken locally (and others if possible) and also in other more accessible formats such as audio tapes or CDs (see also *Written information and information in other formats* in Chapter 4).

Although most women want all the information that screening and diagnostic tests can provide, some do not: they have the right to question or decline any tests, and their decisions must be respected, documented and adhered to.

- Women must always be told if a test might detect an abnormality for which there is no treatment and/or for which they might be offered a termination. Some women may want to decline all or part of the process (ARC 2005);
- Some women may refuse all tests that carry any risk to the baby;

- Some women may consent to a screening or diagnostic test to find out if their baby has a serious condition, even though they would not agree to a termination (Ahmed et al 2006). They should be reassured that this is a legitimate choice.

It is important not to assume that, if there is a lower uptake of antenatal screening by women of minority ethnic and religious groups, and by women in the most disadvantaged social groups, this reflects negative attitudes to screening:

- In relation to screening for Down's syndrome, Dormandy et al (2005) found that health care systems appear to be less effective at enabling informed decisions for these women. Comparing *only women who had a positive attitude towards screening*, they found that women in minority and disadvantaged groups were less likely to be screened than white women and women in the most advantaged social groups;

- Ahmed et al (2006), in a study of the attitudes of a group of women of Pakistani heritage towards antenatal diagnosis and termination of pregnancy, found that, although religious beliefs and precepts were a major factor for many women, other factors also played an important role.

BLOOD TESTS

Women need to know that:

- Some tests, such as screening for infections and identifying the woman's blood group, enable staff to give appropriate treatment that will minimise any risks to the baby and to the woman;

- Other tests involve screening blood for serious conditions, such as neural tube defects, sickle cell disorders and thalassaemia (see below), and for conditions for which further invasive testing might be needed to get a definitive diagnosis. The full implications of these tests must be explained – for example, that in some cases the baby's father may need to be tested as well.

In order to identify the conditions for which to screen, staff may have to ask women about their family origins. Some members of staff are nervous about asking questions that may be seen by women and their partners as intrusive, racist or discriminatory (Dyson 2005: 53). They may also worry about disrupting the relationship of trust that they are trying to establish. As a result they may try to guess a woman's family origins based on her name or physical appearance, or may avoid probing even when they are fairly certain that the answer she has given is incomplete or incorrect. This could result in women not being offered screening when they should be.

Issues of family origins and ethnicity are often very sensitive, especially for members of minority communities who often experience racism, exclusion and discrimination, and may feel that their right to be in the UK, or to receive health care, is being questioned. For refugees, asylum seekers and people whose legal status is unclear, questions about family origins may raise fears about links between the health service and immigration authorities and the police.

Staff who discuss these issues with parents need to understand the differences between:

- *Family origins,* which are a geographical and genetic issue. Family origins refer to the countries or regions of the world in which a person's parents, grandparents and other ancestors may have originated. Family origins indicate the possible genetic inheritance of certain diseases prevalent in these countries;

- *Ethnic group,* which is a question of cultural identity;

- *Religion,* which is a question of faith and identity;

- *Place of birth or childhood,* which may have nothing to do with genetic inheritance; and

- *Nationality,* which is a political and legal issue (Dyson 2005: 50-52).

It is important not to ask whether a person is British – this is likely to cause offence and is irrelevant, as a person's genetic inheritance is not necessarily related to their nationality. Questions about family origins should also not be confused with the question about ethnic group that is asked for health service monitoring purposes (Dyson 2005: 59).

Some Muslim women may decline to give blood samples during the month of Ramadan. During this month many healthy adult Muslims abstain from both food and water from sunrise to sunset. Although pregnant women are exempt from fasting, many choose to fast alongside their families, both for spiritual reasons and because making up a month of fasting at a later date may be difficult. Some women consider that having blood taken while fasting breaks and invalidates their fast. (For more information see Schott and Henley 1996: 139, and for details of festival dates see SHAP in Appendix 2.)

Down's syndrome

Women should be informed that screening and testing for Down's syndrome is a two-stage process and that, at present, there are no non-invasive tests that can give a definite diagnosis. They should be told that, if the blood test results show an increased chance of the baby having Down's syndrome, they will be offered an invasive test to obtain a diagnosis. Having the blood test does not commit them to accepting the invasive test if it is offered.

Sickle cell and thalassaemia disorders

Staff who discuss screening for sickle cell disorders or thalassaemia need to understand:

- That anyone may be affected by sickle cell disorders or thalassaemia. Assumptions should not be made on the basis of a person's skin colour, other superficial physical features, or name (see above). It is always necessary to ask. However, if a parent gives answers that seem unlikely or incomplete on the basis of their skin colour, other superficial physical features or name, staff need to probe sensitively for more information (Dyson 2005: 68);

- The circumstances under which the baby's father should be offered screening and how this will be organised;

- That in some communities there is a stigma attached to being a sickle cell or thalassaemia carrier: the issue must always be handled sensitively and with complete confidentiality (Dyson 2005: 127; Ahmed et al 2002).

Some parents, for example those who have an affected relative, may already be well informed about sickle cell and/or thalassaemia and how it is inherited. Staff should check what women and their partners already know before beginning the discussion. Depending on the level of knowledge, staff should outline the key points about sickle cell and thalassaemia and clarify any misconceptions. They should explain that it is necessary to ask about family origins because sickle cell and thalassaemia are linked to genes more commonly found in people whose families originated in certain parts of the world. It is very important that parents do not feel discriminated against, blamed or stigmatised for possibly carrying a particular gene.

GIVING RESULTS OF SCREENING TESTS

All women having an antenatal screening test must be informed of the result, even if it is negative or if the level of risk identified is very low (NDSSPE 2004: 2.6).

All staff directly involved in the provision of antenatal screening information or services – including midwives, medical staff, general practitioners, sonographers, primary care teams, and laboratory staff – should have an induction course and an annual updating session (NDSSPE 2004: 3.1 and 3.2). They should have received the appropriate education for their roles and responsibilities and for any specific tasks required.

If the member of staff who gives the screening results does not feel sufficiently well informed about the significance and implications of the results, they should explain this and arrange for the woman - and her partner - to see someone who has a fuller understanding of the issues as soon as possible.

The information that women and couples need in order to make properly informed decisions about screening tests can be extremely complicated and difficult to explain, especially to those for whom all of it is new. Workloads should be organised so that staff have enough time for this.

Staff must have easy access to up-to-date, reliable information about all the tests they offer and the conditions they detect, and must be prepared for new tests as they become available (Ryder 1999).

The language of screening results

"Two women with exactly the same results, explained in exactly the same way, will not necessarily perceive their risk in the same way." UK National Screening Committee (UKNSC 2005: 5)

In many cases a screening test provides information about the level of risk that a baby is affected, rather than a clear yes or no. People's perception of the meaning of a certain level of risk is highly individual. It depends on their own life experiences, the severity and implications of the problem that has been identified, and how the statistical risk is explained (Edwards A 2004). Discussing risk should be a two-way process: an *exchange of information* with the aim of enabling the woman to make decisions that are consistent with her own values and wishes.

People's ability to assimilate complex information also varies. Staff need to be able to tailor their explanations and examples to suit the woman or couple they are talking to. It may sometimes be helpful to provide and discuss information over several consultations, though this is not always possible if choices are time limited (Edwards A et al 2002).

The language used when presenting screening results should be chosen with care. Words are "rarely value free and [often] have connotations other than their dictionary definition". Staff need to be aware of how parents may understand words, and to choose those that accurately convey the situation and the level of chance (Abramsky and Fletcher 2002). For example:

- Abramsky and Fletcher found that parents were likely to assume that something "rare" is more serious than something "common"; and that something "abnormal" is more serious than something "unusual";

- The words "syndrome", "disorder" and "anomaly" also worried parents. If a laboratory test identifies a variation from a norm that is unlikely to cause problems in the baby, it is not usually appropriate to use the word "syndrome". On the other hand, if the diagnosis indicates that the baby could have serious problems, the word "syndrome" may be entirely appropriate;

- The word "risk" has negative connotations for many people; "chance" may be more neutral;

- In the context of screening, the everyday implications of "positive" and "negative" are reversed: a positive result is likely to be bad news and a negative result to be good news. In general, the words "negative" and "positive" should be avoided when giving results;

- Giving the chance of a desired outcome is generally more reassuring to parents than giving the equivalent chance of the corresponding undesired outcome (Abramsky and Fletcher 2002). Reframing information from a different perspective – for example, a 20 per cent chance of having an affected child as opposed to an 80 per cent chance of having an unaffected child – may influence people's decision about what to do (Marteau 1989). It is usually helpful to give the chances of both possible outcomes;

- Technical words such as "trisomy" are likely to worry parents more than equivalent, more commonly-used phrases such as "extra chromosome" (Abramsky and Fletcher 2002);

- Some people may understand "high risk" as meaning that the baby is definitely affected, and "low risk" as meaning that the baby is definitely not affected (Ryder 1999). These terms should be clarified. Women also need to understand that, for some conditions, a negative result may still carry a residual possibility of having an affected child (Marteau et al 2000). In addition, a negative result for a particular test does not rule out the possibility of other problems that were not tested for;

- Words such as "likely", "unlikely", "high", "low" and "probable" mean very different things to different people and must be further discussed and clarified (Edwards A et al 2002);

- The technical screening terms "false positive" and "false negative" are unfamiliar to most parents and should be explained;

- Some people prefer verbal or descriptive information about risk while others find numbers easier to understand (Edwards A 2004). In general, the most useful approach is to use both, for example, a verbal probability phrase such as "very unlikely" as well as the corresponding numerical probability (Marteau et al 2000);

- Some people find numbers easier to understand if they are presented visually, for example in a diagram or a bar or pie chart. ARC (2005) suggests that a result of 1 in 100 could be represented by 100 circles on a page, one of which is a different colour from the rest. For larger numbers it may be helpful to have a visual aid to demonstrate the level of risk; for example, an illustration, or a jar of marbles or of beans containing one of a different colour;

- Some people find ratios, for example "1 in X", easier to understand; others prefer percentages, for example "X per cent". Abramsky and Fletcher (2002) found that many people perceived "1 in X" as larger than the equivalent percentage. They may also focus on the "1" and assume that that "1" must be their baby (Personal communication, ARC 2006). In general it is better to present both ratios and percentages. It is also important to be consistent – that is, not to give the chance of one outcome in percentages and of another as 1 in X (Abramsky and Fletcher 2002);

- To people who are unfamiliar with the language of probability, "1 in 300" may sound like a higher risk than "1 in 100";

- Calman and Royston (1997) suggest comparing a specific risk to numbers of people. For example, a risk of 1 in 100 (or 1 per cent) could be compared to one person in a street; 1 in 1,000 (or 0.1 per cent) to one person in a village; 1 in 10,000 (or 0.01 per cent) to one person in a small town and so on. Analogies based on the maximum capacity of well-known local venues such as a local football stadium could also be used;

- Many people find it hard to remember risk information. Each woman should be given a written record of the discussion to take away with her.

ULTRASOUND EXAMINATIONS

For most women, seeing their baby on a scan is an exciting and much anticipated event, often shared with the baby's father. Although many women know that ultrasound is used to check their due date, the size of the baby and the position of the placenta, they may not realise that it also checks for possible structural abnormalities and can find markers for chromosomal abnormalities.

Women must be well informed about the purpose of each ultrasound examination and the possibility of unexpected findings (Mitchell 2004; Garcia et al 2002). They should be given clear verbal and written information beforehand about what the examination involves, why it is done and what it might show (RCOG 2004d), and told how they will be given the results. The sonographer should check that the woman understands the purpose of the examination before beginning the scan.

A woman should be able to have her partner (or a relative or friend) with her throughout all examinations if she wants. However, staff should be aware that some women feel that undressing for a scan is immodest, especially if men are present, and may find the experience humiliating and distressing. It can help to keep the woman's body covered as much as possible throughout the examination, and to ensure privacy by limiting the number of people present, closing the door, and placing a screen between the door and the couch. Some women may strongly prefer the examination to be carried out by a woman: this wish should be complied with if possible.

Transvaginal scanning is increasingly used, especially for assessment in early pregnancy.

However, some women may find transvaginal scanning distressing and even traumatic (Clement et al 2003). It is important to explain the reasons for using it, to describe the procedure, and to acknowledge the possibility of discomfort. Specific consent must always be requested. Again, some women may find a vaginal scan acceptable provided it is carried out by a woman and/or no men are present.

Before the ultrasound examination, the sonographer should ask the woman or couple if they would like to look at their baby. Ideally there should be a second screen, positioned so as to give the parents a good view of the baby and to prevent repetitive strain injuries to staff. If it is not possible to have a second screen, the sonographer should explain to the parents that they will see their baby briefly at the beginning of the examination: the sonographer will then turn the screen away to do the necessary checks; he or she will then invite them to see their baby for a longer period at the end and will explain what they are seeing.

18–20 week screening examination

The main purpose of the 18–20 week anomaly scan (or its equivalent) is to check for abnormalities. It is very important that women understand this and its possible implications before the appointment is made. If a woman does not want to know if her baby has an abnormality, she must be able to decline the scan. All women should know what will be checked at this examination and should also be told that this scan cannot identify all possible significant abnormalities (RCOG 2000). It may be helpful to encourage women to bring their partner or another supporter, and to advise them not to bring other children.

Communication during an ultrasound examination

Information gained from the examination should be communicated sensitively and clearly. Any uncertainties about the findings should be acknowledged.

The most difficult part of the scanning procedure is often what to say during the scan and immediately afterwards. Long silences are very hard for parents. Whenever possible, sonographers should explain what they are doing. If the sonographer needs some time to concentrate, it may be helpful to use phrases such as, "I am going to be quiet for a moment so that I can concentrate on the screen". Staff also need to be aware that parents are often highly sensitive to non-verbal messages and body language: they may become alarmed if the screen is turned away from them without prior warning, or if the sonographer's facial expression and demeanour change (Mitchell 2004).

> *I can remember every detail of the room and the moment the chatty sonographer stopped talking and turned the screen away from me. She then asked her assistant to get a doctor. That is the moment I knew deep inside me that my baby daughter Heather had died, and my heart broke.* Mother

If a problem is discovered during a scan, the sonographer should tell the woman or couple as soon as possible that there is something on the scan that needs to be looked at more closely. It is important not to pretend that all is well or offer false reassurance.

- *If the sonographer is permitted to say* what he or she has identified during the examination and to discuss the implications. This should be done with honesty, tact and empathy. The woman or couple should be asked if they would like the sonographer to show them on the screen what he or she has seen and explain its implications (Mitchell 2004);

- If the sonographer is not permitted to say what he or she has identified, he or she should say that there may be a problem, explain the limits of his or her skills or remit, and say that a second opinion is needed. Phrases such as these may be helpful: "I'm very sorry but I think I might have found a problem ... I will have to get a doctor to have another look ... I may have found a problem with the baby's heart" (Personal communication, ARC 2006). The second opinion should be organised as soon as possible, and the sonographer should acknowledge that the wait is very stressful for the parents.

Women and couples should be given time to begin to take in the results of the examination before the next steps and choices are explained to them. (See also *Before leaving the department* below.)

If another ultrasound examination is needed, this should be organised as soon as possible. Parents are likely to be better able to tolerate delay if there is a reasonable explanation for it. Again, it is important that staff acknowledge the stress and difficulty for them of waiting.

Ultrasound examination when a problem is suspected

Sometimes a woman is sent for a scan because a problem is suspected or to confirm a diagnosis. Some women may also ask for a scan in order to help them accept the reality of the situation. This examination should ideally be carried out by a member of staff who specialises in fetal abnormalities and who can interpret and explain the information obtained straightaway. If this is not possible, the woman or couple must be informed beforehand and must be told what arrangements will be made to explain the findings fully to them as soon as possible. As with the 20-week anomaly scan, women should be encouraged to bring their partner or another person for support, and advised not to bring other children.

When they returned with the scanning machine I could not look at it. I watched my husband's face. When I saw the incredible sadness that spread across his face I knew that we had lost our baby. Mother

The sonographer should speak to the woman – to both parents if they are together – before the scan to make sure that they understand the reasons for the scan and are well prepared. He or she should acknowledge that having a scan in these circumstances is extremely upsetting and stressful, and should make it clear that he or she recognises the likely impact on the parents of the results. It can help to say something like, "I'm sorry. This must be very hard for you ...".

Some parents will appreciate a scan photograph but others will not, so this should be offered tentatively. If the parents do not want a photograph, the sonographer could offer to take one and keep it in the woman's medical records so that they can ask for it later if they want (see also *Photographs* in Chapter 12).

Before leaving the department

When a woman's or couple's anxiety has been raised or bad news has been given, they should be offered support by someone in the department. Every department that carries out scanning should have a "quiet room" and a member of staff available who can support parents in these situations (RCOG 2000).

If the woman (or couple) needs to go to another department straightaway, a member of staff should accompany them, so that they can be seen immediately with no additional unnecessary delay and explanations.

A woman should always have an appointment to be seen by an obstetrician within 24 hours of a problem being detected. If she must be referred to a specialist unit, the reason must be carefully explained and she should normally be seen within 72 hours (RCOG 2000: 4.3.4). She should be given the contact details of a member of staff who can answer questions and offer support in the meantime.

The woman – or couple – should be given verbal and written information about the time and purpose of their next appointment, where it will be, and the name and role (eg radiologist, obstetrician, specialist midwife) of the person they will see. Some parents may also want to contact an appropriate voluntary organisation for information and advice, and it may be helpful to offer information about these (see Appendix 2).

If a woman is alone, she should be invited to bring her partner or another supporter with her to the next appointment. If she is planning to travel home alone, staff should suggest that she may prefer to phone someone and ask them to come and accompany her.

Ultrasound policy and procedures

Every unit should have an agreed procedure for talking to women and, if they wish, their partner or another supporter, about ultrasound examination findings. This procedure should be developed and agreed by a multi-professional group that includes parents or their representatives, sonographers, nurses, midwives, radiologists, obstetricians and genetic counsellors. The policy should ensure that the time between the detection of an abnormal finding, and explaining it to the woman and discussing the next steps, is as short as possible. This will be easier if several members of staff from different disciplines are all trained in ultrasound examination and in the necessary communication skills (see Chapter 4).

In order to facilitate best practice, sonographers should receive information from the relevant department (eg histology laboratory or fetal medicine unit) about the outcomes of pregnancies in which they have identified abnormalities. Wherever possible, they should be involved in case and audit meetings. They must also have good informal and formal support.

FURTHER TESTS AND APPOINTMENTS

If further tests are required to clarify the diagnosis, or more specialist appointments are needed, the woman should be referred for these as soon as possible.

If she needs to go to another department or unit, it is important to make sure that she knows what she is going for, where she is going and how to get there, and whom she will see (both name and role). If necessary, someone should phone ahead to make sure that she is expected. She should not have to explain why she has come to several different staff or in front of other parents (Chitty et al 1996).

We booked in at reception and were asked if we had attended before. Nobody seemed to know or care that we had been referred from another hospital. We were told to wait in a large square bare room with 6 or 7 other women, some with partners and young children. Then we were led to a darkened room with a very large ultrasound machine by a doctor with a soft friendly voice. He asked, "So what can I do for you today?" I couldn't believe that he had to ask. Surely everybody in the world knew that ours had come crashing down around us? Mother

Wherever a woman goes for further tests, the staff should be expecting her and should welcome her (and her partner). She should not have to wait with other pregnant women who are having scheduled scans or tests, but should be offered a private room.

Trusts and Health Boards should be aware of the costs that women – and couples – may incur if they have to travel a long way to access specialist care during pregnancy. Funding should be allocated to assist parents who are on low incomes.

CHORIONIC VILLUS SAMPLING AND AMNIOCENTESIS

Amniocentesis is the most common invasive antenatal diagnostic procedure in the UK. The associated miscarriage rate is 1 per cent (RCOG 2005a). Chorionic villus sampling (CVS), which can be carried out much earlier, has been associated with a slightly higher rate of miscarriage. Both procedures should be carried out by someone who is skilled and practised in them.

Women and couples should be given both verbal and written information in their first language about the procedure. This must include the risks and what to expect afterwards. They must also know that amniocentesis and CVS can detect a range of defects that they may not be aware of. Written consent must be obtained (RCOG 2005a).

PRESENTING AND DISCUSSING DIAGNOSTIC TEST RESULTS

The results of a diagnostic test should always be given to the woman as soon as possible. Staff should have agreed with her when and how she will be given the results. If for some reason the full discussion of the results and their implications cannot take place immediately, the woman should be offered an appointment as soon as possible.

Giving results over the phone

If the results are to be given by phone, staff should discuss with the woman beforehand when this should be done. It may be possible to set a time when she will be at home (rather than at work), and when her partner or another supporter will be with her.

When the woman answers the phone, staff should always check whether it is all right for her to talk before they give the results. Very often the response to being given bad news over the phone is a long silence. This can be very hard for staff, who may be tempted to say something. In general it is better to wait until the woman can speak. Because she may be too shocked to take in much information now, it is important to give her a phone number and a named member of staff to ask for, so that she or her partner can call back later (Personal communication, ARC 2006). She should also be offered an immediate face-to-face appointment to discuss further the results and their implications.

Discussing test results and their implications

An appointment to discuss the abnormality that has been detected is highly stressful for parents and very demanding for staff. Although staff "cannot take the pain of the situation away, sensitive supportive care at this time plays an important part in helping parents come to decisions that are right for them" (ARC 2005).

All staff who give women the results of tests must be fully informed about the condition(s) they are discussing. The information they give about the condition and the woman's options must be accurate, up-to-date and balanced, and unaffected by their own personal views or prejudices about the condition or what they themselves would decide in this situation (Abramsky et al 2001). The possible severity of and impact of the condition should be neither exaggerated nor understated.

Staff should bear in mind that the parents are likely to feel shocked and numb, and to find it difficult to take in the information and to think clearly. They should offer parents another appointment for further discussion (see also Breaking bad news in Chapter 4).

The parents may want the following information:

- A clear explanation of the abnormality or condition;
- How reliable the diagnosis is, what further confirmation might be needed and how this might be obtained. If the findings are uncertain or cannot yet be confirmed, the stressful nature of such uncertainty should be acknowledged;
- How the pregnancy is likely to progress;
- Whether special care or treatment will be needed before the birth;
- What the longer term prognosis is for the baby and what treatment might be available;
- How the condition might affect the baby's quality of life;
- What will happen if they decide to continue or to end the pregnancy (ARC 2005).

Parents should be encouraged to ask any questions they may have at the time, and also to write down questions that may occur to them afterwards, for discussion at the next appointment.

If the baby might be born alive but cannot survive, staff should try to give parents some idea of how long he or she is likely to live. For example, a baby with anencephaly or a severe heart defect may live for only minutes or hours. A baby with Edward's or Patau's syndrome will usually die shortly after birth. Parents should be told what is most likely, but that in rare cases babies may live longer, and it is impossible to predict what will happen. It may be prudent to say to parents that if they look the condition up on the internet they may find examples of children with a very short life expectancy who have lived for several months or even years, but that in reality this occurs very rarely. The parents also need to know that their baby will be given the best possible care after the birth to ensure that he or she does not suffer (see also Chapter 8).

If there is a chance that intensive treatment and intervention might save the baby's life, staff should explain to the parents how the baby will be monitored during labour and the birth, the interventions that could be undertaken, and the possible implications.

If there are grounds for a termination, this should be offered. This can be a very difficult issue to raise. Possible ways to introduce the subject are, for example, "I have to tell you that you could decide ...", "I have to give you the option of ...", or "There are a number of choices open to you/ for you to think about" (Statham et al 2001: 40). If the woman wants to consider termination, she needs to know, at the time or later, how it would be carried out. If the pregnancy is fairly advanced she needs to know how long she has to make her decision.

Whenever possible, parents should be given supplementary written information that has been developed specifically for parents about the condition affecting their baby. This information should include other sources such as ARC, and Contact a Family (see Appendix 2). Information for parents should also be available in other languages and formats.

Choice and decision making

"There are no right or wrong decisions, just decisions that parents can live with." Antenatal Results and Choices (ARC 2005)

Choice is widely seen as empowering and beneficial. However, when an abnormality is suspected or detected in pregnancy, the woman or couple are suddenly forced to make choices that they never wanted to make. They need time to adjust to their situation and to think about what they will do. Staff should give as much objective, factual information as the parents want, and should acknowledge the consequences, risks and benefits of the possible courses of action, as well as any uncertainties. It is important never to make assumptions about what parents will decide to do – for example, on the basis of their religious affiliation, cultural heritage or way of life. (See also *Facilitating informed choice* in Chapter 4.)

Decisions may be particularly difficult and stressful if women – and their partners – have to base their decision on the *probability* that their baby is severely ill or disabled, rather than on a definite prognosis, and staff should acknowledge this. In certain circumstances it may be helpful to offer to refer parents to a fetal medicine unit for a second opinion about the baby's condition. Although there may be little new information to be gained, it may confirm the likely prognosis the parents have been given and provide them with more information. Many parents have found this helpful when they look back afterwards at the decisions they made (Personal communication, ARC 2006).

A few women may have decided in advance what they will choose if their unborn baby has a serious abnormality, though some may change their decision when faced with the actual situation.

Some women – and couples – will want a lot of information in order to make their decision. Some will know immediately what they want to do. Some may need to come back for more information and discussion at a later date. Some parents may want to contact voluntary organisations (see above) or talk to other people. Parents' decisions may also be affected by their religious, cultural and personal values and beliefs, their obstetric history, or by knowing someone with personal experience of the abnormality. Some parents will also want to know about the implications for future pregnancies of what is happening in this pregnancy; understanding these may influence their decision now.

Many women and couples find that they vacillate, changing their minds frequently while trying to come to a decision. This can be extremely distressing, especially for people who are used to being decisive. It can be helpful to reassure them that such vacillation is very common and to acknowledge how difficult it is.

Sometimes a woman will want time to explore her own – and her partner's – beliefs and values before she reaches a decision. Some couples may appreciate the support of a member of staff to help them explore options and see if they can reach a joint decision. A woman who decides on a course of action against her partner's wishes will need additional support, as she will have to cope not only with the anxiety about her baby, but also with the consequences of "going it alone" (ARC 2005).

Some women (and couples) may want to discuss with other family members whether to have further tests, or whether to terminate an affected pregnancy. One advantage of such collective decision making is that, whatever they jointly decide, the woman or couple are likely to feel that they will receive support from other members of the family (Ahmed et al 2006). However, some women or couples will want to make their decision on their own without consulting other people, or will want to make a decision that they know their family or other people will disapprove of. It is particularly important in such cases to maintain strict confidentiality.

Women and couples should be given information about ARC (see Appendix 2). If possible, they should also be offered contact details for a voluntary organisation that deals with the specific abnormality affecting their baby. In the case of a non-lethal abnormality, they may want to find out from other parents how the condition might affect the quality of the child's life, and the impact that caring for that child might have on them and on any other existing or future children.

Once the woman has made her decision, the next steps should be discussed:

- *If she decides to continue the pregnancy,* the member of staff who is caring for her should identify her immediate needs, find out how she would like to be cared for, and arrange the necessary referrals (see Chapter 8);

- *If she decides to terminate the pregnancy,* she may want the termination to be carried out as soon as possible. However, some women may find it helpful to wait for a while. As far as possible, women themselves should determine the timing and the pace of events. To do this they need to understand any medical or other implications of the decisions they make (see Chapter 11).

If tests show that the baby has a severe abnormality and is likely to die in utero, parents who are not having a termination may have to go home and wait for the baby to die. This may mean frequent visits for scans to check the condition of the baby, so that the woman can be offered an induction soon after the death. The pain and stress of this situation should be acknowledged.

She had Down's syndrome which caused her heart to be hopelessly underdeveloped. There was no intervention that could have saved her and we were told she could die in days or in weeks. We watched powerlessly on ultrasound as her heart beat slowed and faded. She died soon after and, perversely, her death was something of a relief. Her struggle was over; she died in the only place she had ever known. We were spared days or perhaps weeks of waiting and frequent visits to the hospital for repeat scans. Father

COMMUNICATION BETWEEN SECONDARY AND PRIMARY CARE STAFF

"Much of the organisation [of maternity care] is determined by the imperative to carry out various investigations to detect deviations from normality, yet when those deviations are actually encountered, the system is not always very good at coping with them."
(Statham et al 2003)

Many women and couples want and expect to discuss their situation with their GP, as he or she is responsible for their long-term care. They may also want to talk to their community midwife or health visitor. However, communication between primary and secondary care staff about abnormalities diagnosed in pregnancy is often poor. Primary care staff may also be uncertain about what they can or should offer to women with a suspected or diagnosed fetal abnormality (Statham et al 2003).

Trusts, Health Boards and managers should have a policy that ensures prompt and accurate communication between secondary and primary care staff about women with a suspected or diagnosed fetal abnormality. Primary care staff should have information about test results, should know what support they are expected to offer to women and couples in this situation, and should be equipped and able to provide it.

CHAPTER 8: CONTINUING THE PREGNANCY

This chapter deals mainly with the needs of mothers – and their partners if present – who know that their baby is very likely to die at or shortly after the birth and who have decided to continue the pregnancy.

If the baby cannot survive

Some women who know that their baby cannot survive may decide to continue with the pregnancy for several reasons. Some may feel that the diagnosis was made too late in the pregnancy for them to accept a termination. Some may wish to plan and prepare for their baby's birth and death, perhaps with the possibility of having some time with their baby after the birth. Some may find termination unacceptable on personal, religious or ethical grounds. Some may not believe the diagnosis or may find it too hard to accept.

> *I do not regret for a moment continuing the pregnancy. It meant that we had 6 precious hours with our beautiful daughter and those hours mean so much to me. And although it was awful knowing so early in the pregnancy that she could not live, it meant we were able to prepare ourselves and other people, and to plan exactly how we wanted her birth and her short life to be. The doctors and midwives were surprised at our decision but they accepted it and supported us.* Mother

Parents who decide to continue with the pregnancy despite the diagnosis of a lethal abnormality need respect, sensitive care and support, and recognition that their situation is special. They need to know that, if their baby is born alive, he or she will receive the best possible palliative care and will be kept as comfortable as possible until he or she dies. For most parents in this situation, the period between the diagnosis and the birth is extremely difficult, a time in which they can do very little but wait for the impending tragedy. It is important that the staff caring for them do all that they can to help and support them and that they respect their decision to continue with the pregnancy, even if they themselves would not have made the same choice (Chitty et al 1996).

> *The staff were great, really supported us and cared for us. There were only one or two people who seemed to think we had made a weird decision.* Mother

Some women may prefer not to have special attention even though they fully understand the situation, and may want to "enjoy a normal pregnancy", knowing that life will not be normal afterwards.

Some women find it hard to believe or to accept a diagnosis of lethal abnormality. They are likely to need time and support to help them take in and come to terms with their situation, unless there are urgent decisions to be made. Some may want to be treated as normally as possible during the pregnancy. However, they should not be given false reassurance (see below).

If the baby might live

Parents who continue the pregnancy knowing that there is a chance, however small, that their baby may live but will definitely require intensive intervention also need continuing sensitive supportive and co-ordinated care. Much of the guidance in this chapter also applies to these parents. However, because there is a chance that their baby might live, the type and intensity of antenatal care that they will receive following the diagnosis is likely to be very different.

PLANNING AND COMMUNICATION

Once a woman has decided that she wants to continue the pregnancy, she and her partner should be offered an appointment for a multidisciplinary meeting with the key staff who will be involved in their care. This meeting should include the consultant obstetrician, the lead midwife who will oversee the care of the mother during the rest of her pregnancy and her labour (see Continuous and co-ordinated care below), and/or the delivery suite manager or her deputy. Other people should be involved as appropriate, depending on the situation – for example, a genetic counsellor and/or a consultant neonatologist. The purpose of this meeting is to develop a plan of care that is tailored to the individual situation and that aims to optimise outcomes – including psychological outcomes – for the whole family (Breeze et al 2006).

The aims of the meeting are to:

- Confirm the diagnosis and prognosis and discuss them with the parents;

- Ensure that the parents understand the most likely outcome for the baby and any other possible outcomes;

- Discuss and agree a plan of care for the mother during the rest of the pregnancy and during the labour (see *Babies born alive at the threshold of viability in* Chapter 11);

- Discuss and agree a plan of care for the baby if he or she lives for a short time;

- Ensure that there will be clear and consistent communication between everyone involved, throughout the pregnancy and birth and afterwards.

The plan of care should be clearly documented: one copy should be kept in the mother's hospital antenatal notes, another given to the mother in her hand-held notes, a third sent to the referring unit, and a fourth sent to the mother's GP. As the pregnancy progresses, any developments and changes in the care plan should be discussed with the mother – and her partner – and with the other specialists involved. The plan of care should be updated and copies of the revised plans issued if necessary.

Because the planning meeting is likely to be extremely stressful for many parents, the lead midwife should take responsibility for ensuring that they understand what is being discussed and are consulted as appropriate. She should offer to go through the care plan with the mother – and her partner if present – after the meeting, and make sure that they have fully understood it and find it acceptable. The mother should be advised to carry the plan of care with her in her hand-held notes in case she goes into labour unexpectedly and the baby is born elsewhere (Breeze et al 2006).

If it is clear that medical intervention cannot save the baby, it may be possible to offer the mother some of her care at a midwives' clinic or from her GP if she would prefer this.

It is important to make sure that no inappropriate intervention is made at the birth: a caesarean section should normally only be performed if it is necessary for the mother's wellbeing. Provided the parents consent, no attempt should be made to resuscitate the baby after the birth (for more about who gives consent, see *Facilitating informed choice* in Chapter 4). It is very important that the decision is clearly written both in the mother's hand-held notes and in her hospital notes, and that it is communicated to the relevant staff, so that the baby is not inappropriately resuscitated, either by junior staff who have not been informed or if the mother goes into labour elsewhere.

A few parents may change their minds about resuscitation when they see their baby at birth. This can lead to difficulties but needs to be sensitively managed by a senior member of staff, ideally someone who was present when the question of resuscitation was originally discussed with the parents. It may be helpful to acknowledge the parents' distress, to gently remind them of the reasons for the decision not to resuscitate, and to re-state what is in their baby's best interests.

If there is a chance that the baby might live and the mother will be transferred to a specialist hospital to give birth, she should be offered the opportunity to visit the hospital beforehand to meet and talk to the staff who will be caring for her and her baby. (See also *Help for parents on low incomes* in Chapter 1.)

Funding to help with travel costs should be made available to parents on low incomes if they have to travel a long way for care.

CONTINUOUS AND CO-ORDINATED CARE

To avoid creating additional stress and anxiety for parents who are already under enormous pressure, it is very important that their care is well co-ordinated (Statham et al 2001: 176 ff). In addition to the obstetric consultant, the mother should be cared for during pregnancy by a small number of staff whom she can get to know and trust. She should not, for example, see a different midwife or junior doctor at every antenatal visit (Chitty et al 1996).

The member of the midwifery team designated as the mother's lead midwife should:

- Guide the parents through the system, explaining, whenever necessary, where they need to go, how to get there, whom they will see and why;

- Ensure that they have as much information as they want about the baby and the pregnancy and that the information is balanced, clear, up to date and specific;

- Make sure that the mother can make informed decisions and choices whenever appropriate and that she is able to feel, as far as possible, in control of what is happening;

- Try to ensure continuity of carers and that all staff caring for the mother are kept informed about the diagnosis and the plan of care, and of any changes;

- Liaise between the different departments and hospitals, with the GP and with community staff and ensure smooth transitions between different departments, hospitals, clinics and the community (see also *The place of care during pregnancy* below);

- Make sure that the parents have verbal and written information about what to do if there is an emergency, both during the day and out of hours;

- Make sure that the mother has the contact addresses of relevant voluntary organisations (see Appendix 2).

The lead midwife should not be the only person who supports the mother – and her partner – but should be there as a "back-stop" to keep an eye on their care, deal with questions and worries, and help sort out any problems. She should also try to ensure that the staff working with the parents are well supported and have opportunities to discuss both the care they are offering the parents and their own feelings.

SUPPORT FOR PARENTS

Many parents who know that their baby will or may die feel very isolated: support from staff is very important. "Even a single, brief positive encounter remained a treasured memory and had a significant impact on parents' coping" (Chaplin et al 2005).

In most cases, family members and friends find it very hard to listen to parents' distress and negative feelings. Parents may also be reluctant to talk about their situation for fear of having to deal with hurtful remarks or inappropriate reassurance, or of having to cope with other people's distress as well as their own. Some parents may find it helpful to talk to staff about what to say to relatives, friends and acquaintances, and how to respond to any insensitive or ill-informed remarks.

Staff caring for these parents need to be sensitive but realistic and to remain focused on the current situation. It can be tempting to try to offer unrealistic reassurance about the outcome of the pregnancy, or to talk about "when all this is over"; for example, suggesting that the parents can have another baby if this baby is certain to die, or talking about special schools if the baby may live but be disabled (Statham et al 2001: 175). Well-meaning attempts to provide unrealistic comfort or to distract parents from what they are going through can increase their distress and isolation and mean that they have no one to whom they feel they can talk honestly. It is important that parents are able to discuss with staff their possibly conflicting feelings about their decision and about the baby, and that they do not feel judged, rebuffed or patronised. They should also be offered an opportunity to see a counsellor. Parents of a baby with an inherited condition may want to see a genetic counsellor.

PHYSICAL CARE DURING PREGNANCY

If it is known that the baby will not live, the mother still needs antenatal care for herself. The father too needs to be acknowledged, both as an expectant father and as a parent facing a very painful situation. Routine antenatal provision is both insensitive and inappropriate for most mothers in this situation (Chitty et al 1996), and they should not be expected to wait with other women in the antenatal clinic. At the same time, care should be taken to ensure that they do not feel stigmatised or isolated.

Some women will not want any more tests or ultrasound examinations unless these are essential for their own wellbeing. For other women, scans, at least, offer a valuable opportunity to see their baby alive and/or may be helpful in confirming and explaining the diagnosis. Scans may also be important, for example, if the father was not present when the abnormality was first identified. Some parents may appreciate having photographs of the ultrasound scan and this should be offered (see also *Creating memories* in Chapter 12).

Women – and their partners if present – should be given as much information as they request about their baby. For many parents it is important to have all the information available, including the baby's sex if this is known, so that they can visualise and develop a relationship with the baby. Others may want very little information.

A woman whose baby has a life-threatening condition also needs to be recognised as an expectant mother rather than just "a container for the baby" (Statham et al 2001: 266). Much of what is said above also applies to her care. Women in this situation have to deal with enormous and prolonged uncertainty. Physical and emotional care for the mother can easily become forgotten in the anxiety and concern for the baby, particularly if she is seeing several different specialists and/or having to travel back and forth to a Fetal Medicine Unit in another hospital.

If there is a chance that treatment or other interventions may save the baby's life and the mother wants them, she may require a constant stream of tests, each of which is both stressful in itself and is followed by an anxious wait for the results. Continuity of care, good communication between staff, and sensitive and understanding support for the parents are essential.

THE PLACE OF CARE DURING PREGNANCY

Whenever women – or couples – are sent to another department or unit, whether for tests, discussions or procedures, or before labour, they should be given clear verbal and written information about where to go and how to get there (including details of parking facilities if they will be travelling by car). The referring unit should ensure that the staff who will receive the parents are expecting them and know why they are coming. A mother should not have to explain her situation to staff and should be received in a sensitive and supportive manner. This will also help her to feel confident that there is an overall plan for her care.

Women should not be put in situations that may cause them unnecessary distress. For example, they should not have to decide whether to explain their situation to other pregnant women and well-meaning enquirers while waiting for scans, tests or consultations. It is also upsetting to be with women whose pregnancies are normal and who are excited or are complaining about trivial (in comparison) things such as back ache. If a woman cannot be seen immediately, she should be asked if she would prefer a quiet place to wait away from other pregnant women and be assured that she will be called as soon as possible.

If a woman whose baby will not live has to be admitted for antenatal care, there should be a balance between giving her and her partner privacy and isolating them. She should be offered a single room wherever possible and asked if she would prefer to have meals brought to her room, rather than sit with other pregnant women. If the mother chooses to tell other women in the ward about her baby's prognosis, staff should be prepared to deal with the anxieties that this may raise in the other women.

SUPPORT FOR PARENTS DURING LABOUR AND BIRTH

Most parents, especially if this is their first baby, will want information about the process of labour and giving birth and their options for pain relief, including self-help techniques and positions for labour. Parents in this situation are unlikely to feel able to attend a standard antenatal class. If possible, they should be offered individual preparation sessions with an antenatal teacher who can empathise with them, understand their distress and help them to prepare for a birth that is likely to end in tragedy.

As part of preparation for coming into hospital for the birth, staff might suggest that the parents might like to bring in a shawl, a baby blanket or clothes to dress the baby in, and also a camera in case they decide that they want to take photographs.

Women should receive continuous support and care during the labour and should have access to the full range of pain relief options. Staff should be aware that the process of pushing the baby out can be extremely traumatic for a mother who knows that her unborn baby is safe as long as she or he remains inside her but that the birth will cause her baby's death.

> *I knew my baby was alive and safe inside me but I also knew that when he was born he would die. It made pushing the last thing I wanted to do. It was a truly horrendous situation to be in.* Mother

Whenever possible, the mother should be cared for in labour by members of the team that has cared for her during the pregnancy. As well as benefiting the parents and helping to ensure that the birth is handled according to the mother's wishes, a team approach can help to ensure that staff are well supported by each other, and so are less likely to distance themselves from the parents in this stressful situation.

If the baby is likely to die at or shortly after the birth, parents may want to plan how they want to welcome their baby and create memories. They need to know that their baby will be delivered gently, kept warm and comfortable, offered fluids by mouth if appropriate, and treated with dignity and love (see also *Late miscarriage and premature labour* in Chapter 11).

Parents should be offered opportunities to see and cuddle their baby and to keep him or her with them after the birth until he or she dies (see *Asking parents if they want to see and hold the baby* in Chapter 12). Others may prefer the baby to be cared for in the neonatal unit, because they find it too distressing to watch him or her slowly deteriorate (see also *Being with the baby at the time of death* in Chapter 14). Parents also need to know that they can keep the baby with them after the death for as long as they want (Chitty et al 1996).

> *I was referred for a specialist heart scan when I was 20 weeks as there is a family history of heart defects. I was very nervous and my worst fears came true - my baby had a serious heart defect. They asked me to decide if I wanted to continue with the pregnancy - for me this was an easy decision as I believe that every life is sacred. When he was born, we were shocked to find that he also had a hole in his skull. He was taken to special care, but then they said that there was nothing more they could do to save him. So they took the tubes out and I held my baby until he died. I do not regret my decision to continue with the pregnancy as I got to spend 3 precious days with my baby boy. Thankfully I now have three healthy children.* Mother

If medical care is planned for a baby with a life-threatening condition, parents need to know in advance what is likely to happen at the birth and who will be there to receive the baby. They should be offered an appointment with a neonatologist to discuss the baby's care, and an opportunity to visit the neonatal intensive care unit (see also Chapter 14). They may want to discuss how they would like the birth to be managed if the baby dies during the labour or birth (see previous paragraphs).

CHAPTER 9: LOSSES IN PREGNANCY – AN OVERVIEW OF EFFECTIVE CARE

OTHER RELEVANT CHAPTERS:
1: PROVIDING INCLUSIVE CARE
2: HOLISTIC CARE
3: LOSS AND GRIEF
4: COMMUNICATION
5: COMMUNICATION ACROSS LANGUAGE AND OTHER BARRIERS
10: EARLY PREGNANCY LOSSES
11: LOSSES IN THE SECOND AND THIRD TRIMESTERS
12. AFTER A LOSS

This chapter discusses some of the issues that are relevant to all childbearing losses, including the involvement of parents, support for partners, the place of care and pain management. The next two chapters make specific recommendations relevant to the care of parents who experience a loss in the first trimester – Chapter 10 – and of parents who lose a baby in the second or third trimester – Chapter 11.

This division between the first trimester and the second and third trimesters is not intended to suggest that there is a qualitative divide for parents between loss at different times, nor that earlier loss is less distressing than later loss. The meaning to parents of any childbearing loss is intensely personal and depends on many factors, only one of which may be the gestation of the baby. No assumptions should ever be made about what parents will feel.

> *The midwife behaved as if he was a normal live baby, she didn't treat me as if this was awful, she was just like, isn't he beautiful, look how much he weighs.* Mother

The care given to a family before and following a perinatal loss is extremely important and can set the stage for the family's entire grieving process (Leoni 1997: 361). Parents do not forget the events surrounding the loss of their baby. They need to be able to remember an experience which, however distressing, was handled with great care and sensitivity. In contrast, poor care can greatly exacerbate parents' distress, both immediately and in the long term.

> *There was a sensitive awareness of our needs and excellent continuity of care in the labour ward. I was cared for by three key midwives throughout my stay who showed great under standing of my needs and who obviously communicated well with each other.* Mother

Continuity of carers should be ensured whenever possible, so that a woman does not have to keep building new relationships at such a difficult and critical time. However, the other staff on the ward should be told that the parents are losing or have lost their baby, so they can react appropriately if they come into contact with them and do not inadvertently cause distress.

INVOLVING PARENTS

Loss of control and loss of certainty are major stressors and are almost inevitably part of the experience of childbearing loss. Parents who feel that they could have been better informed and prepared by staff, or who feel that they were not allowed to make important decisions, are likely to experience additional distress. To help parents retain a sense of control over what is happening, staff should offer them the opportunity to be involved in making decisions and should make sure that they know, as far as is possible, what is going to happen. This can have psychological benefits beyond the immediate decisions to be made (Moulder 1998: 222).

In order to make decisions, parents need to know what choices they have, and the advantages, disadvantages and possible consequences of each. Whenever possible, parents should be given time to assimilate this information and to discuss what would be best for them. However, staff also need to be aware that it can be difficult for parents to make decisions when they are distressed and frightened, and when the mother may be in pain or coping with the effects of analgesia (see also *Facilitating informed choice* in Chapter 4).

To ensure that staff are able to give all parents the information they need to make decisions, and that it is accurate and consistent, the hospital should have:

- A clear plan of care covering each type of pregnancy loss, including any care options where appropriate. This should cover hospital and primary care and should be known and understood by all the staff whom parents will encounter;

- At least one named member of the hospital staff who is fully informed about the relevant care plan, and who takes primary responsibility for ensuring that parents understand it, for overseeing their care and for communicating with the appropriate member(s) of the primary care staff when a woman goes home;

- At least one named member of the primary care staff who takes over responsibility for overseeing care and communication when a woman goes home (see also *Good communication between staff* in Chapter 4).

Preparation

Before any procedure, except in an emergency, staff should explain and discuss with parents what is likely to happen. Even when there is little time, most parents are grateful for efforts to inform and involve them as far as possible.

Many parents are surprised and shocked to find that even a relatively early miscarriage is similar to labour. A woman in later pregnancy whose baby has died in utero or who is having a termination for fetal abnormality may also not expect to labour and give birth. Women in their first pregnancy may not know what labour and birth are like and may need a lot of information.

If there is time to prepare, women whose labour will be induced or who are in spontaneous labour may want to make a birth plan This could state what they would like to happen and also what they fear and do not want.

Women may also want information about what (depending on the gestation) the products of pregnancy or the baby might look like. Most women do not know what to expect, and may find it helpful if staff offer to explain honestly and sensitively what they are likely to see. It may also be helpful to offer to show parents one or more photographs of babies of approximately the same gestation, if these are available. These photographs should not be from textbooks, as these are often unsuitable for parents and are likely to make things worse rather then better. The parents of the babies whose photographs are used must have given written consent.

If there is a chance that the baby might be born alive, even if she or he is unlikely to live for long, staff should explain how the baby would be cared for, and discuss with the parents what they might like to do (see *Babies born at the threshold of viability* in Chapter 11).

Some parents may have religious requirements or want to carry out a special ritual when the baby is born. This may be most likely for losses in the second and third trimester, or if the baby may be born alive. For example, Christian parents may want a naming and blessing ceremony, and staff should offer to contact the appropriate chaplain. Muslim parents may want the baby washed immediately after the birth and may want the father to whisper the Muslim call to prayer into the baby's ears. In the hours after the birth, some parents may want, for example, to pray with family or members of their congregation, to light candles, or to place the body in a certain position. If it seems appropriate, parents may be asked in advance what their wishes might be. If it is not appropriate, this question should be postponed until after the birth.

Most parents prefer to leave detailed discussions about whether they will want their baby to have a funeral until after the birth. However, some parents want to know beforehand. It may therefore be helpful for staff to mention at this stage that the parents will be asked later about what they might want. This opens the way for those who want to ask questions now.

PARTNERS

If a woman wants, she should be able to have her partner, or a relative or friend, with her at all times. This should apply regardless of the stage at which the pregnancy is ending. Some women may want to have more than one person with them, and this should be accommodated wherever possible. A few women may prefer to be alone, provided that they know that they can get help immediately if it is needed. Others do not wish to be left alone at any time, and should not be. Even if a woman has someone else with her, it is important that staff offer support and make it clear that they are available whenever needed.

Partners, when present, should be kept fully informed and should be involved whenever possible. They should receive support in their own right, because, in addition to losing a baby, they are likely to feel fearful for the woman, and powerless and worried about seeing her distressed and probably in pain. It may be helpful to say that, although there is very little that partners can actively do, just by being there they are showing their concern and support. It is also important to acknowledge that most people find just being there very difficult (see also *The place of care* below).

Partners often feel protective towards the woman, and may become very anxious that staff should be doing more to help her and, where appropriate, the baby. In some cases this may lead to aggression towards staff. Acknowledging the partner's concerns and giving clear explanations may help to reassure him that everything possible is being done.

THE PLACE OF CARE

The place of care should be appropriate to the stage of pregnancy and the type of loss that the woman is experiencing. Whether care is in an early pregnancy assessment unit, on a gynaecological ward or on a labour ward, women should always be looked after by staff who are specifically trained to deal not only with clinical care and physical needs, but also with the emotional needs of the women and their partners.

> I was put in a gynae ward because I was only 20 weeks. I wanted my baby to be acknowledged and recognised as a baby, but I wasn't allowed into the labour ward. Everyone around me was having Ds and Cs and hysterectomies. Mother

The facilities provided for parents who are losing a baby should be thoughtfully planned. Wherever possible, parents who are losing a baby should not have to wait or be cared for with others whose pregnancy or labour is progressing normally, or with parents with healthy babies.

The decoration of the rooms in which parents are cared for at the time of and after the loss is also important. For example, posters of women with babies are entirely inappropriate, and reproductions of well-known paintings should be avoided. Many parents find that their surroundings during this time are etched on their memories and that, long after-wards, a particular picture or other image can trigger very painful memories.

> I was wheeled into the delivery suite to deliver my stillborn daughter and was faced with a large photo of a smiling and emotional mother who had just delivered a live baby. I had had an epidural and couldn't turn away. All I could think was, "This is not how it's going to be for me". I asked the midwife and she quickly removed it. Mother

Consideration should be given to the practical needs of partners who may be spending many hours with the woman. Many maternity units have double rooms where couples can stay after a stillbirth, but partners also need to be catered for beforehand. They should not have to go home simply because there is nowhere for them to be. In any ward or room where women who are experiencing a childbearing loss are cared for, there should be:

- A comfortable chair in the same room;
- Toilet facilities nearby for men as well as for women;
- Facilities available round the clock so that partners can eat and drink at any time;
- Ideally, a room nearby with comfortable, reclining chairs and tea and coffee-making facilities where partners can take short breaks.

Policies on place of care

Each Trust and Health Board should have a policy that sets out the place of care for women experiencing pregnancy loss. The policy should cover the different types of loss and the gestations at which they occur. The policy should state that a woman with a later mid-trimester loss should, wherever possible, be offered an informed choice about whether she is cared for on a gynaecology or a labour ward.

Trusts and Health Boards will have different policies about the place of care for different types of loss. However, the basis of all policies should be that the place in which a woman is cared for should not add unnecessarily to her distress or limit her choices. The policies should also ensure that staff in the different wards have the necessary skills, competencies and facilities to provide optimal care for women and their partners.

Early miscarriages All Trusts and Health Boards should provide an early pregnancy assessment unit (EPAU), open at least five days a week, to which GPs have direct access. Dedicated units with a multidisciplinary team of supportive staff can streamline the care of women with pain or bleeding in early pregnancy. They offer both clinical and economic benefits. All EPAUs should have access to transvaginal ultrasound and staff who are trained to use it (RCOG 2006).

Except in an emergency, it is unacceptable to allow a woman to miscarry or deliver in the accident and emergency (A&E) department. Women who are admitted through A&E should be transferred to a ward as quickly as possible. At no time should a woman who is in labour be left on a trolley in a public place. A woman who is miscarrying should also not normally be in a ward where other women are terminating pregnancies for reasons other than fetal abnormality.

Later mid-trimester losses The place of care for women experiencing later mid-trimester losses varies from hospital to hospital. Women who are in labour during the latter half of the second trimester should normally be cared for in the labour ward. However, ideally all women should be able to choose: they should be informed about the types of pain relief that are available in each location. Some women would prefer not to be in a place where others are giving birth to healthy babies.

Care in the labour ward should ensure that:

- Each woman and her partner or labour companion receive appropriate care, understanding, and physical and emotional support throughout the labour and birth and afterwards;
- The full range of pain relief options is available;
- The baby is delivered and handled with care, sensitivity and respect;
- The parents are offered the same opportunities to create memories of their baby as if the baby had been stillborn at or after 24 weeks (see Chapter 12).

If a woman in labour during the second trimester is cared for in a gynaecology ward, she should be in a single room. The nurses caring for her – and her partner – must have the necessary competencies to offer the standard of care described in the list above.
All nurses who care for women in labour should have had training in the necessary skills. Inexperienced nurses who are caring for women in labour should be under the direct supervision of a nurse with the relevant experience. Ideally, nurses should have had an opportunity to witness a normal labour and birth on a delivery suite, so that they can see at first hand how a baby (regardless of whether alive or not) should be handled during delivery and afterwards.

Dedicated rooms Trusts and Health Boards should ensure that each labour ward has – depending on the size of the unit and the number of deliveries per annum – one or more specially equipped rooms in which women who have had an intra-uterine death, and women having a later mid-trimester loss, can labour. These rooms should be a short distance from the main labour rooms. Every effort should be made to ensure that women can remain in them for labour and for delivery. It is very important that parents are not shown into these rooms before they know that their baby has died or is likely to die.

> *We were shown into a very nice, comfortable room and only realised that something might be seriously wrong when we saw a label on the kettle saying "dedicated to the memory of...". We were devastated.* Mother

After the birth, parents should be cared for in rooms that have been specially designed for bereaved parents.

PAIN MANAGEMENT

Many women whose pregnancy ends early are unprepared for the length and pain of their labour (Moulder 1998: 163). Women who are in early spontaneous labour or whose labour is being induced need exactly the same level of information about pain relief as women who will have a straightforward labour. Whenever possible, the different options, and the advantages and disadvantages and side effects of each, should be discussed carefully beforehand and, where appropriate, during labour.

It is important to explain to women the possible benefits and disadvantages – both physical and emotional – of pain relief. Used well (that is, in a way that suits the wishes and needs of the individual) pain relief both reduces pain and can help women to feel more in control of what is happening. There is a risk, however, that some methods of pain relief, for example opiates, may diminish – in a negative way – a woman's ability to take in and participate in what is happening. She may feel confused later on about events that she needs to remember and understand, and this may add to her distress. This is especially important if she wants to see and hold her baby at birth.

It is important to find the appropriate type and level of pain relief for each woman. When assessing the pain relief required, staff should bear in mind that a woman who is frightened, shocked and/or distressed may feel pain more acutely. Without a healthy baby to look forward to following the birth, some women may find it particularly difficult to cope with the normal pain of labour and may fear that they are tearing or being damaged internally. They are likely to need extra encouragement and support to keep going (Woods 1997: 91) and continuity of carers is very important.

CHAPTER 10: EARLY PREGNANCY LOSSES

This chapter deals with specific issues relating to losses in the first trimester of pregnancy, including missed and incomplete miscarriage and early fetal demise, ectopic and molar pregnancies, and multi-fetal pregnancy reduction. Follow-up and ongoing care following early pregnancy loss are discussed at the end of the chapter and in Chapter 19. Additional recommendations specific to GPs' practices are contained in Guidance for GP practices in Chapter 22. The terminology used in this chapter to describe the different types of loss is in line with the recommendations made by the RCOG (2006) (see *Choosing words* in Chapter 4).

HISTOLOGICAL EXAMINATION FOLLOWING EARLY PREGNANCY LOSS

The RCOG (2004e) recommends that all products of conception should be sent for histological examination, so that women who are at risk of malignant disease following a molar pregnancy (see below) can be identified and referred to a specialist centre. Although increasing use of ultrasound has led to earlier diagnosis of molar pregnancies, ultrasound does not always identify partial moles. All women should be asked for their consent, and the value of the examination should be explained.

There should be a clear local policy on histological examination of the products of conception. All relevant hospital and primary care staff should be familiar with the policy. Women who miscarry at home are likely to be distressed if they comply with a request to take tissue to their GP or to the hospital, and then find that it is not examined but is simply disposed of. Arrangements for sensitive disposal of all products of pregnancy should be in place.

MISCARRIAGE AND INCOMPLETE MISCARRIAGE

We lost twins at 14 and 16 weeks. This was hard to deal with, as a miscarriage is considered an "invisible death" with no funeral or place of rest to visit. Mother

Early miscarriage may be seen as a routine and minor medical event by some staff, and a few women may be relieved because their pregnancy was unwanted. However, for most women miscarriage is very distressing and brings disappointment, sadness and grief. All women and couples who are experiencing a miscarriage need to feel supported and well cared for.

I lost our baby before I knew I was pregnant. I couldn't believe how hard this was, losing a baby I didn't even know I had. Mother

The first signs of a possible miscarriage can cause intense anxiety. It is important that staff show that they understand this and that they treat any sign of an impending miscarriage with proper concern. They should be aware that they have an important role to play, even when there may be nothing that they can do to prevent the loss.

I spent a week lying on the sofa pretending that I wasn't bleeding and that my heart wasn't breaking. Mother

The amount of practical care and support that is appropriate will vary: some women do not want much contact with health care staff at this time, others want a great deal. Many will want to know if anything can be done to prevent the loss of the baby, and some may be distressed and feel guilty because they believe that the miscarriage is the result of something they have done or have failed to do. Women who are older, who have undergone fertility treatment, or who have already had one or more miscarriages, are likely to be particularly anxious and may need additional support and help.

When a woman contacts her GP, midwife or health visitor because of bleeding in early pregnancy, she should, if appropriate (see next paragraph), be referred for assessment, ideally at an early pregnancy assessment unit (EPAU) (see *Policies on place of care* in Chapter 9). Some women may feel that they can get enough support and information over the telephone, provided the staff member they talk to can give them as much time as they need and will keep in touch. Whenever possible, the woman should be able to telephone or see the same person if she needs further advice and support.

Because referring women to an EPAU if they are less than 6 weeks pregnant is unlikely to be beneficial, Trusts and Health Boards should have a policy that defines the criteria for referral. This should be disseminated to all relevant primary care staff.

MISSED MISCARRIAGE AND EARLY FETAL DEMISE

The diagnosis of a missed miscarriage (also called a delayed or silent miscarriage), or early fetal demise (formerly referred to as an anembryonic pregnancy or blighted ovum – see *Choosing words* in Chapter 4), often comes as a sudden and complete shock to the woman and her partner, as it is often identified only at the first routine scan.

Women who discover that their baby has been dead for some time can feel ashamed and guilty because they had not realised that anything was wrong. Women who have had a missed miscarriage or early fetal demise should be offered the option of an evacuation of retained products of conception (ERPC - see later) or, if it is available, medical management. However, some may prefer to wait until they pass the products of the pregnancy naturally.

If early fetal demise is identified, the woman may find it hard to believe, especially as she "feels pregnant", her hormone levels continue to rise and a pregnancy test is positive. Recent research studies on early fetal demise suggest that the apparently empty pregnancy sac did once contain an embryo but that it was reabsorbed at a very early stage of development. This means that it is inaccurate to say that the woman has not been pregnant (Regan 2001: 18–19). Women need clear and sensitive explanation and to know that it is likely that the embryo could not continue to develop because something went wrong at a very early stage. They should be told that no special follow-up is needed and should be reassured that, although upsetting and sad, this is likely to have been a random event and unlikely to recur.

MOLAR PREGNANCY

A molar pregnancy, or hydatidiform mole, is the most common type of placental tumour. It can be complete or partial:

- Complete moles are rare in White European women but more common in women whose families originated in south-east Asia. In a small number of cases, a complete mole can develop into a choriocarcinoma;

- Partial moles are much more common and usually result in the same signs as a miscarriage or an incomplete miscarriage. Partial moles rarely become invasive. However, all women should be carefully followed up at a specialist centre (Regan 2001: 22–23).

Few people are aware of the existence of molar pregnancies. Most women only find out that they have had a molar pregnancy some time after their miscarriage, by which time they may be beginning to adjust to their loss. They are likely to be shocked and frightened at the news, and may find it hard to take in. They need a careful and sensitive explanation about what has been found and should be offered an immediate appointment.

At this appointment, women – and their partners if present – need clear information about the findings and their possible implications. They should be told that they will need follow-up at a specialist cancer centre. It is important that women are forewarned about this, so that they are not unnecessarily shocked and frightened when they receive a letter from a cancer centre. They should also be given high quality supplementary information (including information in other formats) to take away.

Women – and couples - now face a situation which, at best, means a delay before they can consider trying to conceive again and, at worst, is life-threatening. They are bound to have additional fears and concerns and should be offered extra support and help.

CARE IN HOSPITAL

"Women often tell us how the care they receive makes all the difference in helping them come to terms with their losses, especially in early miscarriage, where the parents may be the only people who recognise that their loss was a baby." (Personal communication, Miscarriage Association 2007)

If a woman attends a hospital department and leaves again within a short time, her stay and her progression through the system can be distressingly disjointed. It is easy for her to feel that she is simply being processed through an uncaring system. The different members of staff whom she sees may know little about her and may seem to have no time for her. Each staff member may also believe that someone else in the chain will give the woman the information, support and time that she needs.

Each member of staff should try to build a relationship, however brief, with the women they care for. Although some health care staff believe that the expression of sympathy will "open the floodgates", a purely clinical approach is unhelpful and hurtful. Even a few words, such as "I am sorry that this is happening to you", can help a woman to feel cared for and, perhaps, that she has been supported during a painful and difficult experience.

There should be a clear plan of care for early miscarriage, which includes, as far as possible, continuity of carer. Ideally, each woman should have a named member of staff who is responsible for her care, for giving her the information she wants and for ensuring that she moves smoothly between departments (Moulder 1998: 61–65).

Choice of management methods

In the case of an incomplete or missed miscarriage in the first trimester, women should be offered a choice of management methods: having a choice is associated with positive quality of life outcomes (RCOG 2006; Smith et al 2006).

Smith et al (2006) and Ogden and Maker (2004), in qualitative studies of women who had recently experienced early miscarriage, found a wide range of preferences and views about the management of early miscarriage:

- Some women prefer no intervention; others want to bring the miscarriage to completion as soon as possible;

- Some want to experience the miscarriage and grieve for their lost baby; others want to avoid further conscious experience of the miscarriage;

- Some want to see the fetal remains if this is possible; others find this idea frightening and want to avoid seeing anything;

- Some feel safer in hospital; others far prefer to be at home.

- Some women prefer surgical management because it is more predictable and resolves the problem quickly; in contrast, a surprisingly high proportion of women feel that being hospitalised, having a general anaesthetic and undergoing an operation, are frightening and traumatic events to be avoided if possible;

- Many women who opted for expectant management emphasised the importance for them of a natural solution. However, some were unprepared for the amount of bleeding and pain that they experienced and for the time the whole process took (Smith et al 2006).

The studies concluded that there is no "one best way" to treat miscarriage that will suit all women, but that all women consider it very important to have good information about the different options, to be given time to make their decision, and to be cared for by competent and caring staff.

Trinder et al (2006) found that the incidence of infection following surgical, medical and expectant management of first trimester miscarriage was low (2–3 per cent) and that there were no differences in infection rates between the different management methods. However, they also found that there were a significant number of unplanned admissions to hospital and unplanned surgical interventions in women who had had expectant or medical management.

Whenever possible and clinically appropriate, each woman should be offered a choice between expectant, medical and surgical management. In order to make the choice that best suits her and her situation, she needs accurate and understandable information about the different methods, what each involves, the time it is likely to take, and the advantages and disadvantages of each (see below). Women should not feel pressured to make a choice immediately. Unless their medical condition dictates otherwise, those who want to go home to think about their decision should be encouraged to do so. Once a woman has made a decision, she may want more detailed information about what to expect: predictability is important and helps increase women's sense of control over what is happening to them (Smith et al 2006).

Expectant and medical management

All women who are offered either expectant or medical management should be given a clear explanation of what is involved, when they will need to return for further assessments or treatment and, depending on the gestation, what they may see when they miscarry. Women who are returning home during the miscarriage must be given a direct phone number for 24-hour telephone advice and support, and should be encouraged to phone if they are at all worried. They must have immediate access to inpatient care when necessary (RCOG 2006). Each woman should also be given written back-up information and told that, unless she objects, her GP will be informed about the miscarriage (see also *Communication between hospital and community staff* in Chapter 4).

Women who are offered medical management should be informed about the extent and duration of bleeding, which can last for up to 21 days (RCOG 2006); what to expect in terms of pain and how to manage it; and possible side effects and what they can do to alleviate them. They also need to know that, although there is a good chance that medical management will be successful, in some cases surgery may be necessary.

Women who are having expectant management and are at home while miscarrying are often understandably anxious about what is happening, and may need a lot of psychological support as well as regular contact and review. They should be told:

- *That there may be a long period* of time during which they may not know whether they have lost their baby or not. This uncertainty can be extremely hard to bear. Although advice to wait and see what happens may be acceptable for a while, the waiting time should be limited by offering each woman an appointment for further assessment;

- *About the possible ranges of bleeding and pain, and how to manage them.* There is a striking variation in the amount of bleeding and pain that women experience: some have very heavy bleeding for a long time and pain similar to that of labour (Smith et al 2006; Ogden and Maker 2004). It is important that all women know that this may happen and what they can do to alleviate pain;

- *What to do with the products of conception.* Women who lose a complete embryo or fetus at home, and flush it away by mistake, may be distressed at not being able to see it or to dispose of it more respectfully. They should be told how they might collect and store any tissue that they pass and where they could take it (see *Histological examination following early pregnancy loss* above);

Surgical management

I climbed up onto the bed and I remember having the doctor check my name and birth date. Then the mask was put on to send me to sleep and even as I was being put under the anaesthetic the tears were pouring. I did not want them taking my babies. For weeks afterwards the smell of the mask was all I could smell and the memory was terrible.
Mother

Although, in clinical terms evacuation of retained products of conception (ERPC) is a minor procedure, it is a significant and often worrying event for the woman. It marks the end of the pregnancy in a very definite and final way. Afterwards women may feel intensely sad and empty, even if they are also relieved that the miscarriage itself is over.

Before an ERPC, the woman should know why it is considered necessary and what will happen. Many women are more familiar with the term D and C, and may not realise that ERPC is the same procedure and it may be helpful to mention this.

Women should be prepared for some bleeding and pain afterwards, and should be offered pain relief. They may want to know what will be removed during the ERPC and what it will look like. Parents who want to see what has been removed should be sensitively prepared for what they will see, and theatre staff informed of their wishes.

Women should be advised beforehand not to travel home alone after the ERPC: they will need to arrange for someone to accompany them.

A woman's consent should be obtained before samples are sent for examination (HTA Code 1 2006: 66). She should also be told that, unless she wants to make alternative arrangements, the hospital will ensure that the baby (or tissue) receives respectful disposal (see *Policies and practice* in Chapter 17).

Timing Some women will not want to wait for an ERPC; others will appreciate some delay. If possible, a woman's preferences should be respected. It is important that all women receive adequate support from staff at whatever time of day or night the procedure is carried out, and that they are kept informed of any delays in going to theatre. If a long delay is anticipated they should be offered something light to eat and drink.

The rest of this chapter deals with ectopic and molar pregnancies and multifetal pregnancy reduction. Most of what is recommended in *Care in hospital* above also applies to these types of loss.

ECTOPIC PREGNANCY

Ectopic pregnancy affects more than 1 in every 100 pregnancies and the incidence is increasing. Women of childbearing age who are sexually active and who have symptoms such as abdominal or shoulder-tip pain, or a missed or late period, or abnormal bleeding, should be taken seriously. If an ectopic pregnancy is suspected, the woman should be referred to hospital or to an EPAU for immediate assessment (Walker 2002; Tay et al 2000).

Depending on the circumstances, an ectopic pregnancy can be managed medically, surgically and in some cases expectantly. Except in an emergency (see Surgical management below), a woman should receive clear and factual information about the different treatment options and the advantages and disadvantages of each, so that she can participate in choosing the most appropriate course of action (RCOG 2004c). For women who are waiting for confirmation of a suspected ectopic pregnancy, or whose pregnancy is being managed expectantly or medically, the waiting time can be extremely difficult and frightening.

Medical management

Women who are offered medical management should be given verbal and written information (and/or information in other formats) about:

- What medical management involves;
- How long it may take, the benefits, risks and adverse side-effects;
- What to expect in terms of pain and bleeding;
- How often they will need to return for assessment.

They should also be advised to avoid sexual intercourse during treatment and to use reliable contraception for the three months after treatment is completed because methotrexate is teratogenic (RCOG 2004c).

Surgical management

If a woman is admitted as an emergency, she and her partner are likely to be upset, frightened and anxious about the surgery and about her safety. They may also be very sad at the loss of the baby. Women who did not realise that they were pregnant may be shocked both by the discovery and by the loss. Many will also be worried that surgery may reduce their chances of conceiving in the future.

Parents in this situation need the same sensitive and individual care that is needed by all parents facing the loss of a pregnancy. Although there may be very little time before surgery to explain what is happening, it is still important that the woman – or couple – are given as much information and preparation as possible. Partners often have an anxious and frightening wait, usually by themselves, while the woman is undergoing surgery. A named member of staff should be responsible for offering support to the partner while he is waiting for news, and for ensuring that he is not left in suspense for any longer than is absolutely necessary.

Once the woman is fully recovered from the anaesthetic, she and her partner should be given clear information about the reasons for the surgery and what was done. Staff should choose their words with care: although it may be clinically correct to talk about "an ectopic" the woman is likely to see this as the loss of her baby; "removal of a tube", in practice, means significantly reducing the woman's chances of conceiving again. Parents may also want to know what will happen to the baby or to the tissue that has been removed (see Chapter 17).

Before she leaves hospital, the woman should be given advice about taking care of herself during the recovery period, and a follow-up appointment made. Some women will want to discuss the implications for future pregnancies before they go home; others may not be ready to consider this. If the subject is not discussed before she leaves hospital, it should be raised at a follow-up appointment (see below and Chapter 19). Women should be offered information about the Ectopic Pregnancy Trust and other relevant organisations (see Appendix 2).

MULTIFETAL PREGNANCY REDUCTION

If a woman is found to be expecting three or more babies, she may be offered fetal reduction to reduce the risk of losing the pregnancy or of going into very premature labour with consequent risks for the babies. These risks must be weighed up against the risk of the procedure, which may result in the loss of the pregnancy. For many parents this is a very difficult and frightening decision, which raises moral and ethical dilemmas. For some parents, fetal reduction may be out of the question. If the parents decide against reduction, for whatever reason, their decision should be supported (Maifeld et al 2003).

Parents should be given clear information about the possible practical and emotional benefits and the risks to the mother, to the whole pregnancy, and to individual babies, of having or not having the reduction. They need to know how fetal reduction is carried out and that, after the procedure, the fetuses that have died remain in the uterus but do not harm the surviving baby or babies. They also need to know that, if the procedure is carried out early in the pregnancy, there are unlikely to be any visible remains of the fetuses that have died when the surviving baby or babies are born.

Parents may feel very isolated both around the time of making the decision and undergoing the procedure, and after the remaining baby or babies are born. Family members and friends rarely understand the complexity or anguish of the decision: some parents may not feel able to tell them (Bergh et al 1999). For parents who have had assisted conception, deciding to abort one or two fetuses after having gone through so much to become pregnant can seem particularly bizarre and frightening. Even though most parents who have had successful fetal reduction feel afterwards that they made the right decision, they may also experience guilt, a sense of failure, fear of criticism by other people and long-term grief at the loss of one or more of their potentially healthy babies (Bryan 2002).

Parents need time and support to make their decision. If they decide to go ahead, they should be encouraged to think about the implications for the surviving children and what they might tell them in years to come. If the parents are planning not to tell them, they should be aware that that if they have ever discussed the reduction with family members or friends there is always a risk that the surviving child or children may inadvertently discover later on (MBF 1997b). Parents should be reassured that they can get counselling and support at any time in the future to help with telling the children or with any difficulties which may arise.

Some parents may want to see a counsellor to discuss their decision. They may also want to contact the Multiple Births Foundation (MBF) for more information and to discuss the decision with someone other than the health professionals caring for them. Some parents may want to contact the Twins and Multiple Births Association (TAMBA), which can put them in touch with other parents who have faced this difficult dilemma (see Appendix 2).

Many parents who decide to have embryo reduction are upset by the "seemingly (and often actual) arbitrary choice as to which ... should live and which should die" (Denton and Bryan undated). Many find the procedure stressful, frightening and very distressing. They need strong and understanding support before, during and afterwards (Bergh et al 1999). It is important that the staff carrying out the procedure are very sensitive to the needs and feelings of the parents, and do what they can to minimise their distress – for example, ensuring that any discussion about which embryo to select is discreet and cannot be overheard by the parents.

When the surviving babies are born, staff should be aware that parents may still need to mourn the loss, and that this can be very difficult if there is no body, and when they are also celebrating their surviving baby's – or babies' – birth.

FOLLOW-UP APPOINTMENTS AFTER EARLY LOSS

Appropriate support after an early loss can bring significant psychological benefit (RCOG 2006). Women who miscarry early are likely to want information and discussion about why the miscarriage occurred and whether it is likely to happen again. Trusts, Health Boards and managers should ensure that the care pathway for women who experience miscarriage includes the offer of a follow-up appointment either with their GP or with a member of the consultant team, depending on the circumstances.

All women with a history of recurrent miscarriage (normally three or more) should be offered a range of investigations (RCOG 2003). They should be offered referral for an assessment at the nearest specialist centre for the care of parents who have experienced recurrent pregnancy loss.

ONGOING SUPPORT

Miscarriage is seldom taken seriously by those who have not experienced one, and few people understand how distressing it can be (Mander 2005: 42). In addition, because many parents delay announcing a pregnancy until the end of the first trimester, their friends, family members and colleagues may not even have known about the pregnancy. All this can make life doubly hard for parents at a time when they need special consideration and support (see also Chapter 19).

"Even though miscarriage is so common, it's still something of a taboo subject – people just don't talk about it. This can leave women feeling very alone. What's more, most women never find out why they have miscarried, so they often assume that it must have been something they did or didn't do." (Personal communication, Miscarriage Association 2006)

Staff may be able to help parents think through whom they want to tell about the miscarriage, and who within their family and social circle would be helpful and supportive. It can also help to warn parents that they may encounter insensitive and unintentionally hurtful remarks such as, "It was nature's way of telling you there was something wrong with your baby"; "You're young, you can always have another one"; or "At least you can be grateful you've already got two children". Women and their partners may need to be assertive in explaining to family members and friends how they are feeling and what they would find helpful.

> *Everyone said it was for the best, that the baby wasn't growing properly, that it would never have survived. They say at least it happened before it had a chance and that you just have to move on. I know all those things. I know it was only a tiny thing that didn't look much like a baby, but it was my baby, it was Jason, it was part of me, and it took a part of me when it died.* Mother

All parents should be offered information about the relevant voluntary organisations – for example, the Miscarriage Association, Sands, the TAMBA Bereavement Support Group and the Multiple Births Foundation (see Appendix 2).

CHAPTER 11: LOSSES IN THE SECOND AND THIRD TRIMESTERS

The silence is the thing that will stay with me forever, and seeing my beautiful son with his eyes closed. He was so still. Mother

This chapter deals with issues that relate specifically to late miscarriage and premature labour, intra-uterine death, intra-partum death and stillbirth, termination for fetal abnormality and selective feticide. Additional recommendations specific to GPs' practices are contained in *Guidance for GP practices* in Chapter 22.

LATE MISCARRIAGE AND PREMATURE LABOUR

There was fear of losing our longed for children. There was fear of what they would look like and what would happen. I was in complete denial of what, to everyone else, was inevitable. I can still see the shock on the faces of the hospital staff. Father

Late miscarriage and premature labour are often viewed by staff as very different events. However, from the parents' perspective they are very similar. In both cases, parents are likely to be extremely distressed and frightened and to need continuous sensitive and supportive care throughout the labour, during the birth and afterwards. They should be cared for in a ward or department that is equipped and staffed to meet their specific needs. While the term "fetus" is the accurate medical term, it is an inappropriate word to use with parents: the word "baby" is used in most places in these Guidelines.

Babies who will not be born alive
If it is known that the baby will not be born alive, and if there is time, parents might want to begin to think about whether they might want to see, touch and hold the baby. They should be told that the baby will be treated with compassion and dignity during and after the birth, whether or not they want to see or hold him or her (see *Creating memories* in Chapter 12).

Babies born alive at the threshold of viability
A baby of any gestation who breathes or exhibits other "signs of life" - for example, a heartbeat, pulsation of the umbilical cord, or definite movement of voluntary muscles – after expulsion from his or her mother, whether or not the cord has been cut or the placenta is attached, is regarded as born alive (WHO 1992).

Evidence indicates that the outcome for babies who are born alive before 24 weeks' gestation is likely to be poor. Even with intensive care, most of these babies die: a few survive, though almost always with some level of disability:

- For babies born at 22 and 23 weeks, survival to discharge from intensive care is rare;

- Below 22 weeks' gestation, survival is "almost unrecorded": for this reason these babies are sometimes termed "pre-viable" (EPICure study 1995, cited in Nuffield 2006: 9.15, 9.17 and 5.5).

There has been much debate among both professionals and the public about the responsibilities and duties of health care staff in relation to the care of these very premature babies. The Nuffield Working Party report *Critical care decisions in fetal and neonatal medicine: ethical issues* (Nuffield 2006) addresses some of these issues and states that:

- Once a baby is born alive, he or she acquires the same legal status as any other human being, and the parents and staff owe him or her a duty of care. The baby's best interests must be a central consideration in determining whether and how to treat him or her (Nuffield 2006: 2.21, 2.49);

- There is no legal requirement to provide life-sustaining treatment if parents and staff agree that a baby is unlikely to survive because he or she is very premature and/or suffers from such severe abnormalities that it is not in his or her best interests to be given invasive intensive care. Babies should not be subjected to intensive interventions that are unlikely to have any benefit and which may cause suffering (Nuffield 2006: 9.14). The legal obligation is to provide appropriate care (Nuffield 2006: 9.13);

- There are no good reasons to draw a moral distinction between withholding and withdrawing treatment from a baby, provided that these actions are motivated in each case by an assessment of the baby's best interests (Nuffield 2006: 2.33).

The care of babies born at the threshold of viability can present great dilemmas for everyone involved. Many parents are understandably anxious that everything possible should be done for their baby. Some may be influenced by press reports of the 'miraculous' survival of an extremely premature baby, and have unrealistic expectations about what can be done for their baby. Many health care staff think that it is wrong to subject a baby who is extremely unlikely to survive to invasive and painful interventions that they do not believe will be in the baby's best interests. However the guidance from different professional organisations is inconsistent.

The Nuffield Working Party (2006: 9.15) recommends that the relevant professional bodies should consider developing guidelines on deciding whether to institute full intensive care for babies born below 26 weeks' gestation. In the meantime, each unit should have a policy on the management of babies born alive at the threshold of viability. This should be agreed and endorsed by all the professional groups that might be involved in the care of the mother and/or the baby.

Good practice
When it is anticipated that an extremely pre-term baby, with or without an abnormality, may show signs of life after birth, and if there is time, the realistic prospects for the baby and the likely consequences of different courses of action should be discussed within the health care team and with the parents, so that a care plan can be jointly agreed (NMC 2007; RCOG 2001;

BAPM 2000). The care plan should be clearly documented in the mother's notes.

However, a proper assessment of the baby's condition is often not possible until he or she is born. It is therefore important that staff tell parents that the plan of care may have to be adapted once a doctor is able to examine the baby and decide what is in his or her best interests (BAPM 2000).

If no care plan has been agreed and no senior paediatrician is available when a very premature baby is born showing signs of life, the nurse or midwife "must use their professional judgment as to whether the baby is capable of survival" (NMC 2007).

- If the baby is born before 22 weeks gestation (NMC 2007), or has a lethal abnormality such as anencephaly and will die shortly after birth 'in any event', comfort care (see below) should be given (NMC 2007; BAPM 2000);

- If it is thought that the baby is capable of surviving for more than a short period of time, the nurse or midwife "should instigate resuscitative measures". Senior medical staff will assess the baby and decide with the parents whether to withdraw treatment (NMC 2007). If the doctor decides that intervention is not in the baby's best interests, and the parents agree, comfort care (see below) should be given.

If it is known that the baby cannot survive, it is very important that the parents know that their baby will be given comfort care if he or she is born alive - that is, be cared for with respect and tenderness at all times, be kept warm, and be offered fluids by mouth (BAPM 2000). They should be told that, if they want to, they can see, touch and hold their baby for as long as they choose.

Detailed discussions with the mother may be inappropriate before the birth, for example if she is in strong labour or has had analgesia that affects her ability to concentrate. If the father is present, staff should discuss the situation with him and ideally reach agreement about how the baby will be cared for. The mother should always be told about the type of care that is planned for the baby and what to expect when the baby is born. For example, she and her partner should be gently and sensitively warned that some babies who are born too early to survive may make movements at birth, and that in a few babies this may continue for some time, but it does not mean that the baby will survive.

Mothers who were not able to participate in decision-making before the birth should have an opportunity afterwards to discuss with the doctors caring for her and for her baby the decisions that were taken and what happened.

BABIES WHO WILL BE OFFERED INTENSIVE CARE

If the baby might be admitted to the neonatal unit, the parents should, if there is time, be offered an opportunity to visit the unit beforehand and be informed about the care that the baby would receive.

If there is time, the management plan should be discussed with the parents and they should be told what to expect when their baby is born. For example, several additional members of staff will be called, including a paediatrician who will assess and initiate treatment for the baby and in due course transfer the baby to the neonatal intensive care unit. (For more about intensive neonatal care see Chapter 14.)

Good practice
Discussions and decisions about whether to institute critical care for babies at any gestation should be made in partnership with the parents and with the health care team (Nuffield 2006: 2.48; RCPCH 2004; BAPM 2000). If there is time before the birth, a neonatal paediatrician should talk to the parents about the baby's prospects and what should be done. The discussion should cover the baby's likely condition and prognosis at birth, based on local and national statistics for premature babies at this gestation, and should also take account of any specific problems that have been diagnosed or are suspected. However, parents should be told that it is extremely difficult to predict the outcome for any individual baby (Nuffield 2006:9.3).

Depending on the condition of the baby and on the gestation, some parents may not want treatment to be initiated or continued because they do not want their baby to suffer and/or because of the risks of severe disability if the baby survives. Caring for a child who is seriously disabled or ill significantly affects the lives of his or her parents. The implications for them and for other family members should be taken into account during discussions and when decisions are being made (Nuffield 2006: 2.29).

Some parents do not want to decide what should happen to their baby. In this case, doctors should make this decision in consultation with colleagues as appropriate, based on their view of the baby's best interests (Nuffield 2006: 2.47–2.48). They should tell the parents about the decision and offer them an opportunity to discuss it if they want to.

An experienced paediatrician should always be present at the birth to assess the actual gestational age and condition of the baby (Nuffield 2006: 9.16a).

In a multiple birth where one baby will die and the other(s) will live, parents often feel torn between their babies. It may be helpful to encourage them to devote their attention to the dying or dead baby in the short time that is available to them, in the knowledge that they will have much longer with the one(s) that survive.

TERMINATION OF PREGNANCY FOR FETAL ABNORMALITY

The pain of loss, and the pain of being the one to make the decision to create that loss, are the hardest things I will ever have to bear. Mother

Women and their partners who decide to have a termination for fetal abnormality at any gestation are likely to feel extremely anxious and distressed. Research confirms that the intensity of grief experienced by women who terminate a pregnancy for fetal abnormality is as profound as that of women who lose a baby spontaneously (Statham et al 2001: 269; Zeanah et al 1993) (see also *Grief and childbearing losses* in Chapter 3).

She couldn't have lived, and she was only 18 weeks when she died, but I loved her as much as I love my two boys. Mother

Every experience is individual, and the feelings and responses of parents who decide to terminate a pregnancy for fetal abnormality may be influenced by many factors. Many parents experience an agonising combination of sadness, guilt, doubt, anxiety, relief, failure, shame, self-blame, vulnerability, anger and loneliness. For most parents the additional burden of having *decided* to end the pregnancy, however well thought through their decision, makes it even more difficult to come to terms with the loss. They may find the situation particularly distressing if the baby has a non-lethal abnormality (Korenromp et al 2005). For some parents the particularly heartbreaking circumstances of termination for fetal abnormality can lead to severe trauma, intense grief, and post-traumatic stress disorder (Kersting et al 2005; Korenromp et al 2005; Zeanah et al 1993).

It is very important that staff caring for parents who have decided to terminate a pregnancy do not add to their distress by indicating any disapproval or judgement of their decision (Statham 2002) (see also *Conscientious objection* in Chapter 23).

Discussion and planning

I was really scared about how my baby would look. Nobody mentioned it and I didn't dare ask. Mother

Women – and couples – should be gently prepared for what is likely to happen during the labour and birth and afterwards, and for how the baby is likely to look. They should be offered choices about pain relief and how they would like their labour and birth to be managed (see Chapter 9).

Some women may want to have a blessing ceremony for the baby before the termination is carried out. Women having a medical termination may want to plan the labour and birth, and/or to see, touch or hold their baby after the birth, and/or have a blessing. They may also want to create memories of their baby (see *Creating memories* in Chapter 12). Staff may find it very difficult to suggest these possibilities to parents in this situation and it must clearly be done with great sensitivity. However, it may help women to know that many parents who have had a termination for fetal abnormality have welcomed such suggestions and have valued the opportunities this gave them (Statham et al 2001: 81–82; Moulder 1998: 130–138).

Some parents may be grateful for help in thinking about what to say to other people about their loss, whether they will want visitors when they are in hospital after the termination, and whether they will want cards or flowers. If they have decided not to tell family members and friends about the termination, it is extremely important that staff on the ward know this and maintain complete confidentiality (ARC 2005).

Termination of pregnancy before 21 weeks + 6 days' gestation

If a woman undergoes medical termination before 21 weeks + 6 days' gestation, she – and her partner – should be gently and sensitively told that the baby may make movements at birth but that this does not mean that the baby could survive even with intensive care. Parents should be assured that the baby will be given comfort care – warmth and the offer of fluids by mouth – and that they can see, touch and hold the baby if they want to (see *Babies born alive at the threshold of viability* earlier).

Termination of pregnancy at or after 21 weeks + 6 days

The RCOG recommends that "for all terminations at gestational age of more than 21 weeks + 6 days, the method chosen should ensure that the fetus is born dead" (RCOG 2001).

When feticide is discussed, it is very important that the woman understands, before she makes a decision, what is involved, where the procedure will be carried out, and what she is likely to feel during and after the procedure. She also needs to know when and where her labour will be induced. Some women may feel that one advantage of feticide is that they can be sure that their baby does not suffer during the labour and birth.

The parents of a baby who has been diagnosed with a lethal abnormality may decide not to have feticide before the termination. If the baby is, or may be, born alive they may be grateful for the opportunity to hold her or him after the birth and to be together as a family, even if only for a short while, before the baby dies. Staff are not under a legal obligation to take all possible steps to preserve the life of a baby with such serious abnormalities that it is not in his or her best interests to survive. In this situation, the mother's decision to decline feticide should be respected and supported (Nuffield 2006: 4.16). The parents should receive the same information about what to expect when the baby is born as those whose baby might be born alive at the threshold of viability (see earlier).

The parents must also be sensitively told that if the baby lives even for a very short time and then dies, they will have to register the baby's birth and death (see *Certification following a termination if the baby is born alive and then dies* in Chapter 16).

Travelling to a Fetal Medicine Unit
In many cases women have to travel to another unit to have the feticide carried out. Some may want to stay at this hospital to give birth rather than travel back to their local hospital (Statham at al 2001: 79). This should be offered whenever possible.

A woman travelling to a different unit should be given a clear map and careful instructions about where to go. The staff in the unit should be expecting her so that they can welcome her without her having to explain why she has come. If she is planning to come alone, staff should discuss with her whether she might like to come with her partner or another supporter, so that she does have to make the journey alone. Women who plan to travel by car should be told that they should not drive themselves.

> *Travelling to the fetal medicine unit for the feticide was the hardest journey I have ever made. I knew Ella couldn't live but she was my baby and I loved her just as much as I love her brothers. I always will.* Mother

Funding to help with travel costs should be made available to parents on low incomes if they have to travel a long way for the procedure.

The procedure
Complete privacy should be provided for what is an extremely stressful and distressing event for both parents and staff. Careful thought should be given to who, apart from the woman's partner or supporter, is present (Statham et al 2001: 79). If anyone else wants to be present, for example for teaching purposes, the parents must be asked for their consent. They must not be put under any pressure to give it.

The RCOG (2001) states: "Consideration can be given to abolishing fetal movements by the instillation of anaesthetic and/or muscle relaxant agents immediately prior to potassium chloride administration". If a woman feels unable to cope with the procedure, she should be offered sedation.

During the procedure, the ultrasound screen should be placed so that neither the mother nor the father (nor anyone else who is there to support the mother) can see it. Some parents may want to see the screen afterwards so that they can be certain that the baby no longer has a heartbeat and therefore cannot suffer during the labour and birth.

Asystole should be confirmed after five minutes and it is "mandatory to confirm asystole by an ultrasound 30 to 60 minutes after the procedure, and definitely before the woman leaves hospital" (RCOG 2001) (see also *Ultrasound examination when a problem is suspected* in Chapter 7).

SELECTIVE FETICIDE

Women who are expecting a multiple birth and who discover during their pregnancy that one or more of their babies has a serious abnormality may be offered selective feticide. For many women and couples this is a shocking idea when it is first mentioned, especially as the procedure is not widely known about or discussed.

Couples facing this very difficult decision need to be well informed. They need to understand the possible risks of the different courses of action open to them, including the risks to the healthy baby or babies, and the risk of losing both or all of their babies. They need to understand the selective feticide procedure and to know about any physical changes the mother might notice after the baby has died, as well as any side effects of drugs that may be given to the mother to prevent premature labour. For some parents, the idea of the dead baby remaining in the womb beside the living one is disturbing, for others it is comforting (MBF 1997b). Parents also need to know what is likely to happen during the rest of the pregnancy and when the woman gives birth to the surviving baby or babies (see also *Intra-uterine death in a multiple pregnancy* later).

If the feticide is to be carried out after 24 weeks' gestation, parents must also be told that the law requires the baby who has died to be certified and registered as stillborn (see *Certification following a termination after 24 weeks' gestation* in Chapter 16).

Once the feticide has been carried out, other staff who will care for the mother should be informed so that they can avoid causing her unnecessary distress. For example, the mother herself should not have to explain to a sonographer back at the local hospital about the dead baby that is seen during the ultrasound examination. Informing the relevant staff requires a careful communication plan, especially if the feticide has taken place at a specialist centre and the mother goes back to her local hospital to give birth.

Staff should be aware that, even if parents have no doubt about their decision to have selective feticide, many experience very mixed feelings when the surviving baby or babies are born. They may feel intense grief at the loss of the baby who died.

Parents in this situation may want opportunities, both before the feticide and afterwards, to talk to someone who understands the particularly complicated issues surrounding selective feticide about what is happening to them and how they feel. They are likely to have many questions and anxieties, some of which they may find hard to express. They may want to discuss what to say to their family and friends and whether to tell them about the feticide. They may want to give the dead baby a name (see *Creating memories* in Chapter 12). They may want to hold a funeral for the dead baby but not be sure how to manage the situation. They may also want to discuss longer-term issues – for example, what they might say to the surviving child or children as they grow up about the baby who died. Parents may find it helpful to talk to other parents who have faced these problems and they should be given the contact details of the relevant voluntary groups; for example, ARC, Sands, the TAMBA Bereavement Support Group and the Multiple Births Foundation (see Appendix 2).

Much of what is written about late miscarriage and premature labour earlier in this chapter also applies to intra-uterine death, intrapartum death, stillbirth and when a baby is born at or around term with a lethal condition.

INTRA-UTERINE DEATH

When an intra-uterine death is suspected, the mother should be seen and assessed as soon as possible. If the death is confirmed, she should be told straight away (see also *Breaking bad news* in Chapter 4).

Opinions vary on the best time for induction after an intra-uterine death. Geerinck-Vercammen (1999) recommends that parents should be given time between diagnosis and induction so that they can cope with the bad news, make the necessary practical arrangements at home, and think about how they want to say goodbye to their baby. In contrast, Rådestad (2001) found that a long delay can cause mental strain, and states that there is no scientific basis for advising women to delay, nor for the idea that this will benefit them by giving them time to begin to work through what has happened.

> *When I did manage to get to sleep over the next few days, waking up was unbearable. You were still in my belly and I'd hold you thinking I'd had a bad dream. When reality sank in, the devastation would wash over me again and again.* Mother

If there are no contra-indications, some women might appreciate a short delay. Others may find it intolerable to carry a dead baby for longer than necessary and will want to be admitted for induction as quickly as possible. It is important to discuss the options and to give women the information they need to make the decision that is right for them. Staff should suggest to the parents that they may want to plan for the labour and delivery and for what they would like to be done when their baby is born. Some parents may want help and advice in deciding what they want (see also *Involving parents* in Chapter 9).

If a woman goes home and then comes into hospital for the induction, the staff on the labour ward should be expecting her, so that they can welcome her without her having to explain why she has come.

The process of induction and the time it may take should be gently explained.

> *I was not told that it could take so long and had not expected to be in hospital for nearly 6 days. I learnt that at 34 weeks' gestation my body had to be coaxed into delivering.* Mother

Unlike labour with a healthy baby, labour when the baby is known to have died offers no reward at the end. The normal concerns or fears that many women have about labour and birth and how they will cope are likely to be intensified and to loom larger in the face of the knowledge that this labour and birth will result only in the confirmation of a tragedy (Woods 1997: 89-90). It is important that the mother and her partner feel completely supported the whole time and are never left alone unless they want to be.

> *I was induced the next day. The midwife was great. I wasn't able to think at all and she suggested things to me and took control which was a great help. She was so compassionate and respectful – she treated my baby as a person.* Mother

Intra-uterine death in a multiple pregnancy

When one baby in a multiple pregnancy dies, the parents have the complex task of looking forward to the birth of their healthy baby or babies while, at the same time, dealing with the loss of a baby. Some parents may also be distressed about the idea of the dead baby remaining with the live one(s), although other parents may find this comforting (MBF 1997a).

If there is likely to be a body, a fetus papyraceous, or recognisable remains of the baby who has died, parents need to be prepared for the way this might look. They may also want to plan what they want to happen when this baby is born (see also *Creating memories* in Chapter 12). All the staff who will be with the parents during the labour and birth must know whether they have any special wishes for the birth and for the care of the dead baby.

For some parents the relief at having one (or more) surviving baby outweighs the grief they may feel over the loss of the other. However, for many, their grief at the loss is intense. It may overshadow the birth of the healthy baby, affecting their ability to enjoy and develop a relationship with him or her. At the same time, family members and friends may discount the reality of the loss and focus only on the surviving baby, expecting the parents to forget or ignore the one who died and "to be grateful for what they have" (MBF 1997a) (see also *Multiple pregnancies* in Chapter 3).

INTRA-PARTUM DEATH AND STILLBIRTH

The unexpected death of a baby during labour or at birth is extremely traumatic for the parents and also for the staff. The realisation that something is wrong may have triggered a flurry of activity, which is both terrifying and bewildering for the parents, especially as there is usually little, if any, time for explanations. The situation can be especially hard for partners, who may be left standing on the sidelines while all the staff focus on the mother and the baby.

I watched and wondered what my role was, what should I feel, how would I grieve, where I fitted in. Father

I so wanted to hold my baby and to hear his cries, but they did not come. After a strange amount of time that seemed like a second but also like an eternity, a woman doctor came over, put a hand on my arm and said, "I'm sorry, but we have been unable to resuscitate your son. I'm so very sorry". Mother

Parents whose baby has died during or shortly after birth should always be supported and given as much time as they need to let the reality of their loss sink in, before they are asked what they would like to do and before they are required to make any decisions.

WHEN A BABY IS EXPECTED TO DIE AROUND THE TIME OF BIRTH

Mothers who have decided to continue the pregnancy after their baby has been diagnosed with a lethal abnormality need special care and support during labour and birth (see *Support for parents during labour and birth* in Chapter 8) and should be offered opportunities to create memories (see Chapter 12).

In a multiple birth when, for example, one baby is healthy and the other is likely to die very shortly, parents often feel torn between the two. It may be helpful to reassure them that there will be plenty of time afterwards to make up for what they may feel is neglect of the healthier baby, and to encourage them to spend whatever time they can with the baby who cannot or may not survive (MBF 1997a).

CHAPTER 12: AFTER A LOSS

This chapter discusses some aspects of the care that parents may need immediately after a late miscarriage, a late termination of pregnancy, a stillbirth or a death in the minutes and hours after birth. What happens during this time is crucial. How parents are cared for may affect the rest of their lives.

It is the detail of events that matters so much. Mother

TELLING THE PARENTS AND THE STAFF

When a baby dies during labour or birth, or shortly afterwards, the parents should be told straight away. Most parents remember for ever what is said and done at this traumatic and critical time. Although it is not possible for staff to make the situation better or to reduce the parents' distress, they should try to use clear, unambiguous language and to choose words that convey genuine sorrow, warmth and respect (see also *Breaking bad news* in Chapter 4).

Sometimes parents expect or anticipate the death: they still need clear and sensitive confirmation that their baby is dead.

Parents who were looking forward to welcoming a healthy baby may be completely stunned, and may find it impossible to believe that their baby has died. Staff need to be gentle and sensitive and to allow time for them to take in the reality of what has happened.

If the death was completely unexpected, staff too will be shocked and upset and may value the help and support of an experienced colleague in caring for the parents.

Medical and other staff who were involved in the mother's care should make a point of going to see the parents after the loss, to offer their condolences. Junior staff, including doctors who have not done this before, may find it helpful to be accompanied by another doctor or a midwife. Afterwards, managers or colleagues should ensure that all the staff affected are offered support and time to talk before they go home.

Informing other carers

I was on the ward still and someone came in and said, "Where's your baby?" Mother

Midwives, nurses, doctors and health care assistants who will be directly involved in the mother's immediate postnatal care should be informed promptly about the death or loss. This helps to protect parents from well meant but inappropriate comments, and staff from the distress of having caused unnecessary pain. Consideration should also be given to informing ancillary staff who are likely to be in contact with the parents. The hospital chaplain or their own religious adviser should also be contacted if the parents would like this.

If the mother agrees, the front of her medical notes should be marked with a sticker that all staff recognise and understand. This will help to ensure that all staff are aware that she has had a childbearing loss and that she is cared for with tact and sensitivity.

> The Sands teardrop sticker can be used to identify the notes of a mother whose baby has died, both in the time following the death and in any subsequent pregnancies. It can be used on hospital and GP records, antenatal notes and appointment cards to ensure that everyone who comes into contact with a bereaved mother is aware of her loss and does not inadvertently say things that will add to her distress.

TELLING THE FAMILY

At some point, the parents (or the mother, if she is unsupported) will need to tell their family what has happened. Breaking bad news is never easy and is doubly difficult for parents who are themselves shocked and grief stricken.

Then we had to tell our family. How on earth can you tell your loved ones such awful news...I shall never forget the look on Mom and Dad's faces as I told them the baby was dead. There was disbelief, tears and so many unanswerable questions. Their grief and pain was doubled, love for the unborn grandchild and the inability to do anything to ease the pain of their son and daughter. Mother

CREATING MEMORIES

Why create memories?

Normally when a person dies, those who were closest to them have a store of memories to help them remember and remain connected to the dead person. These provide some comfort as well as being a focus for grief. Talking about the person who has died and sharing memories of them helps to confirm their existence and their continuing importance. Physical mementoes connected with the dead person – photographs, clothes, possessions, letters – trigger memories and may bring comfort, enabling those who are bereaved to hold on, in some sense, to part of the person they have loved (Davies 2004).

When someone they love dies, many people also find it important to see the body. This makes the death real and can help people to accept that it has happened. If, as a result of trauma or disaster, there is no body, it may be harder to believe and to come to terms with the fact that the person has died.

Perinatal loss is unique in that it is the loss of someone very important who has already changed the lives of the parents in many fundamental ways, but of whom there are few or no tangible memories and no memories that can be shared with other people. In most cases, the parents have never seen their baby alive: in early pregnancy loss there may be no body. At the same time, most parents feel a strong desire to cherish and remember their baby, and to preserve his or her continuing importance in their lives. Physical items connected with their baby may help to confirm the reality of his or her short existence and provide comfort as well as a focus for their grief (Davies 2004). Staff may be able to help by offering those parents who want, opportunities to create positive memories and physical mementoes.

Parental choice

It is now commonplace for staff to offer parents various ways of creating memories and tangible mementoes of their baby. Protocols, procedures and checklists have been created to ensure that these are offered. However, as Leon (1992) observes, "The current 'management' of perinatal loss is so taken for granted that it has become an orthodoxy without having been examined critically … Procedures that easily turn into rules may dictate a set of interactions with the bereaved, giving these rules priority over empathic listening and responsiveness".

When suggesting to parents that they might want to create memories of their baby, staff should remember that *parental choice is paramount. It is essential to offer genuine choice, and not to steer parents towards a particular course of action in the belief that it will help them.*

Some parents, find the idea of creating memories strange and unnecessary. It is important to listen to individual parents and find out what they would like to do.

Timing is also important. Parents often need time to think about what they want or do not want, especially if the idea is new to them. Women should not be expected to make decisions when they are in shock, straight after what is likely to have been a stressful and traumatic labour, or when they are still affected by opiates or a general anaesthetic. They should be offered time to make decisions and enabled to take important steps at their own pace.

SEEING AND HOLDING THE BABY

The practice of offering parents opportunities to see and hold their babies after the death arose out of the anguish expressed by many mothers who had not been allowed to do so. As a result, it quickly became the norm without any systematic evaluation of the risks and benefits involved.

There is an abundance of anecdotal evidence and some research to confirm that many parents have found seeing and holding their baby and collecting mementoes extremely helpful (Rådestad 2001; Geerinck-Vercammen 1999). More recently, studies have cast doubt on the benefits of seeing and holding the baby, and it has been suggested that this practice is harmful (Hughes et al 2002; Turton et al 2001). However, these studies are not conclusive. Turton et al (2001), in a small study of the possible predictors of post-traumatic stress disorder (PTSD) during and after the pregnancy following a stillbirth, found a "suggestive" relationship between having seen the stillborn baby and PTSD, but state that this link is "not statistically significant". Hughes et al (2002) state that some women in their study who saw and held their baby did not have adverse effects. They speculate (sic) that seeing and holding the dead baby further traumatizes a woman who is already intensely distressed and exhausted. The findings of Turton et al (2001) have been criticised by Lovett (2001), amongst others, who states that "it would be a pity if policy-makers gave this research undue emphasis and abandoned current practice hastily".

Commenting on Hughes et al (2002), Robinson (2002) states that harm may be caused by staff who rely on rote procedures, rather than by the procedures themselves. When the options relating to "creating memories" appear in a detailed checklist with tick boxes, inexperienced staff may feel under pressure to ensure that each item is ticked. As a result, parents may feel that their experience has been so routine and rushed that they have lost control over what happens to them and to their baby, the exact opposite of the aims of good care (Leon 1992) (see also *Checklists* later).

As with any other contentious issue, it is essential to guard against the tendency for practice to swing from one extreme to the other. The current watchword of health care, and of maternity care in particular, is choice. Removing choice from bereaved parents and deciding what will be best for them is paternalistic and damaging. Most people would rather live with the consequences of their own decisions, good or bad, than with the consequences of decisions that are imposed on them by others, however well meaning.

When suggesting to parents that they might want to see and to hold their baby, it is important to remember that:

- To date there is no conclusive research to show that this practice is harmful;
- There is also no evidence to justify telling parents that they will benefit from seeing and holding their baby after death;
- It is impossible to predict who will regret not seeing their baby and who might suffer more intense distress as a result of doing so;
- Being expected to behave in certain ways exacerbates the loss of control and autonomy that parents are already experiencing.

Facilitating genuine choice about seeing and holding a baby who has died is complicated. Parents may have many reasons for being uncertain or refusing. These include:

- Shock at the suggestion, because such a thing has never occurred to them;
- Fear of seeing a dead body, especially if they have never seen one before;
- Fear of what their baby will look like, especially if he or she is known to have died some time before birth or to have a serious abnormality;
- An established personal coping style of dealing with stressful issues by not confronting them directly;
- A cultural or religious prohibition against seeing a dead body (for example, a few very orthodox Jews may decline, as it is considered wrong to see or handle a dead body unless absolutely necessary; some men of certain orthodox Jewish families are forbidden to be near a dead body and may leave abruptly after a baby has died);
- Feeling that seeing and holding the baby is simply not right for them.

Shona was tiny but perfect when she was born. They handed her to me in a tiny blanket and she was so beautiful. Jade was born a bit later and we chose not to see her because of her abnormalities. I wanted to think of her as perfect too, just like her sister. I didn't want to have horrible memories of her. Mother

Discussions with parents

Unless parents have lost a baby before, or been close to someone who has, they may not think of asking to see and hold their baby. It is therefore important that the offer is made, while recognising that some parents will decline. For example, staff could say: "Many parents have said that it helped to see and hold their baby. Others have decided not to. What would you like to do?".

If the parents are unsure, it may be helpful for an experienced member of staff, preferably someone whom they already know, to talk to them and ask whether they would like:

- The baby to be washed and carefully wrapped or dressed first (staff should always ask first if they may wash or dress the baby: some parents may want their baby's body to be washed before they touch it; others may not want anyone who is not of their faith to touch the baby but may want the baby washed by members of their religious community);

- The baby to be placed in a cot or a suitably sized Moses basket beside the parents, so that they can see their baby and then decide, without pressure, whether to hold him or her;

- A member of staff to hold the baby first and stay with the parents for a while;

- A member of staff to take a Polaroid or digital photograph of the baby for the parents to see and then decide;

- The baby to be kept in a nearby room for a while. It can be easier for parents to ask for their baby to be brought to them if they know that he or she is not far away.

These suggestions must be sensitively made: it is important that parents do not feel under pressure from staff to do anything that is against their better judgement.

Some parents will want to see and hold their baby straight away; others may want time to decide. Some parents may choose to see but not to touch or hold their baby. Some parents will decide that they do not want to see or hold their baby, and their decision should be accepted. They should be told where the baby's body will be kept and that, if they want, they can ask to see their baby if they change their minds. Again this must be without pressure. If there are time limits, for example if the body is to be sent for post mortem, this should be explained.

In most cases it is reasonable to make the offer once more some time later. If possible, this should be done by the same member of staff who asked the parents earlier. This will help to avoid repeated offers which may leave parents feeling harassed and unsure. In addition, careful notes must be kept about what the parents have decided and what has or has not been done. This should ensure that all staff know the situation before they speak to the parents.

Good practice

Seeing and holding their baby can be important to parents no matter how small their baby is. It may sometimes be hard for staff to treat a tiny baby of, say, 12 to 15 weeks' gestation in the same way that they would treat a larger, more developed baby. But parents do not compare their baby with others. It is important that all babies are handled respectfully and lovingly.

If there is a visible abnormality or maceration, the parents should be gently warned and told what to expect. It is important that the explanation is factual and without judgement or any implication that the baby looks unpleasant. Parents often see the beauty of their baby rather than what is different or, to other people, unattractive. It can help if the baby is wrapped in a blanket or dressed and the parents look first at the baby's normal features. Some parents may want to see the abnormality. They may find this important in understanding why their baby died. If the pregnancy was terminated, it may help them to feel that they made the right decision. Other parents may want to keep the abnormality covered if this is possible.

If it is appropriate, parents may want to wash their baby, or to watch a member of the staff washing the baby. If there is maceration, skin slippage should be explained first, to prevent further distress to the parents. It is important not to wrap a very premature baby in a paper towel because the paper may stick to the baby's delicate and friable skin and is very difficult to remove. For very tiny babies and some that are macerated, washing may not be appropriate.

Some parents may want to dress their baby in clothes they have chosen. They may need help to do this or may want to ask someone to do it for them. Some hospitals provide clothes, including very tiny ones, in case parents have none, but it is still important that parents themselves are able to choose what their baby wears. Some parents prefer to wrap their baby in a shawl. For very tiny babies who can be difficult to dress, a small knitted poncho or tabard is often a good alternative (see box below). A cot or suitable-sized basket should be available to put the baby in.

We carefully wrapped her in the shawl that Mom had knitted and together placed her in the cot with her toy. I remember kissing her gently on her cold cheek and leaving her forever. It was the hardest thing we have ever had to do. Mother

---

How to knit a poncho

A poncho is very good for dressing a tiny fragile baby. In some hospitals, labour wards and neonatal units have a stock of tiny ponchos and bonnets knitted by volunteers.

- Knit two squares approximately 15 cm x 15 cm in fine wool;
- Place one square on top of the other on a flat surface;
- Turn the poncho so that one corner is at the top;
- To form an opening for the head and neck, fold down a 4 to 5 cm flap of the top corner and stitch it to the top layer only, to hold it in place;
- Then stitch the two squares together, down the top two sides only, leaving enough room at the neck and leaving the bottom two sides open.

With thanks to the staff at the Women and Children's Group, Queen Mary's Hospital, Sidcup.

Time with the baby

We spent a few hours with her to try and remember everything about her, her curly dark hair, round face, ten fingers and ten toes. Mother

Parents should, when they are ready and if they want, be left alone and in private with their baby. They should know that staff are available if needed. Some parents may want to keep the baby with them for some time, perhaps overnight. They should not be asked to part from their baby before they feel ready to do so. They should then be reassured that their baby will be kept safely for them for a stated period of time, and that they can ask to see him or her again if they want (see also *Taking the baby's body home* in Chapter 13).

I combed her soft hair, held her, kissed and stroked her soft sweet cheek, and told her how proud I was of her, that she was mine, and so brave to hang on and fight. I hung onto her as long as I could. I was sure I could feel a pulse as I lay next to her form, holding her tiny palm in mine, willing her back to life. Mother

Multiple births

Special consideration is needed for the parents in a twin or multiple birth if one or more babies have survived.

The emotions that swamped us over the next few days were completely overwhelming. How does one integrate the feeling of grief for one baby with the feeling of joy for the other? After all we had only wanted one healthy baby and we still had that. So why did we feel so terrible? Mother

It is important that staff acknowledge the importance of the baby (or babies) who have died, and avoid focusing only on the baby who is alive (Bryan 2002) (see also *Multiple pregnancies* in Chapter 3). If parents want to see the baby who has died, it may be helpful to see, and perhaps hold, the living and the dead babies together if this is possible. Without this opportunity it can be difficult for parents to grasp the reality of what has happened. Later on, the parents may value the memory of being with all their babies together. Photographs that include both the live and the dead babies can also be helpful in future years, when parents discuss with the surviving children the circumstances of their birth (see *Photographs* overleaf). Staff should also help parents to think about whether they want to create other memories of the baby or babies who have died (Bryan 2002).

The sex of the baby

Most parents are anxious to know as soon as possible whether their baby is a boy or a girl. However, after earlier losses (even up to about 20 weeks' gestation), or if the baby is badly damaged or abnormal, it may be very difficult or impossible to tell what sex the baby is. In babies born at early gestations, female genitals can look very like male genitals. When a baby is born at or under 20 weeks' gestation, the sex should be identified by two members of staff before the parents are told.

If there is any uncertainty, staff should explain to the parents that it is difficult to tell, and that they may have to wait to know the baby's sex until after examination by a pathologist or paediatrician. Although this delay can be difficult, it is better for parents to have to wait than to be given information that they later find out was wrong. If the parents do not want a post mortem examination it may still be possible for the pathologist or paediatrician to examine the baby externally and (in most cases) confirm whether the baby is a boy or a girl.

My twins were born at 18 weeks 5 years ago and lived for an hour. They were named, blessed, registered and cremated as boys. We scattered their ashes as boys. Six weeks later, after the post mortem, we were told they were girls. Up till then we'd been grieving for our boys. All our love, memories, sympathy cards, photos, wrist bands were for "the boys". We talked about the boys and missed them as boys. Suddenly we had to start thinking about them as girls. We had to give them girls' names, mourn them as girls. When people ask me if I have children I don't know what to say any more. This happened 5 years ago and I still feel that I have lost four babies and not two – it's a nightmare. Mother

Naming the baby

Parents may want to name their baby. This helps to give the baby a reality and can help them and their family to talk about him or her in the future. It can also be important for existing and future siblings, especially in a multiple birth where one or more babies survive. Staff should always ask parents whether they may use the baby's name. However, they should bear in mind that some parents will not want to name their baby.

It is easier to choose a name if the baby's sex is known. If there is any doubt about the sex, the parents may want to wait for definite confirmation (see above) before they choose a name. Some parents may still want to give their baby a name, even if it is not possible to identify the baby's sex. They may want to choose a name that could be used for either sex, or a name with a special meaning to them.

Photographs

Many parents cherish for the rest of their lives the photographs that have been taken of their baby. Photographs often also help other family members and friends to understand and empathise with parents. Staff should not assume that parents will not want photographs because their baby is very tiny, or is macerated or abnormal in some way. Most deformities, except facial ones, can be covered, for example by wrapping the baby in a shawl.

However, photographs should never be taken without the parents' knowledge and permission. If, after discussion, they say clearly that they do not want any photographs taken, their wishes must be respected. Some parents may simply find the idea unacceptable or may not feel it is necessary. Some conservative Muslims may regard it as forbidden to make an image of a person, and may not want photographs or hand and footprints taken. However, staff should never assume for any reason that any parents will not want photographs of their baby: photographs should always be offered.

If parents are not sure whether they want photographs, it may be helpful to say gently that many people have greatly valued photographs of their baby, especially in the months and years after the loss. Staff could also offer to take photographs and to keep them safely with the medical records until the parents have decided whether they want to have them. If this offer is accepted, the parents should know that they can ask for the photographs at any time in the future, and whom to contact.

Quality The quality of photographs is very important. For example, blurred photographs or photographs taken with a flash that are very stark can be very hard for parents to look at or to show to other people later. Although it is not easy to take good photographs in this situation, staff should try to make sure that parents have high-quality pictures and to meet any special requests they may have.

Polaroid photographs provide parents with a picture of their baby immediately, but prints from older Polaroid cameras fade over time. Most film processors can make copies of Polaroid photographs and these will not fade, but the quality is generally not good.

> *A midwife took a Polaroid photo of our newly delivered stillborn daughter. The quality of this photo is now very poor and it would be very sad if this was our only picture of her.* Mother

Some hospitals offer parents a single-use camera with a flash so they can take pictures as they wish, but the pictures taken with cheaper single-use cameras is often inferior. Wherever possible, good-quality photographs on 35 mm film, or digital photographs, should be taken. Hospitals should provide cameras and film for parents who do not have their own camera with them.

Digital cameras make it easy to transfer photographs onto a disc, which can then be given to the parents so that they can make copies for themselves and for family members and friends if they want to. In some cases, especially if the baby's skin is bruised or discoloured, parents may prefer black and white or sepia photographs instead of, or as well as, colour photographs. Colour film and digital pictures can usually be converted to black and white or sepia. Some parents may want to take videos.

If film is used, the processing company should be told how precious and unique the photographs are. It may be better not to send the film by post. Some units have an arrangement for photographs to be developed by a local photographic shop. The hospital staff give the parents a leaflet to give to the shop staff which explains the very sensitive and important content of the film. It may be helpful to advise parents to have more than one copy made of each photograph, and to keep the extra copies in a dry, dark, safe place. Photographs exposed to light will fade over time.

Deciding what to take Some parents in this situation know what kinds of photographs they want; other parents may be grateful for sensitive advice and suggestions. Unless they have sophisticated photographic equipment, it may be helpful to advise them to take the photos in natural light if possible, with a simple backdrop.

Some parents may want staff to take some or all of the photographs for them, as it can be difficult to concentrate in such a distressing situation. Alternatively, they may ask a family member or friend. A small number of professional photographers in the UK offer their services voluntarily to bereaved parents (for some contacts see the UK section of the *Now I lay me down to sleep* website in Appendix 2). It may also be possible for a hospital to develop contacts with one or more local professional photographers who would be prepared to give their time to take high-quality photographs for bereaved parents.

Parents may need time to think about the pictures they want and to arrange different shots. They may want to take a lot of photos so that they can select the best. They should be offered privacy so that they can take the photographs they want without worrying about what other people might think. They should not feel under any time pressure unless there is a good reason.

- They may want photos of the baby both dressed and naked, alone in the father's and mother's arms, and lying on the mother;

- They may want close-ups of the baby's hands and feet, and of the baby's hand in the mother's or father's hand;

- They may want to photograph the baby in a Moses basket and on a blanket or shawl;

- They may want family photographs of both parents with the baby, and of each parent separately with the baby;

- They may want photographs of their baby with a brother or sister, and with other members of the family. These photographs may be valuable when parents talk about the loss with their children and other people in the future;

- In a multiple birth if all the babies have died, or if some but not all of the babies have died, parents may want to have photographs of all their babies together if this is possible. This may be the only record of the complete reality of their experience. In later life, a surviving twin, for example, may find photographs a precious, tangible confirmation of his or her twinship. If the parents do not think of it them selves, staff might suggest to them that some other parents have found this helpful.

Photographs taken as part of the post mortem examination should never be considered as a substitute for the photographs described above.

Other mementoes

Many parents want to gather mementoes such as their baby's cot card, name band, a lock of hair, prints or plaster casts of feet or hands, stills from scans, a copy of a fetal monitor tracing, and/or a baptism or baby blessing card. They may value anything that will help them to remember their baby, and staff should offer as much as possible. Some parents may ask for these mementoes to be saved for them so that they can have them later.

It is possible to take hand and foot prints without using ink. This method is more expensive but avoids having to remove ink from the baby's skin (see, for example, *Happy Hands* in Appendix 2). However, if the baby's skin is macerated, it will peel more if hand and footprints are taken and this can make prints rather moist and fuzzy which may be disappointing for the parents. They should be warned about this.

Although many parents find it helpful to have mementoes of their baby, some may decline on personal, cultural or religious grounds. Some parents may find certain specific mementoes unacceptable. For example, some people from the Indian subcontinent may object to cutting the baby's hair: some, such as traditional Sikhs, because they never cut hair; others because the baby's head is usually shaved to remove the pollution of birth. It is very important always to ask parents before a lock of hair is cut, or a foot or hand print is taken.

One way of collecting all these mementoes is to use the Sands Memory Card, a four-page booklet with a place for the baby's name, hand and footprints, a photograph, a lock of hair and space for the parents to record their memories of their baby. Memory cards can be ordered from Sands see Appendix 2.

Religious ceremonies

Whether religious or not, some parents may want to ask the hospital chaplain to give a blessing, hold a naming ceremony, or say prayers for their baby. Some may want to ask their own religious adviser or an older relative. Some parents may want to pray, possibly with other family members or members of their faith community.

CHECKLISTS

In order to ensure that parents are offered all these options, many units incorporate them into detailed checklists that list the many tasks to be carried out after a loss. This has some disadvantages. Checklists inevitably emphasise *what* should be done at the expense of *how* it is done. They cannot reflect the diversity of parents' individual needs or the sensitive issue of when to discuss things with parents.

In addition, when staff are given a checklist with columns to tick or fill in, they generally feel obliged to complete it. There is a danger that they may see their goal as completing the checklist, rather than enabling parents to make their own choices in their own time. A tick in a column, or a Yes/No answer, is an efficient way to record that samples have been sent off, information has been passed on to colleagues, or paperwork has been completed, but it is not a good way to record whether parents have been offered opportunities to create memories of their baby sensitively and at an appropriate time.

It is important therefore to make a clear distinction between essential practical tasks such as collecting samples, completing paperwork etc, and those aspects of care that involve parental choice, such as seeing, touching and holding the baby, taking photos and collecting other mementoes. These latter aspects of care should be listed on a separate sheet of paper, in a way that makes it immediately obvious – for example, copied on coloured paper, though not pink or blue – that this list is qualitatively different from the rest of the checklist, and that its function is simply to remind staff to discuss these issues with parents sensitively and when the time seems right, and to record that they have been discussed (see also *Facilitating informed choice* in Chapter 4). The way the items are set out should also make it clear that parents who decline an option should not be asked repeatedly if they have changed their minds. Using the form overleaf should ensure that this happens.

CREATING MEMORIES – OFFERING CHOICES

This form provides a record for staff and should be kept prominently in the notes. It helps to ensure that:

- parents are offered genuine choices;
- they are given time to reflect and decide what they want;
- parents who have declined previous offers are not asked repeatedly if they have changed their minds.

It is very important to use the form sensitively and flexibly and to take into account:

- any views the parents may have expressed earlier;
- the condition of the baby. If the baby is macerated or visibly abnormal, it may be inappropriate to offer the parents the opportunity to see it. However, this is a very fine judgement and should be made by an experienced midwife or nurse, preferably one who knows the mother and can assess how she is likely to react.

If the parents make it very clear that they definitely do not want to see the baby, the offer should not be repeated, but they should be told that they can change their minds.

CREATING MEMORIES – OFFERING CHOICES							
	First offer made	Accepted	Declined	Postponed	Second offer (if to be made)	Accepted	Declined
Seeing the baby (or fetal remains)							
Holding the baby							
Photographs							
Lock of hair (if baby has hair)							
Foot and handprints (if feasible)							
Naming the baby							

To download a copy from the Sands website, go to www.uk-sands.org and click on **Improving Care.**

CHAPTER 13: POSTNATAL CARE

The recommendations in this chapter are for postnatal care in hospital following late miscarriage, late termination of pregnancy, stillbirth and early neonatal death.

PLACE OF CARE

If a woman is being cared for in hospital after the birth, she should be offered a designated side ward, unless she prefers to be on a ward with others. The room should have a double bed or an additional single bed so that her partner or another supporter can stay with her through the night if she wishes. The room should be large enough to accommodate extra chairs for her partner and other supporters, and a cot or crib so that the parents can have their baby's body with them if they want to. The mother should have her meals brought to her unless she prefers to eat with others (if there is a communal dining table). If she is in a single room designated members of staff should check on her regularly and ensure that she does not become isolated. Partners – or other supporters - should be made to feel welcome, and their need for empathy and support should be acknowledged and met. (See also *Parents' access to their baby* below and *The place of care* in Chapter 9.)

Ideally, each unit should also have a designated sitting room, furnished with a sofa, comfortable chairs, facilities for making tea and coffee, and boxes of tissues. This room can be used for parents to spend time together, to be with their baby and, if they want, to see relatives and friends. It can also be used by staff for discussions with parents.

PHYSICAL AND PRACTICAL CARE

It is essential that women receive excellent practical and physical care after a loss, as well as emotional support (Mander 2005: 5). This includes pain relief and advice about coping with a sore perineum, lochia, stitches, bathing, constipation and other physical problems.

Lactation

Lactation is one of the most distressing physical symptoms that a woman can experience after losing a baby. Engorgement and milk leakage are a constant painful reminder of her baby's death.

Individuals vary, and the stage of pregnancy when the loss occurred is obviously a factor, but some women, especially those who have breastfed before, may lactate even after an early miscarriage or termination. It may be some time before lactation and pain or discomfort stop completely, and women need to know this. They should be given sympathetic support and practical help.

The management of lactation after a loss varies, and there is no conclusive evidence to show that, over all, pharmacological methods are any more effective than non-pharmacological ones. While pharmacological management controls symptoms in the first week, by the second week there is no benefit over self-help approaches, and by the third week women who take medication have more symptoms. Women who use self-help approaches have more pain in the first week but have fewer symptoms in the longer term than women who took medication (Enkin et al 2000: 467–470). Women should be informed of the relative advantages and disadvantages of each approach. Effective self-help strategies include:

- Wearing a good supporting bra;
- Cold compresses;
- Hot showers;
- Oral analgesics.

Expressing a little breast milk can ease acute discomfort, but care should be taken to avoid too much stimulation because this will increase the milk supply. Expressing milk after the loss of their baby is stressful and distressing for many women. Most will need privacy and sensitive support.

If a mother has been expressing breast milk for a baby who has died on the neonatal unit, she should be approached sensitively to find out what she would like to be done with her stored milk. For example, some mothers will want to donate their milk to the milk bank (if there is one) for other sick babies; others may want it to be discarded.

PARENTS' ACCESS TO THEIR BABY

Parents should be able to see their baby's body whenever they want: they need to know whom to ask. The body should normally be kept on or near the ward for as long as the mother is in hospital. Parents may be able to keep the baby beside them in their room for longer if ice-packs are placed under the bottom sheet of the cot or Moses basket.

> *I never thought that the staff would care so beautifully for a baby that had died. Seeing her dressed in proper baby clothes and handled so gently was very comforting.* Mother

In order to facilitate easy access for parents to the bodies of their babies following a childbearing loss, Trusts, Health Boards and managers should ensure that there is a suitable mortuary fridge near the ward in which the mother is being cared for. The staff caring for the mother should have direct access to it. The body must be labelled and the fridge kept locked. The date and time must be logged whenever a baby's body is placed in or removed from the fridge.

If the baby's body must be transferred to the mortuary while the mother is still in hospital, this should be explained to the parents. However, a mother who is still in hospital – and her partner – should not have to go to the mortuary to see their baby. Instead the baby should be brought to them in a place where they can be private and comfortable. This might be in a room on the ward or a quiet room. The baby should be dressed or wrapped according to the parents' wishes, and should be carried in, for example, a suitably sized Moses basket. Staff may need to explain to the parents beforehand that their baby will feel cold and how the body is likely to look and feel. Holding the baby will feel more natural if he or she is wrapped in a shawl. (For more about the transfer and storage of babies' bodies see Chapter 15.)

The parents should be reassured that their baby will be kept safely for a stated period of time. They should be gently told that the body is likely to deteriorate as time passes.

OTHER FAMILY MEMBERS

Some parents want to be alone at this time. They may need staff to restrict visitors and to be firm but tactful on their behalf. Other parents may want their family and friends to visit and comfort them. Visiting hours for other family members should be relaxed so that the family can be together if this is what the mother wants. If the parents are not in a separate room, they will need somewhere private and quiet where they can be with their family. In some cultures it is important for family members and friends to visit parents after a baby's death, so there may be a large number of visitors.

If parents have chosen to see their baby, they may also want other people, including grandparents and other children, to see him or her. It may, for example, be helpful for siblings to see their dead brother or sister, as what they might imagine is often more frightening than the reality. Enabling other family members to see the baby, provided the parents want this, may also help the parents in the longer term, as they will have shared memories to talk about. Parents should be sensitively supported in doing whatever they feel is right for them, and should not be put under any pressure to fit in with other people's expectations.

Some parents may want to take photographs of their baby with other family members (see also *Photographs* in Chapter 12). Some may want to take their baby's body out of the hospital, or home (see *Taking the baby's body home*).

SUPPORT AND LISTENING

My story is all I have got. Father

Many mothers who have given birth to a healthy baby after a problem-free delivery want and need to talk through the details of what happened with different people, often several times over. It is ironic that, although many parents whose baby has died very much want and need to talk about what has happened, they are often given little or no opportunity to do so (Mander 2005: 71).

It can be helpful if the staff who were involved in the events are available to listen to parents, answer their questions and perhaps contribute their memories of what happened. Fathers should receive support and care in their own right.

The hospital staff were very good at making sure that Martin was OK. Every time the midwife came round she'd ask him, "How are you?" Our families watched the midwives taking care of him as well as me. And they took a lead from that. Mother

Some parents may also welcome the chance to talk about the events surrounding their baby's death to a member of staff who was not involved and who is therefore hearing an account of the loss for the first time. Some parents may want to speak to a hospital chaplain, their own religious adviser or a counsellor.

The midwife who delivered our baby was wonderful. She would pop in when she had a minute and sit with us for a little while, just letting us talk and admiring the baby. You could tell she was upset and she really cared. Mother

Although many members of staff feel that there is little they can offer, *simply listening is often more helpful than anything else.* Listening can be very difficult, even more so if the parents are angry or blame the staff for their loss (see *Anger, blame and litigation* in Chapter 3). Giving time to parents after a pregnancy loss or the death of a baby has major benefits for the parents, both in the short and in the longer term (RCOG 2006; Swanson KM 1999; Moulder 1998: 222; Leoni 1997). Staff should give parents as much time as they are able: managers should support the staff who do this and do their best to make arrangements to release them so that they have time to listen. Staff who cared for the mother antenatally and who feel close to the parents may like to offer their sympathy by visiting or sending a card.

Some parents may be anxious about how they are going to feel in the next few weeks and months. It may be helpful to discuss the wide range of feelings that they may experience and the individual and personal nature of grief (see also Chapter 3). It is also important to encourage them to seek help if at any time they are worried about how they are feeling, and to give them details of sources of help and support.

BEFORE THE PARENTS LEAVE THE HOSPITAL

Parents may need a lot of practical information at this time about what they need to do, and this should be communicated sensitively and clearly. It may be necessary to give the same information several times: they should feel able to ask as many questions as they need. They should be given clear written information and/or information in other formats to back up what they have been told.

Before they leave the hospital, and depending on the gestation and the circumstances, parents will need information and discussion about:

- The physical and emotional reactions that they are likely to experience;

- A post mortem or other pathology investigation (see *Post mortem examination* in Chapter 15);

- The need to register the stillbirth or birth and death. The parents should be given clear written information about where and when to register, directions to the Registrar's office, opening hours and telephone numbers (see also *Registration at a register office* in Chapter 16);

- Whether the baby's body should be buried or cremated, and whether they want to organise or participate in a funeral (see *Offering choices* in Chapter 17);

- In circumstances where families are very mobile, it may be prudent to ask parents who have not yet made a decision and who leave the baby (or the remains) at the hospital, to sign a document which states that if, after a stated period of time – for example, six months – they have not told the hospital how they want the baby's remains disposed of, the hospital staff can make suitable arrangements. Parents who sign such a document should be given a copy to take home. They must know whom to contact when they have decided on the arrangements that they want;

- A 6-week follow-up appointment with either the mother's GP or a hospital doctor. The mother needs to understand the purpose of this appointment (see also *Follow-up appointments* in Chapter 19);

- The support that they will be offered by the primary health care team. They should also be given information about relevant voluntary support.

In addition, the mother should be given a phone number so that she can contact the staff who have cared for her.

The designated member of staff responsible for the care of the mother should also make sure that;

- The mother's notes contain the address and phone number where the mother can be contacted in the time immediately after leaving hospital. Parents sometimes go away to stay with relatives, and it may be necessary to get in touch with them, for example for postnatal visits or to let them know when the funeral will be held;

- The appropriate primary care staff are informed immediately, so that they know what has happened and can offer postnatal care and emotional support, and also ensure that the parents do not receive invitations to baby clinics or for immunisation. If there is time, some women may find it helpful to be visited in hospital by a community midwife before they go home (see also *Home visits* in Chapter 19).

Many parents leave hospital fairly shortly after their baby's death. They are likely to be shocked, distressed and exhausted, and may find it very hard to focus on what needs to be done or to make decisions. If it has not been possible to discuss any of the topics listed above, or the discussion was incomplete, the designated member of staff should inform the community midwife and ask her to fill in any gaps.

The designated member of staff should also make sure that all outstanding antenatal and scan appointments are cancelled, and the antenatal class co-ordinator is informed.

She should also cancel the Bounty Pack (see *Entitlement to time off work and benefits* below). Failure to do this causes bereaved parents severe unnecessary distress. Parents may also be grateful for information about the Baby Mailing Preference Service (see Appendix 2). They can register online and prevent, or at least reduce, mailings of baby-related samples, advertisements etc.

> *I spent many months contacting various companies asking them to stop sending information about baby products. I received a lot of free samples and nappies through the post which I found particularly distressing.* Mother

Depending on the length of their stay, the parents may also want to discuss other questions and worries before they leave the hospital, for example:

- *Their chances of having a live, healthy baby in the future.* If there is to be a post mortem or other tests, detailed discussion about a possible future pregnancy will probably be more appropriate when the results are available. However, because the subject of another baby is a major anxiety and concern for many parents at this time, it is important to listen and respond sensitively if and when they raise the subject. Staff should explain honestly that what they can say at this point is limited, and should be careful not to speculate or to present possibilities to parents as though they are facts. If the cause of death is unknown, it is important to warn parents that sometimes no reason can be found for a baby's death even following a post mortem. If appropriate, parents should be offered referral to a genetic counsellor;

- *The timing of a future pregnancy.* In some cases there may be compelling medical reasons for waiting, or it may be advisable for parents to wait for all the test results, in case these have implications for another pregnancy. In most cases, however, there is no medical reason to wait. Nevertheless, although many parents feel strongly that they want to have another baby as soon as possible, it may be important for them to allow time to grieve for the baby or babies they have lost. Parents should be gently warned that the anniversary of their baby's death or due date is likely to be very difficult, and that it may be hard to cope emotionally if a new baby is born at that time. However, it is important to be clear that there are no rules, and that all parents should make their own informed decision. They should not be pressed to delay if they feel strongly that they want to conceive again as soon as possible (see also *Before conception* in Chapter 20). They may also find it helpful to know that it is not unusual for couples to have different views and feelings about if and when to have another baby;

- *Time off work and going back to work.* It is not necessarily best for a woman to go back to work as soon as possible. Many need more time to recover than they, their family members and friends, or employers, anticipate. Some women, including those who have had a miscarriage or an early termination, may need to be encouraged to take time for emotional as well as physical recovery.

Entitlement to time off work and benefits
Second trimester losses

- *Sick leave* A woman whose baby miscarries or is born dead before 24 weeks (legally a miscarriage), or who has a termination before 24 weeks, is not entitled to maternity leave (Tiger 2003). If a woman in this situation does not feel able to return to work immediately, she should be advised to talk to her GP about taking sick leave. Sick leave related to a miscarriage is "protected" in the same way as any sick leave taken during pregnancy: this means that the amount of sick leave that a woman can take is not limited and must be recorded separately from other sick leave she may have taken (Working Families 2006; see Appendix 2). However, some women whose loss occurred before 24 weeks may have to go to back to work out of financial necessity.

- *Benefits* A woman whose baby miscarries or is born dead before 24 weeks, or who has a termination before 24 weeks, is not entitled to Statutory Maternity Pay or Maternity Allowance (Tiger 2003).

Stillbirths (babies born dead after 24 weeks)

- *Maternity and paternity leave* A woman whose baby is stillborn after 24 weeks, is entitled to the full normal maternity leave. She is also entitled to free prescriptions and dental care for one year after the baby's birth. If her partner is entitled to paternity leave, this entitlement still holds.

- *Benefits* A woman whose baby is stillborn is entitled to Statutory Maternity Pay or Maternity Allowance if she is eligible for these. Statutory Maternity Pay is paid by employers to employees who have been working for them since the beginning of the pregnancy. Women who are not eligible for Statutory Maternity Pay may be eligible for Maternity Allowance if they have been employed or self-employed. A Maternity Allowance claim form is available from the local social security office. Women who fill in a claim form but are not eligible for Maternity Allowance are automatically considered for Incapacity Benefit. If the woman's partner is entitled to Statutory Paternity Pay, his entitlement still holds.

  Parents of a stillborn baby who are on a low income may be also eligible for Sure Start Maternity Grants and Funeral Expenses Payments (Working Families 2006; see Appendix 2 and also *Parents on a low income* in Chapter 17.)

Neonatal deaths

- If a baby is born alive at any gestation and then dies, the parents are entitled to the leave and all the benefits described under *Stillbirths* above. They are also entitled to Child Benefit and possibly to other benefits (see *Child benefit and other benefits* in Chapter 14 for more details).

Note: the above paragraphs contain the regulations at the time of going to press (April 2007). For updates, see the Sands website.

Discussing contraception

There is no ideal time to raise the issue of contraception when parents are mourning the loss of their baby. Discussion about preventing another pregnancy can seem extremely insensitive and inappropriate, and grieving parents are often very offended and distressed when the subject is raised (Personal communication, Sands Helpline Staff 2006). Advice on contraception should be offered tentatively and sensitively, preferably by a member of staff whom the parents already know and trust. It may be helpful to start the conversation by acknowledging that although this may not seem to be the right time to talk about contraception, it is important that parents give it some thought. Women should also be aware that if they have unprotected sex before their next period, they could become pregnant. (See also *Couples* in Chapter 3.)

LEAVING THE HOSPITAL

There are no words to describe the utter devastation of walking empty-armed out of the hospital. Of travelling home with the child seat you bought locked in the boot of the car because you can't bear to look at it. Of shutting the door to your baby's beautifully decorated bedroom and not opening it again for months. Mother

Leaving the insulated environment of the hospital and going home to face the world without the baby can be frightening and painful. Some women want to leave soon after the loss. Others prefer to stay a little longer, but some may feel unable to. This may be because of inappropriate facilities or insensitive care; for example, if they do not have the degree of privacy or contact with others that they would like, or if staff are unable to listen and support them. Women should not automatically be sent home as soon as possible: this can lead them to feel abandoned and unwanted when they are already shaken and grieving, especially as support at home is variable and often non-existent (Mander 2005:12; Moulder 2001). Early discharge may also mean that the discussions and decisions mentioned earlier in this chapter are either rushed or omitted.

All parents should be told about the services and support available to them once they are at home. Some may be reassured if they know that a member of the primary health care team will visit them shortly after their discharge from hospital.

Well-meaning relatives should be discouraged from removing the clothing and other items that were prepared for the baby before the mother – or couple – comes home. Although very painful, many bereaved parents find it helpful to deal with baby clothes and equipment in their own time.

We can't come home to a house that pretends he was never there. Father (Hansen 2003)

TAKING THE BABY'S BODY HOME

Some parents find it very helpful to have time with their baby after the death, away from a clinical setting and in a private place where they can be themselves. This can also be an opportunity for relatives and friends to see the baby and to grieve with the parents. Some parents may want to take their baby's body home: for example, to spend a day and perhaps a night in the home where he or she would have lived and grown up. Others may want to take the baby's body to a place that has special significance for them.

There are no legal reasons to prevent parents from taking their baby's body home. Staff should support parents who want to do this, and sensitive and efficient procedures should be in place (DoH 2006a: 2.30).

It was especially helpful to be able to bring Louisa's body home for a few days to the house where she was meant to live and grow up. We let our elder daughter, Natasha, who was then aged 3, hold and care for Louisa, as she was bursting to do. She sang to Louisa, carried her into every room to "show her round", brushed her hair and did This Little Piggy with her toes. It was heartrending but beautiful at the same time. Mother

If parents plan to take the baby's body home for a short time, it is important to take any post mortem arrangements into account. A post mortem may be carried out first – in which case, parents will need to be aware of the condition of the body and may need to tell others in the family about this (see *Restoring the body* in Chapter 15). Alternatively, it may be possible for parents to take their baby's body home for a short time and then back to the hospital for post mortem examination.

There is no legal reason to inform the police if parents take their baby's body home or out of the hospital grounds. However, for the protection of the parents and to prevent misunderstandings, Trusts and Health Boards should issue a form to accompany the body. The form should confirm that the body has been released to the parents and that they will be taking it back to the hospital or making their own funeral arrangements. It should include the name and contact details of the member of staff responsible who can be contacted if any difficulties arise. (For a sample form see Appendix 1: Form 1.) If the parents are collecting the baby's body from the mortuary rather than the ward, the ward should also give them a mortuary release form.

Before they take their baby's body home, parents need to know that it is important to keep the body cool. If they plan to return the body to the hospital before the funeral they also need to know when and where they should go. Alternatively, the funeral director can collect the baby's body from the parents' home before the funeral, to avoid their having to bring the body back to the hospital.

CHAPTER 14: CARE IN NEONATAL UNITS

"The death of a child is one of the most devastating experiences that a parent can have and the quality of care at the end of life and after the child's death can have a major impact on the family's grieving." Royal College of Paediatrics and Child Health (RCPCH 2004)

This chapter deals with the care of babies who are very ill and those who are not expected to live for long.

CARE AND SUPPORT FOR PARENTS IN THE NEONATAL UNIT

Most parents find being in a neonatal intensive care unit frightening and threatening at a time when they are already extremely anxious and distressed. They may feel scared, disempowered, vulnerable and perhaps inadequate for not knowing how to help their baby (Meyer et al 2006; Charchuk and Simpson 2005; Lundqvist et al 2002). They may have little opportunity to feel that they are parents to their baby (or babies).

Cultural and religious variations may influence the way that parents experience and deal with having a baby in the neonatal unit. Staff should be aware of this diversity so as not to view different responses and behaviour by parents as necessarily "abnormal" or uncaring (Fowlie and McHaffie 2004). For parents who are not familiar with Western-style medicine or British hospitals, the experience may be particularly alien and terrifying, especially if there are language barriers (see also *Parents who speak little or no English* in Chapter 5). (For more about cultural and religious issues, see Schott and Henley 1996.)

Providing support for parents is an important part of caring for very ill babies. Staff need to welcome and involve parents and try to help them feel at ease. They should do what they can to help parents feel that they have some control over what is done to their baby. It is important to:

- Explain how the neonatal unit works and what they need to know;

- Listen to the parents and try to understand their values, priorities and concerns;

- Give them as much information as they want (see *Keeping the parents informed* later);

- Acknowledge the extreme stress and the sadness of the situation for the parents, and also the difficulties caused by the nature and pressures of the neonatal unit;

- Invite parents to be present during doctors' rounds, routine medical procedures and when their baby is examined;

- Take parents' observations about their baby's condition seriously and respect them, even if the medical reality is different (Wocial 2000);

- Talk about the baby as an individual rather than just focusing on his or her medical condition;

- Ask if they would like to do normal parental things like touching and talking to their baby, and support them in doing so as necessary (Wocial 2000). Many parents will welcome suggestions and ideas from experienced staff: one way to support parents but avoid pressuring them to do things they do not want to do is to offer examples of things that other parents have done and found helpful (see also *Facilitating informed choice* in Chapter 4). Over time, parents who are initially overwhelmed by the situation and the neonatal unit may feel that they want to play a more active role and should be encouraged to do so (Charchuk and Simpson 2005);

- Suggest that the parents might want to take photographs of their baby in the unit. A camera should be made available for them (see also *Photographs* in Chapter 12). Some parents may want to take a video;

- Use the baby's name when talking to the parents about him or her.

I was by the incubator and was asked if I minded medical students having a look at such a premature baby. I said it would be OK as they have to learn. They asked the consultant questions about Lily-anne but referred to her as 'it'. Lily-anne was a very small but nonetheless human being, and deserved the same respect as any other patient. I didn't complain or say anything at the time because my brain was all over the place. 'It' is not an appropriate way to talk about a child, especially in the presence of a parent. I have been really distraught by this: it has stuck with me for five years. Mother

Some parents may want to bring in a toy or a family photograph to put in the incubator. Some may want to bring in religious items to tie around the baby's wrist or body to help protect the baby from harm. Some may want to bring in holy water with which to bless the baby. Others may want to put drawings, toys or "get well" letters from siblings in or on the incubator. If necessary, parents should be asked to check with staff before they bring anything in so as to reduce the risk of infection. Religious and other valued items should not be disturbed or removed without prior discussion with the parents.

In addition to support offered by clinical staff, parents may value the support of a counsellor, a member of the hospital chaplaincy or their own religious adviser. Christian parents may want their baby baptised.

Spending time with the baby

Parents should be encouraged to spend as much time as they want with their baby, and visiting should be restricted only when absolutely necessary. Nevertheless, it may sometimes be helpful to suggest that parents take a break and get some rest. Ideally, the unit should have a quiet room where parents can relax and make themselves tea and coffee (see *Care around the time of death* later).

We know we are luckier than some, at least we had three bitter-sweet days with our baby. But losing her just broke my heart. Mother

When the baby is unlikely to live for long, there should also be few or no visiting restrictions for siblings, grandparents and other family members, provided that the parents have agreed to these visits. Some parents may also want friends or religious advisers to see their baby in the short time that is available to them, and this should be allowed if possible. Other people can be more supportive to the parents later if they too have memories of the baby (Canadian Paediatric Society 2001). However, restricted space in the unit may mean that the number of visitors present at any one time has to be limited. It may also be appropriate to ask visitors (other than the parents) to leave during doctors' rounds or when procedures are carried out.

Parents are likely to be exhausted after the birth and may find that their sleep is disturbed by anxiety. This makes it additionally hard to deal with the often rapid changes in the baby's condition, try to understand what is happening, and make difficult medical decisions. The emotional and possible financial stresses may take their toll on the parents themselves, on their relationship, and on other family members (Fowlie and McHaffie 2004). Staff need to watch for signs of exhaustion and strain in the parents and take the initiative to offer sensitive help and support if necessary.

It was a six month roller coaster ride. There were periods of great excitement and also fear as Emma's condition took a step forward or back. I also had the added responsibility of supporting Julie and my only son Timothy. Father

Some parents may need special arrangements to enable them to stay in the hospital for any length of time. For example, people who observe religious dietary restrictions may need to bring in their own food or have food brought in for them. Some people may be unable to accept even a drink from the ward kitchen because of religious dietary laws (Schott and Henley 1996: 139).

Some parents cannot spend a lot of time with their baby because they have other commitments and pressures. Others may find it too distressing or frightening. Gentle encouragement and support may help these parents to feel more confident.

Parents whose baby has been transferred to a neonatal unit many miles away may find it especially hard to spend time with their baby. Some women may be reluctant to travel on public transport by themselves. Women who speak little or no English and who fear having to speak to staff may only visit with their husbands. Women who follow the tradition of resting at home for several weeks after giving birth may also be unable to come. It is important to reassure all parents who find it difficult to spend time in the unit that their baby is receiving the best possible care and attention, even though they are not there.

To avoid frightening parents who have come to visit their babies in the unit, it is important always to warn them before they go into the unit if the baby's cot has been moved (MBF 1997a: 15).

Staff should also be aware of the possible interactions between the different families in the unit. Relationships between parents can be supportive but can sometimes also add to the tension or be counter-productive. Parents tend to compare and contrast their baby's progress with that of other babies in the unit. Hearing other people's stories and witnessing the ups and downs of other babies is stressful. It can lead to a highly charged atmosphere that staff may need to defuse.

If the mother is ill

If the mother is in the same hospital but is unable to walk to the neonatal unit, and her physical condition allows, she should be brought to the unit in a wheelchair, so that she can spend as much time as possible with her baby. If the baby is transferred to a regional unit and it is not possible to move the mother with the baby, midwifery staff at the referring hospital should be asked to phone the regional unit regularly to check the baby's progress and pass this information on. The information should be not only about the baby's condition and prognosis but also anything the staff can tell her about the baby's personality and reactions, so that she can picture her baby as an individual.

Some units take digital pictures of babies and relay them to the mother's bedside. Others have a password-enabled site for each baby, where the mother can view computer readings from her baby and on which nurses can enter comments and observations. However, bad news should always be given face to face.

Parents with several babies

In the case of a multiple birth in which, for example, one baby is healthy and the other cannot live, parents often feel torn between the two. It may be helpful to reassure them that there will be plenty of time afterwards to make up for what they may feel is neglect of the healthier baby, and to encourage them to spend whatever time they can with the baby who is unlikely to survive (MBF 1997a).

If parents have two or more babies in the unit, they should be placed near to each other if possible. The babies' incubators should be visually distinguishable from each other. Parents should be told, before they go into the unit, if the incubators have been moved so that they are not worried unnecessarily (MBF 1997a).

For many parents it is very important to see and even hold all their babies together. This may be their only chance to do so if one of the babies is critically ill and so should be offered if possible (Kollantai and Fleischer undated). Photographs might be taken of twins or triplets together, and also with their parents if possible.

> The nurses and doctors who cared for Charlie and Joshua were wonderful. We cannot thank them enough for all that they did for our twins. The neonatal unit helped to provide us with our wonderful memories and allowed us to get to know Charlie and Joshua as individual characters. Mother

If one baby has already died, it is important that the staff caring for the surviving baby or babies in the neonatal unit recognise the importance of all the babies to the parents and listen when the parents want to talk about the baby who has died (see also *Multiple pregnancies* in Chapter 3). Many parents appreciate it if staff bring up the subject of the baby who has died, as this gives them an opportunity to express their feelings.

KEEPING THE PARENTS INFORMED

Parents should be kept informed about changes in their baby's condition and prognosis. For many parents this is an important part of taking parental responsibility, especially when there may be little else that they can do. All mothers – and fathers – should have an opportunity to discuss the care of their baby with a consultant neonatologist within 24 hours of birth (CESDI 2003) and subsequently.

Parents need to feel that information is freely and willingly given as soon as it is relevant, and that nothing is being hidden from them or censored. They need clear, understandable, consistent and honest information about all tests, developments and interventions. Technical terms should normally be avoided or explained in everyday language. All discussions with parents should be documented. It is good practice to have a differently coloured parent communication sheet in the front of the notes where staff can record what parents have been told.

The manner in which information is given is very important: parents are much more likely to believe information if they feel that the person who is giving it cares about their baby (Wocial 2000). Staff should use the baby's first name whenever talking about her or him. Parents should be encouraged to ask questions and to say if they find anything difficult to understand. They should also be encouraged to write down any questions as they occur to them so that they can ask them when the opportunity arises.

It may be necessary to repeat information on several occasions, because stress and anxiety can strongly affect people's ability to take in and remember what they are told (see *Giving information* in Chapter 4). Whenever possible, parents should be offered an opportunity to discuss important matters together and in a quiet place or room. In between formal discussions, parents should have easy access to members of staff who can answer their questions (Wocial 2000).

In order for parents to receive consistent information, it is essential that staff work in a well-functioning multidisciplinary team in which information is shared both up and down the hierarchies and across disciplines. It may also be helpful to have designated members of staff who take the main responsibility for checking that the parents feel informed and listened to, for raising sensitive and difficult issues, and for discussing decisions with them. If a baby is seriously ill or dying, the parents should have opportunities to talk with a senior member of staff.

Some parents may have questions and concerns at times when the consultant team is not there. Others may find it easier to talk to less senior members of staff. In both cases, parents should be encouraged to raise issues with any member of staff with whom they feel comfortable. If their questions cannot be resolved immediately, the member of staff concerned can approach the consultant team on their behalf.

DECISIONS

Most parents want to feel that they have choices and the power to exercise them: without this they may feel they cannot be "proper" parents (Wocial 2000). They should be offered the opportunity to participate in all important decisions about the care of their baby. Whenever possible, staff should avoid implementing a major change in the baby's care without first explaining it to the parents.

If decisions have to be taken in an emergency and the parents cannot be reached, staff must be able to justify what was done, document the reasons for the decision and, as soon as the opportunity arises, explain to the parents what was done and why. In these situations, parents should be telephoned as soon as possible or told as soon as they arrive at the unit (Charchuk and Simpson 2005).

If the baby's prognosis is poor, it may be prudent to suggest that the parents could begin to think about what choices they might want to make if their baby's condition deteriorates. Some parents may not want intensive treatment for a baby who, if she or he survives, would be severely handicapped (Silverman 1992).

Parents should understand that they can withdraw consent for investigations and treatments at any time. If the clinical team believes that this would not be in the interests of the baby they should discuss this with the parents (BAPM 2004) (see also *When parents and staff disagree* later).

WITHDRAWING OR WITHOLDING FURTHER TREATMENT

Decisions about withdrawing or withholding further treatment from a baby are inevitably difficult. The Nuffield Working Party concludes that there are no good reasons for drawing a moral distinction between withholding or withdrawing treatment, provided that these actions are motivated by an assessment of the best interests of the baby in each case (Nuffield 2006: 2.33). Nevertheless, many parents and staff find it especially distressing to withdraw treatment once it has been initiated. This makes it even more important that, wherever possible, the decision to initiate intensive care is based on a realistic assessment of the baby's prospects.

Both parents and staff are likely to have views and opinions about what should and should not be done. It is important for everyone to have opportunities to voice their views and feelings, to listen to each other and, if possible, to reach a consensus.

The parents

> *She was struggling and in great distress and the outlook was dire. My instinct was that keeping her alive was not right. I was desperate for her not to suffer any more or be left trapped inside a body she could not control with an appalling quality of life. I would have gone round pulling out the tubes myself if I hadn't been given the option to let her die.*
> Mother

Some neonatal staff feel that parents should be protected from the onerous responsibility of deciding to withdraw or withhold further treatment, and worry about the long-term effects on parents of having made the decision. However, parents' views and wishes differ a great deal and no assumptions should ever be made about how much they will want to be involved.

Some parents feel strongly that they themselves should take on the responsibility of deciding what is best for their baby, and that this is part of the rights and duties of being a parent. In her study of parents in Scotland, McHaffie found no evidence that parents felt guilty about having taken the decision to withdraw or withhold treatment from their baby, provided they were certain that this had been in the baby's best interests. Lingering doubts about the decision were found only when the parents had not been certain of the wisdom of stopping treatment. This was often because they had not had enough evidence to convince them that the prognosis was poor (McHaffie 2001: 396–397). However, even when parents want to make the decision themselves, they should not be left feeling that they are carrying the burden alone (Chiswick 2001) and they should be strongly supported in their decision.

Some parents want to be fully informed about the issues but feel that they should not make the decision themselves, either because they lack the requisite medical knowledge and the professional experience, or because they are used to a more traditional paternalistic relationship with doctors. Some also do not want to live with the responsibility for having taken such a momentous decision. Some may want to involve senior family members and perhaps their own religious adviser in discussions with medical staff (Brinchmann et al 2002; da Costa et al 2002).

All parents should be given the *opportunity* to be included in the decision about whether to withdraw or withhold further treatment. Even though some – for personal, religious, cultural or other reasons – may choose to delegate the decision, partly or entirely, to the team that is caring for their baby, it is always important that they know that their feelings and views have been heard and taken seriously (Wocial 2000). This requires excellent and co-operative communication between staff and parents – the staff offering their medical expertise, experience and reasoning, and the parents being able to explain their values, preferences and family circumstances and their understanding of the situation (McHaffie 2001: 396-397).

Hospital chaplains may be able to assist some parents – of all faith groups and of none – when life and death decisions are being considered. They can help parents gain a sense of control and offer ongoing comfort and support. They can also help parents reflect on what is best for their baby and encourage confidence in the expertise and experience of the health care team. Many parents feel that a chaplain has more time to sit with them and let them talk about whatever is on their minds (McHaffie 2000).

The health care team

"Neonatal staff have their needs too, and it is easier to be caring and compassionate when we are at ease with our own thoughts and feelings surrounding end of life decisions. This is more likely in neonatal units where there is leadership, teamwork, and a forum for discussing ethical issues. In their absence, end of life decisions challenge staff each time as though it was a new experience, and conflicting and unclear advice may be given to parents, reflecting uncertainties and conflicts between staff members." (Chiswick 2001)

Different members of a health care team inevitably have different experiences, responsibilities and perspectives. If there is disagreement within the multidisciplinary team about continuing or withdrawing further treatment, it is important that each team member is able to state and explain their views openly and honestly in an atmosphere of mutual respect, and to hear, understand and respect the views of others. Some people may feel afraid to voice their opinion, so sympathetic encouragement is important. If they have all shared in the decision-making process, each team member is more likely to be committed to whatever has been agreed (RCPCH 2004: 32; McHaffie and Fowlie 1996: 176).

The timing of the discussions with the parents about withdrawing or withholding treatment can also be a source of tension within a team. Sometimes it is the staff who have most contact with the baby who may feel that continuing treatment or life support is not in the baby's best interests, and that it is time to discuss the issue with the parents. All members of the team should feel able to raise the issue of withdrawing or withholding further treatment with their colleagues, and should be taken seriously when they do. The situation should be discussed within the team and then, when agreement is reached, with the parents.

Nevertheless, there may be a time lag when staff feel that continuing treatment is futile but parents are unable to make a decision quickly. This period can be particularly difficult and the staff most affected may need opportunities to talk about their feelings away from the parents.

Whenever possible, nurses or junior medical staff should not have to carry out clinical procedures that they strongly believe unnecessarily prolong a baby's distress and are not in the baby's best interests. Such situations damage individual and team morale (Chiswick 2001).

Discussions with parents

It can be difficult to raise the issue of withdrawing or withholding treatment with parents. Occasionally, parents raise the subject themselves, particularly if they are concerned that their baby is suffering and that further intervention cannot help. Others may not want to initiate a discussion themselves, but may be relieved if staff do so. Some parents may refuse to consider the idea at all – for example, because they simply cannot believe that their baby will not survive, because they feel that it is wrong to consider any situation hopeless, or because they have strong personal or religious objections to withdrawing or withholding treatment (Roy et al 2004; Garros et al 2003; da Costa et al 2002). Sometimes raising the issue before it is necessary gives parents time to think about it "in the abstract". It may also help them realise that withdrawing or withholding treatment is an option and that their baby is extremely ill.

Parents' decisions about withdrawing or withholding further treatment should not be rushed. Anspach (1993), cited in Cuttini et al (1999), reports that parents were more likely to regret the decision to withdraw treatment if they felt that they had not had enough time to evaluate possible alternatives. Even though waiting can be hard for staff, it is important to respect the parents' decision-making process and timescale. Only the parents can fully understand what the decision means, and they will have to live with the consequences for the rest of their lives (Walsh 2000). However, some parents may find it too difficult to make any decision, and staff may need to gently encourage them to do so in the baby's best interests.

Whoever makes the final decision, the parents should feel absolutely convinced that it was right and was made out of compassionate concern for the best interests of their baby. They must know that the decision is supported by all the staff and should be assured that the staff will continue to provide the best possible care and will keep their baby as comfortable as they can until he or she dies.

> *Thank you for remembering throughout everything that Louisa was a person, not just a body with a complex of medical problems.* Parents

Explaining brain stem death

RCPCH guidelines (2004) suggest that, when parents of children who are diagnosed as brain stem dead see that everything possible has been done, they are more likely to agree to the withdrawal of treatment. However, this is not necessarily true, especially for parents with strongly held religious beliefs. For example, some Muslims and some orthodox Jews define death as the absence of a heartbeat and breathing. Because both of these are present when a baby is on life support, some families may see the withdrawal of life support as murder (da Costa et al 2002; Inwald et al 2000; Goh et al 1999). Parents who do not accept the concept of brain stem death may need more time and explanation to help them understand the reality of their baby's condition. Some may wish to talk to their own religious adviser or to older family members, or to have them present at the discussions.

When parents and staff disagree

If the parents are unhappy with the recommendation of the medical team, several meetings may be necessary at which the different viewpoints of parents and staff can be sensitively explored. If it is difficult for the parents to believe that their baby's condition is very poor or is deteriorating, it may help to show them concrete evidence of a poor prognosis (McHaffie 2001: 413). Some parents find it helpful to see x-rays or scans of their own baby and of healthy babies for comparison (Wocial 2000).

If the disagreement cannot be resolved after genuine and repeated attempts to understand each other's point of view, the parents should be offered a second opinion. To try to ensure independence, they may want to organise this themselves with the help of their GP (RCPCH 2004: 34). If agreement still cannot be reached, it may – very rarely – be necessary to resort to legal proceedings, though this is clearly undesirable for all sides and should be avoided wherever possible.

When there is disagreement it is important that staff who may be expected to continue or to instigate treatment that they do not consider to be in the baby's best interests are well supported. They should be given time and opportunities, away from the parents, to express their views and feelings.

When a decision is reached

Once parents have given their consent to withdraw treatment or not to resuscitate the baby, it is very important that this information is documented and passed on to all staff as soon as possible and that the decision is recorded prominently in the baby's notes (McHaffie et al 2001c).

Care when treatment is withdrawn or withheld

"Infants from whom life-sustaining support is withdrawn or withheld should continue to be kept warm, offered oral nourishment, and treated with dignity and love (comfort care). Their parents should be encouraged to be with their child as much as possible. They should be given every support during this distressing time." British Association of Perinatal Medicine (BAPM 2000)

The way in which the withdrawal of intensive treatment is handled is very important. In particular, it is essential to prepare the parents. Many will not have seen anyone die before and they may feel frightened by the prospect. Before the baby is taken off ventilation, staff should explain what will be done, what is likely to happen, and what they will do to keep the baby as comfortable and free of distress until he or she dies. They should also explain that, although it is very likely or inevitable that the baby will die, the timing is almost always uncertain.

Some babies live for hours or even days after life support is withdrawn, and parents should be warned of this during the discussions beforehand. Although some parents may welcome more time with their baby, it can be traumatic for those who have assumed that the baby's condition and prognosis mean that the death will be swift. They may begin to question whether they were right to withdraw treatment or whether their baby could have survived if treatment had been continued. It is also exhausting for parents to keep saying their goodbyes again and again (McHaffie et al 2001c). Parents whose baby takes a long time to die will need comfort and support, as well as reassurance that the decision to withdraw treatment was correct.

Parents should be told that the baby may appear to gasp when taken off the ventilator. It is important to reassure them that this is normal, but that if they and the doctors feel that the baby is suffering, opiate drugs can be used to alleviate any discomfort.

"Giving a medicine with the primary intent to hasten death is unlawful. Giving a medicine to relieve suffering which may, as a side effect, hasten death is lawful and can be appropriate. It is recognised in English and Scottish law that increasing doses of analgesia necessary for control of pain or distress may shorten life. The giving of opioids is for the benefit of the patient during life not in order to cause or hasten death." Royal College of Paediatrics and Child Health (RCPCH 2004)

All interventions that do not benefit the baby should be stopped. However, fluid and enteral feeds should normally continue if the baby lives for more than a few hours, as both parents and some members of staff may be distressed if these are withdrawn (Roy et al 2004; McHaffie and Fowlie 1998). "Oral nutrition and hydration should only be withheld from a baby when it is clear that providing it causes discomfort and pain, such as when a baby has little functioning bowel due to disease, or when death is imminent" (Nuffield 2006: 9.24).

It is helpful for parents if one or two designated members of staff take the lead and are available to guide and support them until their baby's death and afterwards. The designated members of staff should be responsible for:

- Talking to the parents, explaining what is likely to happen, and answering any questions;

- Discussing what can and cannot be done to meet the needs and wishes of the parents;

- Finding out how the parents feel about being present when the baby dies, and identifying and discussing any particular fears and worries;

- Finding out if they want a religious or other ceremony and helping to arrange this.

BEING WITH THE BABY AT THE TIME OF DEATH

They stopped the ventilator and we sat in a side room and held her. We thought she would die quite quickly, but she didn't. It took forever. Just when we thought she had finally stopped breathing, she took another breath. She was struggling and it was too much to bear. So the doctor gave her an injection of morphine to ease her distress and she died shortly after that. Mother

Most parents will want to be with their baby until he or she dies, and will find this time very precious even though it is also traumatic. Some may feel very anxious about watching their baby die: it may be helpful to say that it is probably more comforting for a dying baby to be out of the incubator, to be held and to feel loved and cherished. Parents should be offered the support of a nurse who will stay with them for the whole time or for as long as they want. However, a few parents may have personal or religious reasons for not wanting to be present. They should be sensitively asked how they would like to be informed that the baby has died. If the baby has been transferred to a specialist unit, consideration should be given to transferring him or her back to the referring unit for terminal care if this will enable the baby to be closer to the mother and other family members.

Whenever possible, parents who want to stay with their baby should be offered a separate room. Staff should remove as much equipment as possible.

Once the decision to withdraw intensive care has been agreed, some parents may want to dress their baby. It may be better to do this while he or she is still on the ventilator. The unit should have suitable clothes available to parents who do not have their own baby clothes. Babies who have been ill since birth may never have been dressed in normal baby clothes and this may be the first time that the parents have seen their baby dressed.

Care around the time of death

Some parents may want to hold their baby before the death and while he or she is dying. This should be sensitively encouraged. However, staff should be aware that at such a traumatic time it can be particularly difficult for parents to refuse what they may perceive as instructions from staff (Lundqvist et al 2002).

Time and privacy are essential. The unit should have a comfortable quiet sitting room, with a settee and soft, non-fluorescent, side lighting where parents can spend time with their baby. There should be a baby nest or Moses basket to put the baby in if they want to, and the room should be large enough and have enough chairs to accommodate several people if necessary.

Many parents find it helpful if family members and friends have the opportunity to see, possibly hold, and say goodbye to the baby. Staff should suggest that parents may like to have their other children with them for at least some of the time, and to take photographs of each sibling holding the baby.

I have a precious photo of my whole family, taken when Sharon came out of the ventilator before she died. All my three children together for the first and last time. Mother

Parents may also want to ask other close family members to be with them, both for support and to look after the baby's siblings when the parents want to be alone with the baby. Some parents may appreciate seeing staff members who have cared for their baby. Some parents may appreciate seeing those staff members who have cared for and been most involved with their baby. The staff concerned may also find this helpful.

Parents may want time alone with the baby in privacy before, during or after the death. They should not feel isolated or abandoned, and should have easy access to a member of staff who can support them, answer any questions and, when the time comes, confirm the death.

Some parents may want to pray alone or with a religious adviser, or to hold a religious ceremony. They should be asked what they would like, and staff should offer to contact whoever is needed and to help with arrangements. The parents should be given privacy to hold whatever ceremony they choose. Some may be grateful if staff will take part.

After their baby's death, parents should be able to be alone with their baby in quiet and privacy for as long as they want. Some parents may want to wash and dress their baby themselves.

> *After he had been disconnected from all his equipment he was placed in my arms for the first time, and as we cuddled him he died peacefully...I never thought that the first time I bathed my baby would also be the last...I wanted to do everything for Charlie; it just didn't seem fair that he wasn't alive...We felt torn between spending time with Charlie and putting our will into Joshua, his twin, to survive.* Mother

Parents may also want to create memories in other ways (see *Creating memories* in Chapter 12).

If the parents were not there at the death

If the parents were not able, or chose not to be, present when the baby died, they may be very worried that their baby may have died alone and unsupported. It is important to reassure them that someone was there to comfort the baby and that the baby died peacefully and without distress. If possible, the person who was with the baby at the time of death should talk to them and gently and sensitively describe what happened.

IF THE BABY IS LIKELY TO LIVE FOR SOME TIME

Some parents may want to take their baby out of the neonatal unit, for example into the grounds or a local park for a while. They can then feel that their baby has experienced more than just the hospital environment and has been a part of the wider world. Some parents will feel able to do this alone; others will want some support.

Some parents may want to take their baby home, either for a short while before returning to the hospital, or with the expectation that their baby will die at home. No matter how caring the staff, hospitals remain public places, and it can be very important for parents to be with their baby in a private and familiar place, even if only for a short time. This can also be helpful for others in the family, especially older brothers or sisters, or for other people who will be important sources of support for parents in the subsequent months and years. Some parents who want to take their baby home will feel confident about managing. Others may need reassurance and support.

If parents want to take their baby home to die, neonatal staff should give them a letter – addressed "to whom it may concern" – explaining the situation and giving the contact details of the unit. The parents should also be given a "do not resuscitate" (DNR) form in case, for example, they call an ambulance team or call out a doctor for help. The parents' GP should also be informed.

Staff should ensure that the parents know that they can telephone or bring their baby back to the unit at any time of the day or night. They should also be told what they will need to do if the baby dies at home, including how to obtain a medical cause of death certificate. If the baby might live for some time and may need nursing or medical care at home, or if the parents want support, the GP and relevant primary care services should be informed (Breeze at al 2006).

LEAVING THE NEONATAL UNIT AFTER THE BABY HAS DIED

It was hard leaving the hospital but they told us we could come back any time of the day or night to see our baby and they would find us somewhere quiet to be with him. Mother

Before they leave the neonatal unit, most parents will need information about:

- A post mortem or other pathology investigation (see *The post mortem examination* in Chapter 15);

- Registering the baby's birth (if this has not yet been done) and death. Parents should be given verbal and written information about where and when to register, directions to the Registrar's office, opening hours and telephone numbers (see *Registering a neonatal death* and *Registering the baby's birth and death at the same time* in Chapter 16);

- The options for a funeral, including whether a hospital-arranged funeral would be offered (see *Offering choices* in Chapter 17).

Most parents will value any memento of their baby's life, no matter how official; for example, the baby's name label from their wrist and ankle and the name label from the incubator. They should be given good copies of consent and other any forms they have signed. They may also want to reassure themselves about what they have signed: sometimes it is hard for people to recall what they did during a time of stress and this can cause them unnecessary worry afterwards (see also *Certificates and forms issued by health care staff* in Chapter 16).

Depending on the situation and on what has already been done, the designated member of staff responsible for the care of the mother – and her partner – should also ensure that, for example, the mother has a 6-week follow-up appointment arranged with her GP or a hospital doctor, and that the parents know what support and help are available to them, both in the hospital and outside, and both professional and voluntary. (See *Before the parents leave the hospital* in Chapter 13 for a full list of everything that must be done.)

All parents should be offered at least one follow-up appointment to see the doctor who was in charge of the care of their baby in the neonatal unit (see *Longer-term support* in Chapter 19).

Before they leave the unit, parents should be given opportunities to ask questions and talk at length with staff about anything that concerns or worries them. Women who have been expressing milk for their baby will need to know about the options for suppressing lactation (see *Lactation* in Chapter 13).

Child benefit and other benefits

Parents whose baby was born alive and then died are entitled to claim Child Benefit. This will be paid from the date of the birth up till 8 weeks after the date of the death. Once the parents have a Child Benefit Number, they will receive a Child Trust Fund payment and (if they are eligible) Tax Credits up till 8 weeks after the death. *They must claim all these within 3 months of the baby's death.* In order to claim Child Benefit the parents must provide evidence of the birth. However, if they have not yet registered the baby's birth, they should be advised to send in the Child Benefit claim form and provide the evidence later.

The Child Benefit Claim form is generally in the Bounty Pack given to new parents. However, this should normally have been cancelled. Staff should therefore sensitively tell the parents about their entitlement and either give them a Child Benefit claim form or advise them to contact the Child Benefit Office (see Appendix 2 for the online claim form address and a telephone number for hospitals to obtain multiple copies of forms).

Although claiming Child Benefit may seem strange to the parents and may be the last thing that occurs to them, it is important that they know that it is an option. The extra small amount of money can be used for a special memento if they wish, and the right to claim may be seen as additional recognition of their baby's existence.

Parents on a low income may be entitled to a Funeral Expenses Payment (see *Parents on a low income* in Chapter 17).

All mothers whose baby was born alive are entitled to full maternity leave and benefits. If their partners are entitled to paternity leave and payments these still hold. (See *Entitlement to time off work and benefits* in Chapter 13 for details.)

INFORMING PRIMARY CARE AND OTHER STAFF

The mother's GP or primary health care team should be informed about the baby's death within 24 hours (CESDI 2003). Provided that the parents consent, other staff in the hospital and the community who have cared for them and their baby should also be informed as soon as possible, so that they can offer their condolences and support and can avoid making inappropriate comments.

It is very important to inform the doctor and the midwives who will see the mother for her postnatal check-up that the baby has died, and also to ensure that the parents are not invited to bring their baby to baby clinics or for immunisation (see also *Before the parents leave the hospital* in Chapter 13). One member of staff in the unit should be responsible for doing this.

KEEPING IN TOUCH

The staff were devastated when Poppy died, they cried - we really felt that they cared. When we left the unit they said phone at any time. They also sent lovely cards which was so nice, you develop such intense relationships with the staff when your baby is in the unit.
Mother

For some parents it is important to remain in touch with the staff in the neonatal unit where their baby died and where so many momentous and life-changing events occurred. They should be assured that they can return to the unit whenever they like during the coming weeks and months. Many parents are also extremely appreciative if, for example, one or more members of staff attend the baby's funeral and/or try to see them at any follow-up visits to the hospital.

> *I was in hospital for several weeks during my next pregnancy and four of the neonatal staff came down to the ward to visit me. They were so pleased when my baby was born strong and healthy.* Mother

Many neonatal units have a book of remembrance in which parents can make an entry (see also Chapter 18). They may not want to do this until some weeks or months after their baby's death. They should be welcomed onto the unit when they come to make the entry, and time should be made for them to sit down and talk with those members of staff who cared for their baby. They may also want some quiet time alone, just to be in the place where their baby lived and died.

Many units telephone or send letters or cards to parents on, for example, the anniversary of their baby's death. Neonatal units should have a system to ensure that this is done. Anniversaries are times when many parents relive what happened and they may gain comfort from knowing that their loss has been remembered and acknowledged by others. A simple card stating that the staff are thinking about them at this sad time is all that is needed. Cards should have no religious content or symbols unless they are specially chosen for a family whose religious faith is known to staff.

An annual remembrance service for all the babies who have died on the unit can give parents the chance to meet with others who have had similar experiences and can give staff the opportunity to share in parents' grief (see also *Memorial services* in Chapter 18). It is important that a service of this kind is acceptable to people from a wide range of religious backgrounds and outlooks (see also Chapter 2). It is useful to ask the parents to let the unit know whether they will be coming, so that, if possible, some of the members of staff who looked after their baby can attend. Ideally they should have time to talk to the parents after the service and to answer any questions or to set up a further meeting to do so.

SUPPORT FOR STAFF

Caring for parents and babies in a neonatal unit can be particularly draining and relentless. It is extremely important that the stresses and demands of the job are acknowledged, and that senior staff and management make it clear that it is legitimate for all staff to ask for and get help and support when they need it. Both formal and informal support must be readily available and staff should be encouraged to make use of it. Debriefing sessions should be offered after a particularly harrowing time to give the staff involved a chance to talk about how they felt (Jennings 2002).

Senior staff, who often have to take very difficult decisions and to deal with the most complicated and difficult situations, may also want to set up personal support networks and systems with other members of staff at their own level (see *Additional support* in Chapter 21).

CHAPTER 15: TRANSFER TO THE MORTUARY AND POST MORTEM INVESTIGATIONS

TRANSFER TO THE MORTUARY

The body of a baby born at a later gestation or who has died in the neonatal unit should, if possible, be kept on the ward, unit or delivery suite in a designated fridge (see *Parents' access to their baby* in Chapter 13). The body should normally be transferred to the mortuary only for a post mortem or when the mother leaves hospital.

Parents should be told before their baby's body or remains are transferred to the mortuary. They should be told what will happen, whether the baby's body will be returned to the ward, and if so when, and assured that the baby's body will be treated with dignity and respect at all times.

Some parents may have personal, cultural or religious preferences about the handling, transportation or storage of their baby's body or remains. These should be documented and accommodated whenever possible (DoH 2006a: 2.2). There must be good communication between the staff caring for the parents and the mortuary staff.

In some cases the baby's body may need to be transferred while the mother is still in hospital – for example, for collection by a funeral director. Before the transfer, the body should be labelled with the mother's name and hospital number, the baby's date and time of birth and death, the baby's sex (if known) and other details, including the baby's name if he or she has been named (DoH 2006a: 2.46). If the baby's last name is different from the mother's, a record must be kept and the mortuary staff must be informed. Items such as clothing, shawls or soft toys that the parents want to accompany the body should also be listed. In some cases the body may need to be transferred to another hospital for a post mortem (see *Location* later).

The baby's body should be transported in a discreet container of a suitable size used specifically for this purpose. A baby born at a later gestation can be transferred in a Moses basket. If the baby is taken to the hospital's own mortuary (as opposed, for example, to a regional paediatric pathology centre), the baby could be carried in the arms of a family member, or by a member of staff possibly accompanied by one or more family members (DoH 2006a: 2.24). If family members accompany the baby to the mortuary, they should be told in advance what to expect and what will happen when they arrive (DoH 2006a: 2.6).

Although most parents should not have to go to the mortuary to see their baby's body, there must be suitable facilities that offer comfort and privacy in the mortuary, so that, if necessary, a family can see and hold their baby there.

Storage and tracking

All babies' bodies and all fetal remains should be kept, regardless of gestational age. There must be adequate and appropriate storage facilities including refrigeration. Bodies and remains must be stored individually and scrupulously labelled and logged. They should be kept in the best possible condition, and protected against accidental damage and avoidable deterioration (DoH 2006a: 2.37). Formalin should be used only when it is necessary to maintain tissue integrity. This may change the baby's appearance but should not prevent the family from seeing the baby.

When a body is incomplete or in pieces, the remains – or if there is no body, the products of conception – should be kept in a separate, clearly-labelled opaque container before disposal. This applies after a termination or an evacuation of retained products of conception (ERPC), as well as after a miscarriage.

It must be possible at any time to track and locate individual bodies and body parts while they are in the care of the hospital – whether on the ward, in the mortuary, in the pathology department or in transit to or from another hospital unit (DoH 2006a: 2.37). Trusts, Health Boards and managers should ensure that hospital departments, including accident and emergency, maternity, and gynaecology wards, have efficient procedures for transferring fetal remains and babies' bodies between them, and systems for tracking the whereabouts of individual bodies and remains. Hospital mortuaries and laboratories must have efficient systems for tracking each body, organ or remains. These systems should be understood by all the staff concerned, including ward and delivery suite staff.

Transporting fetal remains and babies' bodies outside the hospital

Trust and Health Board contracts and arrangements with ambulance services should ensure that the bodies of fetuses and stillborn babies that are transported from home to hospital with the mother are handled and treated respectfully. It is completely unacceptable to place fetal remains or bodies in clinical waste bags. As well as being inappropriate, this could lead to the remains being lost, or accidentally disposed of as clinical waste.

Trusts, Health Boards and managers should also give careful thought to allocating the task of transporting bodies and fetal remains between hospitals. The drivers should know what they are carrying and should be given appropriate documentation so that, if there is a road accident, the presence of human remains can be explained.

POST MORTEM EXAMINATION

The Human Tissue Act 2004 and the Human Tissue Authority Codes of Practice (2006), which apply in England, Wales and Northern Ireland, and the Human Tissue (Scotland) Act 2006, which applies in Scotland, set out strict requirements covering post mortem examination and the removal, storage and use of any body parts, organs and tissue. Parents can be assured that regulations are in place to ensure good practice, that their consent (called authorisation in Scotland) is required, and that they will be kept fully informed.

Most parents want to know as much as possible about why their pregnancy ended or why their baby died. Many also hope that a post mortem can tell them whether there are any implications for future pregnancies.

A post mortem can often provide helpful information:

- It can confirm an existing clinical diagnosis;
- It may identify conditions that might not have been diagnosed;
- It can exclude possible factors such as malformation, infection or growth restriction;
- If the baby died before birth, it can give an approximation of the time of death;
- For some families, it can help them resolve specific questions and may help them to come to terms with what happened;
- In the case of genetic disease, a post mortem may also indicate the need for other members of the family to be offered investigation.

Parents of a surviving baby from a twin pregnancy may want to know whether the baby who died was genetically identical to their surviving baby; however, not all genetic laboratories offer this service unless there is also a specific medical reason for doing so (RCOG and RCP 2001: 25–26).

If it was not possible to determine the baby's sex at birth, parents may want a post mortem examination because they want to find out the gender. Knowing the baby's sex may be very important: it is almost impossible to think about, name or mourn a person whose gender is unknown.

Some parents may also find comfort in the knowledge that a post mortem examination of their baby might benefit other babies and their families, and could contribute towards the prevention of other deaths (Rankin et al 2002).

In addition, post mortem results can contribute to the audit of antenatal and postnatal diagnostic procedures such as ultrasound, and might identify complications of care and treatment. Post mortems are also important for research and training.

Nevertheless, some parents are very distressed by the idea of their baby undergoing a post mortem and find it difficult to contemplate, even if they think it might provide useful information. They may feel that their baby has suffered enough and that he or she should be left in peace.

Some parents may fear that agreeing to a post mortem will shorten the time they can have with their baby. They may be more willing to consent if they know they will have another opportunity to be with their baby after the post mortem (see *Timing* and *Restoring the body* later).

Some parents may refuse a post mortem for religious or cultural reasons. For example:

- A post mortem may be completely unacceptable to most observant Jews and Muslims, because it is important to bury the body complete and whole;

- Parents for whom it is important to hold the funeral as soon as possible after the death, preferably within 24 hours, may refuse a post mortem because this might delay the funeral, although some pathology departments will carry out an urgent post mortem.

Some observant parents may consent to a post mortem despite religious or other restrictions, feeling strongly that they want to understand as much as they can about why their baby died. In such cases, strict confidentiality and meticulous repair of the body may be essential in order to avoid possible conflict with other family members. However, if it is traditional for family members or religious representatives to wash the body before burial, parents need to know that the signs of the post mortem will be visible.

CONSENT TO A POST MORTEM EXAMINATION

No post mortem examination, tests or investigations should be carried out without the parents' knowledge and consent or authorisation, regardless of the gestational age of the baby. The only exception to this is if an investigation is required by a coroner or procurator fiscal. Consent or authorisation is not required for investigations carried out under the instructions of a coroner or procurator fiscal, nor for the retention of tissue, organs or fluids if they are required as part of a criminal investigation (HTA Code 1 2006: 26–27) (see also below).

Specific consent or authorisation must be obtained from the parents before each of the following procedures. In Scotland the standard authorisation form should be used. Consent for one procedure does not imply consent for any others (HTA Code 1 2006: 101–103):

- A post mortem examination;

- Retention of any tissue or organ, including keeping blocks and slides of tissue as part of the baby's medical record (HTA Code 5 2006: 26). However in Scotland, blocks and slides removed during a post mortem may be used for diagnostic or audit purposes without authorisation (The Human Tissue (Scotland) Act 2006);

- Genetic and metabolic testing and the retention of DNA samples;

- Tissue, fluids or organs to be used for medical research, audit, quality control or educational purposes;

- Identifiable photographs of the baby.

Consent for histological examination of the placenta is not covered by the Human Tissue Act 2004. If there is to be a post mortem, the placenta should always be sent with the body. Otherwise, the placenta is usually treated as a surgical specimen in the same way as following a live birth. The placenta should always be sent fresh rather than in formalin, unless otherwise agreed with the pathologist.

Although the parents' consent or authorisation is not required to examine the placenta, they should be informed that this examination will be done. However it is an offence to analyse human tissue for DNA without consent (HTA Code 5 2006: 55). A few parents may want to bury the placenta for personal, cultural or religious reasons. The parents do not need permission to do this, nor is there a need to inform any other authority (see *Releasing the body to the parents* later).

Consent forms

In the past, some staff who asked for consent skimmed over the details of a post mortem examination with the intention of protecting the next of kin from additional distress (Laing 2004). Since the Human Tissue Act became law, this is no longer permissible. In line with the principle of informed consent, most consent forms are very detailed, and parents are asked to make explicit choices and decisions which they often find distressing. It is helpful if staff acknowledge this and say that the forms are designed to ensure that parents understand the extent of their consent (see also *Who asks for consent?* below).

The Human Tissue Authority (HTA) states that "establishments should design consent forms to suit their own local needs and arrangements". Forms can be adapted – provided they conform to certain minimum standards (HTA Code 3 2006: 74) – to make them more suitable for parents who lose a baby during pregnancy or at, or shortly after, birth. Hospitals, Trusts or Health Boards that have already devised consent forms should check them to ensure that they comply with the Human Tissue Act and the HTA's codes of practice.

Who asks for consent?

The request for consent for a post mortem "should only be made in an atmosphere of trust. This involves a close bond between parents and professionals". (Laing 2004)

The member of staff who requests consent should:

- Be a senior doctor, nurse or midwife, or another senior member of staff, preferably someone whom the parents know and trust. Responsibility for requesting consent should never be delegated to junior staff (HTA Code 3 2006: 62–66);

- Have had training on the essential requirements and the implications of asking for consent (HTA Code 1 2006: 96). They should also be aware that they will be liable to prosecution under the terms of the Human Tissue Act (2004: 5.2) if they provide inaccurate information to the pathologist about the extent of the consent that parents have given;

- Understand what a post mortem involves and its potential benefits and that, in some cases, no definite cause may be found for the baby's death, especially at earlier gestations;

- Have read the notes and avoid asking for information that is already documented;

- Be familiar with the consent form and able to take parents through it confidently;

- Ideally have witnessed at least one post mortem on a baby (RCOG/ RCP 2001: 15) and be able to tell the parents, if they ask, what will be done.

The member of staff who requests consent should also understand the purpose of the different procedures, including:

- External examination of the body;

- Examination of the internal organs;

- Photographs and x-rays;

- Tissue sampling;

- The retention of tissue samples for review of the diagnosis;
- Why organs might be retained;
- Restoring the body.

All staff who discuss consent for post mortems with families should be in contact with the pathologist who carries them out. They should regularly exchange information in order to ensure best practice and optimal care and support for parents.

Discussing a post mortem with the parents

Seeking consent is a process that should involve careful listening and discussion. It should be unhurried and honest and should be geared towards helping parents reach decisions that are right for them.

The first step is to establish the parents' willingness to discuss the possibility of a post mortem. It should be made clear to them that no investigations or tests will be done without their consent and that their views and wishes will be respected. This may help to reassure them that consent procedures are open and explicit. They need to know why a post mortem would be valuable (see above) and also that, in some cases, it may not provide answers (Rankin et al 2002). Even in cases when a post mortem would clearly be beneficial, the parents have the right to make their own independent decision, and must be able to live comfortably with whatever they decide (McHaffie et al 2001a). They should have time to consider their decision carefully before they are asked to sign a consent form (HTA Code 1 2006: 84).

In addition to verbal information and discussions, the parents should be offered written information. This should be available in all the main languages spoken locally, and in different formats. A professional interpreter should be involved if the parents speak little or no English.

Whenever possible and appropriate, the parents should be asked together for their consent. They may need time to discuss their individual views and feelings and, if possible, to reach a joint decision. Both parents should sign the consent form if they want to. If only one of them signs, it should normally be the mother. If only the father is available to sign, the reasons for this should be documented and the pathologist informed. Parents should be offered a good-quality copy of the signed form.

Some parents will want to know more about the post mortem than others. It is important that the member of staff who discusses it with them is sensitive to the amount of detail they want to hear. Some will want to know about the actual procedures; others will want to know only what they need to know to give informed consent. Among the points that could be covered are:

- *The possible findings of an investigation and what could be gained* by having the information. Parents should know that, depending on the circumstances, it may not be possible to find a definite cause of death. However, if appropriate, they should also be told that an investigation may also provide valuable information about what did *not* cause the death or loss;

- *What investigations are proposed and how long each would take.* Parents may need to know, for example, that an examination of the brain takes longer than the rest of the post mortem because the brain has to be specially prepared, but that in most cases this should not delay the funeral by more than a few days.
  Parents should be told if and why it would be useful in the case of their baby to carry out longer preparation before examining the brain. Before they consent to the longer preparation, it is important that they understand that they will need either to delay the funeral for several weeks until the examination has been completed, or to bury or cremate the baby's body without the brain. They should also be told what will happen to the brain once the examination has been completed;

- *Where, when and by whom the examination would be performed.* They need to know where their baby's body would be examined and how long this would take, and when they could have access to the body again if they want;

- *That tissue samples would be taken;*

- *That photographs and x-rays are usually taken* as part of the investigation. Parents should be told that any photographs or x-rays would be stored in the medical record. Unless they are anonymised, photographs and x-rays will not be used for teaching purposes without the parents' consent (HTA Code 4 2006: 40);

- *That in most cases they would be able to see or hold the baby's body after the post mortem if they want.* In general, parents who want to should not be discouraged from seeing their baby afterwards. However, if the baby's body is very small, macerated or oedematous, they should be told that the baby's appearance could be distressing and that it might be better not to see him or her again. Parents of very premature babies should be told that it is not normally possible to restore the body, and that it may be better if they say their goodbyes before the post mortem. If the parents are likely to want to see the body again, the mortuary staff must be informed;

- *How the baby's body would look after the post mortem,* including where the suture lines would be (see *Restoring the body* below). Parents who choose to see their baby after the post mortem should not see incisions or other marks that they were not warned about;

- *When the results would be available, and how and when they would be given to the parents;*

- *What would happen to the baby's body, tissue and organs after the examination.* Parents also need to know that if they consent, tissue in the form of blocks and slides may be retained as part of the baby's medical record;

- *How the post mortem would affect the timing of the funeral.*

If the parents are uncertain, anxious or want to know more, it may be helpful to offer them the option of talking to the pathologist who will undertake the procedure. He or she may be able to resolve their concerns.

Parents should be asked if they want to provide clothes, including a bonnet and shawl, for their baby to be dressed in after the post mortem. Hospitals should also have clothes and coverings available (including very small ones) for parents to choose from.

Parents should also be told that they can withdraw their consent at any time before the post mortem is started, or if they have given their consent for research, at any time before tissue or organs are used (HTA Code 3 2006: 72). They should be given the name and phone number of the person to contact if they change their minds.

See *Follow-up appointments* and *Follow-up appointments at the hospital* in Chapter 19 on discussing the post mortem results and their implications.

Parents who do not consent

If, after discussion and explanation of the possible benefits, parents do not consent to all or some of the post mortem investigations, no pressure should be exerted. Their decision should be respected and accepted. However, it may be appropriate to explore with them possible alternatives to a full post mortem if this will offer clear benefits. For example, some parents may consent to:

- External examination only;
- Partial examination confined to a specific region of the body;
- Blood or urine tests;
- Skin biopsy, needle biopsy and aspiration of body fluids.

In some cases, laparoscopic examination or investigations such as x-rays, ultrasound or CT or MRI scanning are available and may be more acceptable (Wright and Lee 2004).

It is important that the staff member asking for consent discusses the possible options and their availability and usefulness with the pathologist, before suggesting them to the parents.

Timing

There is an inherent tension between many parents' need to spend as much time with their baby, and the benefits of carrying out the post mortem as soon as possible after the death. In order to make an informed choice, parents should be told that an early post mortem is more likely to provide better information. However, this depends to some extent on the situation; for example, where the baby's body is kept (eg in a fridge or beside the parents), the gestation of the baby, and how long before the birth the baby died. If staff are not sure how to advise parents, they should discuss the situation and the options with the pathologist. For example, it may be possible to take a small skin biopsy for genetic study, and to delay the full post mortem for a while.

Location

Ideally, all post mortem examinations on fetuses and babies should be carried out by specialists in perinatal pathology. The Joint Working Party on Fetal and Perinatal Pathology (RCOG and RCP 2001) recommends that "perinatal necropsies are best carried out in regional centres". If the post mortem is to be carried out at another hospital, the parents must be informed. The body should not be transferred to that hospital any earlier than necessary, so that the parents can have as long as possible to see the body if they want. The body should also be returned as soon afterwards as possible. This applies as much to babies born at early gestations as to those born later.

If a baby's body is to be sent to another hospital, arrangements should be made for it to be sent safely and handled as respectfully as possible. Parents should be told where their baby's body is being sent and why, how it will be transported, and when it will be returned. The baby's body must be clearly labelled and all items such as clothing and shawls that are sent with the body should be listed, so that pathology staff can dress and wrap the baby's body before returning it.

See also *Transporting fetal remains and babies' bodies outside the hospital* earlier.

RESTORING THE BODY

Mortuary staff should always assume that the parents will want to see the body again. Each baby's body should be restored and carefully dressed. However, it is not normally possible to restore the bodies of babies of early gestations and the parents should have been warned about this (see *Discussing a post mortem with the parents* earlier).

> I was dreading visiting her in the mortuary but I wanted to see her after the post mortem. I was so relieved to find that she was dressed in the same clothes and hat that she had been in when we'd last seen her. It is so comforting to know that people had taken such good care of her. Mother

Unless parents have given explicit permission for certain organs to be retained, these should all be put back and the body should be complete for the funeral. Whenever possible, the brain should be replaced in the skull and not in the abdomen, and every effort made to avoid seepage of body fluids.

RETENTION AND DISPOSAL OF BLOCKS AND SLIDES

Blocks and slides of tissue may be retained as part of the medical record or they may be returned with (but not in) the body. If they are retained or disposed of, the parents should be informed. Some units retain blocks and slides indefinitely. Others intend to dispose of them. The HTA (2006 Code 5: 37–38) states that blocks and slides may be disposed of by burial or incineration. However, some crematoria will not accept them and the best method of disposal has yet to be identified.

DEATHS REPORTED TO THE CORONER/PROCURATOR FISCAL

If a baby dies unexpectedly following delivery, or following or during a medical or surgical procedure during the neonatal period, or if there is any suspicion about why the pregnancy ended or the baby died – for example, if the mother has been involved in an accident or is a victim of violence – the doctor must report the death to a coroner or, in Scotland, a procurator fiscal.

The coroner or procurator fiscal may decide that a post mortem should be carried out to try to establish the cause of death. A medico-legal post mortem is usually carried out as soon as possible. Occasionally this may delay the funeral. The body will be restored to the same standard as following a hospital post mortem.

If the parents want to object to a medico-legal post mortem for any reason, they should be advised to contact the coroner's or procurator's fiscal office immediately to discuss their objections and the situation. The coroner or procurator fiscal, or one of his or her officers, can usually be contacted 24 hours a day. A coroner or procurator fiscal has the legal right to go ahead with a post mortem even if the parents object. However, the parents can, if they wish, apply to the High Court to try to prevent this.

England and Wales Following a medico-legal post mortem, the coroner usually sends a copy of the pathologist's report to the hospital consultant concerned. He or she should offer parents an appointment to discuss the findings. Parents can ask the coroner for a copy of the pathologist's report but they may be charged a small fee.

Scotland Following a medico-legal post mortem, the procurator fiscal normally sends a copy of the report to the parents' general practitioner, who should explain the report sensitively to them. If the parents want a copy of the pathologist's report, they should request this from the procurator fiscal. No fee is charged.

Northern Ireland Following a medico-legal post mortem, the coroner normally sends a copy of the report to the parents' general practitioner, who should explain the report sensitively to them. The immediate family can ask the coroner for a free copy of the report. Coroners' Liaison Officers ensure that families are fully informed and involved.

For registration procedures following a coroner's post mortem, see *Registration in coroner's/procurator's fiscal cases* in Chapter 16.

RELEASING THE BODY OR REMAINS TO THE PARENTS

Trusts and Health Boards should have procedures and paperwork – including a mortuary release form – to enable mortuary staff to hand over a baby's body or remains to parents who want to organise the baby's funeral themselves (DoH 2006a: 2.30). Although no documentation is legally necessary, the hospital should give parents a form that confirms their right to take their baby's body from the hospital. (For a sample form see Appendix 1: Form 1.)

> *I was dealt with in such a professional and sensitive way at the mortuary at my local hospital. The attendant asked me to sign some forms and handed me a white box that he had made containing Noah. He explained what I could do with Noah's remains, the answer being that you can do whatever you want, there are no limitations. I have spoken to several other parents whose babies were born dead before 24 weeks, and they were not given this choice. Not everyone will want it, but some do, and they should always be told.* Mother

Parents of babies who were stillborn, or who were born alive at any gestation, should be told that there are certain regulations about what can be done with the body (see *Releasing the body or remains to the parents* in Chapter 17 for details). There are no regulations governing what can be done with the body or remains of a baby born dead before 24 weeks.

If the body or remains have been placed in formalin or another fixative, the family should be given advice about avoiding accidental exposure to the fixative and what to do if this occurs.

Parents who are organising the baby's funeral themselves should be informed about procedures for releasing the body and for keeping it until the funeral. They should also be given a contact number for a member of staff who can advise them if they need further information or help (DoH 2006a: 2.32). (See also *Releasing the body or remains to the parents* in Chapter 17.)

CHAPTER 16: CERTIFICATES AND REGISTRATION

LEGAL DEFINITIONS

Stillbirth

A stillborn child is defined in law as "a child which has issued forth from its mother after the twenty-fourth week of pregnancy and which did not at any time after being completely expelled from its mother breathe or show any other signs of life".

Relevant laws:

- England and Wales: Section 41 of the Births and Deaths Registration Act 1953 (BDRA) as amended by the Stillbirth Definition Act 1992;
- Scotland: Section 56(1) of the Registration of Births, Deaths and Marriages (Scotland) Act 1965 as amended by the Stillbirth Definition Act 1992;
- Northern Ireland: Births and Deaths Registration Order 1976 as amended by the Stillbirth Definition Northern Ireland Order 1992.

Neonatal death

"Death before the age of 28 completed days." (CEMACH 2006)

The status of the fetus

Under Article 2 of the Human Rights Convention, which was incorporated into English law by the Human Rights Act (1998) and into Scottish Law by the Scotland Act 1998, a fetus has no legal status. Therefore in the UK, the interests of the fetus cannot outweigh those of the mother.

CERTIFICATES AND FORMS ISSUED BY HEALTH CARE STAFF

The forms and certificates that staff give to parents following a childbearing loss depend on the type of loss. Some are required by law, others should be offered by hospitals as part of good practice.

Many parents greatly value copies of certificates and forms. These provide some tangible record of their baby's existence when they may otherwise have few or no mementoes:

- Staff should offer all parents good-quality copies of all the forms and certificates they issue, and should explain what they are and what they are for;
- All locally-produced documents should be worded sensitively and sympathetically.

It is always possible to use plain, non-bureaucratic language without compromising meaning or clarity (see also *Written information and information in other formats* in Chapter 4);

- Locally-produced forms and certificates should also be available, if possible, in the main local languages for parents who do not read English. If these are not yet available, or if parents still need help, an interpreter should explain to the parents what the form or certificate says and its purpose.

CERTIFICATION FOR A BABY BORN DEAD BEFORE 24 WEEKS' GESTATION

When a baby is born dead before 24 weeks' gestation (the legal age of viability), the law does not require or permit the birth to be certified or registered.

- Parents of a baby born dead before 24 weeks may appreciate the offer of *a certificate of birth from the hospital* as one way of creating memories of their baby (see Appendix 1: Form 2, and *Creating memories* in Chapter 12).

- In most cases the baby's remains will be disposed of by the hospital (see Chapter 17). To enable this:

  - a doctor, registered midwife or nurse who was present at the birth and/or has examined the baby issues a *form or letter* confirming that the baby was born dead at less than 24 weeks' gestation. For a sample form see Appendix 1: Form 3;

  - depending on the arrangements to be made (burial, communal cremation, or individual cremation), other documentation may be required – see *Documentation* in Chapter 17, and the sample forms in Appendix 1.

- If the parents are having a private funeral, they need:

- **a form or letter** confirming that the baby was born dead at less than 24 weeks' gestation. For a sample form see Appendix 1: Form 3. If this form is to be given to parents, it should be adapted and the word "baby" should be inserted in place of "fetal remains" (which occurs twice in the form) in order to avoid causing unnecessary distress;

  - (for cremation) a **form for the crematorium.** For a sample form see Appendix 1: Form 6;

- If the parents want to take the baby's body or remains home for burial, for example in their garden, they do not, in law, require a certificate or letter (see *Burial on private land* and *Releasing the body or remains to the parents* in Chapter 17). However, in case questions or suspicions are raised, they should be given an official **form or letter** stating that they have taken the body with the knowledge of the hospital, and including a contact telephone number in case of difficulties (see, for example, Appendix 1: Form 1). A copy of this document should be kept in the records.

CERTIFICATION FOR A STILLBIRTH

When a baby is stillborn, the doctor or the registered midwife who attended the delivery, or who examined the baby's body after the birth, gives the parents a *medical certificate* certifying the stillbirth. This certificate must be taken to the registrar of births and deaths (see later).

If the baby's body is to be cremated, a doctor must verify the stillbirth and fill in a *cremation form*. **In England, Wales and Scotland** only one medical signature is needed; in **Northern Ireland** there must be a second medical signature. No fee should be charged for signing a cremation form for a stillborn baby. (See later for coroner's/procurator's fiscal cases.)

For parents who want to take the baby's body or remains home for burial, see the final bullet point in *Certification for a baby born dead before 24 weeks' gestation* above.

Certification for a baby who was born at or after 24 weeks but had died *before* 24 weeks

If it is known, or is clear from the state of the body, that the baby died in utero before 24 weeks, although he or she was expelled from the mother only after 24 weeks, the baby should *not* be certified or registered as stillborn, but should be certified as described above in *Certification for a baby born dead before 24 weeks' gestation*.

This situation might arise, for example, if there is a delay between a diagnosed intrauterine death and delivery, or following selective or multifetal pregnancy reduction. There should be evidence, usually based on ultrasound imaging, that it was known before the 24th week of pregnancy that the baby (or babies) had died. This evidence should be clearly detailed in the mother's notes in case queries arise later (RCM 2005; RCOG 2005b).

If there is no such evidence, the decision about the baby's gestational age at death should be made by a doctor. It may be appropriate to use the stage of development of the dead baby or babies as an indicator of when the death occurred. The default position is for the doctor to certify the birth as a stillbirth (Jones 2005; RCOG 2005b).

Certification for a fetus papyraceous

If a fetus papyraceous is identified at the birth of one or more other babies, this must be documented in the mother's notes, and the parents should be informed. A fetus papyraceous should not be certified as a stillbirth (RCM 2005). Some parents may, however, appreciate the offer of a certificate from the hospital confirming the existence of this baby (see *Certification for a baby born dead before 24 weeks' gestation* above).

CERTIFICATION FOR A NEONATAL DEATH

If a baby is born alive at any gestation, and dies within 28 days of birth, the doctor who saw the baby before death issues a *medical certificate* certifying the death. This certificate must always be issued, even if the baby lived for only a few minutes. The certificate must be taken to the registrar of births and deaths.

If the baby's body is to be cremated, the doctor who verified the death and signed the medical certificate signs a *cremation form*. A second doctor's signature is also needed, unless there has been a post mortem. Doctors may waive the fees for this. (See later for coroner's/procurator's fiscal cases.)

If no doctor saw the baby while the baby was still alive, the death cannot be medically certified until it has been reported to the coroner or procurator fiscal. The doctor responsible for the care of the mother should contact the coroner or procurator fiscal to discuss the circumstances of the death. The parents must be informed about this, and the procedure and the reasons sensitively explained to them.

In most cases the coroner or procurator fiscal will send a notification to the registrar, so that the death can be registered. However, if the coroner or procurator fiscal decides to investigate further, the doctor should tell the parents that the death cannot be registered until the investigation (which may include a post mortem) has been completed. The registrar will contact the parents when the death can be registered.

CERTIFICATION FOLLOWING A TERMINATION BEFORE 24 WEEKS' GESTATION

Once the termination has taken place, the doctor responsible for initiating it fills out a *termination notification form,* which is sent in confidence to the Chief Medical Officer for England, Wales or Scotland as appropriate.

For a certificate that may be offered to the parents, see *Certification for a baby born dead before 24 weeks' gestation* above.

CERTIFICATION FOLLOWING A TERMINATION AFTER 24 WEEKS' GESTATION

Once the termination has taken place, the doctor responsible for initiating it fills out a *termination notification form,* which is sent in confidence to the Chief Medical Officer for England, Wales or Scotland as appropriate.

If the baby is **stillborn** (see *Legal definitions* above) the doctor or registered midwife who attended the delivery, or who examined the baby's body after the birth, gives the parents a *medical certificate* certifying the stillbirth (see *Certification for a stillbirth* above). This certificate must be taken to the registrar of births and deaths for the stillbirth to be registered.

Cremation – see *Certification for a stillbirth* above.

CERTIFICATION FOLLOWING A TERMINATION IF THE BABY IS BORN ALIVE AND THEN DIES

If a baby is born alive following a termination of pregnancy at any gestation and subsequently dies, both the birth and the death of the baby must be registered with the registrar of births and deaths.

The doctor who saw the baby while the baby was still alive issues a *medical certificate* certifying the death (see *Certification for a neonatal death* above).

If no doctor saw the baby while the baby was still alive, the death cannot be medically certified until it has been reported to the coroner or procurator fiscal. (See relevant section in *Certification for a neonatal death* above.) The parents should be told that the death cannot be registered until any investigations have been completed.

Cremation – see *Certification for a neonatal death* above.

REGISTRATION

Registration is required by law for all stillbirths, live births and deaths. If a baby is born dead before 24 weeks' gestation, the law does not require registration. Information about all stillbirths, live births and deaths must be given in person at a register office. It cannot be given by letter or telephone.

How health care staff can help parents

Many parents find the process of registering the stillbirth or birth and death of their baby very distressing, though many are also pleased that there is tangible evidence in law of their baby's existence. Most registrars do what they can to support parents and avoid causing unnecessary additional distress.

Health care staff can help parents by offering to explain what the process involves, and alerting them to decisions they may want to make before they go to the register office; for example, naming the baby or, if the parents are not married, having both parents' names on the certificate if they wish. (See below for more details about the regulations for each type of loss.)

Staff who discuss registration with parents should have easy access to a well-written reference guide on registration, certification, burial, cremation etc. This should include what parents need to know (including in more complicated situations), key local information (addresses, telephone numbers, opening hours and other details of the registrar of births and deaths, the coroner/procurator fiscal, funeral directors, crematoria, cemeteries etc), and any other information that may be helpful to parents. The guide should be checked and updated regularly.

Before the parents leave the hospital, a member of staff should make sure that:

- *They know how to get to the register office and why they are going.* The parents should be given a specially written leaflet explaining the process of registration and what they need to do (DoH 2005b). This should include full details about the registration office, opening times and a map. There should be separate leaflets for registering a stillbirth and registering a neonatal death. Ideally these should be available in different formats and in all the main languages spoken locally;

- *They know whether they have to make an appointment to see the registrar.* It is generally a good idea to advise the parents to telephone the registrar's office to say that they will be coming to register a stillbirth or neonatal death. They can then usually be seen quickly and will not have to wait with other parents registering births. If parents prefer, a member of staff could make this phone call;

- *They have the medical certificate and any other information that the registrar will need* (see sections below for specific details). It is helpful to the registrar if "Death of a baby" is written, with the parents' permission, in the corner of the envelope containing the medical certificate;

- **Parents who need an interpreter know whether the register offices provides an interpreting service and how to book it.** If no interpreter is provided, parents should be advised to take a relative or friend along to help them understand and answer the registrar's questions.

If there are likely to be any problems – for example, delay due to the mother's illness, or complications with entering the father's name in the register – the parents or, if they prefer, the member of staff who is caring for them should telephone the registrar for advice. In particularly difficult situations, the parents may also appreciate an offer by a member of staff to go with them to the register office.

Urgent burials

Some parents may require, usually for religious reasons, that burial takes place within 24 hours or as soon as possible after the death. Although registration must normally take place before a body can be buried, the local registrar should make arrangements to provide the necessary documents before registration, so that urgent burials can take place – for example, if the death or stillbirth occurs on or just before a weekend or public holiday. Families may need help from health care staff with getting the documentation completed as quickly as possible, and with contacting the registrar out of hours.

If an urgent burial is required, the registrar will normally issue a certificate of burial to allow the burial to go ahead. (This is unlikely to be possible if the death needs to be reported to a coroner or procurator fiscal.)

Formal registration of the death can take place later:

- In **England, Wales** and **Northern Ireland** up to 5 days after a neonatal death (which can be extended to 14 days), and up to 42 days after a stillbirth;
- In **Scotland**, up to 8 days after a neonatal death, and up to 21 days after a stillbirth.

Cremation It is not currently possible to organise an urgent cremation in the same way. In England and Wales the regulations may be amended in the near future to enable a certificate for cremation to be issued before registration in the same way as for burials.

Where to register a birth, death or stillbirth

In **England, Wales** and **Scotland,** information for the registration of a birth, death or stillbirth can be given in any district within the same country. If this is not the district in which the event occurred, the process will take a few days longer because the information must be forwarded to the register office in the district where the event did occur. This office will then post the appropriate certificate(s) (of birth, death or stillbirth) to the parents. In the case of a stillbirth or a neonatal death, this may mean a slight delay to the funeral, because burial or cremation cannot normally take place until after the registrar in the district where the event occurred has issued the necessary paperwork.

In **Northern Ireland**, information for the registration of a birth, death or stillbirth can be given either in the registration district in which it occurred, or in the district in which the mother usually lives. In the latter case there may again be a slight delay.

REGISTERING A STILLBIRTH

In **England, Wales** and **Northern Ireland** a stillbirth should be registered within 42 days and cannot be registered after three months.
In **Scotland** a stillbirth should be registered within 21 days and cannot normally be registered after three months. However, in certain circumstances, a stillbirth can be registered beyond three months with the approval of the Registrar General.

Who can register a stillbirth?

The registrar will normally expect the baby's mother, or, if the parents are married, either parent, to give the information. If the parents are unmarried, and both parents want the father's name in the register, they must normally attend the register office together to sign the register. However:

- If the mother attends the register office alone, but *both parents* want the father's name in the register, the mother must give the registrar a declaration that has been signed by the father in front of a justice of the peace or a notary public acknowledging his paternity;

- If the father attends the register office alone, and *both parents* want his name in the register, he must give the registrar a declaration signed by the mother in front of a justice of the peace or a notary public acknowledging his paternity. If the mother cannot leave the hospital and the time limit for registration is approaching, the registrar should be contacted for advice.

What documentation must the parents take?

- The medical certificate issued by the doctor or midwife who certified the stillbirth (see earlier).

What information will the registrar need?

- The date and place of the birth (and, in **Scotland,** the time) (on the medical certificate);

- The baby's names (if given) and sex;

- The cause of death (on the medical certificate);

- The parents' full names, current or previous occupations, usual address(es), places of birth, and the mother's maiden name if she is or has been married and any other names she might have had. If the parents are not married, and the mother does not want the father's details in the register, her details are sufficient.

What else should the parents know before they go to the register office?

- Parents can have their baby's personal names entered in the register:
  – In **England, Wales** and **Northern Ireland** the baby's personal name(s) cannot be entered later: *parents who have not yet decided on a name may want time to think before they go to the register office;*
  – In **Scotland** the baby's personal name(s) can be entered later.

England and Wales

- The registrar gives the parents a ***certificate of registration of stillbirth.*** This is a small certificate issued free of charge, which shows that the stillbirth has been registered;

- The parents can ask for a ***full certificate of stillbirth*** if they want. This is a certified copy of the complete entry in the stillbirth register. A small fee is charged for it. It is helpful if health care staff tell parents beforehand that they can ask for a full certificate if they want one;

- The registrar will also give the parents a *certificate for burial or cremation* ("white certificate"). They should give this to their funeral director or, if the hospital is arranging the funeral, to the hospital administrator who is dealing with it.

Scotland
- The registrar will offer parents an *extract of the stillbirth entry* in the register. This is a certified copy of the full entry in the stillbirth register;

- The registrar will also give the parents a *certificate of registration of stillbirth.* They should give this to their funeral director or, if the hospital is arranging the funeral, to the hospital administrator who is dealing with it.

Northern Ireland
- The registrar will offer parents a *certificate of stillbirth* when they register the stillbirth. This is an exact copy of the entry in the stillbirth register;

- The registrar will also give the parents a *form to permit the disposal of the body*. They should give this to their funeral director or, if the hospital is arranging the funeral, to the hospital administrator who is dealing with it.

Getting copies later on If the parents did not get a full certificate when they registered the stillbirth, or if they want another copy, they can usually get one by contacting either the register office where the stillbirth is registered, or the General Register Office for England and Wales, for Scotland or for Northern Ireland (see Appendix 2).

REGISTERING A NEONATAL DEATH
All deaths, including neonatal deaths, must normally be registered within 5 days (8 days in **Scotland**). If it is necessary to go beyond the time limit, the registrar should be contacted as soon as possible.

Both the baby's birth and the death must be registered (see *Babies born alive at the threshold of viability* in Chapter 11). For many parents, registration is also very important as recognition of their baby's brief life. If the birth has not yet been registered, this can be done at the same time as the death, or later if necessary. No medical certificate is needed to register the birth. (See below for coroner's/procurator's fiscal cases.)

Who can register a neonatal death?
The registrar will normally expect the baby's mother or father to attend the register office. Either or both parents can register the death, whether they are married or not. Alternatively, another relative, someone else who was present at the death, or a suitable person from the hospital can register the death if the parents cannot do it themselves.

What documentation must the parents take?
- The medical certificate issued by the doctor who saw the baby before death.

What information will the registrar need?
- The date and place of the baby's death (and, in **Scotland**, the time) (on the medical certificate);
- The baby's full name (see overleaf);

- The date and place of the baby's birth (on the birth certificate);
- The baby's age at death (on the medical certificate);
- The cause of death (on the medical certificate);
- The parents' full names, and current or previous occupations;
- The usual address of the baby's mother or parents.

What else should the parents know before they go to the register office?

- The registrar will enter the baby's personal name(s) in the register of deaths at the time of registration:
  - In **England, Wales** and **Northern Ireland** the baby's personal name(s) cannot be entered later: *parents who have not yet decided on a name may want time to think before they go to the register office;*
  - In **Scotland** the baby's personal name(s) can be entered later;
- The registrar will offer the parents a ***death certificate*** (a certified copy of the baby's entry in the death register). There is a small fee. Parents can get more copies of the death certificate later by writing to the registrar of the district where the death was registered;
- The registrar will give the parents a ***certificate for burial or cremation*** ("green certificate"). They should give this to their funeral director or, if the hospital is arranging the funeral on behalf of the parents, to the hospital administrator dealing with it;
- The registrar will give the parents a **certificate** for any social security benefits that may be payable. They need the baby's birth certificate to claim Child Benefit and other related benefits to which they are entitled (see *Child benefit and other benefits* in Chapter 14).

REGISTERING THE BABY'S BIRTH AND DEATH AT THE SAME TIME

By law, all live births must be registered within 42 days (21 days in **Scotland**). If the parents have not already registered their baby's birth, they can do this when they register the death. No medical certificate or other documentation is needed to register a birth.

What documentation must the parents take?

See *Registering a neonatal death* above.

What information will the registrar need?

See *Registering a neonatal death* above.

What else should the parents know before they go to the register office?

- The baby's personal name(s) can be entered in the register of births and on the birth certificate when the birth is registered:
  - In **England** and **Wales** the baby's personal name(s) can also be entered up to one year later;
  - In **Northern Ireland** the baby's personal name(s) can also be entered up to two years later;

- In **Scotland** the baby's personal name(s) can be entered at any later date without restriction:

- The baby's birth certificate (a certificate of registration of birth, an extract from the register or a full certificate) is required for parents to claim Child Benefit and any other benefits to which they are entitled (see *Child benefit and other benefits* in Chapter 14);

- Parents can get more copies of their baby's birth certificate at a later date by writing to the registrar of the district where the baby was registered. There is a small fee.

For more detailed information about registering a stillbirth, birth or neonatal death see the websites under *Registry Offices for England and Wales, Scotland, and Northern Ireland* in Appendix 2.

REGISTRATION IN CORONER'S/PROCURATOR'S FISCAL CASES

If there is any uncertainty surrounding the cause of a neonatal death, or there is reason to believe that a "stillborn" baby was in fact born alive, the doctor must report the case to a coroner or, in Scotland, a procurator fiscal. This does not necessarily delay registration or the funeral. In most cases, the coroner or procurator fiscal will not wish to examine the case further and will instruct the doctor to issue the medical certificate to the parents, so that registration and the funeral can go ahead. The parents should always be informed when a death is reported to a coroner or procurator fiscal.

In a few cases, the coroner or procurator fiscal may order a post mortem. (See also *Deaths reported to the coroner/ procurator fiscal* in Chapter 15). The doctor should tell the parents that the case has been reported, and explain why. He or she should also give the parents the telephone number and address of the coroner's or procurator fiscal's office, and encourage them to contact the office.

England, Wales and Northern Ireland If there is to be an inquest, the coroner normally issues a burial order, or a cremation form, within a few days. This enables the parents to go ahead with the burial or cremation. Once the inquest is over, the coroner sends a certificate to the registrar who then registers the death. The parents can write to the registrar for copies of the certificates as described above. (In the case of a neonatal death, the parents must register the birth as described above.)

Scotland The procurator fiscal is responsible for establishing the cause of death in all sudden, unexpected, unexplained or suspicious deaths. If necessary, he or she will order a post mortem. Once the cause of death has been established, the procurator fiscal normally issues the necessary documentation to allow burial or cremation to proceed. The procurator fiscal can ask for a Fatal Accident Inquiry (FAI) if the death has occurred in circumstances that give rise to serious public concern, and it appears to be in the public interest that an FAI be held. FAIs are not common – there are about 70 a year for the whole of Scotland.

CHAPTER 17: FUNERALS AND SENSITIVE DISPOSAL

> OTHER RELEVANT CHAPTERS:
> 1: PROVIDING INCLUSIVE CARE
> 2: HOLISTIC CARE
> 3: LOSS AND GRIEF
> 4: COMMUNICATION
> 5: COMMUNICATION ACROSS LANGUAGE AND OTHER BARRIERS
> 15: TRANSFER TO THE MORTUARY AND POST MORTEM INVESTIGATIONS
> 16: CERTIFICATES AND REGISTRATION
> 18: MEMORIALS

This chapter deals with the burial, cremation and respectful disposal of the bodies and remains of babies who die at any gestation or shortly after birth. It covers what staff and parents need to know about funerals or disposal – including private arrangements – and the choices that parents should be offered; requirements for Trust and Health Board contracts with funeral directors, cemeteries and crematoria to ensure high standards of service; and the relevant law and other regulations relating to burial, cremation and disposal.

For legal issues and regulations relating to funerals and disposal, see the end of this chapter.

In the natural, logical order of things, parents are not expected to outlive their children. I should not be burying my son, I should not be burying him. Father

POLICIES AND PRACTICE

There is growing awareness of the importance of what happens to fetal remains, as well as to the bodies of babies who are stillborn, or die shortly after birth. The Polkinghorne Report (1989), which reviewed guidance on the use of fetuses and fetal material for research, states that because a fetus has the potential to develop into a human being, it is entitled to respect and therefore, from an ethical point of view, has a status broadly comparable to that of a living person. The RCN (2002: 4) states that "parents should be given the same choice on the disposal of fetal remains as for a stillborn child", and the Human Tissue Authority stresses the importance of handling pregnancy loss with sensitivity, and ensuring that the needs of the woman or couple are paramount: this should be reflected in disposal policies (HTA Code 5 2006: B6).

The importance of sensitive disposal, and respectful burial or cremation, should not be underestimated. The costs to Trusts and Health Boards should be viewed as an investment rather than an expense. Parents who discover afterwards that arrangements were not satisfactory – for example, if the remains of their baby have been incinerated rather than cremated or buried – are likely to be distressed: complaints and emotive publicity, which take up staff time and involve additional expense, are more likely.

Trust and Health Board policies on funerals and sensitive disposal should cover losses at all gestations, as well as stillbirths and neonatal deaths. The basis for all these policies must be that babies' bodies and remains are handled with respect. The policies should be carefully worked out in close consultation with representatives from all the departments that will have to implement them, as well as representatives of bereaved parents (for example, ARC, the Miscarriage Association, Sands and the Multiple Births Foundation). They should be communicated to all the staff concerned, and reviewed and updated regularly.

In addition to arranging and paying for burial or cremation, and for a funeral or other ceremony for a stillborn baby, fetus and fetal remains, Trusts, Health Boards and managers should consider offering to arrange and pay for burial or cremation and for a funeral or other ceremony for a baby who dies shortly after birth (DoH 2005b: 78).

Trust and Health Board policies should ensure that parents are informed about arrangements for funerals and sensitive disposal, and are enabled to express their own wishes about what happens to their baby's body or the products of conception. If parents want to, they should be able to make their own funeral arrangements, or to participate in the arrangements made by the hospital.

All staff who are in any way involved in the management of childbearing loss should:
- Have an overall understanding of hospital policies and practices with regard to funerals and disposal;
- Be well informed about policies and practices in their specific area of responsibility.

They should have easy access to a well-written, regularly updated reference guide (see *How health care staff can help parents* in Chapter 16).

OFFERING CHOICES
Parents' needs and wishes cannot be assumed on the basis of the gestational age of their baby, nor of the nature of their loss. For most parents, it is important that their baby's remains are disposed of respectfully, whatever the gestation.

For some parents, especially of babies who die at later gestations, arranging a funeral or other ceremony for their baby, no matter how simple, helps give reality and expression to their loss and can affirm the significance of their baby's existence and death. A funeral can take many forms and need not be religious. It can be an important way of honouring the baby, enabling parents to do something for their baby, and creating memories for the future. It can also help to make the baby's existence real for family and friends, and help them to understand his or her importance to the parents. It gives them a formal opportunity to express their sympathy and support. However, some parents may simply want their baby's body or remains to be respectfully buried or cremated by the hospital.

Written and other information
All parents should be offered written information relevant to the stage at which the pregnancy ended or the baby died, outlining (as appropriate):

- What arrangements will normally be made;
- What choices they have if they want the hospital to make the arrangements;
- What choices they have, and what they need to do, if they want to make their own arrangements;
- What, if any, costs are involved, and what to do if they might be eligible for a Social Fund Funeral Expenses Payment (see *Parents on a low income later*).

A range of additional options, such as an entry in the hospital remembrance book, or an individual or communal memorial service, should also be mentioned (see Chapter 18). The name and contact details of a member of staff whom parents can contact for more information should be included.

If possible, written information should also be available in other formats and in the other main languages spoken locally. The content should take account of any cultural and religious issues that may be relevant.

The member of staff who gives to parents, should make it clear that they are willing and available for further discussion or questions.

Discussions with parents

Some parents, perhaps especially those who have lost a baby early in pregnancy, may not want further discussion, and may choose to leave all arrangements to the hospital. However, some may change their minds later, or may want to know afterwards what was done.

Other parents will want to discuss the arrangements and their options in detail. They will need to decide whether they want the hospital to make some or all of the arrangements and, if so, whether and how they might want to participate in or enhance the funeral and any likely costs. They may want, for example, to buy flowers, or, perhaps for losses at later gestations, to have a different type of coffin, to have the baby at home before the funeral, to have a car to take members of the family to the funeral, or to put up a plaque or memorial. The options available if the hospital arranges the funeral will depend to some extent on whether the ceremony will be a shared or an individual one. If parents are offered a choice between burial and cremation, they need to know in advance what each option would involve (see *Cremation and burial options* below).

If parents decide to organise the funeral themselves, whether or not they use a funeral director, they may still need information from staff about their options, help with making decisions, and support.

For many parents, the loss of a pregnancy or the death of their baby is their first experience of bereavement. They may know nothing about any practical arrangements that have to be made, nor of the choices that are open to them. Some parents may find it difficult to think about what they could do, and some may welcome tentative suggestions. It is important to create an atmosphere in which parents have time to think, can say honestly what they want and don't want, can ask questions, and can raise any fears and worries. Staff need to listen carefully and try to help parents make choices that reflect their own wishes and values, so that they can look back on a positive experience in the years to come (Daly 2005) (see also *Arranging a private funeral* later).

Staff who talk with parents should have a thorough understanding of the available options for babies of different gestations, and should know what is possible at local cemeteries and crematoria. They should also:

- Be aware of and open to different personal, religious and cultural requirements (see below), including non-religious options;

- Have reflected on their own feelings and attitudes and how these may affect the way they talk to parents and the way they respond to them. Some parents may make decisions that the staff member considers inappropriate, but which may be right for them. It is important that staff do not question what parents want to do unless there are legal or other reasons why their wishes cannot be carried out.

Staff may sometimes find checklists helpful in ensuring that essential questions are asked and procedures are followed . However, *any checklists that staff use when they are eliciting the views and preferences of parents should make it clear that the overriding principle is parental choice.* (See also *Checklists* in Chapter 12.)

> *The nurse insisted that I choose between burial and cremation and that we must attend the funeral, but I didn't want to be involved in any of that. It seemed weird and unnatural to me to be having a funeral for a pregnancy that ended at 12 weeks.* Mother

Cultural and religious considerations

All cultures and religions have different ways of managing death and funerals. However, it is never possible to make assumptions about what any individual will want on the basis of their heritage or religion: the decisions of parents within any group will vary. There may also be differences in practice between different denominations and traditions in the same religion.

Staff should be aware, for example, that:

- In the UK, the options that are offered are often based on the assumption that families are nuclear, and that the parents are the people most involved when a baby dies. In an extended family, the loss of a baby may be keenly felt by a larger number of people, all of whom may want to be involved;

- In some cultures, pregnancy and childbirth and everything associated with them are traditionally women's responsibilities. Some women may expect or prefer their husbands to be excluded, and older female relatives may sometimes be more important in supporting a bereaved mother. On the other hand, formal and public religious events, such as funerals, may involve mainly men, and women may sometimes be excluded;

- Some parents may want members of their own religion to prepare the baby's body for the funeral;

- Although attending a funeral is right for many parents, this is not always an option. For example, some religions or denominations do not traditionally hold funerals or other ceremonies for a baby born dead before 24 weeks, or for a stillborn baby; some do not allow women to go to the graveside;

- For many parents the decision about burial or cremation is a personal one; for some it may be affected by religious requirements. For example, for observant Jews and Muslims, burial traditionally takes place within 24 hours of death. Some observant Jews and some Muslims may also want to bury all products of a pregnancy, whatever the gestation. Although Sikh and Hindu adults are normally cremated, it is traditional in these communities for babies to be buried. Again, burial traditionally takes place as soon as possible after the death.

Cremation and burial options

The member of staff supporting the parents should be well informed about the choices available to them, and about local cemetery and crematorium regulations.

Burial If their baby will be buried in a *shared grave*, parents should be told this in advance. They should be told how many babies will be in the grave (see *Contract with a cemetery* below). This information should also be included in the written information for parents. Parents should be given an estimate of how long it is likely to be before the grave is closed and the ground properly reinstated. Some parents find it comforting to know that their baby will be buried with other babies. Others find the idea upsetting and might prefer to make their own arrangements.

Parents also need to know in advance about any local regulations affecting shared and individual graves, so that they do not discover that they cannot commemorate their baby in the way that they planned when it is too late for them to consider alternatives. These regulations are not enshrined in law, but are decided locally. For example:

- Some cemeteries do not permit headstones of any kind on a communal grave. Others lay down the type and size of headstone that is permitted. If no headstone is permitted, there is sometimes a communal memorial stone nearby, and it may be possible to have the baby's name and dates of birth and death engraved on this;

- Rules in some cemeteries forbid any flowers on a shared grave. Some forbid personal items, such as pictures or a teddy bear, on any grave, whether shared or individual;

- Some cemeteries have a book of remembrance in which the baby's name can be entered.

Once a baby of any gestation has been buried in a shared grave it may not be possible to exhume the body later and bury it elsewhere (see *Exhumation* later). This depends on how the cemetery digs the grave and how and when the coffins are placed in it. It is important that the staff advising parents know the local situation and can tell them in advance what is likely to be possible.

Some parents may decide to pay for a *single plot* in the cemetery, though this may be expensive (see *Costs* later). Many cemeteries also have regulations about the kinds of memorials allowed on single graves, and parents should be told about these in advance.

Some parents may want to have their baby buried in a nearby or familiar churchyard. Whether this is possible will depend on space and on the church regulations. Others (Muslim and Jewish parents, for example) may want their baby to be buried in a cemetery, or an area of a cemetery, specially reserved for members of their faith.

Cremation Parents should be warned that no ashes will be available following a *communal cremation* – that is, if the bodies or remains of several babies are placed in the cremator at the same time.

After an *individual* cremation there may also not be any ashes, because the soft bones of very young babies are usually destroyed by the high temperatures of the cremation process. Parents should be warned about this. Whether or not a crematorium can produce ashes from babies depends on the make and model of the cremator, how it is operated (fully automated or manual override), and the turbulence during the cremation cycle. Parents who receive no ashes and later learn of other parents who, in a similar situation, have received ashes, may understandably be upset.

If there are ashes following an individual cremation:

- Parents can choose, for example, to scatter or bury them at the crematorium, or in a local churchyard or municipal cemetery that is closer to their home, or elsewhere – for example, in a place that has a special meaning for them;

- Alternatively they can choose to keep them at home;

- Some parents may want to scatter the ashes on water. The Environment Agency is sympathetic to individual families who wish to do this, and parents arranging individual ceremonies do not require special approval. (See also *Scattering ashes on water: Environment Agency regulations* later.)

Parents should be reassured that these decisions do not have to be made in a hurry. The ashes are normally available from the day after the cremation and can usually be kept by the crematorium or the funeral director until the parents have decided what to do. Alternatively, the parents may prefer to collect them and take them home while they decide.

Many crematoria have a designated area for memorials to babies that have died. There may be rules about the types of memorial that are permitted. In some places parents can have their baby's name inscribed on a plaque or memorial stone.

All crematoria have books of remembrance in which the baby's name can be entered.

FUNERALS ARRANGED BY THE HOSPITAL

We went to the funeral. We felt we just had to be there even though it was incredibly painful. It was a simple one, arranged by the hospital. I am so grateful they did that for us. I couldn't have possibly done it myself. Mother

Many parents will want the hospital to arrange a funeral for their baby. They should be asked if they would like to attend and (whether they attend or not) if they would like to be informed of the date and time of the funeral. Some parents may not want to attend, but may want, for example, to send flowers. Parents who want to attend the funeral should be given written directions and the number of someone to phone if they have any queries.

- If the hospital has a set time for communal funerals, the parents should be informed of the date and time and of the type of ceremony that will be performed;

- If the hospital offers an individual funeral, and the parents want this, the date and time should be agreed with them before booking, and then confirmed in writing.(See also *Arranging a private funeral* later, for ideas about enhancing the funeral.)

Some parents do not want to be informed of the date of the funeral: their decision must be recorded to ensure that they are not sent this information.

Before the mother leaves hospital, a note must be made of the address and telephone number where she can be contacted (for example, if she is going to stay with relatives). Unless the parents have asked not to be informed, the member of staff arranging the funeral should try to check by phone that they have received the information about the funeral.

If parents want to participate in a funeral that is arranged by the hospital and want advice, they may welcome an opportunity to talk to a hospital chaplain beforehand. Depending on the parents' wishes, the chaplain may also be able to contact a religious adviser of the parents' own faith, or a Humanist adviser, to help them.

> *We had the twins cremated which was arranged by the hospital chaplain. Letting them go was the hardest and most painful thing I have ever had to do in my life. I wish now that I had touched the coffin, but at the time I couldn't think straight … I had ordered two white roses which were tied together with white ribbon and I placed these on the coffin. Ed held the coffin and carried it in. He said he wanted to do it as it was his only chance of giving them a cuddle.* Mother

If the baby is buried and the parents do not attend the funeral, the funeral director or the hospital should inform them in writing where the grave is, and the number of the plot. Both the funeral director and the hospital should keep a record of these details.

NEGOTIATING FUNERAL CONTRACTS

Trusts and Health Boards should appoint a multidisciplinary group of staff that negotiates and monitors contracts with local funeral directors, the manager of a local cemetery and/or the manager of a crematorium. *One or more members of the staff who regularly provide care for bereaved parents should be part of the negotiating team.*

Primary Care Trusts should make their own arrangements for funerals, burials and cremations for losses that occur outside the hospital, and negotiate contracts accordingly. Alternatively, they can arrange to share in the arrangements made by a local hospital.

Contract with a funeral director

The contact with a funeral director should state clearly the hospital's requirements for funerals for all fetal remains and for all babies who are born dead or who die shortly after birth. Many funeral directors have good knowledge of local communities and their needs. They can be an important resource for Trusts, Health Boards and managers in planning and implementing care following a pregnancy or childbearing loss.

The contract with a funeral director should ensure arrangements that parents will find acceptable, whether or not they choose to attend the funeral. Contracts should not be awarded on the grounds of price alone. The standard of a contract funeral should be at least as good as that of a simple private funeral, and parents who ask the hospital to make all the arrangements should not feel that they are choosing a "cheap" and therefore inferior service. A member of staff should attend contract funerals regularly to monitor the standard of provision and ensure that it is acceptable.

The costs of collecting bodies and fetal remains from the hospital mortuary should be included in the agreed fee. The contract should also state that the parents of a baby born at a later gestation should be able to discuss the funeral with the funeral director beforehand, to attend the funeral, and to enhance it by paying for additional features not included in the contract (see, for example, the possibilities listed in *Discussions with parents* above).

The funeral director should also provide facilities for parents who want to see their baby's body at the funeral parlour before the funeral.

It is important to make sure that the contracted funeral director understands the possible range of personal, religious and cultural needs of different families and can accommodate them. Hospitals may sometimes need to arrange additional contracts with specialist funeral directors who have experience in organising funerals for members of a particular religious or ethnic group, and have contacts with the appropriate cemeteries.

Contract with a cemetery

A contract should be negotiated with a cemetery if possible, so that parents can be offered the choice between burial and cremation. In densely populated areas, the cost of burial may be prohibitive.

Even if hospitals cannot offer burial as an option for all parents, arrangements should be in place for those whose religion requires burial. The member of staff responsible should establish links with the relevant religious groups (and, where appropriate, with specialist funeral directors), so that parents who require a religious burial can be referred to them. Most parents who are likely to require their baby to be buried for religious reasons are also likely to need to hold the funeral as soon as possible after the death.

Burials should be in an acceptable area of a cemetery. Many council-run cemeteries have a designated area for babies. Some Trusts and Health Boards or local authorities buy a special plot for the burial of babies of all gestations and ages. In this case, a record must be kept of the site of each grave and the babies it contains, so that parents can visit the grave later if they wish.

Some cemeteries only permit the burial of babies in separate graves, whether the baby has a contract or a private funeral. In other cemeteries, babies who died at early gestations (especially those who have contract funerals) must be buried in a communal grave with a number of other babies, each in his or her own coffin (see also *Cremation and burial options* above). These graves should normally be located in a special children's area of the cemetery with a general memorial stone. There should be a book of remembrance where the names of individual babies can be entered if the parents wish.

The contract should describe the services to be provided for hospital-arranged funerals. It should also state:

- The documentation that will be needed;

- The area that is designated for the burial of fetal remains and babies;

- How many containers of fetal remains may be placed in a single coffin;

- How containers of fetal remains should be labelled: in order to maintain the confidentiality of the mother, a case number rather than a name should be used, so that only the health care staff can trace the remains to the mother (ICCM 2004);

- The gestation after which a baby should be buried in a separate coffin;

- How coffins should be labelled;

- Whether babies will have individual or communal graves, and the maximum number allowed in a communal grave;

- How the coffins will be arranged within a communal grave: coffins that are stacked one on top of the other rather than laid side by side make it almost impossible to exhume a specific coffin (see *Exhumation* later);

- How the exact location of each coffin in a communal grave will be recorded;

- That *lockable* grave covers, which are relatively inexpensive and easily available, will be used instead of plywood sheets to ensure that communal graves are not disturbed until such time as the grave is filled and the ground re-constituted;

- Who will lead the funeral ceremony, and how often funeral ceremonies will take place;

- The responsibilities of the cemetery, and of the Trust or Health Board, for keeping records of when and where burials take place, so that remains can be traced at any time during the next 50 years (ICCM 2004).

If the local cemetery does not accept fetal material for burial, the Trust or Health Board should consider finding another cemetery where this can be done. It may be helpful to contact the Institute of Cemetery and Crematorium Management for advice (formerly known as the Institute of Burial and Cremation Administration) (see Appendix 2).

Contract with a crematorium

This should describe the services to be provided for hospital-arranged funerals. It should also state:

- The documentation that will be needed (see *Documentation* below for a list of the forms required for the cremation of fetal remains and babies born dead before 24 weeks' gestation);

- The type of container to be used for fetal remains to ensure that they comply with crematorium regulations;

- How containers of fetal remains will be labelled: to maintain the confidentiality of the mother a case number should be used, so that only the health care staff can trace the remains to her (ICCM 2004);

- How many containers may be placed in a single coffin;

- The gestation after which a baby should be cremated in a separate coffin;

- The type of coffin, how it should be labelled, and what other items may or may not be placed in it;

- When and how often cremations will take place;

- Who will lead the funeral ceremony;

- Whether there are likely to be ashes and, if so, where they will be scattered;

- The responsibilities of the crematorium, and of the Trust or Health Board, for maintaining records of when and where the cremations of individual babies and fetal remains have taken place. These records must be kept for up to 50 years (ICCM 2004).

Some crematoria will not accept fetal material for cremation, or will not carry out communal cremations. Some will not cremate tissue that results from a molar, anembryonic or ectopic pregnancy on the grounds that it contains tissue from a living person – the mother. In these situations, Trusts and Health Boards should seek out the services of a crematorium that will undertake communal cremation of fetal material, and will cremate tissue from early pregnancy losses. It may be helpful to contact the Institute of Cemetery and Crematorium Management for advice (formerly known as the Institute of Burial and Cremation Administration) (see Appendix 2).

Documentation

Some crematoria do not have standard forms covering the cremation of fetal remains and the bodies of babies born dead before 24 weeks' gestation. It may be helpful to suggest that they use the forms in Appendix 1:

3: *Medical certificate authorising burial or cremation of fetal remains of less than 24 weeks' gestation;*

4: *Form for preliminary application for communal cremation of fetal remains of less than 24 weeks' gestation;*

5: *List of fetal remains for communal cremation;*

6: *Application form for the individual cremation of fetal remains.*

Incineration of bodies and remains

Incineration should be used only as a last resort. Many people feel that it is unacceptable to deliver fetal remains, or load them into an incinerator, with clinical and other waste (RCN 2002: 3 and 4). However, if a hospital cannot arrange for the burial or cremation of fetal remains from a pregnancy that ended before 24 weeks' gestation, it may necessary to incinerate them (HSG 1991 cited in RCOG 2005c). A designated member of staff should be responsible for ensuring that this procedure is carried out as respectfully as possible. Staff should be aware, however, that incineration is unacceptable to some parents on religious grounds.

Fetal remains awaiting incineration should be stored in separate, secure, opaque containers in a safe place, and should be transported in these containers (DoH 2004b).

If fetal remains will be incinerated rather than cremated, parents should be sensitively informed in the written information they are given that:

• The method of disposal will be incineration (which must not be called cremation);

• If they want to, they can make their own arrangements for cremation or burial of their baby's remains.

PARENTS ON A LOW INCOME

Parents of babies who are born dead at or after 24 weeks (stillborn), or born alive at any gestation, who are receiving Income Support, housing or other benefits or tax credits, can usually get a Social Fund Funeral Expenses Payment to help them with the costs of a private funeral (see below) or of enhancements for a hospital funeral. This payment covers the costs of a simple, respectful, low-cost funeral, normally within the UK. It includes the charges of the burial authority or crematorium, certain necessary travel expenses, and up to £700 for other funeral expenses. A Funeral Expenses Payment must be claimed from the date of the baby's death until *up to three months after the date of the funeral.* Parents must attach receipts for the final funeral bill and/or the costs of any enhancements, travel expenses etc with the claim.

Claim forms can be downloaded from the Jobcentre Plus website (see Appendix 2), or obtained from the local social security office or Jobcentre Plus. (For other benefits for parents on a low income, see *Entitlement to time off work and benefits* in Chapter 13, and *Child benefit and other benefits* in Chapter 14.).

ARRANGING A PRIVATE FUNERAL

We decided to arrange our baby's funeral ourselves. It was the hardest thing we've ever done and I can't imagine how we managed it but I'm glad we did. I so wanted our baby to know how much we loved her, how special she was and how much we wanted her to be safe from harm. I just kept telling her that in my head. Mother

Parents may need information and support from staff to help them think about whether they want to arrange a private funeral. They need to know about the choices and decisions they can make. A private funeral need not be expensive or difficult to arrange, and parents on a low income can usually get financial help (see *Parents on a low income* above). Parents can contact a funeral director to organise the funeral, or can contact the cemetery or crematorium themselves. They can also bury the baby on private land (see *Burial on private land* below). If they want specialist help with the ceremony – for example, from a faith community leader or a Humanist adviser – the funeral director should be able to arrange a contact for them.

If the parents decide to use a funeral director:

- The hospital should give parents a list of local funeral directors. This should indicate which firms are members of a professional organisation. Parents need to know that they are free to go to any funeral director, and that they can discuss costs with several funeral directors and find out what each would provide without making any commitment. However, some parents may prefer to use the firm with which the hospital has a contract, because they can be confident that this firm has experience of organising funerals for babies;

- Some parents may prefer the chaplain, a member of the hospital or community staff, or another member of their family, to liaise with the funeral director for them. However, they should still be given every opportunity to make decisions themselves and to become involved. Any decisions should always be checked with them;

- Some parents may want to contact their local Sands or other bereavement support group (see Appendix 2) to find out what can be done locally, and to get personal recommendations for local funeral directors.

Planning

Depending on what is possible under local cemetery and crematorium regulations, whether there is a body, and on the condition of the body, the person advising the parents might gently suggest some or all of the following:

- Parents choose special readings, songs, hymns or prayers for the funeral;

- They and other family members contribute to the ceremony, for example with readings or an address;

- The baby is dressed in his or her own clothes in the coffin. Parents may want to dress their baby themselves, or may want to ask a funeral director to do this;

- The coffin is kept open until immediately before the funeral, or throughout the funeral;

- One or two special things are placed in the coffin; for example, a family photograph, a letter or poem to the baby, drawings or paintings by brothers or sisters, a soft toy such as a teddy bear, something they had bought specially for the baby, a rose, or something else of special value and significance to them. Parents should be warned that environmental legislation and individual crematorium safety rules place restrictions on what can be cremated. If the baby is to be cremated, the funeral director will remove anything that cannot be cremated before the coffin is finally closed and will return it to the parents;

- Parents might like to have the baby at home for a time before the funeral. They could take the coffin to the funeral with them, either in a funeral director's limousine or in their own car;

- Parents could carry the coffin from the car to the chapel and then to the grave or the crematorium;

- The baby could be placed in a Moses basket during the ceremony, or the coffin could be placed in a Moses basket;

- The ceremony could be photographed or videoed to create memories for later;

- There could be a memorial book or card for people attending the funeral to sign;

- People who attend the funeral could be invited to gather afterwards for refreshments and to support the parents.

Costs

It is important that the person who is informing the parents understands the kinds of costs that may be involved and what is possible locally. He or she should also tell the parents whether they might be eligible for financial support (see above). Some parents may need reassurance that the amount of money they spend on their baby's funeral is in no way a measure of their love for their baby, or of their grief.

- Hospital medical staff should waive fees for signing cremation forms for stillborn babies and babies who die shortly after birth;

- Some funeral directors either charge a nominal fee, or make no charge, for the standard private funeral of a baby. However, parents may have to pay for any additional features that they choose;

- Parents whose baby is cremated may have to pay crematorium fees (if charged – see below), the costs of a plaque or any other form of memorial, and fees for a religious service if they have one;

- A Medical Referee at the crematorium must sign the *Authority to Cremate* (Form F) for a stillborn baby, and for a baby who died shortly after birth. There may be a fee for this. In the case of individual or communal cremation of fetal remains or babies born dead before 24 weeks, guidance from the Department of Constitutional Affairs (DCA undated) states that a Medical Referee is not required to sign the *Authority to Cremate* (Form F), so no fee is payable;

- The cost of buying a private burial plot in a municipal cemetery can be high. Sometimes it is possible to buy a smaller child's plot, which is less expensive. Alternatively, it may be possible to buy a place in a communal grave;

- If the family has a family plot the baby can normally be buried there, provided the legal owner of the grave gives written permission. There will be a charge for digging or re-opening the grave;

- Burial in a churchyard, if space and local regulations permit, is less expensive, though there will still be additional fees – for example, for digging the grave;

- Parents may also wish to buy a headstone for their baby's grave if this is permitted. For advice on headstones and memorials, parents can contact cemetery staff, a local funeral director or a monumental mason. (To find a local monumental mason, parents can contact the National Association of Memorial Masons, see Appendix 2.) The local Sands branch or other bereavement support group may also be able to give advice.

BURIAL ON PRIVATE LAND

Some parents may want to bury their baby in their own garden, or in some other place that holds special meaning for them. There is also an increasing number of woodland and natural, or green, burial sites where parents can bury their baby. (For more information about these and details of local sites, as well as information about burial on private land, contact the Natural Death Centre – see Appendix 2). Staff may be able to help parents consider what they would like to do, and could offer to put them in touch with other professionals (such as a funeral director or environmental health officer) and the Natural Death Centre for information.

There is no legal prohibition affecting the burial of a body on private land, provided that:

- The owner of the land gives permission, for example in the case of a rented property;

- There is no interference with any rights that other people may have over the land. If the property is mortgaged, it may be prudent to inform the mortgage company before the burial takes place as it may affect the resale of the property. It may also be prudent to consult the appropriate authority if the property is in a conservation area;

- That no danger is caused to others, for example, through pollution of groundwater, surface water or water courses, or by body fluids leaking into or onto adjoining land;

- The body is buried at an appropriate depth.

Parents need to think carefully about burying their baby in their garden (as they might move house), or on land that could possibly be used for new purposes. They may want to consult their local council's environmental health department and the Environment Agency for advice about the suitability of the site and the depth of the grave (EA 2005). There is no legal requirement to register home burials on private land. However, details of the burial should be noted and kept with the deeds of the property.

In the case of a **neonatal death,** parents who bury their baby themselves must notify the registrar of births and deaths of the date and place of burial within 96 hours. (See overleaf)This is not required in the case of a stillborn baby or other pregnancy loss.

RELEASING THE BODY OR REMAINS TO THE PARENTS

Staff in some areas have been unwilling to release fetal remains or babies' bodies to parents, rather than to a funeral director. However, there is no legal reason why parents should not take the body, or remains, and make their own arrangements. Staff should support parents who want to do this, and there should be sensitive and efficient procedures in place (DoH 2006a: 2.30) An opaque container should be provided for products of conception. Parents of a stillborn baby or of a baby who died shortly after birth should be given information about the regulations relating to funerals and disposal (see earlier).

In law, no documentation is needed to accompany the body, but for the protection of the parents and to avoid misunderstandings, Trusts and Health Boards should give the parents a form. (For a sample form see Appendix 1: Form 1.) In order to minimise unnecessary distress for parents, the mortuary staff should ensure that the body or fetal remains are well presented and that the appropriate paperwork is ready.

> *We left the hospital…bringing Matthew and his tiny coffin with us. Matthew was buried the next afternoon and it was such a sad day. For me the worst part was walking away from the graveyard knowing that I would never get to see my baby again.* Mother

SUMMARY OF LEGAL ISSUES AND REGULATIONS
Losses before 24 weeks' gestation

- There is no legal requirement to bury or cremate fetal material or fetuses (including remains following termination) before 24 weeks' gestation;

- Incineration is permitted under certain conditions (HTA Code 5 2006: B19 and B20);

- Maceration and sluicing of fetal material are not permitted (HTA Code 5 2006: B20);

- Communal burial of fetal tissue or fetuses is permitted (HTA Code 5 2006: B15);

- Communal cremation of fetal tissue or fetuses is permitted (HTA Code 5 2006: B 17, The Human Tissue (Scotland) Act 2006).

The Human Tissue Authority's responsibilities do not extend to Scotland. However, as in the rest of the UK, the overriding principle should be respectful and sensitive disposal. The guidance contained in HTA Code of Practice No.5 (2006), in RCOG Good Practice No.5 (2005c) and in *Sensitive disposal of all fetal remains: Guidance for nurses and midwives* (RCN 2002) should all be regarded as good practice and should be adhered to.

Stillbirths

Common law requires that a baby who is stillborn must be buried or cremated. This requirement also applies in the case of a termination after 24 weeks' gestation.

The legal duty to dispose of a baby's body rests with the baby's parents: with their consent, it can be done by the Trust or Health Board on their behalf.

Neonatal deaths

The law requires that if a baby is born alive and then dies the body must be buried or cremated.

The legal duty to dispose of a baby's body rests with the baby's parents: with their consent, it can be done by the Trust or Health Board on their behalf.

After a neonatal death, the person who carries out the disposal (usually a funeral director, though it can also be the parents) must notify the registrar of the date, place and means of disposal within 96 hours. If the registrar has not been notified within 14 days of the issue of the death certificate, he or she must make enquiries. If the body has not been disposed of, the registrar must inform the officer responsible for environmental health. If it appears that no suitable arrangements for disposal have been or are being made, the local council has a duty to dispose of a body under Section 46 of the Public Health (Control of Disease) Act 1984. There is no legislative equivalent to Section 46 of the Public Health (Control of Disease) Act 1984 in Northern Ireland.

Scattering ashes on water: Environment Agency regulations

Families should not spread ashes:

- Within one kilometre upstream of any drinking water supply;

- From a bridge over a river used by boaters and canoeists;

- Anywhere close to a marina, to anglers or to bathers;

- In windy weather or close to buildings, to avoid the risk of ashes being blown about.

Ashes should be scattered as close to the surface of the water as possible. Non-biodegradable items such as plastic bags, or wreaths that contain plastic or metal, should not be thrown into the water, or left on the river bank (EA 2005).

Exhumation

Occasionally a family might, at some future date, want to exhume a baby's body so that, for example, the baby can be re-buried in the same grave as another family member. It is therefore essential that accurate records are kept, so that the location of the grave and the exact position of the coffin in the grave can be identified.

The exhumation of a baby who died before 24 weeks' gestation does not require a licence. However, it is highly unlikely that permission will be granted to exhume a baby who has been buried in a communal grave, especially if the coffins are stacked one upon another, because the families of all the other babies in the grave would have to give their consent first.

It is an offence to exhume the body of a baby born at or after 24 weeks' gestation without the necessary permissions:

- In **England,** this includes a licence from the Department of Constitutional Affairs or, if the grave is in consecrated ground, a faculty from the Chancellor of the local diocese;

- In **Scotland** an Exhumation Grant from the local Sheriff is required;

- In **Northern Ireland,** if the grave is in consecrated ground, the family should first contact the church authorities, the District Chief Public Health Inspector, and the police, who are authorised to permit exhumation for the purposes of reburial. In the case of a public cemetery, the licence of the Department of the Environment for Northern Ireland is required, and the police and the District Chief Public Health Inspector must be notified. The exhumation should be carried out in accordance with the terms of the Burial Grounds Regulations (Northern Ireland) 1992.

The exhumation procedure must be carried out in such a way that respect for the deceased is maintained and public health is protected. Details of the regulations and requirements are available from the relevant local authority.

Depending on the condition of the body at burial, and the length of time that has elapsed, it may not be possible to find identifiable remains. If this is at all likely, parents should be told before they go to the trouble of trying to get the necessary permissions.

CHAPTER 18: MEMORIALS

OTHER RELEVANT CHAPTERS:
1: PROVIDING INCLUSIVE CARE
2: HOLISTIC CARE
3: LOSS AND GRIEF
4: COMMUNICATION
5: COMMUNICATION ACROSS LANGUAGE AND OTHER BARRIERS
17: FUNERALS AND SENSITIVE DISPOSAL

Many parents want to create some kind of lasting memorial to their baby. Some may choose to have a formal memorial, such as a headstone or a plaque in a cemetery or crematorium grounds. But many want to create other forms of memorial and may be grateful for suggestions from health care staff. They may also like to contact their local Sands, Miscarriage Association, ARC, TAMBA or other bereavement support group (see Appendix 2) to find out from other parents what they have done.

Books of remembrance

All crematoria, and some cemeteries, have books of remembrance in which parents can have their baby's name entered. The funeral director, or the local crematorium or cemetery manager, can tell them how to arrange this.

Many hospitals also have books of remembrance. Some keep a book in the maternity unit and another in the neonatal unit (see *Keeping in touch* in Chapter 14). Other hospitals have only one book, usually kept in the hospital chapel or multi-faith room. Staff should offer all parents of babies born dead at any gestational age, and all parents whose babies die shortly after birth, the opportunity to enter their baby's name and an inscription.

Some maternity and neonatal units have memorial books in which parents and other family members are invited to insert photographs and poems, as well as personal messages about the baby who died.

It is important to ensure that hospital books of remembrance, memorial books, sympathy cards and other similar material are non-religious, so that they do not offend or exclude parents of any faith or of none.

Memorial services

Some parents, especially if they have decided not to arrange or attend a funeral, may wish to organise their own memorial ceremony. This can be held shortly after the death, or later when they feel ready. Many parents find a ceremony helpful and comforting, even many years after their loss.

Parents who want a religious memorial ceremony should be advised to contact the hospital chaplain, or the religious adviser of their choice, to discuss the form of the service and how it can best meet their needs. Other parents may prefer to organise a personal ceremony at home, or in some place that carries meaning for them (Daly 2005).

Some hospital chaplains hold regular communal, non-denominational memorial services in the hospital chapel or multi-faith room, or at a local church. These services should be sensitive to the needs of parents of different religious faiths and none, and to the needs of parents who have lost a baby at any gestation and for any reason. All parents should be informed about these services and should be given an open invitation. All parents must know that they will be welcome, no matter when their baby died, and whether or not they have a religious affiliation.

Some hospitals hold an annual act of remembrance, or memorial service, to which all bereaved parents are invited. Some units send out personal invitations to all parents who have lost a baby since the last memorial service and also advertise the service in the local press. Some Sands, Miscarriage Association and ARC groups around the country organise services to which everyone can come. These services should also be open and suited to the needs of parents of all religious faiths and none. Some local churches hold annual memorial services.

Other memorials

> *Daisy was due on 18th April. We spent the day with our family on the beach where we had had our wedding photos taken, remembering her. We scattered her ashes and then we released a bunch of helium balloons tied to pictures that the kids had drawn. We said goodbye. And now we have some happy memories of her, alongside the pain.* Father

There are many public and private ways in which parents can create memorials to their babies. Sometimes parents welcome reassurance from staff that it is never too late – even years after the loss – to commemorate and show their love and grief for their baby. All bereaved parents, including those who have lost a baby early in pregnancy, or who have had a termination, may find it helpful to know that other parents have honoured and remembered their baby in some of these ways:

- Framing and hanging a photograph of the baby, or a drawing or painting made from a photograph;

- Painting, buying, or commissioning a special picture – perhaps of a special place associated with the pregnancy or the baby, or of something that symbolises the baby;

- Making a book of everything to do with the pregnancy and the baby's life and death – for example, the slip of paper confirming the pregnancy, any test results, the hospital appointments cards, photographs taken during the pregnancy, a scan photo, pictures by siblings, the baby's cot card and name band if the baby died after birth, cards and letters people sent, a photo of the cemetery or the baby's grave;

- Buying or making a special box to keep the baby's treasures in (a toy, some clothes, and other mementoes), or using a Sands Memory Card (see *Other mementoes* in Chapter 12);

- Pressing flowers from their baby's funeral, to keep or to display in a frame;

- Making a special embroidery or piece of patchwork;

- Lighting a candle on anniversaries or other special days;

- Putting flowers on the baby's grave (where this is permitted – see *Cremation and burial options* in Chapter 17) on anniversaries and other important dates;

- Buying a special vase, perhaps with the baby's name engraved on it, and arranging flowers in this on anniversaries, or whenever parents wish;

- Visiting a special place on anniversaries, or sending flowers or some other gift to, for example, a hospital or nursing home;

- Planting a specially chosen tree or shrub in a favourite place, or in the cemetery where the baby is buried.

- Writing a poem or letter to the baby, or choosing a piece of writing or a poem to be written in calligraphy and perhaps framed;

- Writing an account of their experience of loss, remembering what happened. Charities that support bereaved parents, such as Sands, the Miscarriage Association and ARC, publish parents' stories in their newsletters;

- Putting up a bench with a memorial plaque in a well-loved place, or in the cemetery where the baby is buried;

- Making a donation to a charity in memory of their baby.

CHAPTER 19: FOLLOW-UP APPOINTMENTS AND ONGOING CARE

Trusts, Health Boards and managers should agree a policy with local Primary Care Trusts to ensure that both immediate and long-term follow-up and care are available to all parents who experience a childbearing loss. *The criteria for providing ongoing care should be based on the needs of the parents and not on the type of loss, nor on the gestation at which the loss occurred.* Support should also be available for women who have had a termination for reasons other than fetal abnormality if they request it.

Support should continue to be available to all women in a subsequent pregnancy or after the birth of another baby. This requires co-ordination and good communication between hospital and community services.

CARE AND SUPPORT AT HOME

I had thought that terms like "your arms aching to hold him" belonged in trashy romance novels. But they are true. Your arms do ache. Your chest does feel as if a huge stone has settled on it. Your heart does break into a million pieces. It's the loneliest feeling in the world. Mother

I remember the morning after Emma died so clearly. I awoke and after barely a moment realised that she was gone. I sobbed and sobbed. Father

Coming home from hospital was the hardest thing and instead of time healing I believe it is getting harder for me. My husband is back to work and I feel devastated and lost without our little boy. I now have to face returning to work and going back to my old life instead of the happy times we had planned. Mother

In the first few days at home, visits from family members and friends, and perhaps the activities of organising and preparing for a funeral, may cushion the shock of their loss for some parents. However, once other people return to their normal routines, most parents are left to cope on their own. In the days and weeks that follow, they are left alone with what many women describe as empty arms, experiencing the full intensity of their loss and grief. It is at this time that they may most need ongoing care and support from primary care staff (Personal communication, Sands Helpline Staff 2006).

Nothing is ever the same after losing a baby. But people want you to get back to how you were. They expect you to do it fairly quickly. Mother

Some women and couples may appear to be well supported by their family and friends. However, even these parents may not be getting the help that they need. In addition, some may distance themselves from family members to protect themselves from further pain; some may try to hide their grief; some may find that friends and relatives avoid them or are unwilling to listen, possibly because they themselves are experiencing renewed grief for past losses (see also *Grandparents* in Chapter 3). Women who have had early losses may never have told anyone that they were pregnant; women who have had a termination for fetal abnormality may not have told friends or family members in case they disapprove.

Skilled staff may be the only people to whom these parents feel able to talk freely, especially months and years after the loss, when other people may feel that they should be "over it". It is important, therefore, that GPs and other primary care staff take the initiative and offer support to parents, rather than wait for them to ask.

Both my husband and I found out who our friends were. Many have become closer whilst others have disappeared from our lives completely. Some people would cross to the other side of the street to avoid us whilst others would come up and hug you, then walk away. Mother

COMMUNICATION AND CO-ORDINATION
Between the hospital and the primary care team
In most cases, primary care staff should be promptly informed that a woman has had a pregnancy loss, so that the appropriate member of staff can contact her and so that she is not, for example, sent reminders for antenatal appointments. However, a few women may not want their GP or primary care team informed (see below) and it is always important to check.

Provided the woman does not object:

- The hospital or clinic should immediately send a summary of her obstetric history and care to her GP when she is discharged. Depending on the gestation at which the loss occurred, the summary should also be sent to the community midwife and the health visitor;

- Because letters can take some days to arrive, a designated member of staff at the hospital should phone the GP and the community midwife when a woman is discharged;

- The woman should also be given a summary of her care to hand to her GP when she sees him or her. (See also *Communication between hospital and community staff* in Chapter 4.)

A few women, perhaps those who have had early losses or terminations, may not want their GP or primary care team to be informed; hospital staff should explain the disadvantages of this. If a woman still declines, her decision must be respected (see *The duty of confidentiality* in Chapter 4). She should be given a letter summarising her history and treatment to give to her GP or another doctor, in case she needs further medical care.

Some women go to stay with relatives for some time before they return home. Those with a baby in the neonatal unit may be spending a great deal of time in the unit. It is important that, before a woman is discharged from the hospital, staff find out where she is going to be, and pass this information on to the relevant community midwifery team.

> *Because I wasn't at home but on the ward with Joseph who was very ill I wasn't having midwifery care after the caesarean. My health visitor arranged for a midwife to come and check my scar, which was a good thing as I was on bedside vigil and wasn't taking care of myself.* Mother

THE ROLE OF PRIMARY CARE STAFF
GPs

Many parents welcome a phone call or visit from their GP after any kind of loss – including early loss, late miscarriage and termination for fetal abnormality. Having their GP acknowledge the loss, express sympathy, ask how they are, and offer support can be very important (Statham at al 2001: 105; Moulder 1998: 64).

The GP may also be the one health professional who is in touch with bereaved parents over many years, and who can inform newly-arrived primary care staff about the parents' situation. This long-term relationship enables GPs to keep an eye on the parents' physical and emotional wellbeing, and to offer care as appropriate, including:

- Physical care;

- Ongoing emotional support, and a sympathetic ear;

- Contraceptive advice;

- Discussing and clarifying the results of investigations, if the parents have questions after appointments at the hospital;

- Referral to other specialist services, such as genetic counselling;

- Referral to appropriate support organisations and/or counselling services;

- Pre-conceptual advice.

See also *Guidance for GP practices* in Chapter 22. For information on maternity leave and benefits following pregnancy loss, see *Entitlement to time off work and benefits* in Chapter 13 and *Child benefit and other benefits* in Chapter 14.

Community midwives and health visitors

All women who have given birth, including those who have had a late miscarriage or late medical termination, should receive postnatal care and the offer of emotional support from a community midwife.

Some women may also appreciate a visit from the health visitor, especially if they have met her before, or if there are other children in the family. At this visit, the health visitor can ask whether future visits would be helpful.

If different members of the primary care team are involved with the woman, it is important that they communicate with each other to avoid overlap, and also to make sure that one member of staff continues to visit for as long as the woman wants.

HOME VISITS

First contact

It can be very difficult to make a first visit to a bereaved woman or family. Staff are likely to feel more confident, and better able to help, if they have been informed about key details of the loss (see *Communication and co-ordination* above), and if they feel well prepared and supported. All staff who visit or contact parents after a pregnancy loss should have had training in bereavement care, and should feel confident and competent in supporting distressed parents (see *Staff training* in Chapter 21).

Staff should usually telephone (or write, if the woman has no phone) and offer a visit, rather than visit unannounced. If the woman does not want a visit at this point, the offer should be repeated after a couple of weeks.

> *The health visitor wrote and said if we wanted to talk she would be happy to listen. She said a lot of people don't have anyone to talk to and that was what she wanted to offer us. She came a couple of times, once when we were both here, and once when I was on my own.* Mother

It is important to ensure confidentiality in situations where other family members may not know about the loss:

- Staff who telephone should check they are speaking directly to the woman. Letters should be marked "Private and confidential" on the envelope;

- Some women may want to be visited but may fear the reactions of family members or neighbours if a uniformed member of staff arrives at their home. In this case, staff should suggest not wearing a uniform or meeting elsewhere.

If staff are not fluent in the mother's language, they should work with a professional interpreter. They should ask her to make the first contact with the mother by letter or phone (see also *Working well with an interpreter* in Chapter 5).

The purpose of a home visit

> *The local professionals saw us through some hard times. The care that my health visitor gave helped us both through the emotional turmoil of memories of Heulwen's stillbirth that came back to us when Joe was so ill after he was born.* Mother

Often the initial purpose of a home visit is a physical check-up for the mother. Women may want help with physical symptoms such as bleeding, lactation, stitches and pain. They may also want to know about postnatal exercises. However, it is always important to try to avoid imposing a set agenda, and to respond to the woman's – and her partner's – needs. They may want to ask questions about what has happened, and to check their understanding of the information they were given at the hospital. They may also want:

- Help in preparing questions for their consultant or GP;

- Suggestions about dealing with the reactions and questions of other family members – other children, grandparents, a pregnant sister-in-law – and of friends and neighbours;

- Advice about registering the birth and death, or the stillbirth (see *Registration at a register office* in Chapter 16);

- Help with decisions about a funeral and with arrangements (see *Offering choices* in Chapter 17);

- Advice about sex and contraception (see *Contraception* in Chapter 13), and possibly about the timing of another pregnancy, their chances of having a live healthy baby, and how they can reduce or manage any risks (see Chapter 20);

- Information about local or national support organisations (see *Voluntary support* later);

- Advice about maternity leave and claiming benefit payments (see *Entitlement to time off work and benefits* in Chapter 13 and *Child benefit and other benefits* in Chapter 14).

- Advice about coping with or returning to work, including what to say to colleagues, and how to deal with their reactions (see *Before the parents leave the hospital* in Chapter 13).

FOLLOW-UP APPOINTMENTS
Good practice

Parents, especially those who have lost a baby in the second or third trimester, often have very high expectations of follow-up appointments: they are hoping for clear answers that will help them make sense of what has happened. If, as often happens, it is not possible to provide these, the doctor should acknowledge the distress, confusion and disappointment that parents may feel.

Most parents urgently want information about why the pregnancy failed, or why their baby died. It is important to acknowledge the difficulty of not having a definite reason for the loss.

> *One of the hardest things is not knowing why. I am a logical person and I know I could accept it if I could understand it. It has taken me almost a year to accept that we will not find an answer.* Mother

- Parents may want to go over the events surrounding the loss, so that they can clarify and confirm what happened;

- Many will also want to discuss how they are feeling. It is important to ask them, and to offer them an opportunity to talk. Parents who are depressed, or who are unable to cope with daily life, should be offered a referral for help and support (see *Complicated grief* in Chapter 3).

  Nikcevic et al (1998), in a study of 204 women who had had a miscarriage, found that women *who attended a follow-up appointment but were not given an opportunity to express their feelings* had clinically raised levels of anxiety, when compared with women who attended a follow-up appointment and *were* given an opportunity to express their feelings, *and* in comparison with women who did not have a follow-up appointment at all;

- Parents may want an opportunity to talk about implications for any future pregnancies, and for any existing children. They may want to know the chances of the same thing happening in the next pregnancy, and whether anything can be done to ensure that it does not;

- Some parents may want to ask when they can "try again". They may also be worried about how they will cope with the anxiety of another pregnancy, and may need to know what help and support will be available. Others may want to talk about coming to terms with the possibility that they may never have a child;

- Some parents may want referral for investigations, or to the regional genetic services. If they do not want genetic follow-up immediately, they should be told how to access services at a later date if they want to.

It is important to make sure that the parents know what each appointment is for, so that they do not come, for example, expecting to hear post-mortem results, only to find that the appointment is simply for a physical check-up.

- If appropriate, the couple should be encouraged to attend appointments together. Some women may want to bring a relative or friend as well as, or instead of, their partner;

- Parents should be encouraged to write down any questions and worries, and to bring the list with them to the appointment;

- They should be told whom to contact if they need to talk to someone urgently in the time before the appointment, and given contact details.

Follow-up appointments with the GP

Unless a woman does not want her GP informed, a detailed discharge summary must be sent to the GP as soon as the woman is discharged from hospital. Staff should encourage each woman to make an appointment to see her GP if she feels this would be helpful.

In the case of a later loss, or if there are special indications, the GP should initiate contact with the woman and perhaps offer a home visit.

Women who have lost a baby in the second or third trimester should also be advised to make an appointment with their GP for a postnatal check-up about six weeks after the loss of the baby. This appointment should include:

- A physical check-up, and an opportunity for the woman to discuss and ask questions about her physical health;

- An opportunity to discuss contraception (see also *Contraception* in Chapter 13);

- Time to talk about how she feels, and about any other concerns. (See also *Guidance for GP practices* in Chapter 22).

Follow-up appointments at the hospital after a second or third trimester loss

The woman – or parents - should be given an appointment with the consultant obstetrician, usually for a time when all the results from investigations such as a post mortem will be available. (See also *Follow-up appointments after a neonatal death – additional points* below.) The doctor, and all the members of staff seeing the parents, should have read the notes before they see her in order to familiarise themselves with the mother's history, and so that they can refer to her baby by name (if a name was given). They should be prepared and able to provide detailed information, and to answer a wide range of questions as honestly as possible. To alert staff, the notes should have been marked with a Sands teardrop or other sticker (see *Informing other carers* in Chapter 12).

> *When I went back to the hospital for my follow-up appointment the doctor said cheerfully, "Who's watching your baby?"* Mother

Many parents are anxious to have an early appointment with the consultant, and to receive post mortem or investigation results, as soon as possible. They should be told in advance how long it is likely to be before the results are available. If the post mortem results are delayed, the parents should be contacted before they see the consultant, the delay explained and a new appointment offered.

> *We waited 12 weeks for the appointment that would tell us what had gone so incredibly wrong and at times I was so scared they would tell me I had done something wrong, but they found no reason at all and again I found myself asking WHY? I think I will always question why?* Mother

When both an obstetrician and a paediatrician have been involved, they should decide whether one or both should see the parents. If the baby had a complex abnormality which may have a genetic component, it may be helpful for parents to see the local clinical genetics team at the same meeting, so that they get comprehensive information and advice.

Midwifery support It can be very helpful for a midwife who is experienced in bereavement support to be present at the follow-up appointment. She can assess how the woman or couple are feeling, and whether they have further needs that should be addressed. She can also be the main contact for the woman – and her partner – if they:

- Have further questions about what has been discussed;
- Want to find out about counselling;
- Want to discuss the implications for another pregnancy;
- Become pregnant again. Knowing that they have a link with a named midwife whom they can contact as soon as they know they are pregnant, and who knows their story, can help to reassure the parents, who are likely to be extremely anxious.

The consultation The discussion with the parents should cover the issues listed at the beginning of this chapter, as well as the results of any investigations and their implications. Staff should be prepared to allow as much time as possible: the pathology results may raise many issues, and the parents may have a lot of questions. It is very important that any medical terminology used in the results is interpreted to the parents, and that unfamiliar medical concepts and events are explained (Rankin et al 2002).

In some hospitals, the parents are given, or at least offered, a copy of the full pathologist's report. Elsewhere they are given a summary. The full report should be sent to their GP. Parents should be told whom to contact if they have any further questions.

Parents may be particularly concerned about the implications of what has happened for a future pregnancy. Staff should offer to describe the kind of care and support that would be given. If there are indications that further investigations or treatment would be necessary in a future pregnancy, staff should offer to discuss with them, whenever they want to know, how these would be organised.

Organisation

- It is important to make sure that follow-up appointments are offered to parents who might fall through the net; for example, if their baby was transferred out of the area before he or she died, or if they have one or more surviving babies from a multiple pregnancy (McHaffie et al 2001b).

- Some parents may find it too distressing to go back to the place where their baby died. In this case, arrangements should be made to see them in another suitable setting, or outside normal clinic hours;

- The mother's notes should be marked with a Sands teardrop or other sticker (see *Informing other carers* in Chapter 12), so that all staff – including receptionists – are aware that she has had a miscarriage, stillbirth or neonatal death;

- Bereaved parents should not have to sit with other mothers with healthy babies, or attend an appointment in the antenatal or postnatal clinic;

- An interpreter should be booked for all follow-up appointments if the mother does not speak fluent English. The interpreter should be well informed beforehand about the situation and the reason for the visit (see also *Working well with an interpreter* in Chapter 5);

- Staff should offer parents written information and/or information in other formats about appropriate sources of continuing support, both professional and voluntary;

- At the end of the appointment, parents should be told whom to contact if they have further questions, problems or worries. In some cases it may be appropriate to offer another appointment;

- A written summary of the discussion should be sent to the woman, with a copy to her GP and to the referring hospital if appropriate.

After our genetic counselling appointment the consultant wrote to us to confirm what he'd told us. He wrote that it was nice to meet our daughter Rosie (whom we had had to take to the appointment), that he was pleased that we had a pleasant time in Donegal for Daisy's due date, and that he considered us to be a low-risk in terms of future babies being affected by Down's Syndrome. The personal touches in the letter had a tremendous impact: it was very comforting for us that a specialist saw us as a family and not as an abstract de-personalised "case". Father

Follow-up appointments after a neonatal death – additional points

- Parents should be offered an appointment with the doctor who was in charge of the care of their baby in the neonatal unit, or with whom they had the most contact. Many find it helpful if the nurse who was most involved in looking after the baby is also present;

- At follow-up appointments, most parents are looking for a full, compassionate and clear account of why their baby died that makes sense to them. If a decision was made to withdraw care, this includes reassurance that the decision was correct. It is important that they are not given conflicting accounts, or left with unanswered questions. They may also want to discuss the possible risks for any future pregnancy (McHaffie et al 2001b);

- Many parents also appreciate sharing memories of their baby, and of the events in their baby's life, with the doctor, nurses and other staff who were most involved. They are grateful when staff show care and respect for the whole family, and show that they understand the impact that the baby's life and death have had on the parents (McHaffie et al 2001b);

- Although most parents want to know as much as possible about why their baby died, some find the catalogue of problems and impairments that may be listed in a post mortem report extremely distressing and too much to take in, especially shortly after the baby's death. Staff should try to sense when parents have had enough information, and perhaps suggest that they put the written report away to discuss later, or arrange another appointment for a later date (McHaffie et al 2001b);

- Women – with their partners if appropriate – should also have an appointment to see a consultant obstetrician to discuss their own health, to ask questions about the pregnancy and the birth, and to discuss the implications of their loss for any future pregnancies or existing children.

LONGER-TERM SUPPORT

Day and night I have an ache of yearning for him. Even simple tasks seem a big effort as if I am moving through treacle. Mother

The pain is still deep inside, surfacing occasionally, but you get through somehow. You have to. I still cry, with some days being better than others. Seeing all the other mothers passing with toddlers her age and imagining what she would look like, it always brings a tear or two so I have to turn away. Mother

Many parents will grieve for their baby over the following months and years. Many will value continuing professional support, but the kind of support that they need, and the timing will vary. It is important that parents know that they can ask for support even long after their loss, and whom they should contact for support.

As time passes, parents may have more questions about why the pregnancy ended, or why their baby died. In many cases no satisfactory explanation can be found. This can be particularly difficult: some parents may need help in accepting that no cause will be found and, perhaps, in believing that they did not somehow cause their baby's death.

Care around pregnancy loss and the death of a baby is dominated by female staff, and men can feel out of place and marginalised.

Support at home? Almost none at all. The only person who got any support at all was my wife Heather. The midwife visited but at no point asked me how I was. Father

Sometimes support that is given only to the mother helps to strengthen a partnership; sometimes it is divisive. Some couples may find it helpful to see a member of staff together, perhaps in the evening or at weekends. Some fathers may appreciate an offer to see a member of staff alone, so that they can discuss their feelings and concerns without fearing that they are adding to their partner's distress. Support groups such as Sands, the Miscarriage Association and ARC have leaflets for fathers, and also male volunteers whom fathers can contact.

If there were problems and conflicts in relationships within the family before the baby died, these may grow worse, at least for a time. Sometimes professional help with family relationships would be an unwelcome intrusion, but for some families an outsider's support can be invaluable, and can help to relieve tensions and pressures. For example, with the parents' permission, a GP or health visitor may be able to talk to other children in the family. Other family members may want to talk to their own GP or to a counsellor.

Parents who continue to find it very difficult to cope with daily life several months after the loss might benefit from specialist help. They should be offered a referral (see *Recognising complicated grief* in Chapter 3).

VOLUNTARY SUPPORT

> *We are members of a club that we never wanted to join.* Father

> *If you are lucky you find support from other parents. Sands helps keep you sane, to realise that you are not alone. To find out that you aren't going mad when you scream yourself hoarse in the car because you can't keep it in any more. It offers that safe place where you can talk about your child when your family and friends would rather you moved on, like they do in TV soap land. Where you can remember your baby, give thanks for them, find out that other parents hate Christmas just as you do for the presents that are missing, can't function in the weeks after their child's birthday even though no one else mentions it. The discovery that you are not a freak and not going mad is a huge relief.* Mother

Many parents find it helpful to talk to other people who have been through similar experiences, either one-to-one or in a group. However, it is generally better to refer parents to a specialist voluntary group that has trained supporters or befrienders, rather than to an individual local parent who has had a loss. Staff should offer parents information about national organisations and local groups and schemes, and how to contact them. (For addresses see Appendix 2.) It may sometimes be helpful for staff to offer to make the first contact with a group for the parents.

> *No-one can explain the emotions of losing a child, the only people who understand are those who have had a similar experience. Your life is over. The nursery is empty. Your heart is broken and your inside feels empty. You go to the hospital to have a baby, your whole life is geared up for this little person and you come home with nothing but a few memories.* Mother

It is important that voluntary support groups are seen as complementing professional support rather than replacing it, and that staff do not automatically withdraw their support if parents develop local contacts. Staff should also bear in mind the possible limitations of local self-help groups: for example, parents in minority communities or whose first language is not English, fathers, parents on a low income, and single mothers may feel uncomfortable in some groups. In such cases, health visitors and community midwives may be able to help build bridges, or to set up new groups where these parents may feel more at home.

CHAPTER 20: ANOTHER PREGNANCY

People's everyday assumptions that a couple will go on to have children may lead to inadvertently intrusive questions such as, "When are you going to try again?" (Moulder 2005: 54). Well-meaning friends and family members may also offer false reassurance such as "Everything will be OK next time". This can make it very difficult for parents to tell even close friends and family about their fears and difficulties. Health care staff may be the only people with whom they can talk honestly.

For a few parents there is no possibility of another pregnancy. Some may have medical problems that make it impossible or too dangerous for the mother. Medical or genetic problems affecting the baby may mean that the risk of another loss is too high for parents to contemplate. Some parents may have reached the end of their reproductive life. Others cannot face the stresses and worries of another pregnancy that could end in tragedy, even though there is no specific risk or difficulty (Kohner and Henley 2001: 97).

Parents who had treatment for fertility problems in order to conceive the baby who died, face the double blow of pregnancy loss and infertility. Some may decide that they cannot face the stresses and uncertainty of another round of fertility treatment.

> *It was torture to have to face IVF again. Kindly meant advice to "try again" rang very hollow. We were lucky enough to conceive again eventually and to have a healthy second daughter. Later we had a miscarriage. We live with a continuing sense of loss. The pain of infertility endures until you feel that your family is complete.* Mother

Another pregnancy: before conception

The timing of another pregnancy, the risks involved, and the chances of a live healthy baby are major concerns for many parents who hope to have another baby. They may long to be pregnant again but also fear the pain and grief of another loss. They may have lost confidence in their ability to produce a healthy baby. They may feel under pressure to have another baby as soon as possible, sometimes in order to relieve the anxiety of the people who love them and want them to be happy again.

- In some cases the parents have differing views about embarking on another pregnancy. One partner may feel that the risk is not worth taking, while the other wants a baby very badly. Some studies indicate that fathers often want to conceive as soon as possible, while many mothers want to wait longer until they feel physically or emotionally ready (Turton et al 2006; Swanson 2003);

- One or both parents may find sexual intercourse distressing, either because of the memories it brings back or because of the possibility of conceiving, and the prospect of a long and anxious pregnancy. If, for example, the parents' grief is causing problems with their relationship, it may anyway be very hard for them to feel close enough to make love. Many parents, and especially those who have had fertility problems, may also be afraid that they cannot conceive;

- For some parents it is important to find out as much as they can before embarking on another pregnancy about why their baby died, and whether they can do anything to try to ensure a successful outcome. Another pregnancy may be especially difficult if no reason was found for the loss, because there is nothing that the parents can do to try to ensure that it does not happen again.

Staff may be able to help by:

- *Offering time to parents to discuss their feelings* – separately or together – and helping them to reach a decision;

- *Offering them an opportunity to discuss the actual risks, in their specific case, of problems in another pregnancy,* based on what is known about why the previous loss occurred, and the mother's obstetric history. Some parents overrate the risk that the problem will recur. At the same time, it is important to be realistic. For example, older women have a higher chance of spontaneous early miscarriage: they should be warned about this;

- *Reassuring them that there is no one right time to try for another baby:* outlining the possible advantages and disadvantages of delaying or going ahead, encouraging them to think about their own situation, and to decide what is right for them (Hutti 2005; Franche 2001) (see also *The timing of a future pregnancy* in *Before the parents leave the hospital* in Chapter 13);

- *Encouraging both parents to look after themselves* physically and emotionally, and to find practical ways of trying to reduce their anxiety, for example, by encouraging them to learn and practise relaxation techniques;

- *Offering pre-conceptual advice* such as stopping smoking, taking folic acid, eating well and reducing alcohol intake as appropriate. Such measures can help parents feel that they are taking some control and doing something positive;

- *Offering to organise referral* to appropriate medical or genetic specialists and, if the parents want, to a counsellor;

- *Acknowledging that a future pregnancy is likely to be stressful* and outlining any additional antenatal support that would be offered.

CARE DURING ANOTHER PREGNANCY

When I got pregnant after 8 months, I wanted to be delighted but I didn't dare let myself in case all our hopes were dashed again. Mother

She was pregnant ... again. What should have been fantastic news filled me with sheer terror. I did not know if I could go through this again. Father

Although it is never possible to predict how individual parents will feel, the main features of another pregnancy are often overwhelming anxiety and mental anguish (Wallerstedt et al 2003; Rillstone and Hutchinson 2001). Parents' fears are likely to be strongest in the first pregnancy after the loss, but can also recur in later pregnancies, following the birth of a healthy baby.

- Many parents describe the experience of another pregnancy as being like an emotional rollercoaster that they cannot get off. They also describe the exhaustion of trying to keep their hopes and fears in check. One of the most important things that staff can offer parents is sensitive support, to help them deal with the range of feelings and worries that they have. Parents may appreciate the offer of one-to-one sessions at times when their anxiety levels are particularly high. Some parents may be grateful for the offer of an early ultrasound scan to check that all is well.

It's an excruciating time not knowing if your next baby will live or die. You know you have been chosen once and there is no reason why fate will not strike again. It is about understanding, empathy, and a kind heart and smile but very few words - just a giant pair of ears will do! Mother

- Some parents may try to protect themselves from being overwhelmed by fear and anxiety by distancing themselves from what is happening, either throughout the pregnancy, or until the point at which they feel their baby is safe (Rillstone and Hutchinson 2001). They may also prefer to avoid any discussion of emotional issues with staff, and to focus on the practical tasks at hand. However, some are grateful for opportunities to talk to staff about how they are feeling;

- Certain stages or events during the pregnancy may be particularly difficult, depending on what happened before. For example, parents may be very anxious and distressed in the period leading up to the week in which the previous pregnancy ended, or to the test that identified the problem or abnormality. Some feel less frightened after this point, provided all is well. Others remain fearful and anguished until after the new baby is born. Certain dates can also be very distressing; for example, the anniversary of the loss, or the date on which the baby who died should have been born;

- A woman who feels that she was to blame for the loss of her baby is likely to find a subsequent pregnancy particularly hard (Franche 2001; Franche and Mikail 1999). It may be helpful to find out why she believes this, and to discuss the validity of her feelings. If there was no apparent cause for the loss it may be helpful to acknowledge the difficulty of coming to terms with this;

- Many fathers feel that they want to take more interest in this pregnancy, or to be more actively involved, partly to support the mother, and partly because they are now more aware of what can go wrong. Staff can help support fathers by including them – provided the mother wishes – in all discussions, and by encouraging them to voice their questions and concerns about both the baby and the mother (Armstrong 2001). Some fathers are reluctant to voice their anxieties when their partner is there in case they add to her distress. Fathers should be offered time on their own to talk;

- Some parents worry that they will be unable to love the new baby, or that, if they do, this will be disloyal to the baby or babies who died. Parents who have lost multiple babies may feel that no single baby can ever replace the twins or triplets they have lost. Some parents worry about the effects of the fear and anxiety they are feeling on the wellbeing of this baby. It is important that staff acknowledge the validity of parents' concerns, and take them seriously;

- A pregnancy following a childbearing loss can also be extremely stressful for the wider family, perhaps especially for other children and for grandparents. Some parents may welcome discussion about how to cope with the reactions of other family members;

My community midwife was wonderful and did the early booking at my home. We live in a close community and if I had been seen going to the hospital it would have been common knowledge that I was pregnant. Mother

- Some parents tell very few people about the pregnancy, or limit the amount of information they give. Some prefer not to tell anyone until after they have had the results of tests, or after they pass the gestation at which the previous pregnancy ended. Even if they do tell family members and friends, they may not feel able to be open about their real fears, nor to speak about the baby they have lost. Some parents are also unsure how to answer well-meaning questions from strangers – for example, "Is this your first baby?". They may find it helpful to discuss with staff what to say in different situations, how to cope with hurtful comments, and how they might tell family members and friends what support they need (Hutti 2005; Rillstone and Hutchinson 2001);

- For some parents, support from a local parents' group can be very helpful during their next pregnancy, especially perhaps if they can develop a relationship with parents who have experienced situations very similar to their own (see also *Voluntary support* in Chapter 19) (Hutti 2005).

Antenatal care in another pregnancy

Many of the recommendations in Chapters 7and 8 also apply to the care of mothers and couples in pregnancies following a loss.

Place of care Parents who have a good relationship with staff in a particular hospital may want to return there for their antenatal care. Sometimes it is nevertheless necessary to rebuild trust, especially if the parents are unhappy about aspects of the care they or their baby received. Some parents, even if their previous care was good, may prefer to be cared for in a different hospital or by different members of staff (Wallerstedt et al 2003). If parents want, the GP should refer them to another unit, or to another consultant.

I was given a new community midwife. The community midwife I had had when I was pregnant with Heulwen who was stillborn was really considerate. She understood that I felt uneasy seeing her even though she hadn't done anything wrong. When I did run into her she always chatted to me and was so caring. Mother

I got a consultant in a different hospital, a fantastic antenatal midwife, and a great anaesthetist and doctors all of whom buoyed me up all the way through and during delivery of a baby boy by caesarean. The staff thought I would need special care afterwards so they arranged for me to go to a cottage hospital near home. Mother

Special consultant-led clinics for women with high-risk pregnancies can ensure that women are carefully monitored and cared for throughout the next pregnancy. However, attending a high-risk antenatal clinic can also have disadvantages for some parents. Although they are likely to have things in common with the other parents, hearing other peoples' stories can raise new fears and worries. Staff need to be aware that this may happen, and to give all parents time on their own to talk about any anxieties.

At my booking appointment the midwife said, "Absolutely any time if you're concerned about something you just pick up the phone; we'll never think you're a nuisance. Even if it's every single day, just phone. We don't want to think of you sat at home worrying". I haven't phoned but just knowing that I can has taken that worry away. Mother

Continuity of care A key aim of care in a pregnancy following a childbearing loss is to ensure that parents feel well supported. If possible, each woman should have continuity of carers, so that she does not have to keep explaining her situation and the reasons for her anxiety. All staff who care for the woman – and her partner – antenatally and during and after the birth, should be well-informed about her history, so that they can respond sensitively to her anxieties and needs.

At the first antenatal visit, each woman and her partner should be allocated a lead midwife. The midwife should have read the woman's notes beforehand. If the baby who died was named, she should ask if she can refer to him or her by name.

The lead midwife should give the woman an opportunity to talk about her hopes, fears and feelings, and work out an antenatal care plan with her. Some women want to have all the available antenatal screening and diagnostic tests; others may decline all tests, or all invasive tests, and wait to see what happens. Some may want additional scans or antenatal appointments to reassure them about the progress of their pregnancy. Women in another pregnancy may also need longer appointments, so that they can get the information they need and discuss any worries (Hutti 2005).

Discussing the loss Many parents fear that the problem that led to the loss of their baby will recur in this pregnancy. It is helpful to offer to go over the mother's obstetric history and the medical and/or genetic facts, and to make sure that the parents really understand what happened, and have a realistic view of the likely outcome of this pregnancy.

Although all this may have been discussed with the parents after the loss, they may have been too sad and shocked to take it in or remember it. If the parents' fears are medically unfounded, they should be tactfully corrected. However, some have good reason to fear, and will need sensitive support that balances realism with hope throughout the pregnancy. Staff should bear in mind that, for these parents, statistical probabilities may have lost their power to provide comfort (Wallerstedt et al 2003: Rillstone and Hutchinson 2001). It is important not to offer false reassurance, because this increases parents' sense of isolation, and may prevent them from talking honestly about their worries.

I was monitored regularly but nothing anyone said could reassure me. I didn't believe that she would be born alive until I was in the operating theatre awaiting my caesarean section. Mother

Antenatal classes Many bereaved parents feel unable to attend standard antenatal classes. They should be offered individual sessions by a member of the team caring for them, to prepare them for labour and birth. Some parents may want to attend classes, and may welcome help with deciding what, if anything, they should say to the class leader and to the group.

TLC (Tender Loving Care) clinic Some hospitals run a drop-in clinic, where women – with a partner, relative or friend if they choose – who have experienced recurrent early miscarriage, later pregnancy loss or neonatal death and who are pregnant again can meet and support each other in a relaxed and informal setting. Such clinics may be led by, for example, a bereavement support midwife with support from other midwives and gynaecology nurses. It is helpful if they are run at the same time as a consultant-led antenatal clinic, so that women can seek a consultant opinion if they are anxious. Such clinics give women access to regular and ongoing emotional support throughout their pregnancy and are generally highly appreciated (Personal communication, Bereavement support midwife 2006).

I was fortunate in that the midwife who ran the baby loss support group I attended was with me throughout the pregnancy, the time in hospital and was there waiting in the delivery suite when I came out of theatre with my second son. She and another Mum who had lost a child were the only people who understood my fear of another loss. Others just got angry. Mother

Pressures on staff Many parents become strongly attached to the staff who care for them; the understanding, kindness, and continuing interest and concern that these members of staff offer can be extremely important (Rillstone and Hutchinson 2001). Although it can be very gratifying for staff to realise how important they are to parents, such close involvement is also emotionally exhausting. Staff need recognition from their managers and colleagues of the value and the pressures of their work. They may need additional support, especially if the next pregnancy ends in another loss. There should be regular team meetings at which staff doing this work are encouraged to discuss difficult and painful situations (see also Chapter 21).

Labour and birth

My biggest fear was going into the hospital. Though the staff were wonderful, would they understand when I needed the "medical jargon" explained to me? My community midwife was with us when Charlie was born. She explained the scores and that they meant he was fine. She stayed with us that day and helped me with breastfeeding and the initial emotional rollercoaster that I went through once Charlie had arrived safely. Mother

Women who have had a childbearing loss often find it very hard to believe that they can have a healthy baby. Most will need additional support and encouragement during labour.

Women – and their partners – should be asked if they would like to make a birth plan, and staff should offer to discuss with them what they might want. There may be certain things that the woman wants to avoid, or to do differently, this time. It may also be helpful to discuss with parents the mixture of emotions they may feel when their baby is born. The birth plan must be passed on to the labour ward staff who should make every effort to follow it. Women and couples should be offered an opportunity to visit the labour ward, and to meet some of the staff to discuss their anxieties and concerns.

If a baby in a previous pregnancy died during labour or at birth, this time is likely to be especially terrifying for the parents. They should be offered an opportunity to discuss with their obstetrician the mode and timing of delivery well in advance. Women who will labour should be warned that they may experience flashbacks and panic attacks. They should be assured that the staff who will be caring for them will help and support them. During the labour, staff may need to offer constant reassurance and to remind women that this is a different birth and a different baby (Wallerstedt et al 2003).

The woman's notes should be clearly marked with a Sands teardrop or other sticker (see *Informing other carers* in Chapter 12) so that labour ward staff are alerted to the fact that she has had a previous loss and can read her notes carefully. Staff should be prepared for the possible emotional reactions of the parents during labour and at the birth. When the woman is admitted, the midwife who will be responsible for her care during labour should acknowledge that the parents may have particular anxieties and emotions and that these are entirely normal. She should check again whether there is anything that should or should not be done during the labour.

> *I cannot say enough, how wonderful the midwife was when our son was stillborn. She subsequently delivered Charlie and her presence at his birth was a reassurance and felt 'right'. She probably has no idea how important she is to us and how glad I am that she was there at the birth of both my sons.* Mother

ANOTHER BABY

> *The staff were fantastic. One member of staff had also lost a child, a boy, and was great with me. They encouraged me to stay in the hospital as long as possible. They asked if I was supported enough emotionally at home, and were just fantastic. I will always remember them all with absolute fondness, and heartfelt thanks.* Mother

> *Our first son, Jordan, made his entrance into the world. After four years of not being able to deal with how I was feeling, all of a sudden I was presented with a whole new set of emotions.* Father

If the next pregnancy results in the birth of a healthy baby, many parents are surprised and confused by the strength of the renewed grief they may feel for the baby or babies who have died. Their reactions may be more complicated if, for example, the new baby resembles, or is the same sex as, the baby who died. In some cases, it may take time before they can begin to love this baby (Hutti 2005). They may feel bewildered and guilty if they are sad or apathetic, or if they find life difficult. They may try to hide their sadness from other people who so badly want them to be happy. Staff should be aware of the range of feelings that parents may be coping with. Sensitive support and encouragement are very important. It may be helpful to reassure parents that their feelings are shared by many parents in the same situation.

Many bereaved parents have lost their optimism and their faith in life. They feel vulnerable and very anxious (Wallerstedt et al 2003). They may become overprotective towards this baby, and towards any other children they have. Staff should try to reassure them that this too is common. However, if parents feel that their grief, anxiety or other feelings are affecting their relationship with the baby, or with other people, or making it hard for them to cope, they should be offered referral for specialist help (see *Recognising complicated grief* in Chapter 3).

Among those parents who go on to have another pregnancy, a few may experience another loss. This is deeply shocking and distressing for the parents, and also for the staff who are caring for them. These parents are likely to need intensive immediate and long-term support from staff, who may be the only people they can talk to. Family members and friends may be too shocked and horrified to be able to support parents following a further bereavement, and may withdraw, or be unable to cope with the parents' grief and other reactions. Some parents may want to take up the offer of specialist counselling from someone who has not, up till now, been involved with them. The staff who cared for the parents during the pregnancy, and those who continue to support them, are also likely to need a lot of support and help.

CHAPTER 21: STAFF SUPPORT AND TRAINING

THE IMPORTANCE OF SUPPORT

When individual staff are stressed, the whole organisation in which they work, as well as the people they care for and their colleagues, may be adversely affected. In contrast, good morale and motivation have positive effects on care (Finlayson 2002). Stress is most likely to occur in situations where demands are high, the amount of control an individual has is low, and there is limited support or help available (RCGP 2002).

There are many reasons why it is stressful and demanding to care for and support parents when a pregnancy ends or a baby dies:

- The way in which individual parents experience loss and grief is intensely personal and unpredictable: staff have to work with a great deal of uncertainty;

- Staff are aware that what they say and do at this time is vitally important, and that parents may remember it for years to come. They may be very anxious about inadvertently saying the wrong thing and causing additional distress;

- Staff are trained to alleviate pain and distress, and can find it particularly hard to deal with grief – which cannot be alleviated. They may find it difficult to take a less active role, to listen, and to give parents time. They need to exercise patience, self-awareness, and self-control in order to offer parents genuine choices, and to support them in making their own decisions;

- Staff also have to deal with their own emotional reactions, often without acknowledgement or support. They will have their own feelings of shock and distress when a baby dies, especially if they have developed a close relationship with the parents. They may also feel that they have failed, and may blame themselves or others. They may sometimes fear complaints and litigation. Some members of staff may be reminded of losses in their own lives, and may find it very hard to cope.

- Staff with little experience in caring for parents who are experiencing pregnancy loss may be anxious about their ability to cope. In a crisis they may react with shock, panic and fear, and may not know what to do;

- Some staff may find that the policies and procedures in their unit do not accommodate the wishes and needs of individual parents. They may feel frustrated and guilty that they cannot care for parents as they would like to. Caring for parents with childbearing losses may also sometimes raise personal ethical dilemmas for some members of staff;

- Many members of staff work under great pressure and in stressful circumstances. The time that they can give to parents is often limited by other demands. They may feel frustrated and anxious if they do not have enough time to give good care, especially if they worry that the pressures under which they work may lead to adverse events and near-misses (Ashcroft et al 2003);

- Parents may express anger and hostility towards staff if they feel that mistakes have been made. This is stressful in itself, and more so if the parents' accusations have some justification. Staff who are doing their best in difficult circumstances are likely to feel demoralised by parents' complaints (Jennings 2002).

Offering empathetic supportive care is difficult and demanding. It is not possible to get it right for absolutely everyone all the time. This should not be a reason for staff to distance themselves, or to be over-cautious about what they say and do. There are bound to be occasions when a sensitive and thoughtful member of staff "gets it wrong" for a particular woman or couple. When this happens, the member of staff should be actively supported, reassured that they were doing their best, given time for reflection, and encouraged to continue to offer empathetic and supportive care in difficult and uncertain situations. Staff who are inexperienced and find it difficult to give supportive care should be offered opportunities for training.

SUPPORT FOR STAFF

Trusts, Health Boards and managers should ensure that there is provision for good staff support, and that the culture of the organisation recognises that it is both responsible and professional for staff to seek support when they need it.

Basic support for all staff

The quality of care that parents receive depends almost entirely on the staff who care for them. For staff to provide parents with good individualised care, they themselves must feel well supported. This applies to all members of staff – at all levels and in all disciplines – who come into contact with parents during and after their loss. It also applies to all primary care staff, some of whom will have long-term relationships with the family, and who often work in greater isolation.

Basic support and regular supervision should be provided for all staff in primary and secondary care as a matter of course, and should be built into the systems within which they work.

Additional support

The type and amount of additional support that a staff member needs vary, depending on the individual and the situation. It is important to have different support options available for members of staff to use as they need.

All staff need:

- An open and supportive atmosphere in which the stress and difficulty of caring for parents and families who are experiencing pregnancy loss are acknowledged, and in which they can share problems and worries, and talk about how they feel;

- Opportunities to reflect on and discuss particular cases, or areas of their practice, with a bereavement support worker or other experienced practitioner, so that they can improve their skills and confidence (Jennings 2002);

- Opportunities to discuss, in confidence, their own feelings, difficulties or worries about a particular case with someone who has appropriate counselling skills. There should be no stigma attached to doing this;

- Other agreed strategies to help alleviate stress: for example, recognition of the need for time out; organising patient allocation so that staff have a break between caring for parents who are experiencing a loss and moving on to care for another woman; de-briefing sessions; and regular team meetings and case reviews, at which staff can discuss aspects of management and care and can learn as a group.

If a member of staff has to deal with several losses within a short space of time, they risk burn-out or becoming distanced and unable to provide empathic care. It is essential that managers and colleagues are alert to this possibility, and take steps to ensure that the care of parents who are experiencing a loss is allocated fairly, and that no single member of staff carries an undue burden.

In addition, individuals might like to set up personal support networks with two or three people. These might be colleagues or friends who would be prepared to give each other informal support when wanted, either on the phone or face to face. (For more about setting up personal support networks, see Schott and Priest 2002: 248–250.)

THE ROLE OF MANAGERS

Managers and senior staff have a particular duty to provide encouragement and support to those for whom they are responsible, to watch for signs of strain or difficulty in individuals and within teams, and to facilitate discussion between colleagues and within teams.

Managers should ensure that:

- The unit has a shared philosophy of care and shared standards and aims;

- All staff working with bereaved parents feel that they are working as part of a team. If there are problems or communication difficulties within a team, managers need to address these, and if necessary to organise intra-team and inter-professional team-building workshops, using an experienced and skilled facilitator (Statham et al 2001: 65);

- Staff feel valued for their work, and that they receive positive feedback when they provide good care to parents. One of the most important factors affecting staff morale and motivation in the NHS is whether staff feel valued (Finlayson 2002);

- No individual member of staff bears sole responsibility for the care of all parents who are experiencing a loss. Although some members of staff will wish to take a special interest in this area of their practice, reliance on one or two experts can cause other staff to feel that they cannot do this work: those who take exclusive responsibility for bereavement care may be at risk of overload and burn-out (see also *Bereavement nurses and midwives* in Chapter 4);

- Support and training are provided for all staff, and are integrated into day-to-day practice;

- The procedures and guidelines that staff are expected to follow are appropriate for the care of families who are experiencing a childbearing loss. Knowing that they are providing a good service to bereaved parents can enable staff to cope better with their own feelings when dealing with loss (Enkin et al 2000: 481). All staff should have opportunities to influence policy, protocols and procedures on the basis of their experience;

- All staff know how to access staff counselling services.

Managers should also make sure that they themselves get support, so that they can support their staff.

CLINICAL SUPERVISION

Clinical supervision is particularly important for staff who work with loss and bereavement. It should provide opportunities for reflection on practice and for personal and professional development, as well as for support and positive feedback.

Midwifery Statutory Supervision

The Nursing and Midwifery Council recognises the importance of supervision within midwifery. The aim of midwifery supervision is to provide mothers and their babies with the highest quality of midwifery care, and to ensure public protection. Supervisors of midwives can help to ensure that midwives are well supported, so that they can offer excellent care.

"When midwives are faced with a situation where they feel they need support and advice the supervisor acts as a resource." Nursing and Midwifery Council (NMC 2005:26)

STAFF TRAINING

Many health care staff are expected to cope with traumatic events and highly emotional situations without appropriate education and training (Burden and Stuart 2005: 173; Deery 2004). Undergraduate, postgraduate and in-service training and updating should be provided for all staff. All staff involved in giving care during pregnancy loss and the death of a baby need to:

- Learn about the experience of loss and grief in general, and of pregnancy loss and the death of a baby in particular, and develop some understanding of these experiences;

- Learn about the possible needs of bereaved parents, and how to provide flexible and inclusive care that meets the needs of women and families from different backgrounds and communities and with different ways of life (see *Developing flexible and inclusive services* in Chapter 1);

- Understand what is meant by parent-led care, and the implications of providing it;

- Develop appropriate communication skills, including skills in communicating across language barriers, and in using interpreters (see *Communicating if there is no interpreter* and *Interpreters* in Chapter 5);

- Know about local procedures and arrangements, the choices open to parents, and local and national sources of information and support for parents.

Multidisciplinary training, involving both hospital and community staff, provides an opportunity for participants to review and contribute to policy and practice, and to share and solve problems with their colleagues.

All Trust and Health Board policies for the management of pregnancy loss and the death of a baby should recognise the need for staff training and updating. Training and updating should also be specified in staff contracts.

CHAPTER 22: GUIDANCE FOR TRUSTS, HEALTH BOARDS, MANAGERS AND GPs

> This chapter is intended as guidance for all the bodies and individuals who are responsible for commissioning and organising care in hospitals and in the community, and for providing the structure and resources to enable front-line health care staff to work effectively.
>
> The rapid changes in the way that health services are structured and managed make it impossible to use a phrase that incorporates all the bodies and individuals involved. We have therefore referred to Trusts (this covers both Hospital Trusts and Primary Care Trusts in most of the guidance), Health Boards and, where appropriate, managers. The guidance in this chapter is also applicable to Foundation Trusts, independent health care establishments, and all other bodies that may be set up in the future to organise and provide care.

The guidance below summarises all the key policy issues set out in the rest of these Guidelines and will help to ensure the best possible care for all women and families who experience a childbearing loss. Some of the items below require a change in practice and increased awareness of parents' needs, but have no resource implications other than adequate staffing levels. Others may require a change in the way that care is organised. Some need additional resources in terms of training, support or facilities. A few may not be immediately achievable, but all should be regarded as important goals.

Some of the items below are audited more easily than others. Those that relate to many of the most important aspects of caring for vulnerable women and families are often the hardest to measure. This should not be a reason for excluding them from audit.

In order to ensure that care for parents experiencing a childbearing loss moves smoothly and efficiently between the hospital and the community, it is very important that Hospital and Primary Care Trusts work together to develop their policies, plan their services and set standards.

Planning and providing services

1. Central to the whole process of designing and implementing policies, and of reviewing current practice, should be the people for whom the services exist. Trusts, Health Boards and managers should find out the views and experiences of bereaved parents via organisations such as Sands, ARC, the Miscarriage Association, the Multiple Births Foundation and the TAMBA Bereavement Support Group, as well as through discussions with individual parents. They should also make special efforts to access the views of bereaved parents of minority cultures and faith groups, because these may not be represented by local voluntary groups.

Inclusive care

2. Childbearing loss affects all social groups, but is most likely to affect women who are socially disadvantaged, excluded or vulnerable in other ways. Trusts, Health Boards and managers should ensure that services are flexible and can be adapted to suit different needs, and that systems and standard practices do not discriminate – either intentionally or unintentionally – against vulnerable women (see Chapter 1).

3. Trusts, Health Boards and managers should identify and train specialist midwives and nurses with skills in supporting vulnerable women with specific needs such as a sensory impairment, mental health problems, homelessness, domestic violence and substance misuse, as well as young teenage women, refugees and asylum seekers. In addition to offering support themselves, these midwives and nurses should be a resource for other members of staff (see Chapter 1).

4. Trusts, Health Boards and managers should be aware of the costs that women – and couples – may incur if they have to travel a long way to access specialist care during pregnancy or to visit a baby in a specialist neonatal unit. Funding should be available to assist parents who are on low incomes.

5. Trusts, Health Boards and managers should ensure that advice is offered to parents who have lost a baby, especially those on low incomes, about benefits and payments to which they may be entitled (see Chapters 13 and 17). Procedures should be in place to cancel the Bounty Pack for bereaved parents, but to ensure that parents of babies who die after birth receive a Child Benefit claim form (see Chapter 14).

Loss and grief

6. Trusts, Health Boards and managers should recognise that support following pregnancy and childbearing loss is an integral part of effective care for women and their families. Good support can improve long-term wellbeing, and prevent the need for costly intervention later (RCOG 2006; Swanson KM 1999; Moulder 1998: 222; Leoni 1997) (see Chapter 3).

7. Trusts, Health Boards and managers should appoint and train specialist bereavement support staff. These staff should be responsible for offering emotional support and practical guidance to parents, and for training, updating, and supporting other members of staff who care for bereaved parents. They should also be involved in helping to ensure standards of bereavement care, and in establishing policies that ensure excellent co-ordination and communication between departments and with primary care staff (see Chapter 4).

Communication

8. Good communication between hospital and primary care staff is essential to good care. Hospital Trusts, Health Boards and managers should agree policies with Primary Care Trusts to ensure that, unless a woman objects, her GP and other relevant community staff are informed promptly about a loss during pregnancy, birth or afterwards, or the diagnosis of a fetal abnormality, and about treatment and care (see Chapter 4).

9. Many Primary Care Trusts, Hospital Trusts and Health Boards produce their own leaflets and information in other formats, material giving both general and specific information about different conditions, local services and arrangements. Some use material produced by voluntary support groups. All such material should be checked on a regular basis to ensure that the information is consistent, up to date, relevant and easy to read. Information should also be available in the main languages spoken locally, and in formats suitable for parents with a sensory impairment (see Chapters 4 and 5).

10. The provision of interpreters for people who speak little or no English, and of signers for people who are deaf or hard of hearing, is an essential part of safe and effective care. Although it is not possible to ensure that interpreters are always available for all the languages spoken locally, or that signers for the deaf are always available, Trusts, Health Boards and managers should provide the best and most comprehensive service possible (see Chapter 5).

11. Trusts, Health Boards and managers should ensure that all staff who communicate with parents and families who speak little or no English have training in how to communicate better across a language barrier, and in how to work with interpreters (see Chapter 5).

Chaplaincies

12. Trusts, Health Boards and managers, especially those in areas that serve multi-faith communities, should ensure that the chaplaincy has contacts with religious advisers of all faith communities and with non-religious advisers such as Humanists (see Chapter 2).

Termination of pregnancy for reasons other than fetal abnormality

13. To minimise delays in referral for termination, Primary Care Trusts should consider setting up contracts with service providers that enable women to access termination services directly, without having to be referred. Whatever the access route, it should be widely publicised. Where direct access is not possible, referrals should be made without delay (see Chapter 6).

14. Trusts, Health Boards and managers should consider commissioning a centralised booking system to cover all local service providers that carry out terminations after 20 weeks' gestation. This would speed up referrals for women who are nearing the end of the second trimester (see Chapter 6).

15. Trusts and Health Boards should ensure that there is provision within the NHS for women with pre-existing health problems who want or need a termination. These women cannot usually be cared for by independent service providers, because they require specialist medical care as well as a termination. Adequate NHS provision would cut the delay between referral and termination that these women often experience, reducing the number of terminations late in the second trimester (see Chapter 6).

16. Trusts, Health Boards and managers should ensure that women who need a termination because their physical health is jeopardised by their pregnancy have prompt access to services within the NHS.

17. The contracts of some Primary Care Trusts limit the types of contraception that independent sector providers can offer. Wherever possible, contracts should enable these providers to offer women their contraceptive method of choice as part of their care, without their having to go elsewhere (see Chapter 6).

Antenatal screening and testing

18. Trusts and Health Boards should have a protocol covering antenatal screening and testing that stresses the importance of informed choice. The protocol should also ensure that staff provide information that is consistent, reliable, up-to-date and clear. Parents should be given information verbally and in written or other formats, and should be informed of results as soon as possible (see Chapter 7).

19. Trusts and Health Boards should have a policy that ensures prompt and accurate communication between the different specialties involved in screening and diagnostic testing; for example, midwifery, obstetrics, haematology, gynaecology nursing and genetic counselling. Good co-ordination and regular communication between specialties are essential to make sure that policies and procedures are coherent and offer the best possible service to parents, and that the information given to parents by staff in different specialities is consistent (see Chapter 7).

20. Trusts, Health Boards and managers should have a policy that ensures prompt and accurate communication between secondary and primary care staff about women with a suspected or diagnosed fetal abnormality. Primary care staff should have information about test results, should know what support they are expected to offer to women and couples in this situation, and should be equipped and able to provide it (see Chapter 7).

Childbearing losses – general

21. Each Trust and Health Board should have a policy that sets out the place of care for women experiencing pregnancy losses. The policy should cover the different types of loss and the gestations at which they occur. Its starting point should be that the place in which a woman is cared for should not add unnecessarily to her distress, or limit her choices. A woman with a later mid-trimester loss should, wherever possible, be offered an informed choice about whether she is cared for on a gynaecology ward or on a labour ward. The policy should also ensure that staff in the different areas have the necessary skills, competencies and facilities to provide optimal care for women and their partners (see Chapter 9).

Early losses

22. All Trusts and Health Boards should provide an early pregnancy assessment unit (EPAU), open at least five days a week, to which GPs have direct access. Dedicated units with a multidisciplinary team of supportive staff can streamline the care of women with pain or bleeding in early pregnancy. They offer both clinical and economic benefits (RCOG 2006) (see Chapter 10).

23. Because referring women who are less than 6 weeks pregnant to an Early Pregnancy Assessment Unit is unlikely to be beneficial, Trusts and Health Boards should also have a policy that defines the criteria for referral. This should be disseminated to all the relevant primary care staff (see Chapter 10).

24. Appropriate support after an early loss can bring significant psychological benefit (RCOG 2006). Women who miscarry early are likely to want information and discussion about why the miscarriage occurred, and whether it is likely to happen again. Trusts, Health Boards and managers should ensure that the care pathway for women who experience miscarriage includes the offer of a follow-up appointment, either with their GP or with a member of the consultant team, depending on the circumstances (see Chapter 10).

Second and third trimester losses

25. Trusts and Health Boards should ensure that each labour ward has – depending on the size of the unit and the number of deliveries per annum – one or more specially equipped rooms in which women who have had an intra-uterine death, and women having a mid-trimester loss, can labour. These rooms should be a short distance from the main labour rooms. Every effort should be made to ensure that women can remain in them for labour and for delivery, and that, after the birth, they are also cared for in rooms especially designed for bereaved parents (see Chapter 9).

Postnatal care

26. In order to facilitate easy access for parents to the bodies of their babies following a childbearing loss, Trusts, Health Boards and managers should ensure that there is a suitable mortuary fridge near the ward, unit or delivery suite, so that babies' bodies can be stored there (see Chapter 13).

27. For the protection of parents who want to take their baby's body home, and to prevent misunderstandings, Trusts and Health Boards should issue a form to accompany the body (see Chapter 13 and Sample Form 1 in Appendix 1).

Fetal remains and babies' bodies

28. Trust and Health Board contracts and arrangements with Ambulance Services should ensure that the bodies of fetuses and stillborn babies that are transported from home to hospital with the mother are handled and treated respectfully. It is completely unacceptable to place fetal remains or bodies in clinical waste bags. As well as being inappropriate, this could lead to the remains being lost or accidentally disposed of as clinical waste (see Chapter 17).

29. Trusts, Health Boards and managers should make sure that there are procedures for transferring fetal remains and babies' bodies between hospital departments, and for tracking the whereabouts of individual bodies and remains. Hospital mortuaries and laboratories should have an efficient system for tracking each body, organ or remains (see Chapter 17).

30. Trusts, Health Boards and managers should give careful thought to allocating the task of transporting bodies and fetal remains between hospitals. The drivers should know what they are carrying, and should be given appropriate documentation, so that if there is a road accident, the presence of human remains can be explained (see Chapter 17).

31. Trusts, Health Boards and managers should have procedures and paperwork in place – including a mortuary release form – to enable mortuary staff to hand over a baby's body or remains to parents who want to organise their baby's funeral themselves (see Chapter 15).

Funerals and sensitive disposal

32. Trust and Health Board policies on funerals and sensitive disposal should cover losses at all gestations, as well as stillbirths and neonatal deaths. The basis for all these policies should be that babies' bodies and remains are handled with respect. The policies should be carefully worked out in close consultation with representatives from all the departments that will have to implement them, as well as representatives of bereaved parents (for example, ARC, the Miscarriage Association and Sands). They should be communicated to all the staff concerned, and regularly reviewed and updated.

33. In addition to arranging and paying for burial or cremation, and for a funeral or other ceremony for a stillborn baby, fetuses and fetal remains, Trusts, Health Boards and managers should consider offering to arrange and pay for a burial or cremation, and for a funeral or other ceremony for a baby who dies shortly after birth (see Chapter 17).

34. Trusts, Health Boards and managers should appoint a multidisciplinary group of staff that negotiates and monitors contracts with local funeral directors, a local cemetery manager and/or the manager of a crematorium. One or more members of the staff who regularly provide care for bereaved parents should be part of the negotiating team (see Chapter 17).

35. Primary Care Trusts should make their own arrangements for funerals, burial and cremation for losses that occur outside the hospital, and should negotiate contracts accordingly. Alternatively, they could arrange to share in arrangements made by a local hospital (see Chapter 17).

36. Trust and Health Board policies should ensure that parents are informed about arrangements for funerals and sensitive disposal, and are enabled to express their own wishes about what happens to their baby's body or the products of conception. If parents want to, they should be able to participate in the arrangements made by the hospital or to make their own funeral arrangements. These policies should be communicated to all relevant staff, and should be regularly reviewed and updated (see Chapter 17).

Ongoing care and support for parents

37. Trusts, Health Boards and managers should agree a policy with local Primary Care Trusts to ensure that both immediate and long-term follow-up and care are available to all women – and couples – who experience a childbearing loss. The criteria for providing ongoing care should be based on the needs of the parents and not on the type of loss, nor on the gestation at which the loss occurred. Support should also be available for women who have had a termination for reasons other than fetal abnormality if they request it. Support should continue to be available to all women in a subsequent pregnancy or after the birth of another baby. This requires co-ordination and good communication between hospital and community services (see Chapters 19 and 20).

Support for staff

38. Caring for parents around the time of a childbearing loss is stressful and demanding. Trusts, Health Boards and managers should ensure that there is provision for good staff support, and that the culture of the organisation recognises that it is both responsible and professional for staff to seek support when they need it (see Chapter 21).

39. All Trust and Health Board policies for the management of pregnancy loss and the death of a baby should recognise the need for staff training and updating. Training and updating should also be specified in staff contracts. Training and updating in the relevant clinical skills, including communication and understanding loss and grief, should be provided for all staff, whatever their discipline (see Chapter 21).

GUIDANCE FOR GP PRACTICES

GPs are ideally placed to ensure that parents who have experienced a miscarriage, stillbirth or neonatal death get the care and support they need. They do not always need to give this support themselves, but they can make sure that someone does, either a health visitor or practice counsellor or a voluntary organisation such as Sands, the Miscarriage Association, ARC or another local organisation. This support can make all the difference to the future wellbeing of the parents and family.

It is now 2 years since Louis died, and during that time I have always experienced a warm welcome at the surgery, almost open access to my GP, and recognition of the effect such a loss can have on all our family. My husband has received similar support. As a mum the things that have made the care I have received from my GP so fantastic have been that everyone in the surgery has shown real concern and care for my family and me. This starts with the receptionists when I phone and for me has emphasised what an important role they can play. I will never forget our first visit to the surgery after Louis' death and one of the receptionists sitting with us as I shared his photos with her. She was clearly moved and cared about what had happened. This meant so much. Mother

There are several ways in which GP practices can ensure that they offer the best possible care to bereaved parents. Some of these can be organised within the practice; others require liaison and agreement with local hospitals and the Primary Care Trust.

1. The initial contact from the hospital is extremely important. A verbal handover is preferable to receiving only a discharge summary. However, it is difficult and inappropriate for GPs to handle calls of this kind while they are seeing patients. Hospital staff are rightly concerned about maintaining confidentiality and may refuse to talk to practice receptionists. However, receptionists are used to passing messages on to doctors and understand the importance of confidentiality. Practices with one or more experienced receptionists should consider informing the relevant staff in hospitals in their area that messages about childbearing losses can be left with them. The receptionists should ensure that the doctor phones back as soon as possible.

2. Each practice should consider identifying a GP to develop a clear policy for the whole practice that will ensure that all parents who have had a miscarriage, stillbirth or neonatal death are offered the care and support they need.

3. Practices should consider allocating the task of co-ordinating the care that bereaved parents receive from the GP, the health visitor and the midwife to a designated member of staff. An experienced receptionist is well placed to take on this role.

4. Practices should consider marking the notes of all the members of a family that has experienced a childbearing loss (for example, with a Sands teardrop sticker - see *Informing other carers* in Chapter 12), so that all GPs who may see them as patients are alerted to the family's loss. This is particularly relevant in large practices, or where a number of locums are employed. It may also be appropriate to communicate this information to the Out of Hours Service in case the family contacts them. Parents who have lost a baby may become particularly anxious and distressed if one of their other children is ill.

5. GPs should consider offering parents an appointment after their hospital follow-up appointment. This gives them an opportunity to discuss what they have been told and to raise any new questions that they may have. It also gives the GP an opportunity to see how the family is faring.

6. The offer of regular appointments with the GP during the first few months after a loss can help parents through a time of crisis. In the early weeks, GPs should offer parents a double appointment to ensure that there is sufficient time for discussion and questions.

7. GP practices, perhaps in conjunction with the Primary Care Trust, could consider producing a leaflet for parents who have experienced a childbearing loss. This leaflet could suggest:

   • the types of support that are available through the NHS and how to access them, plus the contact details of local voluntary support groups (see Appendix 2).

   • that parents mention their loss when they book an appointment with the GP, so that extra time can be allocated, and also if they call the Out of Hours Service, so that the doctor is alerted to their situation.

CHAPTER 23: LEGAL ISSUES, REGULATIONS AND PROFESSIONAL STANDARDS CONCERNING TERMINATION OF PREGNANCY

ABORTION LAW

Under Section 1(1) of the Abortion Act 1967, and Section 37 of the Human Fertilisation and Embryology Act 1990, termination of pregnancy is permitted up to 24 weeks' gestation on condition that continuing the pregnancy would involve greater risk than a termination:

- To the physical or mental health of the pregnant woman;

- To the physical or mental health of the woman's existing children.

Termination after 24 weeks is permitted if there is evidence of a serious fetal abnormality or if continuing the pregnancy poses a risk:

- To the pregnant woman's life;

- Of grave and permanent physical or mental injury to the pregnant woman.

Except in an emergency, a termination must be agreed by two doctors, performed by a doctor and carried out in a government-approved hospital or clinic (Section 1(1), (3) and (4) Abortion Act 1967).

The Abortion Act does not extend to Northern Ireland, where operations carried out to terminate pregnancies are unlawful unless there is a threat to the life of the mother, or a risk of real and serious adverse harm to her long term or permanent health (Sections 58 & 59 of the Offences Against the Person Act 1861 and Section 25(1) of the Criminal Justice Act (Northern Ireland) 1945, as interpreted by case law).

CONSCIENTIOUS OBJECTION

Section 4(1) of the Abortion Act (1967) includes a clause on conscientious objection which allows health care staff to refuse to "participate in any treatment authorised by the Act" to which they have a conscientious objection. The law does not define "participation". However, under Section 4(2) of the Act, staff are obliged to provide treatment in an emergency when a woman's life is at risk. In Northern Ireland staff can also object to participating in performing a termination unless the woman's life is in immediate danger (DHSSP 2007).

The Royal College of Obstetricians and Gynaecologists (RCOG 1996) acknowledges that Fellows and Members will have differing "but sincerely held beliefs", and states that doctors with a conscientious objection to abortion in general, or to abortion for particular reasons or after a particular gestation, should inform the woman and ensure that their employing authority is aware that they are not willing to provide this service.

The Nursing and Midwifery Council (NMC 2006) states that registrants have a right to object to participation in abortion procedures and in technological procedures to achieve pregnancy. The Council reminds registrants that, if they object to having direct involvement in abortion procedures for reasons of conscience, they are accountable for their decision and could be called upon to justify it within the law. In Scotland, however, the burden of proof does not lie with the objector, provided that he or she swears an oath before a court of law stating that he or she has an objection.

The Royal College of Midwives (RCM 1997) "is of the opinion that the conscientious objection clause solely covers being directly involved in the procedures a woman undergoes during the termination of pregnancy whether surgically or medically induced".

Women who undergo a termination of pregnancy for any reason should not be cared for by staff who might disapprove of the choices they have made (Statham 2002), and who might be ambivalent about providing care (Marshall and Raynor 2002). Managers who allocate staff who are sympathetic to the choices that a woman has made are protecting the interests of the woman as well as respecting the views of the midwife. *The Nursing and Midwifery Council Code of Professional Conduct:* standards for conduct, performance and ethics (NMC 2004) states in Clause 2.5 that those nurses and midwives who object to being involved in certain aspects of care or treatment should report this at the earliest opportunity, so that alternative staffing arrangements can be made.

APPENDIX 1: SAMPLE FORMS AND CERTIFICATES

It is very important that all forms and certificates that may be given to parents are attractively laid out and well reproduced. Forms and certificates suitable for reproducing are available to download free of copyright from the Sands website: go to www.uk-sands.org and click on **Improving Care.**

1: Form to give to parents who take the baby's body out of the hospital
For more information see Taking the baby's body home in Chapter 13.

2: Certificate to be offered to parents of a baby who was born dead before 24 weeks' gestation
For more information see Certification for a baby born dead before 24 weeks' gestation in Chapter 16.

3: Medical certificate authorising burial or cremation of fetal remains of less than 24 weeks' gestation
For more information see Certification for a baby born dead before 24 weeks' gestation in Chapter 16 and Contract with a crematorium in Chapter 17.

4: Form for preliminary application for communal cremation of fetal remains of less than 24 weeks' gestation
For more information see Contract with a crematorium in Chapter 17.

5: List of fetal remains for communal cremation
For more information see Contract with a crematorium in Chapter 17.

6: Application form for the individual cremation of fetal remains
For more information see Certification for a baby born dead before 24 weeks' gestation in Chapter 16 and Contract with a crematorium in Chapter 17.

Forms 3, 4, 5 and 6 have been adapted with the kind permission of Eltham Crematorium Joint Committee.

1: Form to give to parents who take the baby's body out of the hospital

There is no legal reason why parents should not take the remains or body of their baby out of the hospital at any gestation. However, for the protection of the parents and to avoid misunderstandings, staff should give them a copy of this form (available to download on the Sands website).

Hospital address

TO WHOM IT MAY CONCERN

_____

This is to confirm that [name(s) of parent(s)]

of [address]

_____

whose baby was stillborn / died on [date]

has/have taken their baby's body from

[name and address of the hospital.]

_____

Date

They will be: [tick where applicable]

❑ **returning the body to the hospital on** [date]

❑ **making their own funeral arrangements.**

_____

Name of authorising member of staff: [please print]

Position [please print]

Signature [signature]

Date [date]

_____

In case of concern, or if confirmation is needed, please contact:

_____

[Contact details for the authorising member of staff or the relevant department]

2: Certificate to be offered to parents of a baby who was born dead before 24 weeks' gestation

- Some mothers will not want to include the father's name on the certificate. A second version of the form should therefore be available without the space for the father's name (see overleaf).

- Both forms are available to download from the Sands website and they should be printed on special paper, to make them more attractive for parents. If hospitals design their own forms, they should be in an attractive typeface.

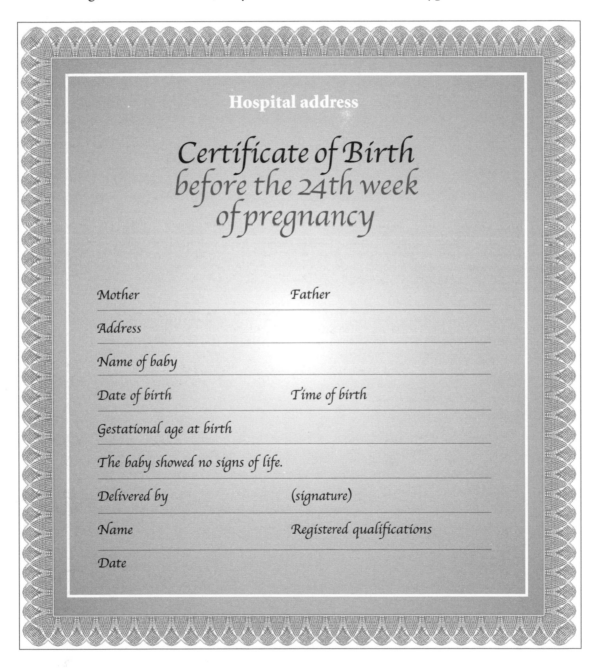

Hospital address

Certificate of Birth before the 24th week of pregnancy

Mother   Father
_____

Address
_____

Name of baby
_____

Date of birth   Time of birth
_____

Gestational age at birth
_____

The baby showed no signs of life.
_____

Delivered by   (signature)
_____

Name   Registered qualifications
_____

Date

Certificate to be offered to the mother only

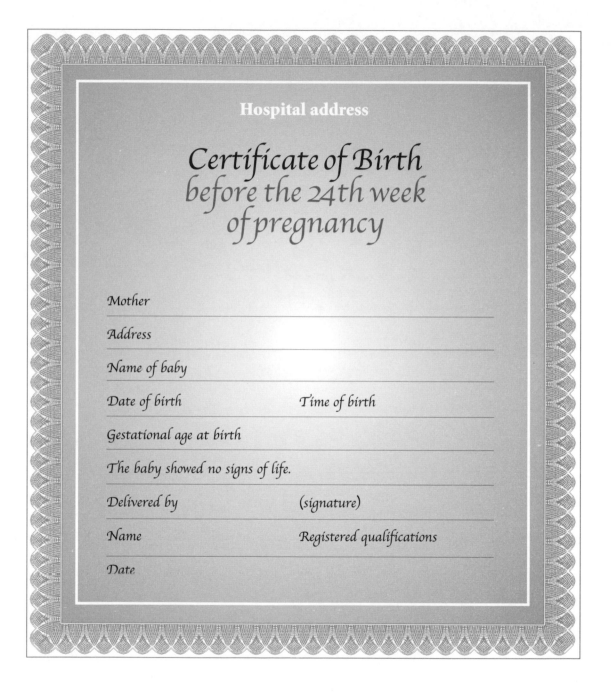

Hospital address

Certificate of Birth
before the 24th week
of pregnancy

Mother

Address

Name of baby

Date of birth   Time of birth

Gestational age at birth

The baby showed no signs of life.

Delivered by   (signature)

Name   Registered qualifications

Date

3: Medical certificate authorising burial or cremation of fetal remains of less than 24 weeks' gestation

This form can be downloaded from the Sands website.

Hospital address

MEDICAL CERTIFICATE FROM DOCTOR OR REGISTERED MIDWIFE
authorising the cremation or burial of fetal remains
of less than 24 weeks' gestation

I hereby certify that I have examined the fetal remains of:

_____

[Mother's name or case number]

Address

_____

_____

_____

_____

Delivered on [date]   at [time]

_____

at   weeks' gestation

_____

and at no time after birth showed any visible signs of life.

I know of no reason why any further enquiry or examination should be made.

Name

_____

Signature

_____

Registered qualifications

_____

Address

_____

Telephone number

_____

Date

4: Form for preliminary application for communal cremation of fetal remains of less than 24 weeks' gestation

This form can be downloaded from the Sands website.

Hospital address

PRELIMINARY APPLICATION FOR THE COMMUNAL CREMATION OF FETAL REMAINS

Date of cremation

Place of cremation

Time of cremation

Originating hospital

Name of person   arranging cremation

Number of fetal remains

Number of coffins

Service required   YES ☐   NO ☐

Organist required   YES ☐   NO ☐

Officiant

Funeral director

Telephone

Address

5: List of fetal remains for communal cremation

This form can be downloaded from the Sands website.

Hospital address

LIST OF FETAL REMAINS FOR COMMUNAL CREMATION

	Fetal remains of /Case number	Name of medical practitioner /midwife
1		
2		
3		
4		
5		
6		
7		
8		
9		
10		
11		
12		
13		
14		
15		
16		
17		
18		
19		
20		

Name   Signature

The medical practitioner or midwife involved in the delivery of each fetus identified above must have completed a **Medical certificate in respect of fetal remains less than 24 weeks' gestation** *for each case. The person authorised by the hospital to make an application for cremation should sign above and attach the medical certificates. Fetal remains may be identified by the name of the woman concerned or the hospital case number in cases subject to confidentiality under the Abortion Act 1967.*

6: Application form for the individual cremation of fetal remains made by staff

For a form suitable to give to parents who will make the application themselves, see overleaf.

These forms can be downloaded from the Sands website.

Hospital address

APPLICATION FORM FOR THE INDIVIDUAL CREMATION OF FETAL REMAINS

Name of baby, if given

Date of cremation

Time of cremation

Family to attend

Service details

Funeral director

Address

Telephone

I, (*name of Applicant*)

Position

Address

apply to
Crematorium to undertake the cremation of the remains
of the baby (described in the attached *Medical certificate in respect of fetal remains less than 24 weeks' gestation*).

The parents have been informed that it is not possible to recover any remains following the cremation.

The parents would like to receive details about the Book of Remembrance ❑
[please tick the box]

Signature of Applicant

Date

This form, together with the Medical certificate authorising burial or cremation of fetal remains of less than 24 weeks' gestation *(Form 3 above), should be received not later than 48 hours before the day of cremation.*

Form for parents applying for cremation of fetal remains

Hospital address

APPLICATION FORM FOR THE INDIVIDUAL CREMATION OF FETAL REMAINS

Name of baby, if given

Date of cremation

Time of cremation

Family to attend

Service details

Funeral director

Address

Telephone

I, (*name of Applicant*)

Address

apply to
Crematorium to undertake the cremation of the remains
of the baby (described in the attached *Medical certificate in respect of fetal remains less than 24 weeks' gestation*).

I/we have been informed that it is not possible to recover any remains following the cremation.

I/we would like to receive details about the Book of Remembrance ❑
[please tick the box]

Signature of Applicant(s)

Date

This form, together with the Medical certificate authorising burial or cremation of fetal remains of less than 24 weeks' gestation *(Form 3 above), should be received not later than 48 hours before the day of cremation.*

APPENDIX 2: USEFUL ADDRESSES

Action on Pre-Eclampsia (APEC)
Helps and supports women who have had or are worried about pre-eclampsia, HELLP Syndrome and pregnancy induced hypertension (PIH).
www.apec.org.uk/

Antenatal Results and Choices (ARC)
Information and support for parents throughout antenatal testing and when a significant abnormality is detected in the unborn baby. (Formerly called SATFA)
www.arc-uk.org

Baby MPS (Mailing Preference Service) online
Free site where parents can register online to stop or at least reduce baby-related mailings of samples, offers, advertisements etc.
www.mpsonline.org.uk/bmpsr/

BLISS the premature baby charity
Support, advice and information for families of babies in intensive care and special care, including bereaved families.
www.bliss.org.uk

British Humanist Association
Has a network of accredited funeral officiants who can help to plan and conduct a non-religious funeral ceremony.
www.humanism.org.uk

Child Benefit Office
The online claim form for Child Benefit can be accessed at
https://esd.dwp.gov.uk/dwp/index.jsp
Hospitals can also obtain small numbers of Child Benefit claim packs from NICO (National Insurance Contributions Office) Stores (Tel: 0191 225 7293)

Child Bereavement Trust
Support, information and resources for bereaved families and for professionals.
www.childbereavement.org.uk

The Compassionate Friends
An organisation of bereaved parents and their families offering understanding, support and encouragement to others after the death of a child or children.
www.tcf.org.uk

Contact a Family
Support, information and resources for families whose child is ill or disabled and for parents facing a diagnosis of abnormality during pregnancy.
www.cafamily.org.uk

Cruse Bereavement Care
Support for people bereaved by death, in any way, whatever their age, nationality or belief. Help includes counselling, bereavement support groups and advice or information on practical matters.
www.crusebereavementcare.org.uk

DIPEx
Website offering a wide variety of personal experiences of health and illness using real-life interviews and including childbearing loss. Users can watch, listen to or read interviews, find reliable information on treatment choices, and look for sources of support.
www.dipex.org/pregnancy

Ectopic Pregnancy Trust
Support and information for people who have had or been affected by an ectopic pregnancy, including health professionals.
www.ectopic.org

Federation of British Cremation Authorities (FBCA)
Organisation of cremation authorities.
www.fbca.org.uk

Happy Hands
Source of the Babysafe inkless system for taking hand and foot prints.
www.happyhands.ws/babysafekit.htm

Infertility Network UK
Advice and support for people dealing with infertility problems and/or facing a life without children. Campaigns for greater understanding of infertility issues and timely and consistent provision of infertility care throughout the UK.
www.infertilitynetworkuk.com

Institute of Cemetery and Crematorium Management (ICCM)
Sets ethical professional and social standards for the management of burial, cremation and related services, and provides education and training. (Formerly the ICBA - Institute of Burial and Cremation Administration)
www.iccm-uk.com

International Stillbirth Alliance (ISA)
International coalition of organisations dedicated to understanding the causes and prevention of stillbirth. Raises awareness, educates on recommended precautionary practices and facilitates research on stillbirth.
www.stillbirthalliance.org

Jobcentre Plus
Online information about Social Fund Funeral Expenses Payments and a downloadable form.
www.jobcentreplus.gov.uk/JCP/Customers/WorkingAgeBenefits/Dev_008260.xml.html

Miscarriage Association
Support and information for those affected by pregnancy loss (including health care professionals). Network of support groups and telephone contacts throughout the UK.
www.miscarriageassociation.org.uk

Multiple Births Foundation (MBF)
Support and information for families with twins and higher multiple births, including support around bereavement, and information for professionals.
www.multiplebirths.org.uk

National Association of Funeral Directors
Advice, a code of practice and addresses for people planning a funeral or looking for a funeral director.
www.nafd.org.uk/

National Association of Memorial Masons (NAMM)
Advice and addresses for people who want a memorial stone.
www.namm.org.uk

Natural Death Centre
Advice for families and others on burial in a woodland or nature reserve site and on organising informal and environmentally-friendly funerals.
www.naturaldeath.org.uk

Now I lay me down to sleep
An American website that puts bereaved parents in touch with professional photographers who will take photographs of their babies at little or no cost. Site shows examples of photographs of babies of all gestations. Click on **Find a photographer > United Kingdom** for a short list of UK photographers.
www.nowilaymedowntosleep.org

Perinatal Institute for maternal and child health
Aims to reduce perinatal mortality and morbidity by distilling and disseminating the evidence for best practice in perinatal care and promoting its implementation.
www.perinatal.nhs.uk/

Plain English Campaign
Free downloadable guides to writing clear information and other material that everyone can understand.
www.plainenglish.co.uk/guides.htm

Registry Offices for England and Wales, Scotland, and Northern Ireland

- England and Wales www.gro.gov.uk/gro/content
- Scotland www.gro-scotland.gov.uk/regscot
- Northern Ireland www.groni.gov.uk/index.htm

RELATE - National Marriage Guidance Council
Confidential counselling for couples, families or individual partners experiencing difficulties in relationships.
www.relate.org.uk

Royal National Institute for the Blind (RNIB)
Offers information, support and advice to people with sight problems.
www.rnib.org.uk

Royal National Institute for Deaf People (RNID)
Offers a range of services for deaf and hard of hearing people and provides information and support on all aspects of deafness, hearing loss and tinnitus.
www.rnid.org.uk

Sands, the stillbirth and neonatal death charity
Support and information for anyone affected by the death of a baby, before or after birth. National helpline, local parent-led support, literature and online support. Works to improve care when a baby dies and promotes research to reduce the loss of babies' lives.
www.uk-sands.org

Samaritans
Available 24 hours a day to provide confidential emotional support for people who are experiencing feelings of distress or despair, including those which may lead to suicide. Telephone 08457 909090 for the cost of a local call. Also face-to-face support.
www.samaritans.org

SHAP Working Party on World Religions in Education
For a calendar of dates of religious festivals – updated each year.
www.shap.org

TAMBA Bereavement Support Group
For families who have lost one or more children from a multiple birth, whether antenatally, postnatally, or at any age subsequently.
www.tamba-bsg.org.uk
(Part of the Twins and Multiple Births Association – TAMBA - www.tamba.org.uk)

UK National Screening Committee

- Antenatal screening: Downs syndrome: Information for women: Leaflets in different languages (English site)
  www.screening.nhs.uk/downs/women.htm

- Sgrinio Cyn Geni Cymru / Antenatal Screening Wales – General (Welsh site)
  www.screeningservices.org.uk/asw/public/about/about.asp

- Screening Choices: learning resource for health professionals offering antenatal and newborn care
  www.screening.nhs.uk/cpd/webfolder/web_nsc.html

Winston's Wish

Helps bereaved children and young people rebuild their lives after a family death. Offers practical support and guidance to families, professionals and anyone concerned about a grieving child.
www.winstonswish.org.uk

Working Families

Campaigns for working families, information leaflets and helpline for families on low incomes.
www.workingfamilies.org.uk/asp/family_zone/f_welcome.asp

REFERENCES

Abramsky L and Fletcher O (2002) Interpreting information: what is said, what is heard – a questionnaire study of health professionals and members of the public *Prenatal Diagnosis* **22**(13): 1188–1194

Abramsky L, Hall S, Levitan J and Marteau TM (2001) What parents are told after prenatal diagnosis of a sex chromosome abnormality: interview and questionnaire study *British Medical Journal* **322:** 463–466

Ahmed S, Green J and Hewison J (2002) What are Pakistani women's experiences of beta-thalassaemia carrier screening? *Public Health* **116:** 297–299

Ahmed S, Green J and Hewison J (2005) Antenatal thalassaemia carrier testing: women's perceptions of 'information' and 'consent' *Journal of Medical Screening* **12:** 69–77

Ahmed S, Green J and Hewison J (2006) Attitudes toward prenatal diagnosis and termination of pregnancy for thalassaemia in pregnant Pakistani women in the north of England *Prenatal Diagnosis* **26:** 248–257

Ahmed S, Valentine S and Shire S (1982) Translation is at best an echo *Community Care* April 22 1982: 19–21

Anspach RR (1993) *Deciding Who Lives* University of California Press, Berkeley, cited in Cuttini et al 1999 (see below)

ARC (2005) *Supporting Parents' Decisions: a handbook for professionals* Antenatal Results and Choices, London

Argyle M (1975) *Bodily Communication* International Universities Press, New York

Armstrong D (2001) Exploring fathers' experiences of pregnancy after a prior perinatal loss *American Journal of Maternal Child Nursing* **26**(3): 147–153

Ashcroft B, Elstein M, Boreham N and Holm S (2003) Prospective semistructured observational study to identify risk attributable to staff deployment, training, and updating opportunities for midwives *British Medical Journal* **327:** 584–588

Bagchi D and Friedman T (1999) Psychological aspects of spontaneous and recurrent abortion *Current Obstetrics and Gynaecology* **9:**19–22

BAPM (2000) *Fetuses and Newborn Infants and the Threshold of Viability: a framework for practice*: *Memorandum* British Association of Perinatal Medicine, London www.bapm.org/documents/publications/threshold.pdf (accessed on 11 May 2006)

BAPM (2004) *Consent in Neonatal Clinical Care: good practice framework* British Association of Perinatal Medicine, London www.bapm.org/media/documents/publications/Staff-leaflet.pdf (accessed on 11 May 2006)

Bennett SM, Litz BT, Lee BS and Maguen S (2005) The scope and impact of perinatal loss: current status and future directions *Professional Psychology: research and practice* **36**(2): 180–187

Bergh C, Möller A, Nilsson L and Wikland M (1999) Obstetric outcome and psychological follow-up of pregnancies after embryo reduction *Human Reproduction* **14**(8): 2170–2175

Birth Control Trust (1997) *Abortion Provision in Britain – how services are provided and how they could be improved* Birth Control Trust, London

BMA (2005) *Abortion Time Limits* British Medical Association, London

Bowlby J (1998) *Attachment and loss: Loss, sadness and depression* Pimlico, Random House, London

Boyce PM, Condon JT and Ellwood DA (2002) Pregnancy loss: a major life event affecting emotional health and well-being *Medical Journal of Australia* **176**(6): 250–251

Breeze AC, Lees CC, Kumar A, Missfelder-Lobos HH and Murdoch EM (2006) Palliative care for prenatally diagnosed lethal fetal abnormality *Archives of Disease in Childhood: Fetal and Neonatal Edition* doi:10.1136/adc.2005.092122 Published online 16 May 2006

Brinchmann BS, Førde R and Nortvedt P (2002) What matters to the parents? A qualitative study of parents' experiences with life-and-death decisions concerning their premature infants *Nursing Ethics* **9**(4): 388–404

Bryan E (2002) Loss in higher multiple pregnancy and multifetal reduction *Twin Research* **5** (3): 169–174

Buckman R (1992) *How to Break Bad News: a guide for health care professionals* Papermac, Basingstoke, UK

Buckman R (1996) Breaking Bad News: why is it still so difficult? In Dickenson D and Johnson M (eds) *Death, Dying and Bereavement* Open University, Sage Books, London

Bulman KH and McCourt C (2002) Somali refugee women's experiences of maternity care in West London: a case study *Critical Public Health* **12**(4): 365–380

Burden B and Stuart PC (2005) Bereavement, grief and the midwife. In Wickham S (ed) *Midwifery Best Practice Vol 3* Books for Midwives, Oxford

Calman K and Royston G (1997) Personal paper: Risk language and dialects *British Medical Journal* **315**: 939–942

Canadian Paediatric Society (2001) Guidelines for health care professionals supporting families experiencing a perinatal loss (Canadian Paediatric Society: Fetus and Newborn Committee) *Paediatric Child Health* **6**(7): 469–476

CEMACH (2002) *Why Mothers Die 1997–1999: midwifery summary and key recommendations* Confidential Enquiry into Maternal and Child Health, London

CEMACH (2004) *Why Mothers Die 2000–2002* Confidential Enquiry into Maternal and Child Health, London www.cemach.org.uk/publications/WMD2000_2002/wmd-01.htm (accessed on 19 June 2006)

CEMACH (2006) *Perinatal Mortality Surveillance, 2004: England, Wales and Northern Ireland* Confidential Enquiry into Maternal and Child Health, London cemach.org.uk/publications/PMR2004_March2006.pdf (accessed on 19 June 2006)

CESDI (2003) *Project 27/28: An enquiry into quality of care and its effect on the survival of babies born at 27–28 weeks* Confidential Enquiry into Stillbirths and Deaths in Infancy Pub: CEMACH, London

Chaplin J, Schweitzer R and Perkoulidis S (2005) Experiences of prenatal diagnosis of spina bifida or hydrocephalus in parents who decide to continue with their pregnancy *Journal of Genetic Counseling* 14(2): 151–162

Charchuk M and Simpson C (2005) Hope, disclosure, and control in the neonatal intensive care unit *Health Communication* 17(2): 191–203

Chiswick M (2001) Parents and end of life decisions in neonatal practice *Archives of Disease in Childhood: Fetal and Neonatal Edition* 85: 1–3

Chitty LS, Barnes CA and Berry C (1996) Continuing with pregnancy after a diagnosis of lethal abnormality: experience of five couples and recommendations for management *British Medical Journal* 313: 478–480

Clare A (2000) *On Men – masculinity in crisis* Chatto and Windus, London

Clement S, Candy B, Heath V, To M and Nicoliades KH (2003) Transvaginal ultrasound in pregnancy: its acceptability to women and maternal psychological morbidity *Ultrasound Obstetrics and Gynecology* 22: 508–514

Cockburn J and Walters WAW (1999) Communication between doctors and patients *Current Obstetrics and Gynecology* 9: 34-40

Condon JT (1987) Prevention of emotional disability following stillbirth – the role of the obstetric team Australian and *New Zealand Journal of Obstetrics and Gynaecology* 27: 323–329

Conway K and Russell G (2000) Couples' grief and experience of support in the aftermath of a miscarriage *British Journal of Medical Psychology* 73(4): 531–545

Coulter A, Entwistle V and Gilbert D (1999) Sharing decisions with patients: is the information good enough? *British Medical Journal* 318: 318–322

Cowles KV (1996) Cultural perspectives on grief: an expanded concept analysis *Journal of Advanced Nursing* 23: 287–294

249

CRE (1994) *Race Relations Code of Practice in Maternity Services* Commission for Racial Equality, London www.cre.gov.uk/gdpract/health_maternity_cop_plan.html (accessed on 14 July 2006)

CRE (2002) *Statutory Code of Practice on the Duty to Promote Race Equality* Commission for Racial Equality, London www.cre.gov.uk/downloads/duty_code.pdf (accessed on 14 July 2006)

CRE (2006) *Gypsies and Irish Travellers: the facts* Commission for Racial Equality, London www.cre.gov.uk/gdpract/g_and_t_facts.html (accessed on 14 July 2006)

Cuttini M, Rebagliato M, Bortoli P, Hansen G, de Leeuw R, Lenoir S et al (1999) Parental visiting, communication, and participation in ethical decisions: a comparison of neonatal unit policies in Europe *Archives of Disease in Childhood: Fetal and Neonatal Edition* **81:** 84–91

da Costa DE, Ghazal H and Al Khusaiby S (2002) Do Not Resuscitate orders and ethical decisions in a neonatal intensive care unit in a Muslim community *Archives of Disease in Childhood: Fetal and Neonatal Edition* **86:** 115–119

Daly N (2005) *Sasha's Legacy: a guide to funerals for babies* Steele Roberts, Aotearoa, New Zealand

Davies MM and Bath PA (2001) The maternity information concerns of Somali women in the United Kingdom *Journal of Advanced Nursing* **36**(2): 237–245

Davies R (2004) New understandings of parental grief: literature review *Journal of Advanced Nursing* **46**(5): 506–513

DCA (undated) *Advice to Medical Practitioners Completing Cremation forms B or C* Department for Constitutional Affairs www.dca.gov.uk/corbur/cremation forms_guidance.pdf (accessed on 23 Oct 2006)

Deery R (2004) An action-research study exploring midwives' support needs and the effect of group clinical supervision *Midwifery* **21:** 161–176

Denton J and Bryan E (undated) *Multiple Birth Children and their Families Following ART* World Health Organization www.who.int/reproductive-health/infertility/24.pdf (accessed on 14 March 2006)

Di Clemente M (2004) *Living with Leo* Bosun Publications/Sands, London

DoH (1998) *National Screening Committee: First Report* Department of Health, London www.nsc.nhs.uk/pdfs/nsc_firstreport.pdf (accessed on 4 December 2006)

DoH (2001a) *Reference Guide to Consent for Examination or Treatment* (Gateway 2001) Department of Health, London www.dh.gov.uk/assetRoot/04/01/90/79/04019079.pdf (accessed on 4 December 2006)

DoH (2001b) *Procedures for the Approval of Independent Sector Places for the Termination of Pregnancy* Department of Health, London
www.dh.gov.uk/assetRoot/04/13/91/05/04139105.pdf (accessed on 4 July 2006)

DoH (2003a) *Confidentiality: NHS Code of Practice* (Gateway 2003)
Department of Health, London
www.dh.gov.uk/assetRoot/04/06/92/54/04069254.pdf (accessed on 8 July 2006)

DoH (2003b) *Families and Post Mortems:* a code of practice (Gateway 2003)
Department of Health, London
www.dh.gov.uk/assetRoot/04/05/43/12/04054312.pdf (accessed on 1 July 2006)

DoH (2004a) *Best Practice Guidance for Doctors and other Health Professionals on the Provision of Advice and Treatment to Young People under 16 on Contraception, Sexual and Reproductive Health* (Gateway 3382) Department of Health, London
www.dh.gov.uk/assetRoot/04/08/69/14/04086914.pdf (accessed on 14 May 2006)

DoH (2004b) *Q and A on Disposal Following Pregnancy Loss before 24 Weeks*
(Gateway 3334)
www.dh.gov.uk/assetRoot/04/09/90/51/04099051.pdf (accessed on 14 December 2006)

DoH (2005a) *Responding to Domestic Abuse: a handbook for health professionals* (Gateway 5802) Department of Health, London www.dh.gov.uk/assetRoot/04/12/66/19/04126619.pdf (accessed on 2 January 2007)

DoH (2005b) *When a Patient Dies: advice on developing bereavement services in the NHS* (Gateway 5578) Department of Health, London
www.dh.gov.uk/assetRoot/04/12/21/93/04122193.pdf (accessed on 7 December 2006)

DoH (2006a) *Care and Respect in Death: good practice guidance for NHS mortuary staff* (Gateway 6831) Department of Health, London
www.dh.gov.uk/assetRoot/04/13/80/79/04138079.pdf (accessed on 7 December 2006)

DoH (2006b) *Abortion Statistics: England and Wales 2004: Statistical Bulletin* Department of Health, London www.dh.gov.uk/assetRoot/04/13/68/59/04136859.pdf (accessed on 1 December 2006)

Don A (2005) *Fathers Feel Too: a book for men on coping with the death of a baby* Bosun Publications/SANDS, London

Dormandy E, Mitchie S, Hooper R and Marteau T (2005) Low uptake of prenatal screening for Down's syndrome in minority ethnic groups and socially deprived groups: a reflection on women's attitudes or a failure to facilitate informed choice? *International Journal of Epidemiology* **34**: 346–352

Duncan D (1995) Fathers have feelings too *Modern Midwife* **5**: 30–31

Dyson L and While A (1998) The 'long shadow' of bereavement *British Journal of Community Nursing* **3**(9): 432–439

Dyson S (2005) *Ethnicity and Screening for Sickle Cell/Thalassaemia: lessons for practice from the voices of experience* Elsevier Churchill Livingstone, London

EA (2005) *Water Quality Policy on Protecting Controlled Waters – funeral practices and the environment* (V5 27.06.05) Environment Agency, London

Edwards A (2004) Flexible rather than standardized approaches to communicating risks in health care *Quality and Safety in Health Care* **13:** 169–170

Edwards A, Elwyn G and Mulley A (2002) Explaining risks: turning numerical data into meaningful pictures *British Medical Journal* **324:** 827–830

Edwards NP (2004) Why can't women just say no? In: Kirkam M (ed.) *Informed Choice in Maternity Care* Palgrave MacMillan, Basingstoke, UK

Eisenbruch M (1984) Cross cultural aspects of bereavement 1: a conceptual framework for comparative analysis *Culture, Medicine and Psychiatry* **8**(4): 283–309

Engelhard IM, Van den Hout MA and Arntz A (2001) Posttraumatic stress disorder after pregnancy loss *General Hospital Psychiatry* **23**(2): 62–66

Enkin M, Keirse MJ, Neilson J, Crowther C, Hodnett E and Hofmeyr J (2000) *A Guide to Effective Care in Pregnancy and Childbirth* Oxford University Press, Oxford and London

EPICure study (1995) *Population Based Studies of Survival and Later Health Status in Extremely Premature Infants* University of Nottingham www.nottingham.ac.uk/human-development/Epicure/epicurehome/index.html (accessed on 2 January 2007)

Fallowfield L (1993) Giving sad and bad news *Lancet* **341:** 476–478

Finlayson B (2002) *Counting the Smiles: morale and motivation in the NHS* King's Fund, London

Flores G, Barton Laws M, Mayo SJ, Zuckerman B, Abreu M, Medina L and Hardt EJ (2003) Errors in medical interpretation and their potential clinical consequences in pediatric encounters *Pediatrics* **111:** 6–14

Fonda Allen JS and Mulhauser LC (1995) Genetic counseling after abnormal prenatal diagnosis: facilitating coping in families who continue their pregnancies *Journal of Genetic Counseling* **4**(4): 251–265

Fowlie PW and McHaffie HE (2004) Supporting parents in the neonatal unit *British Medical Journal* **329:** 1336–1338

Franche R-L (2001) Psychologic and obstetric predictors of couples' grief during pregnancy after miscarriage or perinatal death *Obstetrics & Gynecology* **97**(4): 597–602

Franche R-L and Mikail SF (1999) The impact of perinatal loss on adjustment to subsequent pregnancy *Social Science & Medicine* **48:** 1613–1623

Furedi A (2001) Issues for service providers: a response to points raised *Journal of Medical Ethics* **27:** 28–32 jme.bmj.com/cgi/reprint/27/suppl_2/ii28 (accessed on 2 January 2007)

Garcia J, Bricker L, Henderson J, Martin MA, Mugford M, Nielson J and Roberts R (2002) Women's views of pregnancy ultrasound: a systematic review *Birth* **29**(4): 225–250

Garros D, Rosychuk RJ and Cox PN (2003) Circumstances surrounding end of life in a paediatric intensive care unit *Paediatrics* **112:** 371–379

Geerinck-Vercammen CR (1999) With positive feeling: the grief process after stillbirth in relation to the role of the professional caregivers *European Journal of Obstetrics and Gynecology* **87:** 119–121

GMC (2001) *Good Medical Practice* General Medical Council, London

GMC (2004) *Confidentiality: protecting and providing information* General Medical Council, London

Goh AYT, Lum LCS, Chan PWK, Bakar F and Chong BO (1999) Withdrawal and limitation of life support in paediatric intensive care *Archives of Disease in Childhood* **80:** 424–428
Guirdham M (1990) Interpersonal Skills at Work Prentice Hall, London

Hansen D (2003) *I Hate This (a play without a baby)* www.davidhansen.org First performed at Cleveland Public Theatre, Cleveland, Ohio, February 2003

Henley A and Schott J (1999) *Culture, Religion and Patient Care in a Multiethnic Society* ACE Books, London

Hewson B (2004) Informed choice in maternity care. In: Kirkam M (ed.) *Informed Choice in Maternity Care* Palgrave MacMillan, Basingstoke, UK

Hofstede G (1991) *Cultures and Organizations: software of the mind* McGraw-Hill, London

HSG (1991) *Disposal of Fetal Tissue: executive summary* Health Service Guidelines (91)19 Department of Health, London

HTA Code 1 (2006) *Code of Practice – Consent* Human Tissue Authority, London. www.hta.gov.uk/guidance/codes_of_practice.cfm (accessed on 2 January 2007)

HTA Code 3 (2006) *Code of Practice – Post mortem examination* Human Tissue Authority, London

HTA Code 4 (2006) *Code of Practice – Anatomical examination* Human Tissue Authority, London

HTA Code 5 (2006) *Code of Practice – The removal, storage and disposal of human organs and tissue* Human Tissue Authority, London

Hughes P and Riches S (2003) Psychological aspects of perinatal loss *Current Opinion in Obstetrics and Gynecology* **15**: 107–111

Hughes P, Turton P, Hopper E and Evans CDH (2002) Assessment of guidelines for good practice in psychosocial care of mothers after a stillbirth: a cohort study *Lancet* **360**: 114–118

Hutchon DJ (1998) Understanding miscarriage or insensitive abortion: time for more defined terminology? *American Journal of Obstetrics and Gynecology* **179**(2): 397–398.

Hutti MH (2005) Social and professional support needs of families after perinatal loss *Journal of Obstetric,Gynecologic, and Neonatal Nursing* **34**(5): 630–638

ICCM (2004) *Policy Document for the Disposal of Foetal Remains* Institute of Cemetery and Crematorium Management, London

Inwald D, Jakobovits I and Petros A (2000) Brain stem death: managing care when accepted medical guidelines and religious beliefs are in conflict: consideration and compromise are possible *British Medical Journal* **320**: 1266–1267

Jennings P (2002) Should paediatric units have bereavement support posts? *Archives of Disease in Childhood* **87**: 40–42

Jones SR (2005) Registration of stillbirths: what midwives need to know *British Journal of Midwifery* **13**(11): 691

Kersting A, Dorsch M, Kreulich C, Reutmann M, Ohrmann P, Baez E et al (2005) Trauma and grief 2–7 years after termination of pregnancy because of fetal anomalies – a pilot study *Journal of Psychosomatic Obstetrics and Gynecology* **26**(1): 9–14

Klass D (1996) The deceased child and the psychic and social worlds of bereaved parents during the resolution of grief. In: Klass D, Silverman P and Nickman S (eds) *Continuing Bonds* Taylor and Francis, London

Klier CM, Geller PA and Ritsher JB (2002) Affective disorders in the aftermath of miscarriage: a comprehensive review *Archives of Women's Mental Health* **5**: 129–149

Kohner N and Henley A (2001) *When a Baby Dies* (revised edition) Routledge, Abingdon, UK

Kollantai JA and Fleischer LM (undated) *Multiple Birth Loss and the Hospital Caregiver* Center for Loss In Multiple Birth (CLIMB) www.climb-support.org/pdf/mblnicu.pdf (accessed on 6 June 2006)

Korenromp MJ, Christiaens GC, Van den Bout J, Mulder EJH, Hunfeld JAM, Bilardo CM et al (2005) Long-term psychological consequences of pregnancy termination for fetal abnormality: a cross-sectional study *Prenatal Diagnosis* **25**: 253 260

Laing IA (2004) Clinical aspects of neonatal death and autopsy *Seminars in Neonatology* **9**: 247–254

Leon IG (1992) Perinatal loss: a critique of current hospital practices *Clinical Pediatrics* **31**(6): 366–374

Leonard, L (2002) Prenatal behavior of multiples: implications for families and nurses *Journal of Obstetric, Gynecologic, and Neonatal Nursing* **31**: 248–255

Leoni LC (1997) The nurse's role: care of patients after pregnancy loss. In: Woods JR, Woods JLE (eds) *Loss During Pregnancy or in the Newborn Period* pp 361–386. Jannetti Publications, Pitman, New Jersey

Littlewood J (1992) *Aspects of Grief* Tavistock, London

Lovett KF (2001) PTSD and stillbirth *British Journal of Psychiatry* **179**: 367

Lundqvist A, Nilstun T and Dykes A-K (2002) Both empowered and powerless: mothers' experiences of professional care when their newborn dies *Birth* **29**(3): 192–199

Maifeld M, Hahn S, Titler MG and Mullen M (2003) Decision making regarding multifetal reduction *Journal of Obstetric, Gynecologic, and Neonatal Nursing* **32**: 357–369

Mander R (2005) *Loss and Bereavement in Childbearing* (second edition) Routledge, Abingdon, UK

Marshall J and Raynor M (2002) Conscientious objection 1: legal and ethical issues *British Journal of Midwifery* **10** (6): 392–386

Marteau T (1989) Framing of information: its influence upon decisions of doctors and patients *British Journal of Social Psychology* **28**(1): 89–94

Marteau T and Dormandy E (2001) Facilitating informed choice in prenatal testing: how well are we doing? *American Journal of Medical Genetics* **106**: 185–190

Marteau TM, Dormandie E and Mitchie S (2001) A measure of informed choice *Health Expectations* **4**: 99–108

Marteau TM, Saidi G, Goodburn S, Lawton J, Michie S and Bobrow M (2000) Numbers or words? A randomized controlled trial of presenting screen negative results to pregnant women *Prenatal Diagnosis* **20**: 714–718

MBF (1997a) *Bereavement: guidelines for professionals* Multiple Births Foundation, London

MBF (1997b) *Selective Feticide: a leaflet for parents* Multiple Births Foundation, London

MBF (2000) *When a Twin or Triplet Dies: a booklet for bereaved parents and twins* Multiple Births Foundation, London

McCourt C and Pearce A (2000) Does continuity of carer matter to women from minority ethnic groups? *Midwifery* **16**(2):145–154

McHaffie H (2000) Supporting families when treatment is withdrawn from neonates: parental views on the role of the chaplain *Scottish Journal of Healthcare Chaplaincy* **3**(2): 2–7

McHaffie H (2001) *Crucial Decisions at the Beginning of Life: parents' experiences of treatment withdrawal from infants* Radcliffe Medical Press, Abingdon, UK

McHaffie HE and Fowlie PW (1996) *Life, Death and Decisions: doctors and nurses reflect on neonatal practice* Hochland and Hochland, Cheshire, UK

McHaffie HE and Fowlie PW (1998) Withdrawing and withholding treatment: comments on new guidelines: annotations *Archives of Disease in Childhood* **79**: 1–5

McHaffie HE, Fowlie PW, Hume R, Laing IA, Lloyd DJ and Lyon AJ (2001a) Consent to autopsy for neonates *Archives of Diseases in Childhood* **85**: 4–7

McHaffie HE, Laing IA and Lloyd DJ (2001b) Follow up care of bereaved parents after treatment withdrawal from newborns *Archives of Disease in Childhood: Fetal and Neonatal Edition* **84**: 125–128

McHaffie HE, Lyon AJ and Fowlie PW (2001c) Lingering death after treatment withdrawal in the neonatal intensive care unit *Archives of Disease in Childhood: Fetal and Neonatal Edition* **85**: 8–12

McLeish J (2002) *Mothers in Exile: maternity experiences of asylum seekers in England* Maternity Alliance (now closed) Available from National Childbirth Trust, London www.nct.org.uk

Meyer EC, Ritholz MD, Burns JP and Truog RD (2006) Improving the quality of end-of-life care in the pediatric intensive care unit *Pediatrics* **117**: 649–657

Mezey GC and Bewley S (2000) *An Exploration of the Prevalence and Effects of Domestic Violence in Pregnancy* Economic and Social Research Council, London

Miller S and Ober D (2002) *Finding Hope when a Child Dies: what other cultures can teach us* Fireside books: Simon and Schuster, New York

Mitchell L (2004) Women's experiences of unexpected ultrasound findings *Journal of Midwifery & Women's Health* **49**(3): 228–234

Moulder C (1998) *Understanding Pregnancy Loss: perspectives and issues in care* Macmillan, London

Moulder C (2001) *Miscarriage: the guidelines for good practice* Miscarriage Association Wakefield UK

MSI (2005) *Late Abortion: a research study of abortion between 19–24 weeks* Marie Stopes International, London

Murphy FA (1998) The experience of early miscarriage from a male perspective *Journal of Clinical Nursing* **7**: 325–332

Murray Parkes C (1985) Bereavement *British Journal of Psychiatry* **146**: 11–17

NDSSPE (2004) *Antenatal screening: working standards* National Down's Syndrome Screening Programme for England www.screening.nhs.uk/downs/working_standards.pdf (accessed on 10 December 2006)

Neurologic and developmental disability at six years of age after extremely preterm birth *New England Journal of Medicine* **352**: 9–19

Nikcevic AV, Tunkel SA and Nicolaides KH (1998) Psychological outcomes following missed abortions and provision of follow-up care *Ultrasound in Obstetrics and Gynecology* **11**(2): 123–128

Niven CA (1992) *Psychological Care for Families Before, During and After Birth* Butterworth Heinemann, Oxford

NMC (2004) *The NMC Code of Professional Standards of Conduct: standards for conduct, performance and ethics: Standard 07 04: 6-7* Nursing and Midwifery Council, London

NMC (2005) *Midwives Rules and Standards* Nursing and Midwifery Council, London

NMC (2006) *Conscientious Objection: A–Z advice sheet* Nursing and Midwifery Council, London

NMC (2007) *The care of babies born alive at the threshold of viability: NMC circular 03* Nursing and Midwifery Council, London

NSC (2006) *National Screening Committee policy – Down's Syndrome screening* National Screening Committee http://www.library.nhs.uk/screening/ViewResource.aspx?resID=35689 (accessed on 27 June 2006)

Nuffield (2006) *Critical Care Decisions in Fetal and Neonatal Medicine: ethical issues* Nuffield Council on Bioethics, London www.nuffieldbioethics.org/fileLibrary/pdf/CCD_web_version_8_November.pdf (accessed on 19 November 2006)

Ogden J and Maker C (2004) Expectant or surgical management of miscarriage: a qualitative study *British Journal of Obstetrics and Gynaecology* **111**: 463–467

ONS (2006) *Mortality Statistics: Series DH3 No 37* Office for National Statistics, London www.statistics.gov.uk (accessed on 27 June 2006)

Pector EA and Smith-Levitin M (2002) Mourning and psychological issues in multiple birth loss *Seminars in Neonatology* **7**: 247–256

Peppers L and Knapp R (1980) Maternal reactions to involuntary fetal/infant death *Psychiatry* **43:** 155–159

Permalloo N (2006) Antenatal screening: choices for ethnic minority women *British Journal of Midwifery*14(4): 199–203

Pointon T (1996) Telephone interpreting service is available (Letter) *British Medical Journal* **312:** 53

Polkinghorne J (1989) *Review of the Guidance on Research Use of Fetuses and Fetal Material* The Stationery Office, London

Press N and Browner CH (1997) Why women say yes to prenatal diagnosis *Social Science Medicine* **45**(7): 979–989

Puddifoot J and Johnson M (1999) Active grief, despair and difficulty coping: some measured characteristics of male response following their partner's miscarriage *Journal of Reproductive and Infant Psychology* **17**(1): 89–93

Rådestad I (2001) Stillbirth: care and long-term psychological effects *British Journal of Midwifery* **9:** 474–480

Rankin J, Wright C and Lind T (2002) Cross sectional survey of parents' experience and views of the post-mortem examination *British Medical Journal* **324:** 816–818

RCGP (2002) *Stress and General Practice: information sheet No 22* Royal College of General Practitioners, London

RCM (1997) *Conscientious Objection – Position Paper No 17* Royal College of Midwives, London

RCM (2000): *Maternity Care for Lesbian Mothers: Position paper 22* Royal College of Midwives, London

RCM (2005) *Registration of Stillbirths and Certification for Pregnancy Loss before 24 Weeks of Gestation: guidance paper* Royal College of Midwives, London

RCM (2006) *Domestic Abuse: Pregnancy, Birth and the Puerperium* Royal College of Midwives, London

RCN (2002) *Sensitive Disposal of All Fetal Remains: guidance for nurses and midwives* Royal College of Nursing, London

RCN (2003) *Sex and Relationships Education: signpost guide for nurses working with young people* Royal College of Nursing, London

RCOG (1996) *Termination of Pregnancy for Fetal Abnormality in England, Wales and Scotland* Royal College of Obstetricians and Gynaecologists, London

RCOG (2000) *Ultrasound Screening: supplement to ultrasound screening for fetal abnormalities* Royal College of Obstetricians and Gynaecologists, London www.rcog.org.uk/index.asp?PageID=1185 (accessed on 1 July 2006)

RCOG (2001) *Further issues relating to late abortion, fetal viability and registration of births and deaths* Royal College of Obstetricians and Gynaecologists, London www.rcog.org.uk/index.asp?PageID=549 (accessed on 21 May 2006)

RCOG (2002) *Clinical Standards: advice on planning the service in obstetrics and gynaecology* Royal College of Obstetricians and Gynaecologists, London www.rcog.org.uk/resources/public/pdf/WP_Clinical_Standards.pdf (accessed on December 1 2006)

RCOG (2003) *The Investigation and Treatment of Couples with Recurrent Miscarriage: Clinical Green Top Guideline No 17* Royal College of Obstetricians and Gynaecologists, London www.rcog.org.uk/resources/Public/pdf/Recurrent_Miscarriage_No17.pdf (accessed on 13 January 2006)

RCOG (2004a) *Care of Women Requesting Induced Abortion: Evidence-Based Clinical Guideline No 7* Royal College of Obstetricians and Gynaecologists, London www.rcog.org.uk/resources/Public/pdf/induced_abortionfull.pdf (accessed on 13 January 2006)

RCOG (2004b) *About Abortion Care: what you need to know* Royal College of Obstetricians and Gynaecologists, London www.rcog.org.uk/resources/public/pdf/aboutabortioncare.pdf (accessed on 13 January 2006)

RCOG (2004c) *The Management of Tubal Pregnancy: Clinical Green Top Guideline No 21* Royal College of Obstetricians and Gynaecologists, London www.rcog.org.uk/resources/Public/pdf/management_tubal_pregnancy21.pdf (accessed on 13 January 2006)

RCOG (2004d) *Obtaining Valid Consent: Clinical Governance Advice No 6.* Royal College of Obstetricians and Gynaecologists, London www.rcog.org.uk/resources/Public/pdf/CGA_No6.pdf (accessed on 7 January 2006)

RCOG (2004e) *The Management of Gestational Trophoblastic Neoplasia: Clinical Green Top Guideline No 38* Royal College of Obstetricians and Gynaecologists, London www.rcog.org.uk/resources/Public/pdf/Gestational_Troph_Neoplasia_No38.pdf (accessed on June 7 2006)

RCOG (2005a) *Amniocentesis and Chorionic Villus Sampling: Clinical Green Top Guideline No 8* Royal College of Obstetricians and Gynaecologists, London www.rcog.org.uk/resources/Public/pdf/aminiocentesis_chorionicjan2005.pdf (accessed on 7 July 2006)

RCOG (2005b) *Registration of Stillbirths and Certification for Pregnancy Loss before 24 Weeks of Gestation: Good Practice No 4* Royal College of Obstetricians and Gynaecologists, London www.rcog.org.uk/resources/public/pdf/goodpractice4.pdf (accessed on 7 October 2006)

RCOG (2005c) *Disposal following Pregnancy Loss before 24 Weeks of Gestation: Good Practice No 5* Royal College of Obstetricians and Gynaecologists, London www.rcog.org.uk/resources/public/pdf/goodpractice5.pdf (accessed on 12 July 2006)

RCOG (2006) *The Management of Early Pregnancy Loss: Clinical Green Top Guideline No 25* Royal College of Obstetricians and Gynaecologists, London

RCOG/RCP (2001) *Fetal and Perinatal Pathology: a report of a joint working party* Royal College of Obstetricians and Gynaecologists/Royal College of Pathologists, Pub: RCOG, London

RCP (2005) *Post Traumatic Stress Disorder (PTSD)* Royal College of Psychiatrists, London www.rcpsych.ac.uk/mentalhealthinformation/mentalhealthproblems/posttraumaticstress-disorder/posttraumaticstressdisorder.aspx (accessed on 5 July 2006)

RCPCH (2004) *Withholding or Withdrawing Life Sustaining Treatment in Children: a framework for practice* (second edition) Royal College of Paediatrics and Child Health, London

Regan L (2001) *Miscarriage: what every woman needs to know* Orion Books, London

Rempel GR, Cender LM, Lynam MJ, Sandor GS and Farquharson D (2004) Parents' perspectives on decision making after antenatal diagnosis of congenital heart disease *Journal of Obstetric, Gynecologic, and Neonatal Nursing* 33(1): 64–70

Rillstone P and Hutchinson SA (2001) Managing the reemergence of anguish: pregnancy after a loss due to anomalies *Journal of Obstetric, Gynecologic, and Neonatal Nursing* 30(3): 291–298

RNID (undated), RNID website, Royal National Institute for Deaf People, London rnid.org.uk/information_resources/aboutdeafness (accessed on 5 November 2006)

Roberts C, Moss B, Wass V, Sarangi S and Jones R (2005) Misunderstandings: a qualitative study of primary care consultations in multilingual settings, and educational implications *Medical Education* 39: 465–475

Robinson J (2002) Stilbirth: is seeing the baby harmful? *British Journal of Midwifery* 10(10): 640

Roy R, Aladangady N, Costeloe NK and Larcher V (2004) Decision making and modes of death in a tertiary neonatal unit *Archives of Disease in Childhood: Fetal and Neonatal Edition* 89: 527–530

Ryan, RM (1997) Loss in the neonatal period. In: Woods, JR, Esposito Woods JL (eds) *Loss during Pregnancy or in the Newborn Period* pp 125–158. Jannetti Publications, Pitman, New Jersey

Ryder IH (1999) Prenatal screening for Down Syndrome: a dilemma for the unsupported midwife *Midwifery* **15**: 16–23

Säflund K, Sjögren B and Wredling R (2004) The role of caregivers after a stillbirth: views and experiences of parents *Birth* **31**(2): 132–137

Samuelsson M, Rådestad I and Segesten K (2001) Waste of life: fathers' experiences of losing a child before birth *Birth* **28**(2): 124–130

Schaap A, Wolf H, Bruinse H, Barkhof-van de Lande S and Treffers P (1997) Long-term impact of prenatal bereavement: comparison of grief reactions after intrauterine versus neonatal death *European Journal of Obstetrics and Gynaecology* **75**: 161–167

Schott J and Henley A (1996) *Culture, Religion and Childbearing in a Multiracial Society* Butterworth Heinemann, Oxford

Schott J and Priest J (2002) *Leading Antenatal Classes: a practical guide* Butterworth Heinemann, Oxford

Scrutton S (1995) *Bereavement and Grief: supporting older people through loss* Edward Arnold/Age Concern, London

Shackman J (1984) *The Right to be Understood: a handbook on working with, employing and training community interpreters* Available from Jane Shackman, 28 The Butts, Chippenham, Wilts, SN15 3JT, UK

Sheikh A, Gatrad AR, Sheikh U, Singh Panesar S and Shafi S (2004) The myth of multifaith chaplaincy: a national survey of hospital chaplaincy departments in England and Wales *Diversity in Health and Social Care* **1**: 93–97

Sheldon H (2005) *Language Support in Neonatal Care Research Project: Stage 4: Interpreters' views* (Unpublished interim project report, Pictor Institute Europe, Oxford). Available from Helen Sheldon at helen.sheldon@pickereurope.ac.uk

Silverman WA (1992) Overtreatment of neonates – a personal retrospective *Pediatrics* **90**(6): 971–976

Smith L, Frost J, Levitas R, Bradley H and Garcia J (2006) Women's experiences of three early miscarriage management options: a qualitative study *British Journal of General Practice* **56**: 198–205

Statham H (2002) Prenatal diagnosis of fetal abnormality: the decision to terminate the pregnancy and the psychological consequences *Fetal and Maternal Medicine Review* **13**: 213–247

Statham H, Solomou W and Green JM (2001) *When a Baby has an Abnormality: a study of parents' experience* Centre for Family Research, University of Cambridge, Cambridge

Statham H, Solomou W and Green J (2003) Communication of pre-natal screening and diagnosis results to primary-care health professionals *Public Health* **117**: 348–357

Stroebe M and Schut H (1999) The dual process model of coping with bereavement: rationale and description *Death Studies* **23**: 197–224

Swanson KM (1999) Effects of caring, measurement, and time on miscarriage impact and women's well-being *Nursing Research* **48**(6): 288–298

Swanson KM (2003) Miscarriage effects on couples' interpersonal and sexual relationships during the first year after loss: women's perceptions *Psychosomatic Medicine* **65**: 902–910

Swanson PB, Pearsall-Jones JG and Hay DA (2002) How mothers cope with the death of a twin or higher multiple *Twin Research* **5**(3): 156–164

Tay JI, Moore J and Walker J (2000) Regular review: ectopic pregnancy *British Medical Journal* **320**: 916–919

Tiger (2003) *Maternity Rights in the Event of a Stillbirth or Miscarriage* Tailored Interactive Guidance on Employment Rights www.tiger.gov.uk (accessed on 10 April 2006)

Trinder J, Brocklehurst P, Porter R, Vyas S and Smith L (2006) Management of miscarriage: expectant, medical, or surgical? Results of randomised controlled trial (miscarriage treatment (MIST) trial) *British Medical Journal* doi:10.1136/bmj.38828.593125.55 (accessed on 23 May 2006)

Trompenaars F (1993) *Riding the Waves of Culture* Nicholas Brealey Publishing, London

Turton P, Badenhorst W, Hughes P, Ward J, Riches S and White S (2006) Psychological impact of stillbirth on fathers in the subsequent pregnancy and puerperium *British Journal of Psychiatry* **188**: 165–172

Turton P, Hughes P, Evans CD and Fainman D (2001) Incidence, correlates and predictors of post-traumatic stress disorder in the pregnancy after stillbirth *British Journal of Psychiatry* **178**: 556–560

UKNSC (2005) Understanding and communicating risk. In: *Screening Choices: a resource for health professionals offering antenatal and newborn care* UK National Screening Committee www.screening.nhs.uk/cpd/webfolder/units/understanding-risk.pdf (accessed on 5 April 2006)

UKNSC (undated) *Resource Cards for Midwives to Support the National Screening Committee Antenatal and Newborn Screening Programmes* UK National Screening Committee www.screening.nhs.uk/cpd/resource_cards.pdf (accessed on 15 December 2006)

Walker J (2002) *The ectopic pregnancy: diagnostic guidelines* Ectopic Pregnancy Trust, Uxbridge UK

Wallerstedt C and Higgins P (1996) Facilitating perinatal grieving between the mother and the father *Journal of Obstetric, Gynecologic, and Neonatal Nursing* **25**(5): 389–394

Wallerstedt C, Lilley M and Baldwin K (2003) Interconceptional counseling after perinatal and infant loss *Journal of Obstetric, Gynecologic, and Neonatal Nursing* **32**(4): 533–542

Walsh A (2000) Can a life ever not be worth living? (Editorial) *British Journal of Midwifery* **8**(9): 537–538

Walter T (1999) *On Bereavement: the culture of grief* Open University Press, Maidenhead, UK

WHO (1992*) International statistical classification of diseases and related health problems (tenth revision)* World Health Organisation, Geneva

Williams C, Alderson P and Farsides B (2002) Is nondirectiveness possible within the context of antenatal screening and testing? *Social Science and Medicine* **54**: 339–347

Wilson AL, Fenton LJ, Stevens DC and Soule DJ (1982) The death of a newborn twin: an analysis of parental bereavement *Paediatrics* **70**(4): 587–591

Wilson R (2001) Parents' support for their other children after a miscarriage or perinatal death *Early Human Development* **61**: 55–65

Wocial LD (2000) Life support decisions involving imperiled infants *Journal of Perinatal and Neonatal Nursing* **14**(2): 73–86

Woods JR (1997) Pregnancy-loss counselling: the challenge to the obstetrician. In: Woods JR and Esposito Woods JL (eds) *Loss during Pregnancy or in the Newborn Period.* pp 71–124 Jannetti Publications, Pitman, New Jersey

Worden JW (1991) *Grief Counselling and Grief Therapy: a handbook for the mental health practitioner* Routledge, London

Worden WJ (1996) *Children and Grief – when a parent dies* Guilford Press, New York

Working Families (2006) *Factsheet: stillbirth* Working Families, London www.workingfamilies.org.uk/asp/family_zone/fs_pr8_stillbirth.asp (accessed on 3 January 2007)

Wortman CB and Silver RC (1989) The myths of coping with loss *Journal of Consulting and Clinical Psychiatry* **57**(3): 349–357

Wright C and Lee R (2004) Investigating perinatal death: a review of the options when autopsy is refused *Archives of Disease in Childhood: Fetal and Neonatal Edition* **89**: 285–288

Zeanah CH, Dailey JV, Rosenblatt M and Saller DN (1993) Do women grieve after terminating pregnancies because of fetal anomalies? A controlled investigation *Obstetrics and Gynecology* **82**(2): 270–275

Zolese G and Blacker CV (1992) The psychological complications of therapeutic abortion *British Journal of Psychiatry* **160**: 742–749

INDEX

Sands, the stillbirth and neonatal death charity

Supporting anyone affected by the death of a baby

We offer support and information when a baby dies during pregnancy or after birth:

- *National helpline* Provides a safe place where there is someone to listen and offer support.
  020 7436 5881 helpline@uk-sands.org

- *Support forum* A place where people can connect with others whose baby has died.
  www.sandsforum.org

- *Website* Offers information, resources, personal stories and help with the many choices that parents need to make.
  www.uk-sands.org

- *Support and information leaflets* Practical information and emotional support for all family members and for the days, months and years after bereavement.
  020 7436 7940 www.uk-sands.org

- *Books Written* from both personal and professional perspectives on bereavement.
  020 7436 7940 www.uk-sands.org

- *Local support from others whose baby has died* Many parents find that only others who have experienced a baby's death can offer real understanding.
  020 7436 5881 helpline@uk-sands.org

Our services are for anyone affected by a baby's death, including stillbirth and death during or soon after birth. We offer support when a baby has spent time in special care, if a baby has died at an earlier gestation, or when parents have had to make the difficult decision to end a pregnancy. We offer support whenever a baby dies, whether the death occurred recently or long ago.

As well as supporting mothers and fathers, we are here to help other family members, especially grandparents and other children. Many people can be affected by a baby's death, including friends and health professionals, and all are welcome to contact us.

Improving care when a baby dies

No-one can take away the pain that parents feel when their baby dies. But sensitive, supportive care in hospital can help to ease the grieving process. We have worked in partnership with health professionals for over 25 years to improve understanding of what it means to lose a baby, and of what professionals can do to support and care for parents when their baby dies. The Sands Guidelines for professionals are an essential element within that partnership.

Promoting research to reduce the loss of babies' lives

17 babies are stillborn or die shortly after birth every day in the UK. We believe this figure is unacceptably high, and we want to ensure that as few parents as possible have to experience this devastating loss. We are developing strong links with researchers and organisations in the UK and internationally. Together we are working to promote changes in practice which could help to save more babies' lives, and to identify and fund research which could further advance our understanding of stillbirth and neonatal death.

Sands

28 Portland Place, London, W1B 1LY.
Office: 020 7436 7940 Open Mon to Fri 9.30 am to 5 pm.
support@uk-sands.org

In order to ensure that staff are aware of any new issues and changes in regulations, professional guidance and practice relevant to the Sands Guidelines, essential updates will be posted on the Sands website. To access the webpage, go to www.uk-sands.org and click on **Improving Care** and then on **2007 Guidelines updates.**